The WPA Guide to 1930s
NEVADA

Vintage West Reprints

Eureka and its Resources
by Lambert Molinelli, 1879

Report of Explorations Across the Great Basin . . . in 1859
by Captain James H. Simpson, 1876

An Editor on the Comstock Lode
by Wells Drury, 1936

Frémont: Explorer for a Restless Nation
by Ferol Egan, 1977

Sand in a Whirlwind: The Paiute Indian War of 1860
by Ferol Egan, 1972

The Town That Died Laughing:
The Story of Austin, Nevada
by Oscar Lewis, 1955

Silver Kings . . . Lords of the Nevada
Comstock Lode
by Oscar Lewis, 1947

Wells, Fargo Detective: A Biography
of James B. Hume
by Richard Dillon, 1969

The WPA Guide
to 1930s
NEVADA

*Nevada Writers' Project of the
Work Projects Administration*

FOREWORD TO THE NEW EDITION BY
RUSSELL R. ELLIOTT

University of Nevada Press
Reno and Las Vegas

VINTAGE WEST SERIES EDITOR: ROBERT E. BLESSE

The WPA Guide to 1930s Nevada *was first published in 1940 as*
Nevada: A Guide to the Silver State *and was copyrighted that year by*
the Nevada State Historical Society; the book was part of the American
Guide Series. The text was compiled by workers of the Writers'
Program of the Work Projects Administration in the State of Nevada,
and the work was sponsored by Dr. Jeanne Elizabeth Weir, director of
the Nevada State Historical Society, Reno. The present volume
reproduces the original edition, published by Binfords & Mort,
Publishers, except for the following changes: a new foreword has been
provided by Russell R. Elliott, and the front matter has been modified
to reflect the new publisher.

Library of Congress Cataloging-in-Publication Data

Nevada, a guide to the Silver State
    The WPA guide to 1930s Nevada / Nevada writers' project of
the Work Projects Administration; foreword to the new edition by
Russell R. Elliott.
        p.   cm. — (Vintage West reprints)
    "Compiled by workers of the Writers' Program of the Work
Projects Administration in the state of Nevada"—Copr. p.
    Reprint. Originally published: Nevada, a guide to the Silver
State. Portland, Or. : Binfords & Mort, c1940.
    Includes bibliographical references and index.
    ISBN 0-87417-170-9 (pbk. : alk. paper)
    1. Nevada.   2. Nevada—Description and travel—Tours.
I. Writers' Program (Nev.) II. Title. III. Series: Vintage West
reprint.
F841.N495   1991
917.9304'33—dc20   90-25810
                                                              CIP

University of Nevada Press
Reno, Nevada 89557 USA
Copyright © University of Nevada Press 1991
All Rights Reserved
Cover Design by Dave Comstock
Printed in the United States of America

Contents

Part III. Appendices

Illustrations

GOLD, SILVER AND COPPER—*Continued*

Ruth Copper Pit

> *This pit, in the Steptoe Valley, is one mile wide, a distance that can best be approximated in the airview. Its depth can be judged by the relative size of the ore train in the workings*

Mill where gold and silver extracted, El Dorado

A classifier tank, used in milling gold and silver ores, El Dorado

Settling Tank in Gold Mill

Ore as it comes from the mill

Modern Mining Camp, Rio Tinto

Old Silver Peak Revives

IN THE TOWNS   *Between pages* 102 *and* 103

Airview, Reno

Night Club District, Las Vegas

University of Nevada, Reno

Residential Street, Reno

The Capitol, Carson City

Eureka

Winnemucca, Stock and Mining Center

Stores on Main Street, Elko

Reno Mansion Built by George Nixon, Millionaire of the Second Great Boom

Mansion built near Reno by Sandy Bowers, First Comstock Millionaire

St. Mary's in the Mountains, Virginia City

Typical Architectural D e t a i l, Reno

ALONG THE HIGHWAY   *Between pages* 130 *and* 131

Landscape

> This primitive is the work of an old prospector who disappeared into the desert about 1920. It is in the Nevada Historical Museum

Near Virginia City

Stokes Castle, near Austin

Genoa, the Oldest Settlement

On the Edge of Tonopah

The Bottle House, Rhyolite

Piper's Opera House, Virginia City

Austin

Old Mine Office, Virginia City

Miner's Union Hall, Silver City

Lunch Time, Indian service day school

Basket Maker, Moapa Reservation

A Protest from the Cradle Board

Home of a Shoshone on the Walker River Reservation

Tractor Driver, a modern Paiute

Lost City Museum, Overton

Prehistoric Petroglyphs

FLORA   *Between pages* 160 *and* 161

Desert Thistle

Joshua Trees

The Rare Foxtail Pine, in Charleston Mountain

Creosote Bush in the Clark County Dunes

Ruby Lake (10,000 Altitude)

Aspens on Charleston Mountain

FLORA—*Continued*

Sagebrush
    This variety, notable for its
    height, is found in several
    sections of the state. It was
    sometimes used in the early
    stamp mills for fuel until
    wood could be carried in.

June Snowdrift in Jarbidge Road
Pogonip (Hoar-Frost)
Springtime
Bitter Root
Douglas Phlox
Timberline

ON THE RANGE

Between pages 190 *and* 191

Elko Beef
Sheep
Sheepherder packing to leave Sierra camp
Lambing Time
    The ewe is following her new
    born twins from the lamb
    ing shed

Buckaroo
The Remuda
On Pyramid Lake Reservation
A Prize 4-H Calf
Fallon Turkeys
Washoe Indians Baling Hay
Buying Chaps for Use on the
    Range
A Critical Customer

SPORT AND RECREATION

Between pages 220 *and* 221

Bull-dogging, Heldorado Rodeo,
    Las Vegas
Riding in the Charleston Range
Dudes
Bucking Contest, Reno
Aquaplaning, Lake Mead
A Day's Catch, Lake Mead
Skiing on Mount Rose

Tobogganing
In the Firehouse, Carson City
California Beer Hall, Tonopah
    (c. 1902)
Dance Hall, Las Vegas
Watching a Prize Fight, near
    Reno (c. 1904)
An Early Tonopah Banquet

Maps

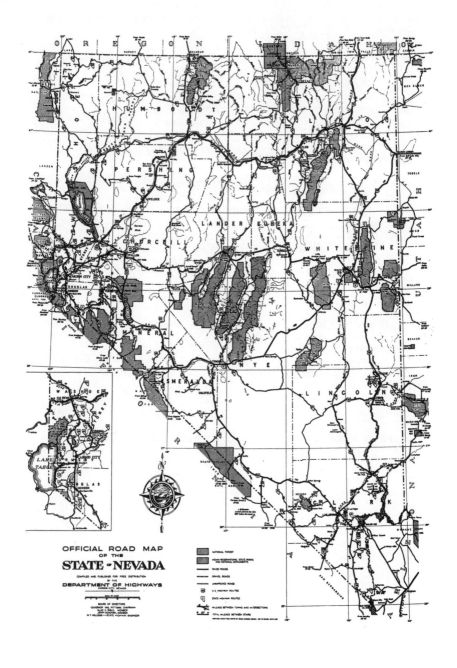

OFFICIAL ROAD MAP
OF THE
STATE ⚬ NEVADA

COMPILED AND PUBLISHED FOR FREE DISTRIBUTION
BY THE
DEPARTMENT OF HIGHWAYS
CARSON CITY, NEVADA

BOARD OF DIRECTORS
GOVERNOR VAIL PITTMAN, CHAIRMAN
ALAN H. BIBLE, MEMBER
JERRY DONOVAN, MEMBER
W. T. MELLORE——STATE HIGHWAY ENGINEER

NATIONAL FOREST

INDIAN RESERVATIONS, STATE PARKS,
AND NATIONAL MONUMENTS

PAVED ROADS

GRAVEL ROADS

UNIMPROVED ROADS

U.S. HIGHWAY ROUTES

STATE HIGHWAY ROUTES

MILEAGE BETWEEN TOWNS AND INTERSECTIONS

TOTAL MILEAGE BETWEEN STARS

Foreword to the New Edition

IT IS GOOD news for the reading public when a useful, out-of-print volume is to be republished. The news was particularly pleasing to Nevada readers when the University of Nevada Press announced that the WPA guidebook for Nevada was to be reissued. The fact that such an announcement could be made in the face of strong competition from more recent guidebooks is testimony to the vitality of this long-out-of-print work.

The WPA guidebook for Nevada was spawned, as were those for other states, by the Work Projects Administration during the 1930s. As Arthur Link points out in his *American Epoch*, 78 percent of WPA money was spent for public construction and conservation while the rest went for a variety of community projects that enrolled musicians, actors, writers, artists, and even historians, on the assumption that they also needed federal assistance during the depression. The plan was known as the Writers' Program of the Work Projects Administration. At the peak of employment the program supported over six thousand journalists, free-lance writers, novelists, poets, Ph.D.'s, and other jobless persons who knew how to put words on paper. It brought forth hacks as well as trained specialists and creative artists such as John Steinbeck, Richard Wright, and Vardis Fisher. Members of the program completed 378 books and pamphlets, which were then published through commercial channels.

One of the most useful of the projects completed by the Writers' Program was the one that produced a series of guidebooks for the several states. It was known collectively as the *American Guide Series*.

Nevada's contribution to the series, *Nevada: A Guide to the Silver State*, was compiled by workers of the Writers' Program in the State of Nevada. The book was sponsored by Dr. Jeanne Elizabeth Wier, director of the Nevada State Historical Society and chairman of the history department at the University of Nevada, thus ensuring that the volume would be supervised carefully and intelligently (no one in Nevada knew more about the state's history than Professor Wier). Much of the research and writing and the overall supervision of the project was in the capable hands of Sheila Rast, who was state supervisor of the project. The volume was published by Binfords & Mort, Portland, Oregon, in 1940.

In its final form the Nevada guidebook consists of three parts. The first part, an introduction to Nevada, includes material on the geography and geology of the state, with additional sections on the plant and animal life, the native population, mining, ranching, the press, churches and schools, the arts, and sports and recreation.

The second section of the book, the essential part, is a tour guide. Here the state is divided into eight touring regions that generally follow the pattern of the major highways through the state. For example, Tour 1 covers the area of northern Nevada along old Highway 40 (now Interstate 80). The description for this tour, like all the others, begins with information about the character of the road (whether paved, graveled, etc.), about accommodations available, and other such items. Since this tour, in a general way, follows the Humboldt River, the authors provided a well-researched four-page description of the emigrant trail, which followed the Humboldt River route through Nevada.

The tour begins at Wendover on the Nevada-Utah border and from that point westward each item of interest, be it mountain, river, pass, valley, or town, is marked out in exact mileage from the state line or some other nearby focal point. All side roads leading from the main highway to points of interest are carefully marked off in miles and each site's interesting historical material is covered. What sets the Nevada guidebook apart from other, later tour books is its simplicity. One can spend as little or as much time as is convenient. The experience is most rewarding if one is traveling with a companion who can read the text and keep up an oral commentary on the progress of the trip.

The book covers the state of Nevada from east to west along Interstate 80 and Highway 50, and from north to south along Highways 93 and 95. The details for each focus of attention are well-researched, and although some items such as figures on population, mineral production, and other statistical data are outdated, the general and specific historical data are surprisingly accurate.

One should be careful when using the volume to check the present highway alignment with that of the 1940 period. One noted realignment occurring since 1940 concerns the route of Highway 50 between Austin and Fallon. The old route, the one covered in the 1940 guidebook, went by way of the rugged Carroll Summit and Eastgate. The present route is a much easier journey, going directly west from Austin over Mt. Airy pass and New Pass, joining the old route a few miles east of Middle Gate.

Another change was the one that took place along part of Highway 93. A new route, sometimes called the Sunnyside Cut-off, follows State Route

318 from near Ely, bypassing Pioche and joining Highway 93 a few miles
north of Ash Springs. Old Highway 93 still goes through Pioche, but
State Route 318 is a more direct route from Ely to Las Vegas and consequently is now used by most travelers.

Other highway realignments include the following: short segments
where Interstate 80 bypasses business districts rather than follow old Highway 40 through towns; the straightening of Highway 395 through Washoe
Valley; the change in Highway 50 to circumvent Glenbrook; and the re-
location of Kingsbury Grade east of Stateline.

The third section of the guidebook consists of two useful appendixes.
One is a chronology of the state from 1775 through 1938, and the other is
a supplementary reading list.

The photographs, spread throughout the volume, reveal a moving picture of Nevada as it was in an earlier part of the century. Many of the
photos are from WPA sources and give an excellent picture of conditions in
the United States during the depression.

Why republish a fifty-year-old guidebook in view of the fact that two
excellent guides for Nevada have been issued in the last few years, one by
Mary Ellen and Al Glass and the other by David Toll? Neither of these fine
volumes approach the subject in quite the same manner as the WPA
guidebook.

The Glass volume, *Touring Nevada*, divides the state into seven regions,
Northwestern Nevada, Northeastern Nevada, East-Central Nevada, Central Nevada, Southeastern Nevada, Southern Nevada, and Southwestern
Nevada, thus covering the state on a regional basis. The historical notes to
each section are excellent, as are the descriptions and the maps. The photographs, nearly all of them by Al Glass, are also excellent. The tourist, once
having decided which section to visit, is given a nearly inclusive tour of the
area by the Glasses.

The work by Toll, *The Compleat Nevada Traveler*, follows a slightly different approach. He divides the state into five regions as follows: Covered
Wagon Territory, Reno-Tahoe Territory, Pony Express Territory, Pioneer
Territory, and Las Vegas Territory. This division makes good sense since
much of the publicity from the state tourist bureau follows the same organization. The author does not attempt to follow the highways mile by mile,
but carefully describes specific sites. The advantage of the Toll book is the
amount of careful research that is demonstrated in the write-up of each site.
The photographs and other illustrations are excellent.

The WPA guidebook, now retitled *The WPA Guide to 1930s Nevada*, offers a different perspective. It provides the modern reader with a vintage snapshot of Nevada as it existed on the eve of World War II, allowing easy comparisons between then and now. It is a well-written account of the state's history, and it provides the background necessary to help today's visitor interpret the past when following the well-traveled routes and the obscure roads that criss-cross the state.

The book offers convenience and simplicity and is at its best when taken along as the traveler moves from one destination to another. It indicates where to stop and explore further, or suggests what sites should be catalogued for another trip. It is just as intrusive as the traveler wants it to be, opening new vistas to explore or simply pouring out interesting information. Anyone who keeps it convenient and available cannot help but enjoy hours of rewarding sightseeing in the beautiful state of Nevada.

Russell R. Elliott
Emeritus Professor of History
University of Nevada, Reno

Note: The reader should be aware that many Nevada highway numbers were changed in the late 1970s. The WPA guidebook uses the old numbering system; the list below compares the old numbers with their new counterparts, to make it easy for readers to locate themselves on recent maps.

OLD	NEW		OLD	NEW
2	722		41A	167
3	208, 266		42	116
3A	264		44	485
3B	428		46	228
5B	602, 740		47	265
5C	599		48	399, 854
6	604		50	400, 858
7	168		51	225, 278, 536
8A	305, 376		52	156, 372
8B	290		53	161
10	360		57	758
11	226		58	374
17	341		59	397
19	207		60	165
20	379		62	118
21	306		63	652, 674
22	338		65	513
23	361		66	398
25	319, 375		67	663
27	431, 900		68	164
29	373		69	377
30	233		71	774
31	359, 839		72	267
32A	646		73	487
33	445, 446, 659, 660, 663		74	488
33A	659, 660		77	163
34	447		80	342
35	489		85	322
36	518		91	844
38	318		92	378
39	157, 613			
41	146, 147, 166, 564			

Preface

THIS BOOK is a story of Nevada and its people, past and present, and a mile by mile description of its natural wonders and points of interest. Every effort has been expended to make this story accurate and comprehensive. The staff has had the warm and full-hearted co-operation of all people and agencies in obtaining information on every phase of State life. So the book can be regarded as the product of all Nevadans. Much of Nevada history is still unwritten and many events are subjects of controversy, because full records are lacking or are contradictory. No book covering so much material can be completely accurate on every point. It is requested that, if errors are found, the discoverers report them to the compilers for use in correcting future editions of the book.

Special acknowledgement is made to Federal, State, and local governmental agencies, commercial and civic associations, and automobile clubs, for their sincere interest and helpful co-operation in this work. Great appreciation must be expressed for the courtesies extended by the Washoe County and University of Nevada libraries.

The staff is particularly grateful for generous aid in special fields to the following people, who graciously gave very much time and energy to reading and rereading manuscripts and checking them for accuracy: Robert A. Allen, State Highway Engineer, who has given much personal time as well as time for the department he represents; Dr. Vincent P. Gianelli, Head of the Department of Geology, Mackay School of Mines, University of Nevada; Florence B. Bovett, Executive Secretary, Nevada State Farm Bureau; Dr. J. E. Church, Emeritus Professor of the Classics, University of Nevada; S. B. Doten, Director of the Agricultural Experiment Station, University of Nevada; James Hendricks, Agent of the Bureau of Plant Industry, United States Department of Agriculture; G. H. Hansen, District Agent of the Biological Survey; Louise Lewers, Associate Secretary of the State Department of Agriculture; Lillian Borghi, art critic of the *Reno Evening Gazette;* Roger Corbett, principal of the Winnemucca School District; George P. Annand, district judge, Ely; Lester Mills, instructor of history in

the Elko High School; William Wright, President of the Nevada State
Cattlemen's Association; Gordon Griswold, President of the Nevada
Wool Grower's Association.

Dr. Jeanne Elizabeth Wier, Secretary of the Nevada State Historical Society and Head of the Department of History and Political
Science of the University of Nevada, is the sponsor of the book, but
her services to it go far beyond actual reading of the manuscript, in
that many people who gave assistance to preparation of the book were
stimulated long ago to an interest in Nevada history by Dr. Wier.

Much credit for the volume is also due the late T. D. Vandervort,
first supervisor of the Nevada Writers' Project, and to his successor,
David E. W. Williamson, who did splendid work in the earlier preparation of this book.

Grateful acknowledgment is made to the workers of the Nevada
State Writers' project for their conscientious effort in the compilation
of the manuscript.

Special gratitude is felt to the many people who gave photographs
for use in the book.

Final work on the guide was done with the editorial co-operation of
Katharine A. Kellock of the W.P.A. Writers' Program.

SHEILA RAST, *State Supervisor,*
Nevada W.P.A. Writers' Project

General Information

(State map showing highways, railroads, and air lines, in pocket, inside back cover.)

Railroads: Southern Pacific Lines (SP), Union Pacific Railroad (UP), which operate a branch of the Oregon Short Line Railroad (OSL), between Twin Falls, Idaho and Wells, Nevada, a branch line between Las Vegas and Boulder City, and the Los Angeles and Salt Lake Railroad (L.A.& S.L.), Nevada Northern Railroad (NN), Western Pacific (WP), Virginia and Truckee Railroad (V&T), and the Nevada Copper Belt Railroad (N.C.B.); the three trunk lines (SP), (WP), and (UP), between Salt Lake and Los Angeles.

Highways: No State border inspection; State has highway patrol. Gas and water at intervals not exceeding 40 miles on Federal-numbered highways; State gasoline tax 4c, Federal gas tax 1c. *Warning*: If going more than a short distance off main highways carry drinking water and water for radiator. Do not drink from any but marked springs. Advisable to carry towrope on all long side-trips. If caught in sand put sagebrush under rear wheels to provide traction. On all mountain grades up-car has right of way. When leaving main highways be sure to make local inquiries on road conditions. Keep out of dry washes when heavy rains begin; the run off comes with incredible speed and may stall the car or overturn it.

Bus Lines: Burlington Transportation Co. (between San Francisco, and Chicago through Reno); Boise-Winnemucca Stages (between Boise, Idaho and Winnemucca); Feather River Stage Co. (between Loyalton, Portola, Calif., and Reno); Inland Stages (between Reno and Los Angeles); Mt. Lassen Motor Transit (between Reno and Westwood, Calif., and between Reno and Portola, Calif.); Nevada-California Stage Lines (between Reno and Sacramento, Calif.); Overland Stages (between Salt Lake City, Utah, and Los Angeles, Calif., through Ely and Las Vegas); Phoenix-Kingman-Boulder City Stages (between Las Vegas and Kingman, Ariz.); Pierce Arrow Stage Line seasonal from approximately June 1 to Oct. 15 (between Reno, and Sacramento,

Calif., through Cal-Neva and points around Lake Tahoe). Nevada
Central Motor Lines (between Reno and Ely); O.C.& N. Stages (be-
tween Reno and Klamath Falls, Ore.); Pacific Greyhound Lines (be-
tween San Francisco and Salt Lake through Reno); Virginia & Truckee
Transit Co., (between Reno and Lake Tahoe through Virginia City,
also between Reno and Hawthorne); Reno-Loyalton-Calpine Stage;
Las Vegas-Tonopah Stage Line (between Reno and Las Vegas); M.
D. Curry, (between Winnemucca and Denio, Ore.); Julio Laucirica,
(between Winnemucca and McDermitt); Mountain City-Elko Stage;
Hubert Welch (between Tonopah and Round Mountain); Yosemite
Park & Curry Co., (between Lake Tahoe and Yosemite, Calif.); J. L.
Personius (between Wells and Twin Falls, Idaho); Interstate Transit
Lines (between Salt Lake City and Los Angeles through Las Vegas);
Lewis Bros. Stages (between Ely and Salt Lake, Utah); Red Bus
Transportation Company (between Caliente and Pioche).

Air Lines: Transcontinental & Western Air Lines (TWA) stops at
Boulder City; United Air Lines at Reno and Elko; Western Air Ex-
press (between Los Angeles and Salt Lake City, Utah) stops at Las
Vegas.

Motor Vehicle Laws: It is unlawful to drive a motor vehicle at a
greater speed than is reasonable and proper, taking into account traffic,
surface, and width of highway. Nonresidents must apply within five
days for visitor's permit; no fee. License plates must be conspicuously
displayed. Minimum age for drivers, 15 years. Lights must be dimmed
when passing other vehicles; two headlights and one tail-light required;
spotlights permitted. Collisions must be reported to a sheriff or highway patrolman, or proper municipal authority. It is unlawful to de-
scend grades in neutral, park on highway, drive on wrong side when
approaching a curve or crest of hill, run motor when gas tank is being
filled.

Accommodations: Excellent hotel and cafe service in all larger towns.
Restaurants and lunchstands in most small towns. Tourist camps in all
towns on main highways. Some kind of accommodation on all roads.
Accommodations scarce in Las Vegas during Heldorado celebration in
April and in Reno during rodeo celebrations, July 3, 4, and 5. Dude
ranches throughout the State, though chiefly around Reno.

Clothing: In summer, dress for hot weather; medium weight topcoats
needed in high elevations. Heed weather reports in winter; never at-

tempt to cross desert stretches when blizzard is forecast. Heavy wearing apparel needed when motoring in winter.

Fires: In National Forests camp fires allowed only in designated areas.

Poisonous Snakes and Parasites: Rattlesnakes are found throughout the State but are rarely seen. The Gila monster, found only in the Virgin River Valley, is venomous but its bite is not fatal. The black widow spider is also present. Species of woodticks, carriers of Rocky Mountain fever, are found in the sheep raising areas; search body carefully after being in brush and remove ticks with tweezers and burn them; if spending much time in brush innoculation is advised. Tularemia can be contracted by contact with the flesh or blood of the rabbit, and, occasionally, that of deer and other game; always wear leather gloves when handling game.

Information Services: State Highway Dept. in Carson City and its division offices in Reno, Las Vegas, Elko, Ely, and Tonopah. Nevada State Automobile Association, Washoe County Library Building, 100 S. Virginia St., Reno. California State Automobile Association, Nevada Division, 237 S. Virginia St., Reno. Boulder Dam Tourist Bureau, Nevada Blvd., Boulder City.

Fishing Laws: Game fish are river trout, rainbow trout, lake trout, brook trout, whitefish, landlocked salmon, royal chinook salmon, perch, bass, and catfish. *Season*: Variable from district to district and year to year; usually starts about April 15 and ends about October 1. *Licenses*: No license required for person less than 14 years old. Nonresident $3; issued by county clerks or agents in each county. *Limit*: Ten pounds of any game fish or 25 fish. *Prohibited*: Use of seine, net, spear, set line, set hooks, grab hooks, trot line or snag line, or any manner of fishing known as snagging; use of wire fence, trap, giant powder, or any other explosive; fishing within 100 feet of dam or fishway; night fishing.

Hunting Laws, Season (dates inclusive): Deer (antlered horns must be branched), 30 days between October 1 and November 15, except in Washoe County, where 30 day period is between October 1 and December 31; cottontail rabbits and mountain hare, November 1 to December 31; pheasant, mountain quail, grouse, partridge, sagehen, 15 days between July 15 and December 1. After these seasons have been set by the Fish and Game Commission, the county commissioners of each county may shorten or close the season entirely. The open season on migratory birds is set each year by presidential proclamation and cannot be changed in the State except to shorten or close it entirely. Under international treaty the opening date on doves cannot be before September 1, and the opening date on ducks before October 1. *Limits*: During season, 1 deer, during one day's hunting, 15 ducks, 5 sagehens, 10 snipe, 4 geese, 4 brants, 3 grouse, 3 pheasants, 10 valley quail, 5 prairie chickens, 5 mountain quail, 25 doves, 3 partridges, 5 cottontail rabbits, 2 mountain hare. *Licenses*: Nonresident $10, aliens $25, $1 additional fee for deer tag; issued by county clerks or agents in each county. *Prohibited*: Night hunting and hunting before sunrise and after sunset; hounds; selling of game. Deer legally killed in State may be transported, provided the tag is countersigned by officers of the Fish and Game Commission.

Wild Flowers: Picking of wild flowers is prohibited, and offenders are heavily punished under State laws.

Part I
Nevada's Background

The Silver State

NEVADA is the great unknown. A land of incredible beauty, it covers more than a hundred thousand square miles of brilliantly colored terrain rising in chain after chain of mountains. Many of them lift snow caps ten to thirteen thousand feet or ascend to pinnacles sculptured into weird or striking forms.

Yet relatively few Americans are familiar with this land. If the citizen of other States is asked what he knows about Nevada, he is apt to laugh and mention gambling and divorce; on second thought he will add Virginia City, which he remembers from Mark Twain's exaggerated account in "Roughing It". Pressed for the State's physical characteristics, he will usually mention the Great Basin—envisioned as a huge hollow bowl—and then, drawing on his memory of pioneer stories, will say: "Isn't Nevada pretty much desert?" That the State is a mountainous region with a flora rivaling that of California in richness and variety, comes to him as astonishing news. He is further amazed to hear that most of the Boulder Dam-Lake Mead Recreational area is in Nevada; that Californians in large numbers come up to the Reno and Las Vegas areas for winter sports; that the Nevada mountains near the Utah line have well developed lake side campsites at elevations much higher than that of Lake Tahoe; and that the State has a number of towns with populations of less than two thousand where social life has a metropolitan character.

There are various reasons for this vast ignorance about the sixth largest State in the Union, but the chief one has been the reticence of the Nevadans themselves. They have always known their State's great beauty and are unusually sensitive to it, but humbled by long neglect on the part of the vast traveling public, it is only recently that they have begun to tell the world about Nevada.

Hatred of hypocrisy is an outstanding characteristic of the people of the Silver State, a characteristic which has given rise to misunderstanding. The State had a six-months divorce law long before the rest of the country knew about it. Many Nevadans hold marriage a private contract and believed that if the partners made a mistake they should be given an opportunity to remedy it; furthermore, they believed that the details of a partnership dissolution concerned only the persons involved. However, because of the widespread publicity about Reno divorces, the world does not realize that Nevadans take marriage seriously. Actually, they are as impatient with those who flout marriage as their general tolerance for the world's foibles permits.

The Nevada attitude on gambling is further evidence of their lack of hypocrisy—and is equally misunderstood. Like every other State in the Union, Nevada has always had its games of chance, and was no more successful than any other place in suppressing them. Faced with the great economic collapse and hunting for new sources of revenue that would not burden the population, it decided in 1931 to cut out the costs of ineffective attempts at suppression and at the same time increase State and local incomes by licensing the gambling devices. The law regulating open gambling had teeth, however, and the State keeps no gambling laws on its statute books that it does not enforce. Only certain games and devices are permitted. The revenue is divided between the State and the counties, or between the State, county, and city or town in which the license is granted. The statute provides a maximum penalty of one thousand dollars and six months imprisonment for anyone convicted of running a crooked game. Any proprietor of a gambling house who allows a minor to gamble at his tables, or even to enter his establishment, is liable to the same punishment.

The results of the policy are illuminating. Though visitors occasionally put up large stakes, the local citizens stick to small amounts and, with many opportunities to observe the workings of the law of averages, are restrained in their gambling. Young Nevadans show relatively little interest in the sport when they reach the age that permits them to place counters on the roulette boards and pull slot machine handles. Further, the State is completely free of racketeers, in spite of the large sums handled by some of the clubs, and no Nevada prosecuting attorney has had a chance to make a name for himself by exposing corrupt relations between politicians and gambling club owners.

The State's forthrightness occasionally rouses misunderstanding among visitors, some of whom approach it as though they were entering a scene of vice; and old ladies motoring out to winter in southern California have been known to ask timidly whether it was safe for them to go out on Nevada streets after dark. Such attitudes are totally unjustified. Visitors outside the gambling club districts shortly forget that gambling exists, and in the gaming areas and clubs themselves, law and order are strictly observed.

Nevadans never force themselves on visitors or bombard them with inducements to visit this or that place in the State. Their courtesy is expressed quietly, and when they offer favors they do it with sincerity.

There are a few other characteristics of the Silver Staters that aid in identifying them. First is an unusual interest in mines and prospecting. Hardly a man in the State goes off for an afternoon picnic without inspecting every outcrop and stone he sees. And almost all—lawyers, doctors, and store-keepers, as well as those attached to the mining industry—keep a few chunks of ore on hand.

Another Nevada trait is an addiction to eating at counters. It is doubtful whether there is a restaurant in the State without one; even the smartest places feature counters. Usually the board is high and the stools are mounted on a small platform. No Nevadan is quite sure why he likes "counter-eating"; but the counter offers company—and the true Nevadan is gregarious, as his passion for clubs and other social circles indicates.

The most characteristic Nevada institution is the "club"—even the smallest community has one or two. But the gilded hot spots of the Reno and Las Vegas area are not typical. Basic equipment of the true Nevada club, which is usually in a former store, consists of a bar, a few slot machines, and one or more big round poker tables with low-hanging, green-shaded lamps over their centers. In addition there may be other gaming facilities and a dining counter. Primarily, the club is neither a gambling hall nor a saloon; rather, it is a social center similar in some ways to the continental cafe or beerhall. While a few habitues take at lest one drink daily, or drop a coin into the slot machines—in lieu of club dues—they often wander in and out several times a day without spending money. As a rule windows are uncurtained and passersby need not even enter to discover whether friends are inside. While the majority of those frequenting the clubs are men, the presence of women draws neither comment nor notice.

Nevada offers many variations from the national pattern, both in its physical aspects and in its people. There is no monotony of scene and though the towns are scattered, most of them have an individuality that repays exploration, a few a charm that makes their discoverers want to keep them unknown lest they be spoiled. But Nevada is large, its people content with their way of life, so it is unlikely that even large numbers of visitors will change its essential quality.

Natural Setting

MOST of Nevada lies within the Great Basin—a great depression whose floor is scored by numerous mountain ranges trending north-south and lying athwart the natural east-west flow of travel. With a few exceptions in the extreme northern and southern parts, all rivers draining its 110,690 square miles flow into sinks and lakes within the State. The exceptions are the Bruneau, Owyhee, and Salmon, and their tributaries, in northern Elko County, flowing into Snake River and thence into the Columbia; and the Muddy, and the Virgin, in Clark County, which flow into the Colorado. The Amargosa is in Nye County and disappears in Death Valley, California. All others lose themselves in the basin of ancient Lake Lahontan, in western Nevada, or in sandy desert wastes. The largest streams are the Humboldt, crossing northern Nevada from east to west, traversing deep gorges cut into the north-south ranges crossing its course; in the western section the Carson, now emptying into Lahontan Reservoir; the Walker, rising like the Carson and Truckee, in California, and emptying into Walker Lake, which lies along the eastern flank of the Wassuk Range; and the Truckee, fed by Lake Tahoe and flowing into Pyramid Lake in Washoe County—at times of extreme flood some of its waters formerly found their way into the neighboring Winnemucca Lake. The major part of the Truckee's flow is diverted through a canal into Lahontan Reservoir. The Colorado River flows along the southeastern border of the State, through a series of deep and picturesque gorges.

The salts dissolved in the waters of the in-flowing streams accumulate in the lakes, or are left in the great evaporating pans called sinks, as the waters disappear. Through the ages this process had increased the alkalinity of the valley soils and created the great arid alkali flats.

The dry lakes found in large number throughout the State are vast level expanses of white sediment devoid of vegetation. The most noteworthy dry lakes, in the black Rock and Smoke Creek deserts of Humboldt and Washoe Counties, are more than one hundred miles long and from five to twenty miles wide. Northwestern Humboldt County has remnants of a petrified forest with some stumps and logs two feet in diameter.

The State's highest mountain is Boundary Peak (13,145 altitude), in the Inyo Range of western Esmeralda County, on the Nevada-California boundary. Other lofty peaks are Mount Wheeler in the Snake Range in White Pine County, Mount Grant in Mineral County, Charleston Mountain in Clark County, Mount Rose in Washoe County, Pilot Peak in Elko County, Roberts Creek Mountain in Eureka County, and Toiyabe Dome and Mahogany Mountain in Nye County. A small part of the Sierra Nevada extends into the extreme western part of the State and attains some elevations of ten thousand feet in Nevada. The average elevation of the State is about fifty-five hundred feet.

In the southern part of the State, particularly in the extreme southeastern corner, are areas of metamorphosed pre-Cambrian rocks. Beginning with the Cambrian period, and extending to near the close of the Paleozoic era, eastern and southern Nevada was submerged at different periods, and a great thickness of Paleozoic sediments accumulated. Western Nevada, in all probability, was then a land mass drained by streams flowing eastward into the sea that then covered western and southern Nevada.

In a later period the early Mesozoic conditions were reversed; western Nevada was submerged by the waters of the Pacific, and this submersion continued through the following period—the Jurassic—and eastern Nevada became an elevated land mass, and sediment from the east was deposited in the western part of the state. Intrusion of granite during the Jurassic accompanied by faulting and folding resulted in the formation of the mountain ranges.

In the northern part of the State are the Columbia River Miocene lavas—basalts and rhyolites—making a rough, rugged terrain similar to that in adjacent California.

Most of the mountain ranges have scanty soil and rather limited amounts of timber and vegetation. The eastern and southern parts of the State contain soils largely of sedimentary origin. Those of the eastern section are derived from granite and porphyries of the Sierra Nevada, while those of the northern section originate from lava, porphyries, and the sedimentaries of old Lake Lahontan.

The Jurassic-Cretaceous deposits, associated with intrusions of granitic rocks, are of two types—contact-metamorphic (the deposit in or close to the contact of igneous and sedimentary rocks) and replacement deposits in the sedimentaries usually associated with intrusive masses (a type that is very productive of valuable minerals). A few early Tertiary veins are associated with granitic intrusions.

During the latter part of the Tertiary period, mineralization occurred on a large scale and with a diversity unequaled in any other western state; it resulted in such deposits as the Comstock Lode, and those in the Tonopah, Goldfield, National, Fairview, and other districts. Most gold and silver had been mined from veins of the middle and late Tertiary period. Much of the brilliantly colored rock exposed all over the State is the result of this mineralization followed by weathering.

In some instances valuable metallic deposits have been discovered from outcrops at the surface, though often merely an indication of such deposits has been found.

Prominent geological features of western Nevada are the terraces, bars, and sediments formed by prehistoric Lake Lahontan. This lake, the surface of which once covered eight thousand four hundred square miles in western Nevada and northeastern California, had a maximum depth of nearly nine hundred feet at the point where one of its remnants, Pyramid Lake, now is. The highest terrace is five hundred and twenty feet above the present level of Pyramid Lake. The Pinnacles along the northwestern shore of Pyramid Lake offer a striking example of a picturesque formation resulting from tufa, a calcium carbonate formation deposited from the waters of the ancient lake. Geologists have concluded that the history of the lake dates back not more than a few thousand years and evidence obtained by drilling indicates that Lake Lahontan represented the last three stages of forty or more lakes of Pleistocene and later times. Honey Lake, Carson Sink, Pyramid, Winnemucca, and Walker Lakes are the only permanent bodies of water at present found in the Lahontan basin.

Steamboat Springs (*see Tour* 4), in Washoe County, outstanding geological phenomena, is one of the few places in the world where ore occurrences are found in the course of deposition. These and other hot springs along the Sierra Nevada have their origin in the heated depths of the earth and rise to the surface along fault fissures generally parallel with the range. The terraces at Steamboat Springs have been built up by silica deposited by the hot waters and the white terraces against dark lava rocks are a conspicuous feature in the landscape. Many of the pools are of boiling temperature and the sinter deposited by them contains several minerals common to ore deposits, as well as small quantities of rare metals, including a trace of gold and silver. Geologists are of the opinion that many mineral-bearing veins have been formed by similar hot waters rising from great depths, bringing their metallic content up in solution and depositing it in fissures. There is a notable high terrace with erupting springs about eight miles south of Beowawe in the northern part of Eureka County (*see Tour* 1).

Numerous caves are found in the sedimentary formations, particularly in the eastern part of the state. The most noteworthy of these are the Lehman caves in White Pine County, Gypsum Cave in Clark County, Whipple Cave in Lincoln County, Goshute Cave in White Pine County, and Lovelock Cave in Pershing County.

Lehman Cave (*see Tour* 6a), now a national monument, is considered one of the most interesting in western America. In its many chambers are beautiful stalactites, stalagmites, and grotesquely colored formations. Gypsum Cave (*see Tour* 3) is of particular interest because of numerous fossils, among them the remains of a giant sloth, that has been found there. Evidence indicates that man existed contemporaneously with this prehistoric animal. Whipple Cave (*see Tour* 2), the mysteries of which have not been fully explored, has many beautiful and fanciful formations. Its main attraction is a chamber five hundred feet long, more than one hundred feet wide, and about one hundred feet high. Northumberland Cave in Nye County, though known to be of considerable size, has been little explored. Lovelock Cave (*see Tour* 1b), a short distance southeast of Lovelock, is near the shore of ancient Lake Lahontan. It offers a rich field for investigation of the culture of primitive man. Many objects have been excavated, ranging from human mummies to crude household articles.

The extreme length of 484 miles spanning seven degrees of latitude, a maximum of 321 miles, and elevations ranging from about 800 feet, near the Colorado River, to more than 13,000 above sea level, gives Nevada a very great variety of climate. Local precipitation depends chiefly on elevation and position in relation to mountain ranges. The eastern slope of the Sierra Nevada, on the western border of the State, receives the greatest rainfall, and the low plateaus in the lower parts of Humboldt and Pershing counties extending southward to the Amargosa and Ralston deserts, receive the least. Mina has the lowest recorded at present. The infrequent thunderstorms are usually light and local though heavy downpours occur occasionally over small areas. These storms, locally termed cloudbursts, may bring as much rain in a few hours as would normally fall in several months. Hail and dense fogs sometimes occur in some sections. A most unusual dense fog, known as pogonip, appears at times during the winter, covering everything with beautiful radiating frost crystals. Snowfall is heavy in the higher mountains and light at lower elevations, ranging from 255 inches at Marlette Lake in the extreme western part, at an elevation of 8,000 feet, to 1 inch at Logandale in Clark County, and at Clay City in Nye County. The common characteristics of all parts of the State are dry, clear air, low annual rainfall, and long periods of brilliant sunshine. Around Las Vegas the winters are very mild while in summer temperatures sometimes rise well above 100° at mid-day; but even in this area the low humidity prevents the heat from being oppressive and the temperature drops rapidly after the sun sets. Winters are coldest in the northeastern part of the State, the temperature sometimes going far below zero near the Idaho line.

In the Reno area winters are mild with light snowfall in the valleys even when the passes in the nearby mountains are deep in snow. Because of the mild winter climate of both Las Vegas and Reno, and their nearness to snow-covered slopes, both cities are becoming centers of winter sport activities.

Prevailing winds are from the south, southwest, and west. Wind velocities are generally moderate, though in a few places, as around Mount Davidson, there are sometimes winds of almost legendary ferocity; the Washoe Zephyr has attained international fame through the tall tales that had their origin during the bonanza days of the Comstock Lode.

Plant and Animal Life

A RID Nevada is a phrase used only by those who do not know the State. Meadows so densely covered with wild iris that they resemble lakes, roadsides banked with the native wild peach in a display that rivals Washington's famed cherry blossoms, late snowfields splashed with the brilliant red of snowplant, mountain trails almost obscured by the profusion of blue lupine, red Indian paintbrush, and wild rose, deserts aflame with the bloom of cactus—this is the true Nevada.

From the highest peaks to the lowest valleys, vegetation is abundant. It covers at least six distinct life zones—the alpine, the sub-alpine, the yellow pine, the pinon-juniper, the sagebrush, and in southern Nevada the creosote bush (*Covillea*). Because of diversified topography, Nevada has within its borders nearly all the plants characteristic of the Southwest and West. Noticeable in the valleys is the line of demarcation between the flora typical of the Western United States and the flora typical of the Southwest, which runs irregularly from near Tonopah to the southern section of the Nevada-Utah line. The dominant species over much of the territory north of this line is the sagebrush, and south of it the creosote bush. Although there are many species of sagebrush, the three-dented leaf sagebrush (*Artemisia tridentata*) is the most common—hence the nickname, "the Sagebrush State." Under favorable conditions this shrub grows to a height of ten feet and in the fall its silvery green leaf and inconspicuous lemon-yellow flower stalk is a familiar sight. The creosote bush (*Covillea tridentata*), a striking shrub with glossy leaves and attractive flowers, forms a sea of yellow when it bursts into bloom.

So diversified is the State's topography that only a single hour of travel is needed from any of the larger towns to make the transition from the sagebrush to the creosote bush zones, and in many places into the yellow pine and aspen belts as well. On Charleston Mountain, near Las Vegas, it takes less than an hour to pass from cactus and creosote bush to the alpine zone; and in the western part of the State a trip from Reno to Lake Tahoe over the Mount Rose road passes through four of the six life zones.

In mountainous areas all over the State the alpine belts, with their peculiar tundra-like vegetation above timberline, contribute few flowers; many of the peaks are snow-capped the year round and the growing season of plants near the snow is very short. Yet species of Eriogonum, Phacelia, and Hulsea occur, all of them extremely hardy and able to withstand the nightly frosts prevalent most of the year. Close below the alpine, in the timberline belt, are sparse thickets of willow and alder— along stream banks; there, also, are the evergreen white-barked pine (*Pinus albicaulus*), mountain hemlock (*Tsuga mertensiana*), an occasional red fir (*Abies magnifica*), and stands of false hellebore (*Veratrum californicum*), Senecio, larkspur (*Delphinium*), shooting stars (*Dodecatheon jeffreyi*), monkey-flower (*Mimulus guttatus*), white and yellow violets, with here and there a patch of chinese-red paint brush. These are scattered among forage grasses and elderberry, currant, and gooseberry bushes. In sheltered spots stand clumps of the white-limbed quaking aspen (*Populus tremuloides*) that form such incredibly brilliant spots of yellow against bright blue autumn skies. The flowering season in these upper zones is between the latter part of June and early October. Unfortunately for the flower-lover, grazing stock in unprotected areas is apt to leave the alpine and sub-alpine meadows denuded before the season is far advanced.

The belt converging into the sub-alpine is probably richer in color and has more numerous species than the one above it, for there the longer growing season fosters many herbaceous plants. The soil of the zone is usually fertile and produces bunch wheat grass, fendler blue grass (*Poa fendleriana*), red crooked-stem, and the manzanita (*Arctostaphylos nevadensis*), whose small but attractive pink flowers give way to a brick red berry during the winter. Also in this zone are the glossy-leafed snow bush or tobacco bush (*Ceanothus velutinus*) and its prostrate relative, the squaw mat (*Ceanothus prostratus*), whose beautiful blue flowers form a delicate carpet for the forest floor. On stream banks monkshood (*Aconitum columbianum*), columbine (*Aquilegia formosa*), meadow rue (*Thalictrum fendleri*), and woodland ferns grow among thickets of wild rose, dogwood, and willow with green forest for a background.

A magnificent tree found in this yellow pine belt is the "queen of the Sierra" (*Pinus lambertiana*), the sugar pine, a tree of great commercial value; the outstretched, horizontal branches, drooping at the ends, hold long slender cones. Scattered in the woods at the northern end of Lake Tahoe are pure stands of the lodge-pole pine (*Pinus con-*

Photograph courtesy State Highway Department

THE CAPITOL OF A NEW STATE (c. 1871; pop. 40,000)

FORT CHURCHILL, NEVADA TERRITORY

EARLY GOLD HILL

A TWENTY-MULE-TEAM FREIGHTER OUT OF ELY

PRIMITIVE STAMP MILL AND WATERWHEEL, DUTCH CREEK (1903)

THE RAILROAD ARRIVES AT ELY (1904)   *Photograph by courtesy Jean Dubravac*

FIRST STANLEY STEAMER AT TONOPAH
Photograph courtesy Tonopah Times-Bonanza

A SIXTEEN HORSE-TEAM DRIVES THROUGH LAS VEGAS (c. 1905)

TONOPAH (1902)

PROSPECTORS AT GOLDFIELD (1903)

JIM BUTLER (SECOND FROM LEFT), HIS WIFE, AND HIS FIRST LEASERS, TONOPAH, (FEBRUARY, 1901)

TONOPAH'S FIRST FOURTH OF JULY (1902)
Jim Butler's Mule (above) was the leading exhibit,
and a drilling contest (below) was a main attraction

Photographs courtesy of Tonopah Times-Bonanza

THE FIRST RIVERSIDE HOTEL IN RENO (LAKE'S CROSSING)

FIRST STAGECOACH TO MANHATTAN (1905)

Photograph courtesy Tonopah Times-Bonanza

torta). In the early spring, as the snow begins to melt, the blood-red snowplant pushes its way through snow banks in clumps of from one to twenty plants. These patches of vivid color are startling to those who see them for the first time. The snowplant is found only in the Sierra Nevada and dies if transplanted.

Below the yellow pine belt, in the lower valleys, the vegetation belongs to another world; there grow the scrub junipers and single-leafed pines—the nut pine, with numerous species of sagebrush, rabbit brush, and other desert flora. The northern and western boundary of the nut pine range is about thirteen miles south of Reno near Steamboat Springs, though scattered trees are found northward. The plant furnished the aborigines with one of their most delectable foods, and still holds favor with the Indians, as well as with white Nevadans. Associated with the pine-nut pine or pinon pine, and sometimes forming characteristic belts, are the western juniper (*Juniperus utahensis*) and (*Juniperus menosperma*). These dull-green, shrubby trees with scaly leaves, standing solitary or in large patches, are in striking contrast to the grey-green of the rabbit brush and sagebrush. Also in the foothills is found the antelope brush (*Purshia tridentata*), whose yellow flowers are sure signs of early spring. Another shrub among sagebrush, antelope brush, and rabbit brush, particularly near Reno, is the wild peach (*Emplectocladus andersonii*), whose pink flowers make the roadsides flame. Also in the spring come the desert sego lily, sprengel's frittillaria, the white or yellow Indian potato, the mahogany-colored wild peony, violets, the delicate creamy pink star of bethlehem, and almost endless varieties of onions, desert lilies, and monkey flowers to form a bright carpet over the earth. In the summer and fall the carpet changes color constantly as the lupines, Astragulus (loco weed), California bee plant, citrus plants (*Dalea polyadenia*), sagebrush, rabbit brush, balsam root, and wild sunflower—representing a variety of genera—appear in the valleys.

In the supposedly barren desert, the alkaline beds of extinct lakes, is another distinct type of vegetation. True, it is not as extensive as the belts that extend about it, nor do the flowers appear in such profusion, but against the white alkali the blooms are brilliant spots of color, as is the foliage in the fall. The desert plants are the salt bushes (*Atriplex canescens and Grayia spinosa*), grease wood (*Sarcobatus vermiculatus*), seep weed (*Dondia occidentalis*), iodine bush (*Allenrolfea occidentalis*), and samphire (*Salicornea europea*). The last is especially beautiful in October, when the whole plant, turning red, is vivid against the dry white alkali. The seeds of the salt bushes are very salty and were at one time used to give flavor in cooking. It is the concentration of salts in the soil that prevents most species from growing in the desert and the type of plant found in an area depends more or less on the percentage of salts in the soil.

In the Covillea belt the vegetation is characteristic of the Southwest. Here are the joshua and other yuccas, the cacti, the cliff rose (*Cowania stansburiana*), the fern bush (*Chamaebatiaria millefolium*), mesquite (*Prosopis chilensis and Prosopis glandulosa*), and ocotillo (*Fouquieria splendens*), all adding beauty to the country. The ocotillo, or candle flower, which grows along the Colorado River, is sometimes as much as twenty feet high and has long slender stems with a basal armor of spines; these are topped with hundreds of flame-colored flowers resembling immense candles.

Among Nevada's twenty-eight species of cacti, one of great interest is the barrel cactus, which, when the top is cut off, reveals a pulp that can be mashed and squeezed to provide a refreshing drink. Indians often resorted to this plant to quench their thirst in the desert.

The joshua tree (*Yucca brevifolia*), largest of the yuccas, is one of the most grotesque plants; it often reaches a height of forty feet and on moonlight nights its branches seem like imploring arms. When in bloom its creamy white flowers form an unforgettable sight.

The herbaceous plants are numerous in this lowest belt and from early spring, sometimes as early as February, to May and June they add to the desert color. By the time the hot summer days arrive some of the lower valley plants are nearly gone, but then the blooms are arriving at the higher elevations and valley dwellers need drive only a short distance to prolong their spring.

The panorama of flower color lasts till late fall, but even in winter vegetation gives the landscape sharp accents: dried brown leaves, and brilliant red and yellow stems and tree trunks stand out against the desert sands and mountain snow.

ANIMAL LIFE

Although fossils have been found in Nevada since the 1870's, very little orderly paleontological exploration has been carried on. The first field worked was the Eureka (*see Tour 7*), midway between the Lake Lahontan and Lake Bonneville basins, at an elevation of six thousand feet. This region is still exceptionally rich in specimens after having produced more than five hundred identified species from Cambrian,

Devonian, and Carboniferous rocks, and many previously unknown forms, principally mollusks and fresh-water shells. Some of the specimens are probably twenty-five million years old.

In the Virgin Valley (*see Tour 1*), a semiarid and practically treeless region of northwestern Nevada, the remains of many extinct mammals were discovered early in 1900, including those of two types of horses, two cameloids, a mastodon, a large cat, and fragmentary remains that were probably those of a rhinoceros. These specimens were found in three formations. In the upper and lower deposits faunal remains are common, and in the middle one large petrified logs, stems, and leaves are abundant.

From the McKnight ranch (*see Tour 1*), forty miles northeast of Elko at the head of the North Fork of the Humboldt River, fragments of footbones, teeth, and cheekbones of indeterminate camels, and the remains of a horse have been recovered, besides a number of reptilian specimens.

The largest fossiliferous area in Nevada is the Esmerelda Field in the middle western counties, where mammalian remains were buried in shore deposits bordering former fresh-water lakes. In the Cedar Mountain beds southeast of Walker Lake a slab discovered in 1912 contained the scattered parts of a type of anchiterium horse, besides remains of other mammals and of plants, mollusks, and fishes. From Stewart and Ione valleys, in this same formation, fossil plants, fish, and fresh-water mollusks have been obtained, and at Black Springs near the line between Esmeralda and Nye counties important finds have been made. Fifty miles south of Mina (*see Tour 5*) remains similar to those at Cedar Mountain have been discovered. It was here that two of the three fossil hedgehogs discovered in the United States were found, besides more of the cameloid type than in all other groups combined.

Fragmentary fossil remains of the rhinoceros, mastodon, and numerous fresh-water mollusks were taken from the Truckee beds in 1914. These beds (*see Tour 1*), which are of the Miocene period, lie in the Kawich Mountains and in the Virginia Range northeast of Reno.

Excavations made for railroad construction uncovered mammalian remains at Astor Pass (*see Tour 1*), near Pyramid Lake, in a gravel deposit evidently formed along the shore of Lake Lahontan. They consisted of a horse skull, several other large skulls, large leg bones, and other fragmentary remains of an elephant, a bison, and a camel. The evidence indicated that the animals lived and died along the shore of the lake and were buried in its sediments. A spearhead was found among the bones of the mastodon.

On Prison Hill in Eagle Valley near Carson City are the best examples of fossil footprints yet found in the West. Among them are mammoth tracks measuring twenty-two inches at the greatest diameter and two to six inches deep. There are several other series of tracks, resembling huge human footprints, from eighteen to twenty inches long and six to eight or nine inches wide. The largest group in this series consists of twenty-four tracks, imprints of the giant sloth. Other series containing fossil remains of an early horse, a mammoth, a mastodon, a ground sloth as large as a rhinoceros, lions, tigers of huge proportions, and birds, were unearthed at depths of twenty to twenty-five feet. Footprints of large four-toed birds, the long toe five or more inches in length, were also found.

The numerous caves of the State have revealed material of paleontological interest, of which the finds in Gypsum Cave are notable (*see First Nevadans*).

Few of the recovered materials have been retained in Nevada, though some are in the State Historical Society Museum in Reno and others in the museum of the University of Nevada.

Notwithstanding the aridity of parts of present-day Nevada and the scarcity of vegetation in some sections, there is still a surprisingly wide variety of animal life. Through protection and encouragement, including the establishment of bird and animal refuges, wild life is probably more abundant today than when white men first entered the region.

Although the State has provided for the establishment of twenty-five game refuges, only eighteen have so far been set aside; these are particularly for antelope, deer, sage grouse, quail, and pheasant. There are also five Federal refuges—the Charles Sheldon Antelope Refuge in the northern part of Washoe County and the northwestern part of Humboldt County; the Anaho Island Refuge for pelicans in Pyramid Lake; the Railroad Valley Bird Refuge in the southeastern corner of Nye County, for which water has been provided through artesian wells; the Ruby Lakes Migratory Game Refuge in Ruby Valley; and the Desert Wildlife Refuge for Nelson big-horn sheep in the Sheep Mountains of Clark County.

Of all Nevada animals none is of greater interest than the pronghorn antelope, the only species of antelope indigenous to North America. Large numbers of pronghorn roamed the continent as late as fifty years ago, but today less than thirty thousand are in the United States. The largest protected herds—about ten thousand animals in all—are on the table-lands of the Charles Sheldon Antelope Reserve (*see Tour* 5), and in the national forests of the eastern part of White Pine County. The pronghorn is found in small numbers in about nine other areas of Nevada.

The mule deer, roaming through all mountain forests of Nevada, is a long-eared species and the largest member of the deer family in the West. There are no native Nevada elk, though since 1932 two car-loads that were shipped in and turned loose on a reserve in the eastern part of White Pine County have increased considerably in numbers.

Several thousand wild horses wander over central and northern Nevada, the biggest herds in the fertile, well watered section south of Eureka. In order to conserve forage for cattle, the wild herds are gradually being rounded up and killed or sold.

Fur-bearing animals are not numerous, though the western badger is found in all heavy sage-covered areas, and beaver on the Humboldt River in such numbers that an open season was declared in 1935—the first in many years. The small spotted skunk is seen in all parts of the State, the Great Basin spotted skunk occasionally in the mountains and along creek bottoms, and the ordinary spotted skunk in the Ruby Mountains alone. A few red fox live in the Sierra and the eastern part of the State, the American mink in western Nevada—particularly along the east and west forks of the Walker and Carson rivers—and along the creeks in the north central part of the State, the Nevada muskrat in considerable numbers in the streams and lakes, a few mountain weasel in the moist timber areas, the Great Basin coyote in the Sierra Nevada, and the desert coyote all over the State. The Nevada cacomixle, a raccoon, is seen in Eldorado Canyon, Clark County, porcupine live in the timbered areas, marmot, pika, the wandering shrew, and numerous species of rats, mice, chipmunks, gophers, squirrels, rabbits, hare, bats are everywhere, and bobcats are in the intermediate mountain ranges and ledgy country.

The Great Basin—and particularly Nevada—is one of the last large areas of the United States where the bird life has been little studied. In general the same factors that tend to restrict the human and animal population also keep the bird population relatively small. The most extensive summary of birds observed in Nevada was compiled by Jean M. Linsdale and published by the Cooper Ornithological Club of Berkeley, California, in February 1936. This list, which gives three hundred and thirty-eight species that have been identified, is considered far from complete.

One of the most interesting of game birds is the sage hen, officially called the sage grouse, which is indigenous. Although belonging to the grouse family, it stands alone in both genus and specie. It formerly ranged over much of the State, but its habitat is now confined to the northern section, and its existence is threatened because it has been ruthlessly hunted. As it will not breed in captivity, its propagation cannot be aided. The pallid grouse lives in the northeastern section and the dusky grouse along the western border; neither is numerous. The big blue grouse and the smaller willow grouse are fairly plentiful in the big timber of Elko County.

The pheasant, imported and bred to stock the State, is becoming sufficiently numerous to be hunted in Washoe, Churchill, Douglas, and Lyon counties. There are several species of quail, of which the valley quail, also an imported bird, is well established in many parts of the State. Mountain quail are found in the western ranges but are scarce. The Gambel quail is common in the southern counties. Propagation of the chukar partridge, which thrives in a wide range of temperatures, is being tried out in Nye County; Hungarian partridge are migrating from Oregon into Humboldt and Washoe counties. This bird, which is twice the size of the California quail, may replace the sage hen. Other game birds are duck, geese, plover, ibis, rail, brant, snipe, and swan.

Birds that are protected include the white pelican, which breeds by thousands on Anaho Island in Pyramid Lake and is found at times at Walker Lake, Topaz Lake, and along the Humboldt River and Willow Creek. Both the golden eagle and the southern bald eagle—the American eagle—are found in Nevada, and prairie falcon, many species of hawk, the turkey vulture, cormorant, heron, crow, raven, and magpie are numerous. Of the many species of duck, some remain in the State throughout the year, and breed wherever there is water.

Common birds are the horned lark, jay, swallow, lark, wren, mockingbird, robin, thrasher, thrush, flycatcher, bluebird, nuthatches, chicadees, warblers, vireos, blackbirds, western meadowlarks, orioles, grosbeaks, finches, sparrows, and buntings; flickers, kingbirds, owls, sandpipers, stilts, terns, gulls, avocets, and snowy egrets; herons, cranes, rails, phoebes, swifts, juncos, cowbirds, gnatcatchers, shrikes, and towhees and in Lincoln, Esmeralda, and Clark counties, the road runner. Several species of humming birds are found all over the State.

There are seventy-eight species of birds in the Charleston Mountain region (*see Tour* 5), but the range of most is more or less limited by temperatures and other barriers. Four new sub-species were found in this region—the southern Nevada jay, the Nevada pigmy nuthatch, the Nevada creeper, and the Nevada junco.

Many of the streams and lakes of Nevada teem with fish. In Lake Tahoe on the Nevada-California line in the Sierra are the Mackinaw trout, which weigh as much as thirty pounds, and the silver trout, weighing up to fifteen pounds. The Mackinaw trout, the State's single deep water fish, can be caught only by trolling. The Truckee River, flowing out of Lake Tahoe, abounds with rainbow; and Pyramid Lake, into which the Truckee empties, is inhabited by the cutthroat, also called the black-spotted, the largest trout species known. The cutthroat of Pyramid Lake is a species of land-locked salmon, now becoming rare because of uncontrolled fishing and a lowering of the water level. Though the average weight of the cutthroat is from twenty-five to thirty pounds, the largest of record weighed sixty-five pounds and the smallest one and one-half. Cui-ui and carp are plentiful. In Topaz Lake, also on the Nevada-California line, are black-spotted, lake, and Loch-Leven trout. In Walker Lake the Walker Lake bass, also known as the crappie, is the most popular game fish. Carp abound there also.

Within easy reach of Reno are some thirty fishable streams, and in Elko County alone there are twenty-eight hundred miles of stream water in which rainbow and brook trout are numerous. The abundant red suckers are not popular as food fish because of their boniness. Sunfish—a kind of mudfish found in the swampy country of White Pine County—whitefish, and catfish also abound. In the northern part of Nevada, in the Owyhee and Salmon rivers, and in Goose Creek, flowing north into the Columbia River, are the steelhead and Pacific Ocean salmon.

Much is being done to propagate and conserve the fish supply. Close to Reno are trout hatcheries, at Galena Creek, Verdi, and Idlewild Park, from which fresh stock is annually planted in the streams of the central and northern counties. The Duck Creek hatching ponds, northeast of Ely, supply the streams of the Schell Creek and Egan ranges, and there are five black-bass spawning ponds at Las Vegas to supply stock for Lake Mead and the Colorado River.

Fresh-water shrimp abound in the irrigation ditches and fishponds of some parts of the State to the extent that it is sometimes necessary to drain and scrape the ditches. Fresh-water mussels are found in the rivers and fresh-water lakes, and snails in moist cultivated areas.

Of the four classes of Nevada reptiles—snakes, lizards, turtles, and toads—the snakes are the most interesting though seldom encountered. The rattler, of which there are three distinct species in the State, and a variable number of so-called sub-species, is the commonest of the poisonous varieties. The most deadly rattler is the rare western diamondback, which usually attains a length of six feet and a weight of about fifteen pounds; it is beautifully marked with symmetrical black rhombs on a gray background and has a whitish to blue belly and a tail with black and white rings. When frightened it quickly throws its body into a coil, sounds the rattles, and then strikes. Essentially a southern snake, it lives in the ledgy canyons along the Colorado River.

The horned rattlesnake or sidewinder, another deadly species, is also of interest. This desert species, small in size and pallid in hue, is found only south of Goldfield along the edge of Death Valley. A large scale over each eye is developed into an upright horn. The sidewinder grows to a length of about eighteen inches; when moving it carries two-thirds of its length on the ground and the other third at an oblique angle to its line of direction. It progresses by lateral forward undulations of the body, and instead of coiling to strike as does the diamondback, it whips from side to side.

Other species include the Panamint rattler, a pallid desert form that is gray, tan, pinkish, or distinctly red, and the Great Basin rattler, which has dorsal blotches of typical form but small and faded in color. Both species are found all over the State. The prairie rattler inhabits central Nevada, the Pacific rattlesnake the northern and western sections, and the tiger rattlesnake the desert mountains.

The valley gopher snake is in the Sierra Nevada and the desert gopher snake in western Nevada; the silver or Pacific rubber snake, also called the two-headed snake, in northern and western Nevada; the striped whip snake in western Nevada; the western striped racer throughout the State; the red racer, the western yellow-bellied racer, the blind snake, the coral snake, Graham's flatnosed snake, the western patch-nosed snake, and Boyle's king snake, in the southern part. Several varieties of garter snake are widely distributed, including the spotted night, the bull, the red and black ground snake, and the yellow gopher.

Lizards, found everywhere, are of two families, one scaly and the other smooth skinned. The Gila lizards of the Virgin River Valley near the Colorado are a sub-species; the bite of this surly creature is venomous but not fatal.

Turtles include the western pond species and the desert tortoise of the Pahrump Valley. Toads include Girard's short-horned and desert-horned species, found throughout, and the pigmy horned toad, found only in Elko County.

Insects are plentiful but none is of greater interest than the insectlike spiders, including the tarantula. This large, venomous, hairy creature lives in all the hot dry deserts of Nevada.

First Nevadans

NEVADA has made important contribution to support the conclusion that what is now the southwestern part of the United States was inhabited by human beings as far back as eight to ten thousand years ago. The oldest evidence of such habitation in Nevada was found in Gypsum Cave, about twenty miles northeast of Las Vegas, during excavations carried on in 1930 and 1931. This cave had been discovered about the time white men first began to settle in Nevada but had attracted attention merely because of its gypsum deposits until someone began to dig down through the many layers of deposits on the floor of its five deep chambers. The upper layers revealed relics of fairly recent Paiute occupation; farther down relics of earlier cultures were found—the Pueblo III and, lower, the Basketmaker. Eventually the excavators reached layers of excrement deposited by the long-extinct ground sloth. There among fossil remains of the ground sloth—bones, claws, and wisps of coarse, yellowish hair—were found charred pieces of wood, worked flint dart points, and primitive ropes of twisted sinew—sure evidence of man's presence in the cave during the lifetime of the prehistoric beast. Of especial interest was the discovery of short, painted wooden shafts, possibly primitive *atlatls,* or spear-throwers.

Also in the southeastern part of the State, in an area roughly coinciding with, though slightly more extensive than the creosote bush zone (*see Plant and Animal Life*), are several sites revealing occupation during the Basketmaker and up through the first three Pueblo cultures. The latest and most extensive of the settlements yet discovered was that of Pueblo Grande de Nevada—called Lost City. The site, now largely hidden beneath the waters of the northern arm of Lake Mead, probably flourished some time between 600 and 900 A. D. Excavations at this site, which was five or six miles long, brought to light skeletons, and thousands of pieces of pottery—some intact and some broken—as well as turquoise jewelry, bits of basketry, scraps of cotton textiles, stone and bone implements, and shell beads. Vestiges of irrigation ditches were traced and ruins were found that indicated houses, or storage rooms, built below ground, as well as flat-roofed houses erected above ground.

The full sequence of primitive habitation in the State has not yet been traced; it is not known whether the Basketmaker and Pueblo peoples had any relationship to the early Gypsum Cave users, but the periods of later occupation can be dated definitely and relationship between contemporary peoples of northern Arizona and of southern Nevada is clear. The time when the villages of northern Arizona were developed has been established by a study of tree rings. While there is no written record or well-established tradition as to why these populous cities were deserted, there is good reason to believe that they were abandoned during a period of great drought. Probably the arrival of other tribes from the north prevented a return of the Pueblos to this region.

Just when human habitation began in the northern part of Nevada is still unclear. There are a great many camp sites and other evidences of early occupation but too few have been studied to establish beyond question whether these were left by tribes that inhabited the region during the past two thousand years, or whether they are the vestiges of peoples who may have been drifting eastward during some more remote period. Some students contend that primitive peoples were living on the shores of ancient Lake Lahontan when it covered a large part of western Nevada; but the date when the waters of the lake receded has not been determined—the final great recession probably began sometime between a thousand and five thousand years ago.

Work at Lovelock Cave, in the Humboldt Valley south of Lovelock, began in 1912. Cultures of three distinct periods were found; surface finds were easily identified as belonging to the latest Paiute period while the oldest artifacts showed Basketmaker influence, which roughly coincided with the beginning of the Christian era.

Well-preserved, desiccated human bodies, as well as skeletons of men, women and children were unearthed in Lovelock Cave. One mummy was that of a man six feet six inches in height; the female remains were of shorter stature. The hair of some of the mummies had a reddish tinge, which gave rise to stories of "red haired Indians"; the color, however, was the result of chemical change after death. Among the artifacts were grinding implements, cutting and scraping implements of obsidian and flint, fishhooks and other domestic implements of bone, also wearing apparel made from the skins and feathers of birds and the hides of animals, and articles of personal adornment made from shells. There were also weapons of war and the hunt, including atlat' of the Basketmaker period, and bow and arrow fragments of later tim·

In or near the Humboldt Valley are the sites of many other former habitations of aborigines, including Ocala Cave, three miles southeast of Ocala, in which seventy-seven early artifacts were found under a guano layer. At the northern end of Humboldt Sink patches of ground are strewn with fragments of rock used in making obsidian and flint implements. Other sites are near Troy and Granite Point and around Pyramid Lake.

An important find made in the vicinity of Walker Lake, farther south, was a spearhead among the bones of a mastodon.

Petroglyphs are found on flat rock surfaces in many sections of the State; these designs were made by gouging the rock surface with tools fashioned out of harder materials such as quartz. The modern Indians can give no clue to the meaning of the symbols, and their interpretation has baffled all scientific investigators; they are not unlike the petroglyphs found in other parts of the world.

In the Valley of Fire near the Colorado River are many petroglyphs showing crude outlines of turtles, lizards, deer, mountain sheep, and men, as well as circles, or straight and wave lines. In the Forty Mile State Park in Crater Valley, northeast of Beatty, are thousands of ancient symbols on boulders, on mesa rims, and the rims of some craters. Cut in the rocks ten miles south of Pioche are fifty figures resembling sheep. Near Kane Springs, eighty miles southwest, some of the most carefully executed and best preserved petroglyphs were found; these represent men on horseback pursuing animals and were certainly made after white men arrived in North America. Some petroglyphs in southern Nevada seem to have been the work of the Pueblos and their recent ancestors.

Four miles east of Sparks is the Court of Antiquity, on whose walls are animals (mostly reptiles), and the usual rows of concentric circles. North of Sparks on a ledge in a steep canyon on the side of Spanish Spring Mountain, where the Truckee River has cut off the point of a hill, designs have been found that suggest a square and compass and a woman holding a branch with outstretched arms.

Eight miles below old Fort Churchill, by the Carson River, on a big basaltic rock with a broad smooth top, shapes have been incised that may have had some magico-religious significance. The figures combine parts of the bodies of animals and birds, and among these wavy lines and figures are interspersed. At Reveille are many incised characters of various kinds. On the rocky walls flanking Walker River, near Walker Lake, are rings, plants, human forms, footprints, waving lines, and circles.

South of Fallon are two caverns with petroglyphs on their walls, and in Pershing County walls and cliffs with ancient picture writings are numerous. The Indians living in the northern region when the Yankee trappers appeared were Plateau Shoshoneans, including some Bannock and more Paviotso or Northern Paiute, who also lived in northern California and eastern Oregon; Shoshone and Southern Paiute were scattered across Nevada from southern California to Utah. The Washoe, living around Lake Tahoe in Nevada and California, possessed a similar culture, though their language was not related to that of the Shoshone or of their neighbors. Some of the tribes were subdivided into smaller groups or bands. Among the Northern Paiute (Paviotso) the bands varied in size from five to ten families, numbering as many as one hundred persons; each needed fifty to one hundred square miles of land for subsistence. In winter the band would congregate in one or two fairly large semipermanent settlements, but in the spring small family groups scattered over the country in a continuous hunt for food. Private property rights were almost unknown, but some western Nevada families claimed rights over certain pine nut groves. For the most part, however, all families were free to wander over the lands controlled by their band.

The winter hut, or wickiup, was conical or domed, with a hole in the top for a smoke vent. The frame, of poles, was covered with bark, dried brush, or tule matting, depending on what was available. In the winter settlements a sweat house was generally erected—a small domed structure covered with grass or skins and placed near a spring or stream. Water poured on hot stones filled the house with steam. The sweat baths were taken for therapeutic purposes, but were frequently cere-monial as well. For summer shelter the Paviotso merely erected four poles to support flat roofs of grass or brush.

Explorers and trappers, as well as later travelers crossing Nevada, were appalled by the extreme poverty and cultural backwardness of the Paiute. Fremont wrote in 1844 that the Indians he met represented "humanity . . . in its lowest form and most elementary state." The early visitors also reported that the Indians were too weak to force their way into lands where game and foodstuffs were more abundant, and that they exhibited none of the boldness characteristic of the Plains Indians; the Indians would attack from ambush for the most insignifi-cant booty and would run great risks to get a single ox. This driving need for whatever they could manage to steal—a far different thing from the Plains Indian's game of pilfering—made the northern Paiute far more troublesome to travelers than their numbers warranted. The Bannock, near the headwaters of the Humboldt, were friendlier.

Large game was scarce in most of the region in early days, and the food supply consisted of plants, small game, and insects. Berries and the seeds of many kinds of grasses were beaten to a paste as were roots and bulbs, which were dug up with pointed sticks. In the western part of the Territory pine nuts were gathered on the wooded ranges in the late fall and stored for winter use, and in the south the pods of the mesquite were also relied on to furnish a food reserve for the winter. Lizards (chuckwallas) and tortoises were prized articles of diet and a swarm of grasshoppers was the occasion for a great feast; a circle of beaters would drive the insects into a central pit where they were boiled or roasted. After the feast, if any grasshoppers were left, they were pounded into paste, formed into cakes, and dried for storage.

Gathering food stuffs, aside from meat, was the women's work, though the men did assist in the pine nut harvest, particularly by climbing trees and knocking the nuts down. Seeds, collected in tall conical baskets, were freed from their husks by beating, then winnowed on trays, and parched; hard seeds and nuts were crushed on a flat stone or in a mortar. Food for winter was usually stored in grass-lined pits near the winter villages.

The Indians were particularly dependent on game in the winter, when the number of men in the bands made communal hunts possible. Rabbits, gophers, and squirrels were equally prized. With infinite patience the Indians would make fiber nets about one hundred feet long and four feet high, which were set up in a semicircle or strung across a canyon. The rabbits driven into this trap were killed by clubbing or with arrows. Antelope were occasionally caught by the same method but a shaman directed the antelope hunts and decreed when his time would be propitious. As a rule the few mountain sheep were hunted by individuals. Sometimes the ducks, mud hens, and geese on the lakes were hunted from rafts of tule, but more often the Indians would divide into parties and snare the birds with nets stretched between stakes in the water. They also made clever decoys to bring the birds within reach of their arrows. In addition to bows and arrows these Indians used various types of clubs as weapons.

The Paviotso and Washoe were particularly dependent on fish and had various ingenious devices for catching them with nets, spears, and weirs. They also dammed pools and poisoned them with a mash of leaves to kill the fish.

Because of the scarcity of skins and fiber plants, little clothing was worn in summer except the breech cloth of the men and the double apron or fiber skirt of the women. In winter, those who could manage it usually had a garment made of strips of rabbit fur; skins of thirty to fifty jack rabbits were needed for a single robe.

The most highly developed and elaborate craft of the Paviotso was basketry. Both twining and coiling were employed and a variety of forms was produced, including large conical burden baskets, water jars coated with pitch, winnowing trays, cooking baskets, and cradle baskets.

Marriage was usually accompanied by an exchange of gifts between the families concerned. The young man lived with his wife's family and his labor contributed to their household economy until the first child was born. A widow could be claimed by the younger brother of her deceased husband, and a widower could marry the younger sister of his late wife. Plurality of wives sometimes occurred, since a man had the privilege of marrying his wife's younger sisters also.

A puberty ceremony for girls, observed by all Nevada Indians, was primarily a purification rite with the addition of magical rites to insure the girl's industriousness. There was no corresponding rite for boys.

None of the highly-developed religious rituals of the Plains type or of the types common in the Southwest existed among the hard-pressed Nevada Indians. Supernatural power was claimed by some individuals through dreams, but never by fasting or self-torture. Persons who established recognition along such lines became shamans and used their powers as leaders of the hunts or in curing the sick. The treatment involved both exorcism by singing and a sucking out of the disease, as among many other North American tribes. Herbs were also employed.

When death came to a member of the Washoe, the corpse was burned with some of his property. At a mourning ceremony held a year later more property was destroyed by fire. On the other hand the Northern Paiute buried their dead in shallow graves or in niches among the rocks. Frequently the mourners cut their hair, and the name of the deceased was taboo for several years. The Southern Paiute of the Moapa region held a wailing ceremony, following cremation, that lasted from one to five nights.

Most ceremonies were linked with the social life of the tribe and took place during the winter. The Southern Paiute of today have acquired the Bear Dance from the Ute; it is largely a social affair, however. The principal diversion of the Indian men was gambling, but they had numerous elaborate games, in which the women only occasionally participated.

With the arrival of white men in numbers a rapid change took place in the life of the Nevada Indians. After several Indian attacks on whites along the travel routes military outposts were established. The Pyramid Lake affair (*see Wilderness to Modern State*) resulted in establishment of Fort Churchill and many Indians fled to the deserts. Others hung about the new mining camps and were occasionally employed as manual laborers.

In 1874 the Government established the Pyramid Lake and Walker River reservations; the year before the small Moapa River Reservation had been set aside and three years later the Duck Valley was created. The 1939 census conducted by the Indian Bureau found 5,395 people in the State who were classified as Indians, more than half of them in non-reservation areas. The majority are Paiute and the second largest group is composed of Shoshone; about 10 per cent are Washoe; slightly more than a hundred belong to Pueblo and other tribes.

In 1892 the Washoe were given individual allotments, but many sections of the area were so barren that they could be used only for sheep raising. In 1916 Congress had to appropriate ten thousand dollars for the purchase of further land and water for these Indians, and five thousand for their support; of the five parcels of land bought, the largest contained only a little more than one hundred acres and only three families were living on them in 1924. Today the Washoes live for the most part around Reno and Carson City; many work on ranches and some go to Lake Tahoe in the summer to act as boatmen and guides. Their wives make baskets for the tourist trade. Before Datsolali, an old Washoe basketmaker, died in 1925, she had achieved a high reputation for artistry of her work, which has rarely been equaled in fineness and regularity of stitches, symmetry, and blending of colors. One of her baskets is in the Carnegie Museum of Pittsburgh.

There are now three reservation hospitals for the Indians of Nevada with approximately one hundred beds in all. Education is available to all Indians, and various rehabilitation projects are being developed.

Wilderness to Modern State

NEVADA, sixth in size among the States of the Union, is bounded on the north by eastern Oregon and the western half of Idaho, on the east by Utah and the northern section of Arizona, and on the west and south by California. Although its boundaries were fixed within five years after it became a State, its territorial history is bound up with that of four other States—New Mexico, Arizona, California, and above all, Utah.

At that, more than half the story of Nevada, both territorial and State, is found in the histories of gold and silver mining. The Spanish, arch-conquerors of peoples who revealed the presence of silver and gold, long ignored this region whose natives had a Stone Age culture. The first large bands of people to cross Nevada, and know it to a limited degree, were the hordes seeking the shortest path to huge gold lodes in California. The first great influx of immigrants to Nevada was the result of the discovery of silver, and the increases in population of the next twenty years came with new discoveries of silver and gold. The sharp decline in population toward the end of the nineteenth century was the result of the falling price of silver and of failure to find new, rich deposits of the precious metals. And the rapid increase in population in the first decade of the twentieth century came with spectacular new discoveries, first of silver and then of gold.

EXPLORERS AND TRAPPERS

The territory that was to become Nevada was slow to attract the attention of explorers, and the first white men to enter it, so far as the record shows, were concerned merely with finding a way across it. In 1774 the Spanish priests and the viceroy of New Mexico became interested in finding a travel route between the New Mexico missions and the ranching chain being developed in upper California. Captain Bautista de Anza and Father Francisco Tomas Garces made a preliminary trip toward the Colorado, and later Father Garces made a second trip in the same direction, during which he may have entered the southern tip of Nevada—the records are confused on this point. After discovery of the deserts and other handicaps in the way of a more or less direct route westward, the next exploring expedition, that led by Fathers Francisco Atanasio Domingues and Silvestre Velez de Escalante, attempted to discover a roundabout course north of the Grand Canyon of the Colorado River. This group first traveled as far north as Utah Lake, then sharply south. Reaching the chaotic mountainous area along the Colorado, they found the region impassable because of snow and abandoned the journey.

Although this expedition probably did not reach Nevada it produced a map that was to help draw attention to the territory, since it indicated a large river reaching westward and labeled the San Buenaventura, which may have been the Green and the Sevier, incorrectly united. The Escalante map, and others showing California streams flowing into the Pacific, led later cartographers and explorers to assume that some stream crossed the Great Basin and cut its way through the Sierra Nevada. The A. Finley map of 1826, then considered reliable, not only marked the course of the Buenaventura, but also that of another stream, called the Rio San Felipe, both flowing through the mountains of eastern California to the Pacific Ocean. The Chapin map of 1839 repeated the error. So strong was the belief in this westward-flowing river that Fre'mont searched for it diligently in 1844 and was not convinced of its non-existence until he had examined nearly every stream on the west slope of the Sierra.

For nearly half a century after the expedition of Dominguez and Escalante no one, so far as the records show, made another attempt to penetrate the forbidding region along the Colorado west and northwest of the Virgin River. But Santa Fe traders in time began to make annual expeditions to Utah over the general route of the Escalante expedition. In 1830, eight years after the American trade with New Mexico began, a group of traders, led by William Wolfskill, followed the lower part of this Santa Fe-Utah trail and then turned westward, crossing Nevada on a course that ran in the neighborhood of Las Vegas. Their success in reaching Los Angeles started other traders over the route, and every year thereafter caravans went overland to buy up jacks and jennies on the California mission and other ranches. The route was called the Old Spanish Trail because it was an extension of one the Spanish had discovered.

The real exploration of Nevada did not begin until 1825, when the fur trade was moving to its peak and trappers and traders were penetrating every valley of the west in their search for beaver streams. How many trappers explored the territory, and where, is unknown, for they were concerned only with fur and few recorded their wanderings.

In the spring of 1825 Peter Skene Ogden led Hudson's Bay Company trappers from Fort Vancouver up the Columbia and Snake rivers and by way of the Owyhee, a Snake tributary, down into northeastern Nevada. For four years Ogden visited the Humboldt Basin and one year went as far west as the Big Bend (near Winnemucca). In the following years this stream was generally called Ogden's River, though Ogden had suggested it be called Paul's River for one of his men who had died near it. Fre'mont in 1845 ignored the name and decided to call it the Humboldt, in honor of the German scientist and explorer.

In 1826 Jedediah S. Smith, a partner in a fur-trading company, and fifteen trappers who had left St. Louis with him in the early spring, went south from the Great Salt Lake and crossed the southeastern corner of Nevada on their way to San Gabriel Mission in California, which was reached in December. During this trip of 1826 Smith entered Nevada just to the east of the site of Panaca in Lincoln County, found Meadow Valley Wash and followed its rocky, winding course, plodding for ten days before coming to an Indian village at Moapa. There he rested for a couple of days before continuing down the Muddy River to the Virgin. Near the junction of these streams, Smith took a trail along the Virgin to the Colorado.

One very curious expedition of the fur-trading period was that led down the Humboldt and across to California by Joseph Walker in 1833. An abbreviated and vague story of this expedition was first given to the world in 1837 by Washington Irving in his *Adventures of Captain Bonneville*. Irving explained that he had purchased the manuscript of Captain Eulalie Bonneville's adventures and had merely given it literary polish; and the story the captain chose to tell was that he had taken a two-year leave from the army in 1832, had raised funds to make a try at fur trading, gone to western Wyoming, and penetrated a certain distance into Oregon. According to his account he had sent Walker and about three dozen men to explore and trap in the vicinity of the Great Salt Lake, and he indicated considerable annoyance because the men had made a long frivolous expedition across to California and had had a very gay time on the plazas there. Bonneville's adventures were entertaining, but he seemed to have very bad luck as a trapper—though he was efficient in bringing all his men safely through the two and a half years in the west. Moreover, he always had plenty of supplies—

enough to entertain passing traders and trappers bountifully, especially if they were British. Later historians have been much puzzled by the story, particularly since the discovery of a simple journal kept by one of the men on the expedition and published soon after his return in an obscure Western Pennsylvania newspaper; the diarist, Zenas Leonard, made it quite clear that several members of the party had joined Bonneville with the understanding that they would be detailed to the California expedition, and that the party was fully—even elaborately—equipped for it. Obscurities in Bonneville's story were explained by some historians as the result of Bonneville's having been dropped from the army for overstaying his leave and by his attempts to re-enter, which were going on at the time the story was written.

The mystery was explained in the 1930's when the Government began to sort out its vast accumulation of papers. Evidence was found to prove that Captain Bonneville had not been dropped from the army for overstaying his leave, but because the army had believed him dead; further, that Bonneville eventually received pay and subsistence for himself and "servants" for a period that ended a year after his leave was supposed to have expired; and that in 1831 Bonneville—a captain—had written a letter to the General-in-Chief of the United States Army referring to the coming expedition and explaining that he had "made arrangements to collect information" as agreed. The British were sharing Oregon at the time, and the Mexicans had title to everything south of Oregon and west of the Rockies, so an army officer and his employees "collecting information" in either area were somewhat *de trop*. Although Bonneville's reports—which must have contained some account of Nevada—have never been found, the War Department apparently considered his services valuable, since he became the first American military commander on the Columbia after the United States had wrested the territory from the British. It was he for whom Bonneville Dam was named.

The next American expedition to enter Nevada was led by John Charles Fremont—and he came within an ace of being called back before he reached it. Fremont was the son-in-law of Senator Thomas Hart Benton of Missouri, who thundered day in and day out on the "manifest destiny" of the United States to have both Oregon and the Mexican Southwest. Fremont's first expedition took him merely to the Rockies, but the second was planned to go into Oregon and work discreetly southward. While Fremont was outfitting for this expedition in 1843, near what became Kansas City, he received an urgent message from his wife in St. Louis, telling him to leave immediately, without questions. Fremont obeyed. Mrs. Fremont, caring for his mail, had opened a letter from the War Department ordering him to return at once to Washington. Sharing her husband's interests, she was very proud of the acclaim created by his first report—most of which she had written for him—and she attributed the order to jealousy and the desire of the commander to send his son on the expedition. It is probable, however, that the War Department had learned that Fremont was taking a small cannon with him for protection from the Indians and feared that the act would increase the already tense feeling between Mexico and the United States. This cannon was dragged with much difficulty on the roundabout course through Oregon, down into Nevada along Pyramid Lake, across the Humboldt Sink, along the Truckee and Carson rivers, and up the steep Sierra, only to be abandoned near the crest at a spot where it was discovered many years later—and from which it was taken to Virginia City for use in celebrations. On the return trip Fremont crossed the Mojave, cut up along the trail used by the Santa Fe traders and made one camp at a place they used—Las Vegas.

In August, 1845, Fremont again started west, this time to explore Nevada more thoroughly. Entering near Pilot Peak at the end of October, he soon divided his party; one section under command of Joseph Walker went down the Humboldt and the other, under Fremont's leadership, made a central crossing to what Fremont named Walker Lake, where he waited for the other party to join his. The united company continued to Owen's Valley and through Walker Pass on the way to coastal California, where Fremont seriously endangered his army position by participating in the Bear Flag Revolt.

WESTERN UTAH

Fremont's reports greatly stimulated interest in the West, already whipped high by various propagandists—expansionists, demagogues, missionary and other real-estate developers, romanticists, and political schemers. The propaganda had found fertile soil in the great unrest blanketing the country since the economic collapse of 1837, brought on by unsound banking and wild speculation in public utilities. The Fremont reports were particularly valued because they contained the first accurate maps of the West and detailed accounts of the terrain.

Interest at the time was chiefly centered on western Oregon, which the missionaries had painted as a paradise with fertile meadowlands and brief mild winters. Every Eastern farmer worried by low prices and the decline in production occasioned by early exhaustion of virgin soil, every workman thrown out of a job by the closing of factories and decrease in construction, every restless and dissatisfied dreamer, had begun to look on the country beyond the Mississippi as offering a new chance for getting ahead. The Great Basin had no appeal whatsoever to the average emigrant, for he judged the value of new land by the lushness and greenness of its grass.

A few Yankees had already wandered into California and managed to obtain ranching lands there, but they were having trouble with the Mexican courts and had started a publicity campaign to induce other Yankees to join them, in order to form a bloc that could force recognition of American expansion.

The result of the various publicity campaigns was that in the spring of 1841 five hundred emigrants gathered on the banks of the Missouri. The great majority, however, fell away for one reason or the other and only about an eighth started off with California as the goal; the leader was John Bidwell. Bidwell's plan had been to leave the Oregon Trail near Fort Hall and cut across to the Humboldt, taking a direct route to California. But the party split when the time came for leaving the well-known trail and only half took the Humboldt route. Many of those who reached California were to return dissatisfied with the dry hot country they found. In 1842 about one hundred people went to Oregon. In 1843, with conditions still very bad in the East, nearly nine hundred started for the West Coast, most of them for Oregon. One party decided to go to California over the Humboldt route with Joseph Walker as their guide. In 1844 nearly fifteen hundred left the Missouri; of these, only the Townsend-Murphy party was sure it wanted to go straight to California and accepted the guidance of agents sent by Captain Sutter to induce would-be settlers to choose the country he was interested in developing. In 1845 three thousand started west, with Oregon as at least the first objective. In 1846, after a year in which there had been a revival of business, only two thousand left the Missouri. Among these emigrants were the Donners (*see Tour 1a*), who traveled with a party that misguidedly took the Great Salt Desert route so much misrepresented by Lansford Hastings (*see Tour 1a*); their journey ended with a tragedy that was to discourage travel along the Humboldt for two years.

In the bitter winter of 1845-6 the Mormons were driven from Nauvoo, Illinois, after having lost their leader, Joseph Smith. Early in 1847 Brigham Young, one of the most able statesmen of American history, took command of the scattered forces and led a small band west along the Platte and over the Divide to find a spot where the Latter-day Saints could build up a state in peace. Young was armed with Fremont's reports and maps, and he had already considered the possibility of settlement in the Great Basin. At the time Young left the Missouri the Great Basin belonged to Mexico, and the fact that it was beyond the borders of the United States, where the Mormons had endured so much persecution, was important in turning his attention to it. After crossing the Divide he had a long talk with the old scout, Jim Bridger, considered the ablest of all the mountain-men though he never received the publicity accorded Carson and Walker. Jim agreed that there were many fertile spots in the Basin, particularly near the Great Salt Lake, and he also said that the mountains of the region held gold and silver. The conference with Bridger settled the question for Young and before fall the Saints were busily putting in crops and digging irrigation ditches by the great inland lake.

When the Saints were driven from Nauvoo they were able to save very little property and the problem of merely providing foodstuffs was overwhelming. Young conceived numerous plans for obtaining the necessities, including agricultural equipment and stock. Some of his followers were left near the Missouri to make what profit they could by selling crops from various little plots of land hastily put to seed; others were told to join a battalion for war on the southwestern border, their army pay to swell the community fund. Yet others were assigned to running a ferry to carry the swelling stream of Oregon-bound travelers across the Upper Platte. Some were sent to work land in various isolated spots; and numbers were stationed along the overland trails to trade with travelers, exchanging one good ox or horse for several jaded ones that might be fattened up to increase the trading and working stock. At one time Young even had a couple of his men at Independence Rock to satisfy the emigrant passion for immortality by carving names high on that landmark, at from two to five dollars a name, according to the difficulty of the position. The carvers did a very good business.

Some of the men who had joined the Mormon Battalion followed the Old Spanish Trail eastward when they were demobilized, then switched to the Escalante Trail to reach the colony by the Great Salt Lake. This combined route was to become known as the Mormon Trail. After the gold rush to California began, numerous people, particularly those who had started west late in the season, availed themselves of Mormon guide-service over this trail, which could be used in the winter and was now in the United States. By the treaty of February 2, 1848, Mexico had reluctantly given up all claim to New Mexico, Upper California, and lands north of them.

One party of 1849, starting southwest over the Mormon Trail under guidance of Jefferson Hunt was particularly headstrong in its belief that the circuitous route was unnecessary. At Mountain Meadows in Utah about one hundred wagons left the train to cut west over an uncharted course, leaving only seven with Hunt. After a few days of extreme hardships most of the deserters returned to the Mormon Trail at the place they had left it and from there they followed Hunt to California without mishap. The rest of the headstrong contingent, including two families with children and a group of young men, the Jay-hawkers, continued westward across Nevada. Some of the wagons were stranded in the mountains, a few found their way through the dry sandy valleys, and two got as far as the great depression the rash adventurers were to name Death Valley. Somehow, most of the party eventually reached the Coast, though all had given up hope before they found a place where they could cross the Panamints.

It was not until March 18, 1849, that Young formally announced the organization of the State of Deseret, which included Nevada.

With the discovery of gold in California in 1848 the route along the Humboldt became important. The fortune-hunters, many of them half mad in their dreams of quick riches, were utterly heedless of how they reached California as long as they did it quickly. The trip overland, however, was not a poor man's expedition. Joel Palmer, who went west in 1845, had published a book in which he advised that four yoke of oxen for every wagon was the minimum for safety and that one or two horses were also needed, for hunting and other purposes. He strongly urged against the carrying of more tools and household equipment than were absolutely necessary, and estimated that one wagonload of the essential goods, largely composed of foodstuffs, would weigh twenty-five hundred pounds. Palmer said that in making up the estimate of the necessary food supply he was assuming that travelers would supplement it with game along the route; this was practical only until 1849, when the great numbers on the trail—twenty thousand left the Missouri in April alone—soon killed every bird and animal in a wide band along the routes.

While some forty-niners rashly attempted further to shorten the distance westward by coming down to the Great Salt Lake and crossing the dreadful Salt Desert to reach the Humboldt, the great majority turned up toward Fort Hall and Soda Springs and then south to the river. Yet others went north around the Great Salt Lake, avoiding the worst of the Salt Desert but still experiencing hardships.

Thus it was that when the forty-niners reached the Humboldt they and their animals were already exhausted and their food supply was usually low. The first wagon trains, moreover, exhausted all the wild hay near the river and many later trains lost animals through starvation. The Humboldt, with its twists through canyons cut in mountains that had to be crossed on steep rocky slopes, was not a stream to meet the travelers' approval. By the time they reached the alkaline pools and sinks at its lower end most of them were in a state of exasperation with the whole region, particularly if they had passed through it during the hottest season. It took some time before more than a very few pioneers were aware of the fertile pockets along the overland road in Nevada, and even longer before numbers came to realize that other land of the region was valuable.

Trading posts soon appeared along the Humboldt Road, one of the first at Ragtown (later Leeteville) by the Carson River. In June, 1849, H. S. Beatie, one of the traders sent out by Brigham Young, built a log stockade and a corral for horses and cattle at the base of the Sierra by the trail. This place, first called Mormon Station, later became Genoa. In 1850 the United States Government, ignoring Young's State of Deseret, announced the creation of the Territory of Utah, which included Nevada, then called Western Utah. At the same time southern Nevada was placed in the Territory of New Mexico. Within three years a sprinkling of farms surrounded Mormon Station and extended into the neighboring Washoe and Eagle valleys.

In 1851 George Chorpenning and Absalom Woodward won the contract to carry mail between Salt Lake City—which already had service from the East—and Sacramento. The first eastbound mail, carried from Sacramento on mule-back, reached Carson Valley on May 17, 1851, but as the traders and settlers of that year had not yet arrived there was no one on hand to cheer the riders on their way. The difficulties the contractors met were enormous and service was far from regular; in winter the mail was sometimes taken south over the Mormon Trail. In 1853 mail service over the Sierra was provided by men on snowshoes. Three years later a powerful man who gained the affectionate nickname of "Snowshoe" Thompson began to carry the mail back and forth, and during deep snows he was sometimes the only means of communication between Carson Valley and the outside world. At first the mail route between Carson Valley and Salt Lake City followed the Humboldt throughout and then Goose Creek, but in 1855 it was shifted south to avoid the snows and other impediments north of the Rubies. In 1854 a road was cleared across the Sierra and a four-mule team began to haul mail and passengers between Salt Lake City and California. By 1857 there was tri-weekly passenger service across the mountains and travelers could use stages the whole way from the Missouri to the West Coast. In the meantime the Government had begun to explore again, looking for the best route to the coast, and in the summer of 1854 the Forty-Second Parallel Expedition had reached the western part of Western Utah.

Settlers in Carson Valley noted these advances in transportation facilities with interest, and wondered whether the clamor of Californians for a railroad would ever be satisfied. But they took little part in the agitation, being much too busy with the construction of irrigation ditches and the building of simple shelters for themselves and their stock. Moreover their primary concern was for a government of their own kind. Even the Mormons, though accustomed to church government, felt at a disadvantage with the seat of territorial government five hundred miles away across mountains and desert.

After Brigham Young, Governor of Utah Territory, heard that the settlers of Carson and neighboring valleys were beginning to agitate to have the area east of the Sierra Nevada attached to California, he erected most of Western Utah into huge Carson County and sent out Orson Hyde, one of the Twelve Apostles, to preside over the county court. Hyde arrived in 1855 and made Mormon Station the county seat, renaming it Genoa. Soon afterward he laid out Franktown in Washoe Valley, built a saw mill, and prepared to build up a second Salt Lake City close to the Sierra.

Young continued to scatter his colonies over the Basin wherever there was water for irrigation; Las Vegas was settled by the Saints in 1855.

Then in 1857 Young recalled all Saints to Salt Lake City in order to mass his forces in the conflict with the national government—a call to which nearly all responded. The settlers looked on their departure with glee and bought up the Mormon farms and other possessions for as little as competition would permit. Orson Hyde later cursed them heartily (*see Tour* 4) for the prices they paid. The remaining farmers and traders vainly petitioned Washington for a new government; if

California would not accept them they wanted an independent territory erected.

NEVADA TERRITORY

In 1857 residents of Genoa and Carson, led by Isaac Roop of Susanville—which was in California but was then believed to be in Utah Territory—convened at Genoa, adopted a constitution for what they called the Territory of Nevada, and asked Congress to recognize their independence. The plea was ignored. After the Mormons and the Federal government called a truce in 1858 an effort was made to reestablish Utah territorial government here, but in the absence of the Mormon settlers Utah officials could not find any respect for their orders.

A second effort to obtain official territorial government for Nevada was made in 1859. On September 7, just after the stampede to Washoe began, Roop was elected governor. He met with a rump legislature on December 15, 1859, and theoretically continued with the duties of governor of the provisional government after adjournment.

A year before the goldrush to California began a member of the Mormon Battalion who had worked for Sutter after demobilization panned some gold near the Carson River while on his way home to Deseret. Later other travelers did the same, but reports of these discoveries attracted no attention; they were too insignificant to compete with the vast treasure being uncovered on the western side of the Sierra. After a few years there was a semi-permanent camp near a canyon at the southern end of the Virginia Range; here men disappointed in California would stay for a few weeks or months on their way back home, panning and prospecting, though with little real hope of uncovering wealth comparable to that which they had missed beyond the mountain. Only a few Chinese, who had come from California to dig an irrigation ditch, had the patience to pan steadily for small returns. The camp of the whites moved slowly up the canyon, followed by the Johntown of the Chinese. None of the returning forty-niners knew any metal but gold and it did not occur to them that there might be other values. Though one Latin-American did recognize traces of silver no one understood what he was trying to tell until the Grosch brothers (see Tour 8) arrived in 1856; they worked secretly and apparently found silver. Both died, however, before they could realize on their discovery.

The long and secretive activity of the Grosch boys had aroused the curiosity of Henry Comstock, an old trapper and trader of Carson Valley. After the boys were gone he tried vainly to discover what had held their interest—he believed it was gold. When in 1859 two miners found an unusually good outcrop of gold he immediately insisted that the claim belonged to a friend, and then arranged to share it himself. Other claims were staked and profits began to mount, though the gold was mixed with some "black stuff" that made recovery difficult. Finally one man sent out a sample of the strange ore for assay, and almost overnight all California knew that silver of unbelievable richness had been found in Washoe.

Immediately the stampede back over the mountains was on; it seemed as if every man who had rushed into California in the course of ten years took part in it—miners, prospectors, lawyers, middlemen, engineers, all mixed up with the dregs of the California camps, which had become less hospitable to them. The result was chaos. No government with any authority existed and the newcomers outnumbered the old-timers of the valleys ten to one in a short time. The discoveries had been made on public land and there were no mining laws, except those laid down by rule of the camp. As the ground began to give up millions, claims and counter-claims grew hotter, and in the absence of responsible authority men enforced their rights with guns if need be—and the need was always there, the rowdies and hoodlums being uncontrolled. For five long years this situation went on, with every man having to gamble on the safety of any investment he chose to make in development. The returns were so high, however, that many took the risk.

The presence of thousands of newcomers who were killing their game, burning down their pine nut trees, and driving them from their accustomed resorts, had the Indians in turmoil by 1860. In the spring the natives of the whole region, largely Paiutes, gathered at Pyramid Lake for a war council. This was still going on when the post of James Williams, a trader living about twenty-five miles east of Carson, was burned by Indians; three white men were shot and two others were burned to death. The generally accepted story on the cause of the attack is that one or more of the men had stolen a couple of young Bannock squaws and thirty other Bannocks had joined the husbands in recapturing the women and punishing the captors. The news of this attack sent fear up and down the valleys; no one bothered to ask whether the Indians had acted under provocation. One hundred and five men hastily volunteered to go after them and popular William M. Ormsby (*see Tour 4*) took command of the Carson unit. The Indians in council were undoubtedly as disturbed as the whites by what had happened and noted the approach of the volunteers with alarm. The whites had almost reached the lake before a single Indian was seen; when the two groups met, however, the Indians determined to take the offensive and the whites suffered heavy losses. Among those killed were Ormsby and another prominent leader, Henry Meredith.

The return of the survivors threw the whole white population of the Far West into panic. Volunteers from Nevada gathered and were soon joined by others from Downieville, California. San Francisco raised money and arms and the Governor of California sent muskets and ammunition. The commander of the Presidio in San Francisco ordered cavalry at Honey Lake to undertake a punitive expedition. On May 11 the cavalry met about five hundred and fifty volunteers at the Big Bend of the Truckee and scouts were sent ahead toward Pyramid; they reported about three hundred Indians advancing, and the regulars and volunteers went forward to meet them. A three-hour battle took place. The Indians fled at dusk after a loss estimated at forty-six men; three white men were killed and four were wounded. The main force later followed the Indians but all had disappeared. After this the Indians staged various raids on the Pony Express and stage stations, and Pony Express service from San Francisco was interrupted for ten days. As a result of this outbreak Fort Churchill (*see Tour* 7) was established along the trail near Carson. Further trouble came in eastern Nevada in 1862, at the time when Indians all over the country were seizing the Civil War as an opportunity to drive out the whites. The outbreak resulted in the establishment of Fort Ruby (*see Tour 1A*). The majority of the Indians fled into the deserts, where they nearly starved.

Throughout 1860 Congress paid no attention to pleas that a separate territorial government be set up for Nevada, but early in 1861 a territorial organic act was passed, and on March 2, 1861, a day before the end of the session, President Buchanan signed it. All that part of Utah Territory west of the 116th meridian became Nevada Territory. The authorized boundaries included a section of California, but that State refused to transfer the land involved. A year later an act of Congress conveyed a further piece of Utah to the new Territory, pushing its boundary eastward by one degree of longitude. In 1869, a third piece of Utah was added, fixing Nevada's eastern boundary on the 114th meridian; at the same time the State acquired from Arizona the triangular southern area below the 37th parallel.

One of President Lincoln's earliest acts on taking office in 1861 was to commission James W. Nye, a New York politician, as governor. Nye at once proceeded to the Territory by sea and on July 11 proclaimed establishment of the Territorial Government. In November the legislature convened at Carson City, which was made the capital.

In *Roughing It,* Mark Twain, whose brother had been made territorial secretary, gave a burlesque account of the trials of setting up a government in a vast region that only two years before had had less than a thousand people and at the time probably had only about twenty thousand—exclusive of large numbers of transients. But his account could not have been far from fact; the legislators and most of the territorial officers had had no experience in statesmanship and there were problems that would have puzzled Solomon. This was a new kind of community; only a very small minority of the population had homes and farm lands—the kind of property owned by most law-framers. No one knew who really owned the mines, since they were on public lands, and no way of acquiring this type of land legally had as yet been worked out. One of the first acts of the territorial legislature was establishment of a prison to meet the much crying need of the time.

The legislature organized nine counties at its first session—Ormsby, Storey, Esmeralda, Humboldt, Churchill, Douglas, Lyon, Lake, and Washoe. Lake was renamed Roop County, but this was no advantage to it, because when the survey was run to establish the boundary between California and Nevada part of the county was given to California, including the farm of Isaac Roop, and little land of value was on the Nevada side. Roop County soon became part of Washoe.

Although Governor Nye was personally popular, within a year the territory was in revolt against other members of the Territorial Government. Practically all had been given their jobs for party service, not for fitness, and their salaries were extremely low in a land of very high prices. Judicial procedure became a farce and men despaired of getting justice; even the juries were flagrantly in the business of selling their verdicts—juries selected by some occult procedure satisfactory to the judges. William Stewart, ablest of all silver-rush lawyers, took an active part in exposing these conditions and stirring up sentiment for statehood, which would make the executive and judiciary dependent on approval of the electorate.

The national and international situation was responsible for most of the curious events of Nevada's political history during the next three years. With the outbreak of the Civil War the mining of silver and gold became of vital importance to the country, and it was exceedingly

Rothstein: Farm Security Admin.

A DRY LAKE BED

Photograph by Charles D. Gallagher

MOUNT WHEELER

U. S. 95, NORTH OF LAS VEGAS *Photograph courtesy Nevada State Highway Dept.*

PYRAMID LAKE

THE SQUAW AND HER BASKET, PYRAMID LAKE

Photograph courtesy Nevada State Highway Dept.

CATHEDRAL GORGE

Photograph by Charles D. Gallagher

Photograph courtesy Smithsonian Institution **THE SITE OF BOULDER DAM (c. 1871)**
This, the first photograph of Black Canyon,
was made by T. H. O'Sullivan, photographer of the Wheeler Expedition to the
Territories.

Photograph courtesy Department of Interior **BOULDER DAM AND LAKE MEAD**

LONG VALLEY, NEAR OREGON LINE

THE HUMBOLDT—ROUTE OF THE '49ERS. *Photograph courtesy George Schwartz*

**THE ELEPHANT—
VALLEY OF FIRE**

ROCK FORMATION, NEAR JARBIDGE

DESERT DUST STORM   *Rothstein: Farm Security Admin.*

LIGHTNING STRIKES TONOPAH (1902)   *Photograph courtesy Mrs. Key Pittman*

important to keep valuable producers loyal to the Union. Southerners were in a minority in Nevada, but that minority was vociferous and clashes between Unionists and "Rebs" were sometimes violent. Washington listened anxiously. The North was not by any means united and the administration was anxiously looking about for supporters. A movement was initiated to give statehood to Montana, Colorado, and Nebraska, as well as Nevada, after Nevada had held a poll on the question in September, 1863. Only Nevada came in during the war. That the territory at most had less than a sixth of the population then required for a single representative in Congress was brushed aside by advocates of statehood.

Once Nevada had demonstrated its Union sentiment there was a further reason, carefully guarded, why President Lincoln worked hard to have it admitted. One of England's leading industries was cotton spinning and weaving, and England was practically dependent on the South for raw materials. With production wrecked by the war, with shipments irregular or cut off by the blockade, one cotton mill after the other was closed. As the clamor of mill-owners and mill-workers increased in bitterness, Her Majesty's government began to show a partisan attitude, and before two years had passed it was apparent that Britain might come out openly with aid for the South. President Lincoln was deeply concerned, because the South might win independence if powerful foreign aid reached it. In an attempt to ward off the danger a friendly demonstration to the United States Government by the Tzarist government was arranged, a visit by Russian ships to New York Harbor. Another move was the Emancipation Proclamation of January 1, 1863. Although Lincoln was opposed to slavery he had wanted to abolish it by some means that would not wreck the economy of the South; but Britain had abolished slavery and British public opinion was strongly against it. To that time the war issue had been States' rights; the effect of the proclamation was to make the issue slavery. But a presidential proclamation was not completely satisfactory, since it was questionable whether a president could abolish enormous property rights, even as a war measure. A constitutional amendment was absolutely necessary. The proclamation had made Britain pause and the firm stand of the American Government against furtive help was having temporary effect. The problem then was where a sufficient number of senatorial votes could be obtained to pass the amendment. Lincoln dispensed patronage liberally but did not quite reach the required number of senators. The admission of one more State of proper sentiment met the need nicely.

Proponents of the enabling act to set up the State of Nevada argued that though the Nevada population was small this must be a temporary condition, since the Territory was producing twenty-four million dollars a year and under a stable government would undoubtedly do much better. The act was passed on March 3, 1863, under executive pressure.

The Nevada constitutional convention met eight months later, and the make-up of the convention gave an enlightening view of the population. Only four members had not been in California and more had come originally from New York than from any other State. Although the passionate interest of everyone in Nevada was the mines, the delegates included eight lawyers, five merchants, one hotel keeper, one physician, one banker, one notary public, one sign-painter, and two farmers. The average age was thirty-nine and only half the members were married.

The section of the constitution that caused most argument concerned taxation; William Stewart said one clause, seemingly innocent, would soon kill mining in the Territory by taxing every mine whether it was producing or not. After Stewart failed to have the section modified— perhaps because of the non-mining make-up of the convention—he took to the field to prevent approval of the constitution by the electorate. His success in January, 1864, forced attention to the taxation question and arrangements for a new enabling act were made in short order. Additional worries made for unity; some congressmen in Washington, faced with additional war levies, had hit on the idea of the Government forcing the mine claimants to operate on lease, the royalties they paid to go into the Federal treasury. Another act authorizing a constitutional convention was introduced in Congress and after much debate was passed; it was signed by the president on March 21, 1864. This time the convention members were elected, assembled, and through with their work in four months. A date in October had been set for submitting the new constitution to the electorate for ratification, but when it was discovered that this would leave too little time to organize election districts for the coming presidential election, Congress was persuaded to set a date in September. With this agreed to, a territorial Republican convention was held in August. Judiciary corruption had reached a peak at this time and nearly everyone was anxious to hurry establishment of a government responsible to the people of Nevada. So great was the haste for admission to the Union that the entire constitution was telegraphed to Washington—a feat that cost $3,416.77. Nevada was proclaimed a State on October 31. Six weeks later the first legislature met to set up house—and also to clean it up.

The territorial period had been one of continuous mining development, with new districts being organized all over the region and camps appearing in almost every section. Also, settlement had been progressing in the more fertile valleys. As a territory Nevada had raised a regiment of infantry for the Union Army in 1861, and later enlisted six troops of cavalry and six companies of infantry, none of which, however, was ordered to the front. The Gridley sack of flour (*see Austin*) was the Territory's most notable contribution to the war. When R. C. Gridley of Austin lost an election bet, he had to carry a fifty pound sack of flour on his shoulders down the main street. The sack was then offered at auction for the benefit of the United States Sanitary Commission, predecessor of the American Red Cross. The purchaser returned it for sale and it was auctioned off later on the Comstock, and in many places on the Pacific Coast and in the eastern states, producing two hundred and seventy-five thousand dollars for the aid of the war wounded.

THE STATE OF NEVADA

During the long struggle for an elected government, channels of communication had been increasing rapidly in number and efficiency. The Pony Express had hardly begun its career when Congress took a step that eventually made it unnecessary, ordering a call for bids on construction of a telegraph line from the Missouri River west. After the rush to Washoe a line had been strung across the Sierra to Carson and this had soon been extended to Fort Churchill. As construction progressed westward Salt Lake City was for a time the terminal and the Pony Express filled the gap between it and the post. By 1862 Ben Holladay had taken over and reorganized stage service between the Missouri and the Coast, and his Overland Stage company had begun to send off daily coaches, a service that continued until 1869, when the first transcontinental railroad was completed and began carrying the mail.

Agitation for the building of a railroad between the Mississippi and the West Coast had been going on for years, with Senator Benton, Fremont's father-in-law, as one of the strongest proponents. The greatest barrier had been the question of its course; the southern faction controlling Congress had insisted on a southern route and northerners had been divided in opinion between a central and a northern route. Surveys had been made and only a decision was needed. Soon after the Civil War removed the objecting southern senators, the Omaha-Sacramento route was adopted. Construction did not actually begin until after the war was over. Though Congress had handed out princely grants of land and made the Government first mortgagee, this was not enough to satisfy the financiers who wanted to enter the game and later the grants were greatly increased. Two companies undertook the work—the Central Pacific and the Union Pacific.

The original provisions ended Central Pacific construction at the California-Nevada Line. Theodore Judah, who organized the Central Pacific, died while in the East, and Leland Stanford, Collis P. Huntington, Mark Hopkins, and Charles Crocker then took charge. Under pressure, the original provisions were amended to permit the Central Pacific to build one hundred and fifty miles eastward across Nevada, then amended again to permit each company to build as far as it could to meet the other. This provision produced the race that was to absorb national attention. The chief incentive for the struggle lay in the vast Government grants of bonds and lands alloted on a mileage basis. The Union Pacific company, angry about the change, which gave not only land but also the rich Comstock freighting to the Central Pacific, determined to reach the Salt Lake first in order to ensure the profitable Mormon trade to itself.

By the end of 1868 the Central Pacific was out of the Humboldt Valley and the Union Pacific was at the foot of the Wasatch Range, each racing for Ogden. The Union Pacific entered Ogden first, with some of its track laid on the hard snow. The two roads met at last on April 18, 1869, at Promontory, Utah, 690 miles from Sacramento and 1,080 miles from Omaha, with rival locomotives facing each other on a single track. On May 10 the last rail was ceremoniously laid on a polished block of California laurel and fastened with a spike of solid gold.

Nevada's enthusiasm over the Central Pacific soon gave way to controversies over rates and fares. The company was properly accused of "charging all the traffic would bear." This source of friction did not decrease until the Interstate Commerce Commission was created in 1887. Establishment of the State Railroad Commission in 1907 ended the trouble. In 1885 control of the Central Pacific had passed to the Southern Pacific Company.

Long before the Central Pacific was completed, freighting was an important business in the territory and by the time the railroad arrived long lines of teams were in service to bring ore and bullion to it.

As large mining camps developed to the north and the south of the Central Pacific numerous plans for branch roads were proposed. But only a few of importance were ever built. The Virginia & Truckee, tapping the Comstock, was completed in 1869. White Pine production declined before plans crystallized for a road to serve that temporarily important district. The branch that reached Eureka in 1875 saved the town's existence when mineral production fell a few years later by making it a distribution center for the east central part of the State. The branch tapping Austin, unfortunately for the builders, was not completed until 1880, when the richest silver deposits had been exhausted and the mining of lower-grade ores had become unprofitable. The third important branch road, serving the Ely district, was not constructed until 1906.

At the period when Nevada's belief in a long period of mining prosperity was highest, a movement had begun that was to have serious effects on the State's history. The problem of a sound monetary system, which had been a factor in the American Revolution, had never been solved. It was, however, inextricably tied up with international monetary problems. England had first adopted the gold standard in 1816, though the rest of Europe had retained silver as the basis of its currency. The United States had been using both silver and gold as legal tender, and had, in 1834, fixed the value of gold at sixteen times that of silver. But this arbitrary rating had not settled the matter. The value of gold and silver bullion on the London market, which determined prices all over the world, fluctuated with the supply.

From the beginning the money question was a political foot-ball in the United States, with debt-burdened farmers fighting deflation by the holders of bonds and mortgages, who wanted to have a national bank and a strictly controlled currency system backed by a fixed percentage of a single metal. And the farmers had been in control until the Civil War, as the southern plantation owners were powerful representatives of the debtor class. Early in the Civil War the Republicans had abolished the State banks, which had largely contributed to inflation by their note issues, and had established a national banking system. Then the great costs of the war had forced the Republicans to inflation; they helped authorize the printing of great quantities of greenbacks unsupported by metal.

After the war, deflation became an acute problem, and the crisis in the United States coincided with international troubles over the same question. In an attempt to bring about the adoption of an international monetary standard in the interests of world trade a conference was held at Paris in 1867, and it adopted gold as the basis for its proposed system. The Franco-Prussian War of 1870-1 forced France, a leader in the conference, from the adopted standard, by turning over the great French gold stores to Germany in the form of indemnities. The United States, however, adopted the gold standard in 1873 and in 1875 Congress enacted a law providing for resumption of specie payment at the end of four years. At the time the silver-producing States paid little attention to the first act, which they later referred to as "the Crime of '73."

In 1873 silver was valued at $1.29 an ounce in London; by 1879 it brought only $1.12. With a decline of fifteen cents by 1876 the silver-producers began to unite politically with the debtors, and they demanded unlimited coinage of silver; though they failed in their objective, in 1878 they did manage to have the Bland-Allison Act passed, ensuring the purchase and coinage of not less than two million dollars worth of silver annually by the Treasury and a possible purchase and coinage of four million.

This measure failed to save Nevada. The great deposits of ore rich in silver had been mined and the gold still being found was either limited in quantity or so mixed with other minerals as to give little profit. The result was an exodus of population from the camps in Storey, Lander, Eureka, and Lincoln counties, and the gradual closing of the great mines of the Comstock.

In the meantime cattle-raising had gained considerable importance in the State, though it did not add materially to the size of the human population for it was carried on largely by big outfits and employed relatively few people. These outfits waged deadly war with one another for some years, then more or less united to drive out newcomers who wanted to share the public grazing lands. With the decline of mining the cattle barons took control of the State. They met their Waterloo in the late 1880's, when an unusually severe winter found them with little hay. Cattle lay dead all over the Nevada range that year and many former cattle barons faced the spring penniless.

On top of this calamity came others. Low prices and decreased industrial production lessened demand for all Nevada products—cattle and minerals—after the financial difficulties that began with the British Baring Brothers late in 1890. Then, in 1893 President Cleveland called a special session of Congress and forced repeal of the silver purchase act. Again there was a sharp drop in Nevada population and the older political parties practically disappeared in the State, to be replaced by the Silver Party, which co-operated with the Populists and elected a senator previously Republican in politics. A "silver member" was also elected to the House of Representatives. But in 1896, when William Jennings Bryan held the Democratic Convention spell-bound with his "Cross of Gold" speech and became the convention's nominee for the presidency, the Silver Party of Nevada merged with the Democratic Party.

There was hardly a Nevadan who did not feel that Bryan was speaking for him when he cried:

"There are two ideas of government. There are those who believe that if you will only legislate to make the well-to-do prosperous their prosperity will leak through on those below. The democratic idea, however, has been that if you legislate to make the masses prosperous their prosperity will find its way through every class which rests upon them.

"You come to us and tell us that the great cities are in favor of the gold standard; we reply that the great cities rest upon our broad and fertile prairies. Burn down your cities and leave our farms, and your cities will spring up again as if by magic; but destroy our farms and the grass will grow in the streets of every city in the country.

"Having behind us the producing masses of this nation and the world, supported by the commercial interests, the labor interests, and the toilers everywhere, we will answer their demand for a gold standard by saying to them: You shall not press down upon the brow of labor this crown of thorns, you shall not crucify mankind upon a cross of gold."

By 1902 silver had ceased to be an intra-state issue; Republicans and Democrats alike bore the silver label in Washington and the parties have more or less alternated in control of the State.

Except for the silver issue, few public questions have stirred Nevadans, but occasionally strong sentiment has been manifested, as on the Chinese exclusion question and on that of establishing a permanent lottery in the State. Although the exclusion of Chinese could be accomplished only by national legislation, the State in 1889 expressed its view by voting to exclude them, with 17,259 for the measure and only 183 opposed. A bill to allow a lottery, passed by the legislature in the 1880's, was vetoed by the government. In 1893 the legislature adopted a resolution amending the state constitution to permit organization of a lottery, but the amendment was never submitted to the voters, since a consitutional amendment must be passed at two successive sessions before being submitted to the people at a general election and when the time came for the legislature to act a second time, public disapproval of the measure was so strong that it was dropped.

During the twenty-five years in which Virginia City controlled State politics, senators were chosen by the legislature and senatorial elections were the principal source of political excitement, with charges of bribery common.

After the discovery and mining of great silver deposits at Tonopah (*see Tour* 5) in 1900, and the uncovering of Goldfield's wealth in 1903, the ebbing tide of population turned and many thousands of men and women came into the State. Although the price of silver had dropped to 63 cents in 1894 and the average price by 1909 was 52 cents, the ores of Tonopah were so rich that huge profits were possible even at the low price. The Tonopah discovery stirred prospectors to new activities and the whole State was again fine-combed for promising outcrops, with the result that many new camps appeared and a few had some years of profitable production. In the long run the most important strike of the period was made near Ely, where vast quantities of copper were found. When the great silver and gold deposits were exhausted Ely copper moved to the front as the State's leading mineral product.

The mining revival started much new railroad-building. Minor roads had been built to tap the soutl *a* stern part of the State but the region did not have real service until after the Tonopah boom. In 1903 construction was begun to connect Salt Lake City and Los Angeles by way of Las Vegas; this Los Angeles and Salt Lake Railroad was eventually absorbed by the Union Pacific. Former Senator W. A. Clark of Montana early began to build the Las Vegas and Tonopah, but the Tonopah and Tidewater, backed by the F. M. Smith borax interests, was constructed, and was extended to Goldfield before Clark's railroad reached the area; this extension was achieved by purchase of the little Bullfrog and Goldfield Railroad. When Clark's road was abandoned soon after the World War ended, it had already paid for itself. The Tonopah and Tidewater was abandoned in 1939. The Tonopah and Goldfield, between Mina and Goldfield, is still in operation.

The Western Pacific Railroad Company, which built the third trunk line across the State, had its genesis in the mind of Walter Bartnett, a young lawyer of San Francisco; the road was constructed across the Sierra Nevada and then extended with the support of George Gould and the Missouri Pacific. It is now the western unit of the system that includes the Denver & Rio Grande and the Missouri Pacific. For most of its distance in Nevada it closely parallels the Southern Pacific main line.

The Virginia & Truckee now operates only between Reno and Minden with service to Virginia City abandoned; the Eureka & Palisade ended its career in 1938. The Nevada Central Railroad, which served the mines of the Austin District, has also ceased operation. But the Nevada Northern still serves the copper producing region around Ely. The Nevada Copper Belt line from Wabuska to Ludwig serves the Yerington and Mason districts, and several short branches of main lines reach smaller communities.

Development of the extensive stock industry of Nevada has been largely dependent on railroads and the new roads lessened the need for long cattle drives by southern stockmen and gradually localized operations. The stock business, like copper mining, has become exceedingly important in supplying an industry independent of gold and silver mining with its great fluctuations in production.

An unusual political event of the revival period took place in 1910, when young Key Pittman, who had come to the State during the Tonopah rush of 1902, ran for election as the Democratic candidate against Republican George S. Nixon, an old timer and banker who had already held the seat for one term. At that time senators were still being chosen by the legislature. During the pre-election campaign the rival candidates stumped the State and reached a public agreement to submit their names to the electorate, though neither the Federal nor State constitution provided for such a course. Nixon won the popular vote but the Democrats won a majority in the legislature, which had to meet in joint session for selection of a senator. Pittman accepted defeat and asked his backers to make Nixon's re-election unanimous. Moved by this act, the Republican faction then proposed a resolution in which, carefully labeling itself the minority party, it "resolved . . . to congratulate the Democratic members for the way they had bowed to the will of the people"; further resolved to congratulate the loser on the "unequivocal manner in which he carried out his part in the 'gentlemen's agreement' "; and finally resolved that "the election of a Republican who was chosen by the popular vote, as against a candidate for the same office, with a Democrat majority in control of the Legislature, emphasizes an epoch in American politics of which the Senate of the United States may well take heed."

Nixon died in June, 1912, and Judge W. A. Massey, a Democrat long in politics, was appointed to fill his place until the next meeting of the legislature, when Pittman was elected. In May, 1912, the Federal amendment calling for the election of senators by popular vote had been "proposed to the legislatures of the several States." Nevada had already shown its mind.

The second mining boom had begun to decline with the exhaustion of the richest mines when, in 1914, the declaration of war in Europe started a third great boom with demand for copper, tungsten, zinc, and other minerals needed for munitions. The mines employed five thousand eight hundred men in addition to those in reduction plants.

Since the 1860's labor has had an important role in Nevada life. In general early mining was carried on by Cornish, Irish, Scottish, and English workers; canal-building by Chinese and French; railroad construction by Chinese and Mexicans; lumbering by Chinese and Irish; stock raising by men of mixed American blood; and sheep herding by Basques.

Miners' unions were organized in all early mining camps of the State, and on the whole maintained fair hours, fair wages, and safety measures. But the locals have not operated continuously because of fluctuations in production.

Since 1861 wages have necessarily been higher than in some other States because of high living costs, result of the need for importing most food stuffs and lumber. In Virginia City miners at first received from three and a half to four dollars a day; laborers "on top"—around the surface workings—were also paid four dollars a day. The ten-hour day was considered the standard working period until the 1870's when an eight-hour day for some mine laborers was established by law. In the 1870's farm laborers received from forty to fifty dollars a month with board and room, while the Chinese, at the bottom of the wage scale, received thirty-five dollars a month for railroad grade-work and boarded themselves.

Nevada has had relatively few periods of labor violence but in 1879 a battle between charcoal burners and officers of the law occurred at Eureka; five charcoal burners were killed and six others badly wounded. The second notable trouble came during the second great boom. At Tonopah in 1906 labor was organized as the Tonopah Mine Operators' Association and set up a scale of wages and working hours for all mine laborers that was accepted by all operators in the Tonopah district; underground laborers were limited to eight hours a day, and surface-men, including ore sorters, blacksmiths, carpenters, engineers, electricians, and machinists to nine hours a day. Wages ran from four dollars to five and a half. The Tonopah agreement did not cover Goldfield, where in 1907 a serious labor clash took place; before it was settled the Governor of Nevada asked, and received, aid from Federal troops to protect property.

In 1939 the mining wage scale was higher than it had been during the three preceding years and reports of January, 1940, showed the average earnings above those of the previous year. In general the 1939 wage of an experienced miner was five dollars and a half for an eight-hour shift; muckers and trammers received from fifty cents to one dollar less. The scale is linked with the price of metals and varies from product to product. Thus, the price of copper was so low in 1937 that producers in the big new Mountain City District shut down for several months, but by 1939, when quotations rose, miners were being paid on a higher scale than when the mines first resumed production. A drop of three or four cents a pound necessarily curtails employment, and hence the annual income of the workers.

On the whole, mining wages are higher in the southern part of Nevada than in the northern and central regions, since another factor that determines the pay rate is the cost of transportation to smelters.

Most mining has no seasonal fluctuations, the chief variable, in addition to price, being the amount of ore available, a factor inevitable in the industry. Mechanical and other inventions promoting greater efficiency have affected mining employment very little in recent years, though there had been a large reduction when new machinery was installed at Ruth and McGill.

There is no set wage scale in ranching operations. The chief seasonal employment is for haying and grain harvesting and the same groups of workers return year after year. The large stock outfits maintain a permanent staff the year round in addition to the harvest crews. The permanent workers average fifty dollars a month with board, sometimes a trifle less. Haymen in some instances receive slightly more, the average man getting two to two dollars and fifty cents a day with room and board, while stackers obtain three to three dollars and fifty cents; mowers, rakers, and wagon men draw an intermediate wage. During the World War stackers received five to six dollars a day. Pay is slightly higher on ranches around Reno, Fallon, and Carson City than in the more thinly settled southern region. The ranchers of the Moapa and Virgin River country harvest their asparagus, tomatoes, and other crops co-operatively, and little outside labor, if any, is employed, members of the association dividing the work as well as the profits.

Although haying machinery and shearing methods have improved, the changes have had little effect on the wage scale. The machinery has, however, reduced the demand for labor. In the Elko ranching district, for example, it is estimated that one tractor with two men can now do the work formerly done by twenty horses and seven men. Machine men, who must be trained in the operation of such intricate equipment as threshers, draw higher pay than the general hands. In threshing, where the pay varies from two to five or six dollars a day, according to the locality and demand, a man owning a threshing machine handles grain by contract, taking along with him a crew consisting of a separator-tender, an engineman, and a sack-sewer. Although ranch wages have improved over those of 1930-35, in 1939 they were approximately one-fourth less than in 1929.

As late as 1937 herders for the sheep outfits were receiving only sixty dollars a month, but in 1939 there was a substantial increase.

American Federation of Labor affiliates predominate in the mining field though the Committee for Industrial Organization has gained a foothold in Ely and Pioche. Workers in other industries are also organized, including the office and restaurant employees of Reno.

Nevada is still governed under the constitution adopted when it became a State in 1864 but the clause requiring officials to take oath they had never fought a duel was repealed in 1914. In 1904 the referendum was introduced and in 1912 the initiative. An amendment giving women suffrage was ratified at the election of 1914, many years before the Federal amendment was made. Nevada became dry a few months before the national Prohibition Amendment was adopted. The government is headed by a governor and has the usual State officials and legislature of two houses, which meets every two years for a period limited by law.

Mining and Mining Jargon

THE history of Nevada can roughly be divided into four twenty-year periods, each of them more or less coinciding with a mining cycle. The first period was characterized by the discovery and mining of the Comstock Lode and other deposits of silver and gold, some unbelievably rich and others of less importance. The next period saw a rapid decline in mining as a result of the exhaustion of rich deposits and the demonetization of silver. The third period, which began with the great silver discovery at Tonopah, followed by jewelry-ore gold at Goldfield, copper at Ely, and many scattered strikes of lesser value, continued to be highly profitable even after the richest silver and gold mines became unproductive, for the outbreak of war in Europe created a demand for many Nevada minerals.

At the beginning of the fourth period there was another rapid decline in demand, as well as a lack of large known deposits of ore rich in silver and gold. The price of silver, which had risen during the war above its 1873 level, dropped a third within a year. But the pattern of the second period, with its great loss of population and virtual cessation of mining activity, was not repeated. Introduction of the cyanide recovery process saved the day. Up to about 1921 nearly all silver and gold recovery in Nevada had been by the ancient amalgamation process, in which the values were extracted from pulverized silver ores by amalgamizing the metal with mercury; the mercury was afterward expelled. This process recovered only part of the values, sometimes less than half. The cyanide process, invented in 1887 to enable more complete recovery of gold, and later tried on silver ores, had been little used in the State. Although more expensive than the amalgamation process, it enabled the profitable working of low grade ores and the reworking of old tailings. Copper, undiscovered at the time of the first mining collapse, also gave considerable income in the post-war period, though profits dropped sharply.

The international price of silver continued to decline after 1921 and in 1932 reached an all-time low of 24½ cents—with an average for the year of 28 cents—with such serious results to world trade, as well as to the silver producers, that the United States in 1933 requested an international monetary conference. Sixty-six governments participated and to prevent a further debasing of silver, the chief silver-producing countries, Australia, Canada, Mexico, Peru, and the United States, agreed, for a period of four years, to absorb thirty-five million ounces of silver annually; the share of the United States was to be at least twenty-four and a half million. The price of newly minted silver was then fixed at 64.64 cents a fine ounce, and in 1934 Congress passed an act with the declared policy of increasing to one-fourth the proportion of silver to gold in the Nation's monetary stocks. These measures have been heavily supported by Nevada members of Congress and have stimulated the mining of the State's low-grade silver ores. New discoveries of rich gold and copper deposits have also provided Nevada with sources of profit for its fifth period of mining, whose beginning has coincided with the outbreak of a second great European war.

Since 1859 Nevada has sent out approximately one billion six hundred million dollars worth of mineral, but with mining production dependent on three very unstable factors—demand, price, and the discovery and exhaustion of deposits—the reports of a single year on the value and quantity of production are apt to be highly misleading.

Nothing better illustrates the fluctuations of the mining industry than the reports of Nevada production in 1937, 1938, and 1939. In 1938 the total Nevada output of gold, silver, copper, lead, and zinc was valued at only $23,529,064—slightly more than two-thirds of the return for the previous year. Gold accounted for 44 per cent of the production, copper 38 per cent, silver 12 per cent, zinc 4 per cent, and lead 2 per cent. Because of the low price of copper the three leading producers had sharply curtailed production, and the lead mines in Nye County had exhausted their deposits. But preliminary figures for 1939 showed production of gold, silver, copper, lead, and zinc to a value of $29,321,587. With the new copper-producing center active and the price of copper rising, owing to the war demand, copper had risen approximately 42 per cent in quantity and 50 per cent in value since 1938. Gold production in 1939 was higher than at any time since 1916 and its value exceeded that of any year since 1912, when Goldfield was still active. This increase in production came largely from expansion at the Getchell Mine, which began bringing up ore in the spring of 1938, from gold-dredging at Manhattan, and from renewed activity near Ely. In spite of somewhat better silver prices in 1939 production of silver went off 7 per cent, with Silver Peak accounting for a third of the total.

The Lincoln County Pioche District in 1939 produced three-fifths of the lead and nine-tenths of the zinc going out of the State.

Of the nearly six million tons of Nevada lode material sold or treated in 1938, more than 70 per cent was sent to mills where the ores were concentrated with the aid of water or air and specific gravity, and 17.5 per cent went to amalgamation and cyanide mills.

Large quantities of ores and concentrates, largely lead and copper, are sent out of the State, principally to mills of Utah, because Nevada does not have the fuel necessary for operation of smelters. McGill remains the single Nevada smelter though plans had been made for another in the Ely district and construction was abandoned only after the great copper interests had made an agreement early in 1940 that called for smelting of Nevada copper elsewhere.

One Nevada mineral in great demand at the end of 1939 was quicksilver; though only $25,000 worth was produced in 1938 the war in Europe sent prices rocketing as the mineral is used in connection with explosives.

Tungsten mining was also very active at the beginning of 1940, after production in 1938 had fallen off two-fifths from the reported value of about $2,500,000 in 1937.

Thus, minerals remain of very great importance to the State and Nevadans have considerable property interest in the State's mines; none the less, only a relatively small part of the millions that have come from below the ground have remained in the State and most of the larger present-day properties are owned by outside companies.

NEVADA MINERAL PRODUCTION

	1859-1937	
Churchill County	29 districts	$6,750,000
Clark County	22 districts	$34,996,767
Douglas County	13 districts	$100,000
Elko County	52 districts	$60,503,014
Esmeralda County	30 districts	$109,925,632
Eureka County	21 districts	$79,980,164
Humbodlt County	24 districts	$8,750,000
Lander County	30 districts	$70,372,758

Lincoln County	20 districts	$72,955,370
Lyon County	16 districts	$25,313,858
Mineral County	26 districts	$81,284,123
Nye County	67 districts	$181,757,913
Pershing County	40 districts	$35,622,402
Storey County	7 districts	$405,000,000
Washoe County	21 districts	$3,753,537
White Pine County	30 districts	$384,062,183

State Total $1,560,127,621

MINING JARGON

Nevada was born of a mineral discovery and mining is so much a part of the State's life and history that its people speak a language often bewildering to outsiders.

Strikes (discoveries) have been chronicled annually in almost every district of the State, commencing with that in Gold Canyon in 1859. But there has been a wide difference in the extent of the discoveries and in the quantities of rich ores exposed. Some of the strikes died almost aborning, others continued to produce for a decade; in a few cases production has continued to the present. Results of development are variously described. The rich bodies of ore found on the Comstock Lode were known as *bonanzas*. In some other districts—Aurora, Austin, Eureka, Candelaria, Tuscarora, National, Goldfield, and Tonopah—the same word has been used, though no other bonanzas ever equaled those of the Comstock. *High-grade* is another term for ore of great richness. *Jewelry-store ore* and *jewelry-ore* mean about the same—exposures of rich ore beautiful in color and high in metal content.

Prospecting is an incurable disease and Nevada is full of its victims. Even those who have managed to settle down begin to move restlessly when word of a new strike spreads. The chronic cases never settle down; but even when they do make a discovery, they are sure to sell out quickly in order to avoid the dull routine of development. Most of them boast of some spot where rich float or a deposit of ore was found and lost; they are sure they will find it again some day and *make a stake*.

In earlier times prospecting was done with pack animals, either horses or burros, or with a buckboard and team. The burro is still the favorite, and every camp is full of tales about the diminutive donkey—of how he "kicked off a piece of rock" that led to an ore discovery, or of how his wanderings led his master to a bonanza. A *buckboard prospector* (he usually has an auto now) is the fellow who does his prospecting almost entirely from the seat of his vehicle; he travels along a valley road, other prospectors tell scornfully, scanning the hills for *formations* (various rock structures) and even when there are distinct indications of a mineral area he will say, "Nope, I don't like it. Giddap," though only a short hike may be required for investigation.

Almost without exception prospectors have individual theories about formations and geology, and are likely to disdain advice, both lay and professional. The prospector's *outfit* is usually limited to bare necessities—one or two *drift picks* (light weight, two-pointed mine picks), a shovel, two or three drills, a light-weight single-jack, a spoon, a wooden ramrod (to tamp powder in drill holes), a small mortar, a pestle, a pan, a magnet, a small prospector's pick (combined hammer and pick), or a pole pick (larger and heavier than a prospector's pick), and possibly a compass and a magnifying glass. Occasionally he carries a few chemicals for testing in the field, and a few sticks of powder, some caps, and fuse.

When a prospector admits he is "bitten by the bug," or has "itchy feet" the man he approaches stiffens himself against an appeal for a *grubstake*—food, money, transportation, or all three, in return for an oral or written contract that the prospector will share whatever he finds *fifty-fifty* with the man who stakes him.

Prospectors in the old days could enter one another's cabins or tents in the absence of the owner, and stay as long as they liked, provided they left the camp as they found it, and indicated their names. Larders at best were scanty—even today they often consist merely of *sow belly* (salt or smoked pork), beans, and the makings for flapjacks and sourdough bread. A few cooking utensils and dishes, a canvas-covered roll of bedding, occasionally a small tent, one or more canteens, a sheepskin jacket, and enough extra clothing for an occasional change, is all that the veteran needs for his comfort, in addition to his grub.

A *one-stamp mill* is a mortar and pestle used to grind pieces of rock to a *pulp* for *panning* (washing by agitation with water). If the resulting concentrate shows *color* (gold, horn-silver, lead sulphide and so on), or a *heel* of metal, it is said to *pingle, pan,* or *prospect.* A metallic element is traced to its source (*in place*) by means of *float* (loose pieces of surface ore), or by panning loose gravel or soil. A mineral deposit is said to *pan out* when favorable results follow its development. *Live quartz* is mineralized quartz. A *coyote hole* is shallow *diggin's* not large or deep enough to establish definite proof of a favorable prospect. The badger in particular, and gophers, squirrels, and other burrowing animals, are regarded as friends of the prospector, because their *dumps,* when panned, may disclose one of the prized minerals. It is said that a prospector is *married to a prospect* when he continues development over a long period without obtaining appreciable results.

To *locate* a lode mining claim or group of claims the claimant must place a *location* or *discovery monument* at the point of discovery—the point where evidence has been found of one of the numerous minerals, precious, semi-precious, or common, used in the trades and industries. The discovery monument may be a wooden stake supported by loose stones or earth, or it may be of stone or earth without the stake. A *notice of location* is placed with the monument, generally protected by stones, in a small can to prevent its blowing away. The notice follows a prescribed form. The claim cannot be for more than 1,500 feet along the vein or lode, or have a width of more than 600 feet—300 feet each way from the vein. The notice must give the position of the claim in relation to some permanent feature of the landscape, name of the claim, the date of location, and the name of the locator. Names of witnesses may also be inscribed.

The law allows twenty days for establishing boundaries, which is done by placing stakes or monuments at each corner and at each side center of the rectangular bit of land. Ninety days are allowed to dig a *location* or *discovery shaft,* four by six by ten feet, or an equivalent, such as an open cut or trench, and to record a certificate of location.

Placer locations are similar to the lode, except that the claim may be either square or rectangular and cover twenty acres. No individual can claim more than one, though locators may unite to acquire contiguous claims. *Assessment work,* consisting of labor or improvements worth $100, must be done on each claim—lode or placer—annually.

If the prospect responds favorably to development the work may be continued indefinitely; if not the owner may at any time decide to *kiss it goodbye* (abandon the claim), and leave it open to location by the next prospector. In the case of a property of merit, he may either sell it directly or through a promoter, who takes a commission. Most deals are made on a time payment basis, with a bond and lease in effect during the intervening period.

Although all mine employees are known as miners, there are numerous sub-classifications. A *hard-rock* miner works on a lode or underground; a *placer miner* or *gravel miner* works in superficial gravel deposits; *muckers* are shovelers; a *machineman* operates a drilling machine, which is used to *put in a round of holes* to be loaded with *powder* (dynamite). The charges are fired by *spitting* (lighting) the fuse, with the aid of a detonating cap. The *powder-monkey* has charge of the explosives; *chuck-tenders* assist the machineman; other workers are *drill sharpeners, blacksmiths, timber framers, pumpmen, trammers, timber-, men, shaftmen, cagers, top workers,* and *hoistmen.* The *supe* is the superintendent, the *shifter* a *shift boss;* the *graveyard shift* is generally from midnight to eight in the morning, *mud* is the end of a shift. "She's deep enough" is a notice of quitting. *Face* in general indicates the end of a drift or tunnel.

Rats and mice are common in metal mines; it is said that "When the rats move out, so does the miner." *High-grading* denotes the clandestine acquisition of rich pieces of ore (*high-grade*), a practice some miners of the past considered a legitimate perquisite—similar to the tote of Negro cooks in the south. *Rocks on the chest,* or *miner's con,* is tuberculosis induced by the accumulation of silica dust in the lungs of miners.

A *muck-stick* is a shovel, a *drift pick* a light-weight sharp-pointed pick; a *steel* is a drill, a *steel churn drill* a long, straight-bit drill used without a hammer; a *single jack* is a light drilling hammer used in single hand work; a *double-jack* is a heavier hammer used in double-hand drilling; a *spoon* is a rod having a concave end used to clean a drill hole; a *picky-poke,* a small bar with offset points on both ends, is used to work ore out of narrow crevices or a narrow raise; *moils* and *gads* are short-pointed pieces of steel used to break or wedge out ore, or to *cut samples* across an ore deposit.

In certain mines *swelling ground* is encountered—an actual swelling caused by chemical action from exposure to air or water; it occasions great strain on mine timbers. *Drummy ground* produces a hollow sound when struck and indicates loose rock, which must be removed or supported by timbering. Broken-up ground, old, filled in workings, and caving ground frequently require the use of *spiling* (planking sharpened on one end), which is driven ahead and supported by a *false set* of timbers until a permanent set can be put in place.

Connective openings in underground workings, when development is by shaft, are known as *crosscut* (at right angle to the vein), *drift* (along the vein), *level* (measured depth and starting point of a crosscut or drift), *winze* (interior shaft sunk from drift or crosscut), *raise* (upward opening from drift of crosscut), *underhand stope* (downward opening from a level to extract ore), and *overhand stope* (upward opening to extract ore). *Waste* is valueless discarded rock, a *station* is an enlargement of a level at the shaft for a landing, pumps, and so on. *Sump* is the extension of a shaft below a station so that the floor of a cage or top of a bucket can be made level with the drift or crosscut, and to serve as a water reservoir.

The *manway* and *ladderway* are in a narrow compartment of a main shaft, and provide emergency passageways; water and air pipes, and wire cable for electric current, are usually in the manway; resting platforms are provided on the ladders in shafts at regular distances. An *ore pocket* is an underground bin; it may be filled with either waste or ore.

Timbering and timbers include the *square set,* so mortised that units may be extended in any direction, the *false set* (temporary timbering), and *lagging* (planking placed on the outside or on top of a timber set). The *collar* is the mouth of a shaft, and the *collar set* is composed of timbers on the surface and provides a protective curbing. *Stulls* are either sawed timbers or unhewn logs, of varying length, used to support an overhanging wall after ore has been removed from a vein; *cribbing* refers to timbers or logs piled crosswise to support either loose or solid ground. Ground *breaks good* or *bad* according to the effectiveness of the blasting; a drill hole is said to *shotgun* when the powder charge blows out without breaking down any rock or ore; a *round of holes* is the variable number drilled before loading and blasting, the number depending upon the size of shaft, tunnel, drift, stope, and so on; a *pop or popshot* is the blasting of a shallow drill-hole with a light charge of powder to square up a shaft or drift.

A *tunnel,* which has two *portals,* may be driven either to crosscut a vein or along its *strike* (direction). *Adit* is a single portal.

Many geological terms are used by miners and prospectors, sometimes with non-professional looseness. *Vein, lode, lead, ledge,* and more rarely *dike,* have the same general meaning (a rock fissure filled with ore).

Vein is most commonly used and, like *lode,* applies chiefly to filled fissures of great width and length. The Comstock, like the Mother Lode of California, extended for many miles. Few, if any, lodes or veins are vertical; they dip at an angle of so many degrees, and are said to *strike* toward certain points of the compass. Ores of commercial value do not occur along the entire length of such lodes, but are found in segments of varying length. A *blind vein* is one covered by eroded material; a true *fissure vein* is between rock walls of the same formation; a *contact vein* is between walls of different formation. *Talc* and *gouge* are usually thin layers of finely ground material between a vein and its hanging wall and foot wall; an *ore shoot*, or a *pay shoot*, is that part of a vein containing ore of commercial value; the ore shoot *rakes* in a certain direction and has a *pitch* of so many degrees; *barren ground* is the part of a vein containing non-commercial ore; a vein has a *strike, pitch, dip, break*, or *fault;* a *horse* (mass in the vein of the same character as the wall rock) is of common occurrence, and the vein may *pinch out* (come to an end); veins are termed *pocketty*, or *bunchy*, when the pay ore occurs in deposits of irregular size; *stringers* and *knife-blade* seams are small veinlets where the metallic content may be highly concentrated; a *frozen vein* or *gash vein* is one in which the ore is cemented to the adjoining wall rock.

Ranching and Stock Growing

FOURTEEN of Nevada's seventeen counties derive a major part of their income from stock-growing and from farming—principally the production of wild hay, alfalfa, and some grain, all for cattle-feeding. In many counties cattle and sheep are of almost equal importance. In the four western counties some diversified farming, including dairying and poultry-raising, is carried on, though stock-growing is predominant there also. In this area numerous outfits handle both cattle and sheep, which is not usual elsewhere in the State. A limited number of small ranches near the Colorado River in Clark County produce vegetables, the Fallon district grows melons and tomatoes, and the western valleys a considerable quantity of potatoes; but a large part of the foodstuffs consumed in the State must be imported and even beef and mutton for the most part comes from out-of-state slaughter-houses.

The large ranches are chiefly in Elko, Humboldt, Eureka, and White Pine counties, with acreages running from six thousand to more than one hundred thousand acres. But the privately owned lands of the State comprise only about one-seventh of the total, the cattle ranches being principally meadow along streams, some winter range, and varied lands ensuring control of water. Nearly all the grazing area is public domain. The United States Forest Service administers most of the higher lands, where stock is summered, and the United States Grazing Service the remainder. All grazing on the public lands is now carried on by individual permits specifying the number of stock that can be taken into an area and the length of time the herds and bands may remain. The fees charged for use of the public lands are usually less than the tax assessments on adjoining privately owned tracts. To a considerable extent, priority on the use of areas belongs to the outfits that can prove they have used them for a number of years, and cattle and sheep men are busy amassing affidavits from prospectors and other nomads to prove long continued use of this and that valley, slope, and water-hole, in hope of obtaining permits for more than one season at a time.

With all public lands virtually withdrawn from entry and all meadowland privately owned, the only way a newcomer can enter the cattle business is by purchase of a home ranch; and under general practice such a purchase at present includes transfer of use-rights in the public domain. This practice, which is supported by strong public opinion, has created numerous problems in administration of the Taylor Grazing Act of 1934, under which the Grazing Service was established. How much effect the new form of administration will have on this and other methods of operation in the cattle business can not be foreseen.

Conditions vary from place to place, but the methods of handling cattle follow the same general pattern throughout the State.

There are two types of cattle operators: one winters out—runs most of his stock on the open range in winter—the other keeps his herds on the home ranch in winter and feeds them hay. Some operators combine the two methods.

In northern Nevada, where winter lasts from December to March, operators who keep their stock under fence need one ton of hay for each head of cattle during this four-month period, and one acre of meadowland is needed to produce a ton. In southern Nevada, because of milder weather conditions, half a ton of hay is sufficient. But the lower feeding costs prevalent in the southern area do not necessarily imply a greater margin of profit, for the potential gain is offset by poorer ranges and poorer quality of stock. Heavy losses are suffered whenever an unusually severe winter occurs, for it often finds the southern operators unprepared to feed their cattle over an extended period. In addition to hay land a rancher who winters in must own some low range and own or control land providing him with a suitable water supply. It is estimated that five hundred head of cattle form the smallest unit that can be economically operated.

The low carrying capacity of the open ranges in the State forces operators to scatter their stock over a wide area, a situation which makes them reluctant to practice controlled breeding, for it is difficult to get the bulls properly distributed throughout the herd when they are not turned out with the rest of the cattle. In northern Nevada calves born in December, January, or February are almost certain to *winter kill* (die from exposure to cold); in the south such losses occur most frequently in January and February. Nowhere in Nevada is range stock pampered as it is in some other sections of the United States.

The West raises some of the best beef cattle produced in the United States, and that of Nevada compares favorably with beef from other range States. Shorthorns are well represented in areas where the stock is kept under fence a good part of the year and wintered in feed lots. Elswhere, the Hereford is especially popular for it has been found to be the best rustler, fattening better than other cows on poor range and requiring less attention than the shorthorn. The Angus, hardiest of the beef breeds, is not raised in considerable numbers, for it becomes so wild under range conditions that it is difficult to handle. The prevailing dairy cattle are Holsteins, though Durhams, or dual-purpose shorthorns, are kept on some diversified farms.

Brands and the branding of cattle are subjects of inexhaustible interest in the range country—and beyond, wherever the American language is spoken. They are so closely interwoven with the story of the West that the very words have a magic quality. They are redolent with the smell of sweat and scorched hair; they conjure up the sight of wide plains rimmed with blue hills shimmering in the heat; in them is the thunder of hoofs on sunbaked earth, the protesting bellow of hard-driven cattle coming in through the dust, the slow drawl of tired voices by a campfire beneath the stars.

Brands—the X-Bar-X, the Flying A, the Lazy S, the 71—these unite romance and business, for the picturesque devices have always had a very utilitarian purpose. They came into use—as every one familiar with range life knows—to enable owners to identify their stock. Little of the range is under fence, cattle graze far into the hills, and when the fall round up of beef occurs, it would be impossible to establish ownership if there were no brands. Brands, therefore, must be easily identifiable by cattlemen, buyers, and others connected with the business.

In the old days brands were registered at county offices, and the record was a square of leather on which the owner had burned, or branded, his particular symbol. A number of these leather records have been preserved.

The county registration system gave rise to a certain amount of duplication of brands, and to put an end to this confusion—source of endless disputes—an act was passed in 1923 providing for a State cattle registration office. The few duplicate brands that still exist belong to pioneer families, who registered them under the old county system and cling to them as they would to family crests. Today brands are no longer filed on leather. The symbols, ranging from letters of the alphabet to animal tracks, scissors, stars and coathangers, are drawn on cards that are kept in prosaic filing cabinets. Sheep brands are still recorded in the counties. In all 2783 brands were on file in the State in 1940, many of them used on both cattle and horses, and in some cases on hogs.

Old brands must be re-recorded every five years at a cost of one dollar; recording a new brand costs two dollars, a transfer of ownership one dollar.

These symbols of ownership are not lightly disregarded. They have a property value, just as an acre of land has value, and banks will not lend money on stock unless the cattle bear a recorded brand.

A story often told to illustrate the importance of the brand relates how, during a drive, the foreman of a trail herd allowed his cowhands a free evening when they camped for the night near a large town. The buckaroos not only made the most of the occasion—they made so much of it that when the following day dawned not one of them was fit to straddle a horse. The irate foreman fired the whole crew and rode to town to get enough money from the local bank to pay the men off. The banker did not know the foreman, who was far from his base, but he was willing to make the loan if his visitor could prove that he was really foreman of the outfit. The foreman tried in vain to find someone who could vouch for him. Then he had a bright idea. He galloped back to camp, rounded up the *remuda,* hitched up the chuck wagon, with the outfit's brand burned all over it, and drove *remuda* and wagon back to town. The banker was asked to look out the window. He saw the brand on hide and wagon and asked for no more. The foreman got his money.

Operators who keep their cattle under fence during the winter generally turn out their dry steers, yearlings, and dry cows around April first, cows and calves about two weeks later, keeping in only a few old cows and the calfy heifers, which are turned out about May first, after they have calved.

Spring branding of calves starts between the middle of May and the first of June. The leading operator in the district usually determines the way in which the range is to be covered and the date when work will begin, after communicating with the other ranchers in the district and those adjacent to it. On the date set the cowboys meet at a ranch or in a pasture at one end of the range. The large operator may send as many as ten riders, the others one or more apiece; the adjoining range users send *reps* (representatives) to gather in their strays and return them to their own range. One rep may look after the interests of several outfits.

Each rider has from four to ten saddle horses which, as a group, are called a *cavy* or *remuda.* One man acts as boss and each day designates the area to be covered, and the place where the cattle are to be gathered. The cowboys as they spread out from camp cover an area roughly circular in shape, and because of this the day's ride is referred to as a *circle*. Sometimes two circles are made in a day, one in the morning, the other, usually closer to camp, after a hastily eaten noontime meal.

The boys start out shortly after daybreak and before noon meet at the *bunch ground* with the cattle they have found. Here the cattle are worked and branded. Some outfits, however, prefer to take their cows and calves to the nearest corral for branding. Operators who brand at a corral generally use *stamp irons* (already made up) but operators who brand at the bunch ground carry *running irons* (rings or bars with curved ends) as they are much easier to carry and fewer irons are needed. The procedure followed depends on the amount of help available, the distance from camp, and whether it has been decided to work the cattle before or after the calves have been branded. The reps and small operators usually want to take their cattle back to their own ranges without delay; stockmen with plenty of pasturage may be in a hurry to put their beef on pasture for the summer so that it will be in condition for an early market, while some stockmen pasture for the summer to avoid having to ride again during the beef roundup.

When the cattle are bunched the cow boss looks over the herd in order to determine roughly what stock has been brought in. He then designates two men to rope the calves, two or three more to hold the herd, the balance to throw and brand. The roping must be done by careful, experienced men, who must be sure of each calf's rightful mother before they rope the calf. When they make a mistake and put the wrong brand on an animal, it must be replaced with one from the brander's outfit or the erroneous brand must be *vented* (nullified) and the calf rebranded on some other spot. A good cow boss keeps mistakes of this kind down to a minimum for they easily create suspicion among neighbors and, even without this complication, cause extra work for everyone.

When a calf has been thrown the brand is applied on either shoulder, either side, or either hip. The left hip is greatly preferred, because, according to the buckaroos, an animal usually falls with its left side up. Calves are *marked* at the same time they are branded—that is, their ears are cut in such a way as to help establish ownership; these earmarks, as a rule, are recorded as well as the brand. Most operators also use a *wattle*—a piece of skin cut loose on the neck, brisket, or rump to help identify the animal.

The reason for this use of several methods of identification is that *rustlers* (cattle thieves), are, and always have been, numerous on the western ranges. Operators do not see their stock for months at a time, and rustlers have ample opportunity to alter markings. Brands can be altered but it is a risky undertaking, for if an operator becomes suspicious he can determine which brand was put on first by killing the animal and examining the skin from the inside. With only the brand to go by it is impossible by late fall, when the animal's hair is long, to establish ownership without throwing the animal and clipping its hair to reveal the brand, whereas the earmark and wattle are always easily discernible.

After the calves have been branded the cow boss gives each outfit an opportunity to *cut out* (separate) that part of its own stock that it wants to drive back to its home ranch. As soon as these cattle have been removed, the remaining cowboys trail the rest of the stock toward the high summer range.

With only slight variations this procedure is followed day after day, rain or shine, as the outfit works its way across the range. Some cowboys drop out, others take their places, as the days go by, but the cow boss stays on, keeping track of the number of calves branded, supervising the work, and—not least of his duties—keeping peace among the riders. His word is law and is seldom disputed.

There was a time when the round-up was tinged with a happy-go-lucky fiesta spirit. Despite the fatigue and the hardships they had to endure the cowboys found energy and time for horse racing and boisterous amusements. They had a great fondness for practical jokes, and as sure as a greenhorn was along they would, as initiation, catch his horse by the tail and tumble both horse and rider in the sand. Today the round-up is as strenuous as it ever was, but the buckaroos are a little less addicted to horse-play. When the last circle of the day has been ridden, and the range cattle have been turned loose, they ride back to camp at a leisurely pace. After they have eaten—and their appetites are good—if it is not quite dark, some shoe their horses or train the younger horses in their *remuda*. The others play cards or are satisfied to loll around until the time comes for them to roll up in their blankets.

By late June the calves have all been branded, the public range permits filled, and the horses used in haying gathered in. For a short time the cattle on the range are forgotten as all hands turn to harvesting the hay for winter use.

Toward the end of August the beef round-up starts, and the same routine is followed as in the spring; all the late spring calves must be branded. Fat steers and cows are cut out and taken to camp. Every few days some are driven off to their respective owners' ranches, for if they were concentrated in one place any length of time, the forage needed by the owner or leaser for his own herd would soon be stripped bare.

The picturesque chuck wagon is no longer the common sight it once was at Nevada round-ups. With pasturage now available at close intervals throughout much of the range country, the cowboys can eat and sleep at ranches and a truck moves their belongings from one place to the next. The breakdown of the large outfits, however, is the principal reason for the disappearance of the chuck wagon. When a wagon was run, some one rancher usually had to carry the burden of the expense for the small outfits, which, though they made full use of this convenience, made no contribution toward the cost of its operation. The result was that the rancher who paid for the chuck wagon was gathering and working everyone else's cattle until he reached the center of his own district, where—his neighbors having gone their many ways—he had to work most of his own stock without outside assistance. But there are areas in which a chuck wagon could still be used to advantage if only the operators could reach some agreement on sharing the expenses.

Most of the cattle coming off the Nevada ranges do not carry enough flesh to be sent direct to market for beef, and are generally rated as *feeders* (cattle that require fattening); consequently, they are sold to speculators and packing companies who ship them to California or the Mid West. There they are fed a special fattening ration for from 90 to 120 days before being sent to the slaughter houses.

By mid-October the last of the beeves are gone and it is time to wean the calves and start putting the cattle into the fields as they drift down from the hills. All calves seven to ten months of age are separated from their mothers, put in a *feed lot,* and given the best hay and concentrates. This is a critical stage in the animal's life, for if he does not make the proper growth as a weaner he is likely to be undeveloped as a two-year-old—the age at which most Nevada steers are marketed. By the first part of December this work is over and the cattle are then classified, according to age and flesh, the poorer ones to be put on hay and the stronger fed little or no hay until snowfall. If an operator has winter range he puts the strongest dry cattle on it, and if the snow becomes deep he may supplement the forage with concentrates, generally cotton seed cake, which is easily handled and high in protein.

During the winter the experienced rancher feeds his cattle in groups. In addition to the weaners is the *hospital bunch* (the oldest and poorest cattle and calfy cows), which must be kept close to the house as they require a great deal of care and supplementary feeding. The *main bunch*, composed of cows, calves, yearlings, and some of the poorer steers, and dry cows, are fed hay but do some grazing. The *dry bunch*—the strong cows and steers—requires little or no special feed and, if the winter range is good, grazing carries them through to spring.

The stock industry was in serious difficulty after the drought years of the later 1920's, but there is evidence that it is now recovering from the effects of those years and is adopting new methods of operation and improving the breed of the herds. With increasing frequency huge trucks and trailers are seen transporting both sheep and cattle between the summer and winter ranges; this saves them from the long exhausting drives and sends them to market with less need for fattening.

Sheep-raising presents a different set of problems. Although sheep range most of the year on the public domain or in the national forests, and sheepmen need own little land for a home ranch, many Nevada operators nowadays own enough land for lamb sheds and shearing pens. A band of a thousand is considered the smallest unit for efficient operation.

The spring activities begin at various times according to the district, but the average date is May 1. Most operators shear before lambing starts, about the last of April, if the weather permits. The shearing is done by groups of trained men who go from one outfit to the other on contracts made by the leader of the gang, who pays his men and is responsible for the efficiency of their work. Shearing time is a period of intense activity, one man or two dexterously shearing an animal at top speed, another gathering the shorn wool and carrying it to men who tromp it into sacks about eight feet long.

When a sheep is released from the shearer the outfit brand is painted on its back or flank with a solvent oil paint, which must be renewed twice a year. This oil brand washes off when the wool is scoured. Lambs are branded and earmarked when they are docked. Some operators also put a special brand on all bucks, and on blooded sheep. This brand is put on the nose or foot. The practice is not general, however.

While dipping all sheep in a strong disinfectant is only resorted to when inspection shows scabbing, it is mandatory that all bucks be dipped once a year, which is done in the spring or in the fall.

Sheep lamb once a year, in the spring. The bands are sometimes brought to sheds for lambing. Sheep have multiple births, the increase averaging from one hundred to one hundred and eighty per cent. Twins are the rule, rather than singles, and triplets are not rare. Lambing of a band takes from four to six weeks, after which the sheep are moved to the summer range. Bucks are not commonly run with the band except from the middle of November to the end of December, in order to control the lambing period.

Sheep are usually driven to the summer range though some operators now transport them by truck. In September or in the early fall, dependent on market conditions, the bands are brought down from the summer range and separated. Healthy lambs and old sheep are sold; the weaker lambs are held for winter feeding. Bands are then made up again and sent to the winter ranges.

Summer bands of the large operators number approximately one thousand ewes with lambs, winter bands about two thousand to twenty-five hundred ewes. The average band has one herder, occasionally two. With the herders is a camp tender, who brings them their supplies and aids them when necessary. A herder places great reliance on his dogs for handling the band and as a general rule no amount of money will induce a sheeptender to sell a well trained dog.

The herder, almost always a Basque, rises before dawn and brews himself a huge bowl of coffee, into which he breaks bread and strong cheese. At break of day the band begins to browse over the hills; as the day grows warmer, about nine or ten in the morning, it settles down to a siesta. While it rests the herder prepares his second breakfast. His third meal is taken in the late afternoon, and the last after dark, when the woolies have been bedded for the night.

Under grazing control the old feud between the sheepmen and the cattlemen is disappearing, but at one time the feud was so bitter in some parts of the State that murder resulted frequently. Both sides poisoned waterholes, causing great loss of life among the animals.

Army remounts are bred to some extent in Nevada and numerous ranchers breed riding stock for their own use and for sale. The wild horses, which formerly bred with the other horses, are now thinning out; for the past few years the Forest Service and other agencies have cooperated to pick them up in order to save the range for cattle and sheep. They are sold at public auction, shipped to dog and cat-food canneries, or used for coyote bait. A few hunters in the Pyramid Lake and other regions have used airplanes to round them up. The plane flies low over the running band and the roar of its engine drives the wild horses in headlong flight toward the corral.

The by-products of the cattle industry do not greatly increase the income of stockmen as cattle are sold on the hoof and medicines and

Rothstein: Farm Security Admin.   **PROSPECTOR TESTING ORE SAMPLES**

RUTH COPPER PIT: *Photograph by Charles D. Gallagher*

This pit, in the Steptoe Valley, is one mile wide.

a distance that can best be approximated in the airview. Its depth can be judged by the relative size of the ore train in the workings.

Rothstein: Farm Security Admin.

MANHATTAN GOLD DREDGE

MINE AND MILL, NEAR LAS VEGAS

ASSAYING SAMPLES OF ORE CONTAINING GOLD AND SILVER

POURING BULLION TO FORM BRICKS

Rothstein: Farm Security Admin.

MILL WHERE GOLD AND SILVER EXTRACTED, EL DORADO

A CLASSIFIER TANK, USED IN MILLING GOLD & SILVER ORES, EL DORADO

ORE AS IT COMES AS CONCENTRATES FROM THE MILL

MODERN MINING CAMP, RIO TINTO *Photograph courtesy State Highway Department*

OLD SILVER PEAK REVIVES *Rothstein: Farm Security Admin.*

serums, manufactured from certain parts of both sheep and cattle, are processed outside the State. The hides are also marketed elsewhere. Wool, however, is sold directly and is an important factor in the State's economy. A woolen mill at Las Vegas, to be operated by Boulder Dam power, has been proposed but its construction is unlikely as wool must be worked in a more humid climate.

In 1938 Pershing County began to grow sugar beets and in 1939 had about 2,000 acres under contract with one of the leading sugar refineries. Increased acreage was not permitted for 1940 under the Federal production control. In the western counties alfalfa is grown to finish (fatten) cattle for market within the State and in Pershing County sugar beet tops are also used for this purpose.

Nevada remains primarily a livestock State, because eighteen inches of rainfall are necessary for successful farming; crop-raising is thus a hazardous gamble except in the few places where irrigation is possible. In the canyon of the Colorado there is evidence that the pre-Columbian Nevadans faced the same problem and built canals and contrivances for raising water from lower to higher levels. The first white men to reach the Walker River Valley reported that the Indians there irrigated patches of land to raise an edible root that formed a great part of their food supply.

In territorial days the Utah Territorial Government granted the privilege of taking irrigation water from the Carson River to settlers in Carson Valley; and at Franktown in Washoe Valley, and at Las Vegas, the Mormons early undertook irrigation projects. Travelers passing through these places paid high prices for hay, grain, and root crops on sale there. The successors of the Mormons, having extended the irrigation systems, sold produce to the mining camps especially to Virginia City, at incredibly advanced rates, for California, the main source of foodstuffs, was far away, and the freight charges were exhorbitant.

Since 1866 irrigation dependent on the appropriation of water from lakes or streams, or on the ownership of springs, has been subject to legislation. The law of 1866 required that anyone desiring to construct a ditch or flume should record the fact in the county in which the ditch was to be built. The recording was intended to deter waste, and to give ample warning to all whose rights might be affected, but this law, like so many western irrigation laws, permitted the indiscriminate filing of indefinite and ridiculous claims.

Many of the laws intended to settle priority of water claims were experimental, and litigation over water rights increased until a law passed on February 16, 1903, gave the State engineer the necessary authority to deal with the situation. Since then not only has litigation over water appropriations become negligible, but Nevada has been able to cooperate with the Federal government to develop irrigation systems. But in aggregate extent and value, the privately or cooperatively developed irrigation facilities far exceed those developed with Federal aid. First of all Federal irrigation projects in the country was the Newlands, which began diverting water from the Truckee to the Carson River in 1907. Much later Rye Patch Dam was constructed to impound the waters of the Humboldt. There have been several lesser undertakings of a similar nature. Although the State has been alloted a share in the waters impounded by Boulder Dam the fertile valleys near Lake Mead are few and relatively small.

Stock Jargon

THE livestock industry, one of the most important of the State, has its own jargon, bewildering at first to the uninitiated.

The man who rides the range, watching the huge herds of cattle, is known variously in this State as *cowboy* or *buckaroo;* the term *vaquero,* with its many spellings—*vacqueros, yaucero* (from *yaucca,* Sp.)—is rarely used in Nevada. Other names used in referring to these cattle artisans are *waddie, cow puncher, hand,* and *cow poke.* The man who has achieved great skill in this field is known as a *top hand* and commands a higher wage. On the other hand a *flat-heeled peeler* or *pumpkin roller* is an amateur cowboy, or a farmer who has turned cowboy. The buckaroo who holds a large herd of cattle from straying at night, the *night herd,* is known as a *night hawk.* The buckaroo who herds the saddle horses is the *rango,* and the one who takes the night shift with horses is the *night rango,* the *night hawk* or *owl.*

A buckaroo's paraphernalia includes the following: the saddle, which the cow-country calls *cactus, hull, chair, centerfire, kak, pack,* or *rigging;* the horn of the saddle, called the *biscuit, grandma, old Susie,* the *handle,* or the *pig,* all indicative of the contempt of true cowhands for the flat-heeled *peeler* who must *pull leather* (grasp the saddle horn) in order to remain with his mount; the cinch or girth, which is the binder holding the saddle in place. Thus a *cinch-binder* is a horse that when cinched too tightly refuses to move or falls over backwards.

The bridle, consisting of headstall, bit, and reins, has several appendages—the *bozal* or braided rope band, the *romal,* a heavy whip attached to the end of the reins, the *feador,* the knotted rope holding the reins, and the *martingale* or the adjustable neck-band to hold the horse's head down. A *hackamore,* a rawhide nose-band used in place of a bit, is a type of halter consisting of a *headstall,* a *feador,* and rope band, and is sometimes known as a *McCarty.*

A *bear trap* is what the old-fashioned ring or spade bit is called by cowboys using lighter, more humane bits. The *tapederos* is a leather covering of various shapes and sizes that fits over the stirrup to protect the rider's foot. The tapederos is not as commonly used in Nevada as in some other cattle states. The buckaroo's spurs are referred to as *steel, gads, hooks, gut lancers,* or *chihuahuas.* The guns often carried by the cowmen are *smoke cannons, hip cannons,* or *hog legs.*

The vocabulary of the *round-up* is a language apart. The wagons taken out are the *bed wagon,* and the *chuck* or *grub wagon.* The chuck wagon carries the food and utensils for the range kitchen. *Man-at-the-pot* is the first buckaroo to pick up the coffee pot when out with the chuck wagons. It becomes his duty to pour the coffee for the outfit. "Come and get her before I throw her out" is the time honored mess call.

The bed carried by the cowboy is known as his *hot roll* or *cama.* The individual quilt in the roll is a *soogan.* On moving day the morning call is "Roll out and roll up."

The horse the cowboy rides is his *cabello (kavayo), cayuse, mustang, broomtail, fuzztail, pungo,* or *hay burner,* and to mount him he climbs upon his *summit, steps upon him,* or *forks him.* A *broncho* or *bronch* is an unbroken horse, and the rider who breaks him is the *peeler.* A horse that is an outlaw is known as a *wassup.* A wild horse is also called a *mustang* or *broomtail,* but more commonly a *bangtail.* A horse that likes to buck is *salty.* Other names for mean horses are *snake, plain hell, hard to sit, outlaw, renegade.* A spotted horse is a *pinto* or *painted* horse. One that refuses to leave camp in the morning is a *camp-staller,* and a horse that has never learned to respond properly to the bit is *hard-mouthed.*

The horse that bucks *turns on, breaks in two, swallows his tail, leaves the world, pitches, weaves, spins, sunfishes, prints tracks, unwinds,* and *turns a wild cat.*

A *roughstring,* the spoiled, unbroken horses taken on the roundup, are usually assigned to the care of one or two men. The *cavvy* or *caviatha* is the band of saddle horses, while the *peratha* is any large band. The cavvy is often called the *remuda.* The round-up of the horses in the morning for the day's ride after cattle is the *circle.* And at round-ups cowboys from other outfits are known as *reps* (representatives). The horses each brings form his *string.*

To *lasso, throw a wicked loop, dab it on, front foot 'em,* or *lead 'em in,* is the duty of the roper. The ropes used have several classifications— the *white line* applies to a manila or linen rope, a *riata* to one of braided strands of rawhide, and a *Macarte* or *McCarty* is of twisted horse-hair (mane or tail). A rope is sometimes *seagrass, twine, string, Tom Horn,* or *maguey.*

In pursuit of his work a cowboy *dallies,* or holds an animal on the rope by wrapping it around the horn of the saddle counter clockwise. *Coffee grinding* is the incorrect way of taking dallies; it means that the rope is wound clockwise. To *tie hard and fast* is another term used to describe holding an animal on the end of a rope attached to the saddle horn.

The cattle are *longhorns, dogies,* or *cows.* A bunch of cattle is a *herd, round-up,* or *rodeo,* each term with a different shade of meaning. A bunch separated from the main herd is a *cut* or *preada.* Moving cattle from one range to another *throws* or *drifts* them, and separating them for prime beef condition, for outfit ownership, or other like reason is to *cut, part* or *knock out.* A *leppy* or *buttermilk* is a motherless calf—described by buckaroos as "a calf whose mother died and whose daddy ran off with another cow." Leppy also refers to a colt that has lost its mother. A *maverick* or *slick-ear* is an unbranded, unclaimed calf. The first term originated in Texas where a man named Maverick went to war for the South and never returned with a result that his cattle wandered the ranges unbranded for a number of years. The term gradually grew more general until any unbranded critter became known as a *maverick. Dogs* are poor, weak calves, while *rawhides* are weak cows. When the female stock claim their young they *mother-up.*

A *branding iron* other than the type used to stamp on hide is a *running iron.* The *ring* is a small iron carried on the saddle to brand calves on the range. The ring is heated and held between crossed sticks.

A *dewlap* is one method of marking calves so that they can be identified by the owner; the skin on the brisket, or lower neck, is cut in different ways so that it hangs down. This mark is easily spotted in a large herd when the *earmark* or *brand* might be difficult to read. A wattle is similar, but the skin-cut hangs down on some part of the body. A *sleeper* is an animal earmarked but not branded. This is a mark used by petty cattle thieves; the calf is marked with their ear identification, and, if it passes as theirs, it is branded later. An *oreana* is an unbranded animal old enough to have strayed from its mother, making identification impossible. The finder usually brands it for himself.

A *nester* is a homesteader or small farmer, much hated by cattlemen because he settles on or near a waterhole.

Nevada ranchmen have the saying "The *riders* come from the north, the *ropers* from the south," and this is generally true. In the north country, Wyoming, Montana, Northern California and Northern Nevada, owing to snow conditions and the fact that in winter the riders wear heavier clothes—chaps, tapaderos, and so on—they ride larger horses, and usually larger horses are harder buckers. Then, too, the northern cattle are fed in the winter and are more domesticated, and branding is mostly done in *corrals*. Thus the average northern buckaroo becomes a better rider than roper. In the south the buckaroos ride smaller horses, cattle range out all the time, and calves are branded on the range—which makes the southern cowboy a skilled roper.

The northern men generally use rawhide riatas. These ropes will not stand a severe sudden jerk. Thus the northern men dally so that they can let the rope slip on the saddle horn and not subject it to the jerk. The southern cowhands use the manila or linen rope, which is very strong, and they tie hard and fast.

A term that is common to both sheep and cattle is *leppy,* sometimes spelled *leppie,* for a motherless lamb as well as a calf or colt. A *bummer* is another name for these baby lambs, which are frequently given away by sheepmen, because of the difficulty of hand-raising them on a bottle. A *granny* is a ewe with such an instinct for motherhood that she steals all the lambs in the vicinity from other ewes. Perversely enough, instead of granny as the mark of age, *gummer* is the label for the old ewes— those without teeth. A *spreader* is a ewe whose teeth are worn and starting to spread. The *bell wether* is the leader of the band, with a tinkling bell strapped on its neck.

A *drop band* is a band of ewes about to lamb. The *bed ground* is the place of the night's stay. *Sheep ropes* are used to tie ewes that do not at first claim their lambs, and a *gancho* is the sheep hook for catching the animals.

The *herder* or *jockey* is the man who cares for the sheep, and the *camp tender* or *camp jack* is the one who cooks and cares for the camp, assisting the herder when necessary.

During shearing season common terms are: *high roller,* a shearer who works fast but poorly; *pink 'em,* an animal sheared so close to the hide that the skin shows pink; *wool tier,* the man who ties fleeces after they are shorn; *wool tromper,* the man who presses the wool into sacks; and *wool wrangler,* the one who carries the tied fleece to the sacking frame for the wool tromper to drop into sacks.

Press, Church, and School

IN NEVADA, as elsewhere, the three great institutions forming public opinion—the press, the church, and the school—have been supplemented in recent years by two others, the movies and the radio. Numerous small towns have at least one movie show a week, attended by audiences largely composed of people from widely scattered ranches. The radio is probably more influential, however, for it can be heard seven days a week without the inconvenience of a long trip to town and ninety-five per cent of the ranches have radios. Nevada has certain reception difficulties; there are a few small areas where no radio will operate, and in the western parts of the State it is sometimes difficult to get any station but Reno's KOH and in the northeastern part Salt Lake's KSL—at least during the day. In the evening it is usually possible to tune in stations in Los Angeles, San Francisco, Salt Lake City, and Denver, and occasionally stations much farther away. KOH, which is the only Nevada station and operates on 630 kilocycles, was set up in 1931 as part of the Columbia network, but in 1940 it joined the red and blue NBC net.

While the publication of newspapers has had its difficulties, the building of churches and schools in Nevada has been a particularly heroic business. Clergymen and teachers would labor to organize churches and schools, promote the building of structures apparently justified by the size of the population and its prosperity—and wake up some morning to find that most of the citizens and their families had disappeared in a rush to some new mining discovery. The State is dotted with deserted public buildings, their window panes broken, the paint peeling from their doors—all monuments to public-spirited people whose zeal survived the wrecking of their plans. Though unable to take their plants with them, as the State's pioneer editors did, they themselves could and did move on to the new camps and start their work over again.

THE PRESS

Of the three influential agencies of the early years, the press was the first to reach a large part of the population. Interest in news was so great that even the little peripatetic camps at the southern end of the Virginia Range had hand-written news sheets in circulation. These were the *Scorpion* and the *Gold Canyon Switch* of 1854. Nevada's first printed newspaper was the *Territorial Enterprise,* which Alfred James and W. L. Jernegan began to publish at Genoa on December 18, 1858, when the population of the whole region that was to be Nevada was less than a thousand.

The *Enterprise* was also first of the many presses that moved from center to center, shifting with the population when mining excitement developed in a new zone. The *Enterprise,* unlike some other papers, took its name as well as its equipment, when it moved. The files of the *Enterprise,* which in the beginning was brought out with a hand-press, provide the most complete record of Nevada's early years. In the beginning the contents consisted largely of dry little items on the outside world that had been collected from passing travelers. Then, as Nevada came to life with the great strike in Washoe, the tone of the writing was adapted to the tempo of the day. Before long there were fiery editorials filled with tart, intemperate statements, chiefly personal, and such matter as would lead to the belief that the editor must have written them while balancing his pen against a six-shooter. Between accounts of rich new discoveries and predictions of more wonderful ones to come were articles that trace the political opinions and events of the period culminating in statehood at the end of October, 1864.

The *Enterprise,* in November, 1859, was moved from Genoa to Carson City, seat of the reorganized Carson County of Utah Territory. A year later it was purchased by Jonathan Williams and I. B. Wollard and moved to Virginia City, which almost overnight, after the discovery of rich silver ore, had become the center of Western Utah. On March 2, 1861, Joseph T. Goodman and D. E. McCarthy bought out Wollard's interests in the publication and in a short time Williams sold out to D. Driscoll. The publication became a daily on September 24, 1861, and steam power was installed on July 31, 1863. In October of that year Goodman and McCarthy became the owners, but two years later on September 15, McCarthy sold out to Goodman, who remained the owner until early in February, 1874.

Some of the journalists of the early Virginia City period were brilliant men and the genius of Mark Twain was fostered and developed by his association with them. Notable were R. H. Daggett, who on occasion could prove himself a happy, lovable liar, able to smooth troubled waters with a preposterous story; Joseph T. Goodman, who employed him; and Dan DeQuille (William Wright), who wrote stories on any subject, and whose vocabulary was truly remarkable. In fact, the expert use of forcible words was characteristic of the *Enterprise* office; there were typesetters who could hurl anathemas at bad copy that would have frightened a Bengal tiger, and the news editor could damn a mutilated dispatch in twenty-four languages.

Dan DeQuille, usually the most painstaking and accurate of reporters, could, when faced with lack of news and empty columns, invent an item that would take the country by storm. An example of this is his story of the "solar armor". The contraption, DeQuille wrote, consisted of a suit of India rubber equipped with a compact air compressor operated by a pocket battery. According to DeQuille, when the wearer found himself uncomfortably warm he had but to touch a button to get air-conditioning, and when sufficiently cooled he could touch another button to turn off the power. The inventor, according to the story, undertook to test the suit one afternoon when the thermometer was registering 117 degrees in the shade. Putting on the outfit he started across Death Valley. After he had failed to return a party started to search for him. Four or five miles out on the desert lay his body. He had apparently started the compressor, but, unable to stop it, had frozen to death. The machine was still running and an icicle eighteen inches long hung from the dead man's nose.

The London newspapers accepted this tale as fact and heartily endorsed the invention.

To "Semblins" (W. J. Forbes) of the *Enterprise* is attributed the remark: "I know Governor Nye has a dam by a mill site but no mill by a dam site," when the State spent a $75,000 appropriation on an inadequate dam, leaving no funds for the proposed mill.

That Mark Twain was not merely an unknown cub-reporter when working for the *Enterprise* is evidenced in the pages of rival papers, which took a continuous series of potshots at him. In 1863 he seems to have been a pet subject of abuse for the *Virginia Evening Bulletin,* which, among other disparaging remarks, said: "At the solicitation of about 1500 of our subscribers we will refrain from again entering into a controversy with that beef-eating, blear-eyed, hollow-headed, slab-sided ignoramus, that pilfering reporter, Mark Twain." The *Bulletin* had apparently come off second best on some point of reporting against the man whose remarkable imagination was even then working at full speed.

In 1874 the *Enterprise* went under control of the Enterprise Publishing Company, of which R. M. Daggett was the brains, and William Sharon the financier. Sharon (*see Tour* 8) wanted to go to the United States Senate, and bought the newspaper to further his ambitions. In 1872, when he had returned from California to push the matter, Goodman had published a "Welcome":

". . . . Your expected return, Mr. Sharon, has offered no opportunity for public preparation, and you will consequently accept these simple remarks as an unworthy but earnest expression of the sentiments of a people who feel that they would be lacking in duty of self respect if they failed upon such occasion to make a deserved recognition of your acts and character. You are probably aware that you have returned to a community where you are feared, hated, and despised . . . ."

". . . . Your character in Nevada for the past nine years has been one of merciless rapacity. You fastened yourself upon the vitals of the state like a hyena, and woe to him who disputed with you a single coveted morsel of your prey . . . you cast honor, honesty, and the commonest civilities aside. You broke faith with men whenever you could subserve your purpose by so doing . . . ."

When Sharon failed of appointment by the legislature he organized the company to buy Goodman out. Under the new owner the paper changed its tune:

"Mr. Sharon has lived in Nevada for ten years. By his sagacity, energy, and nerve, he has amassed a fortune. This is his crime. He has done what he has without once breaking his plighted word, without once violating one principle of business honor. While doing this he has carried with his own, the fortunes of hundreds, and never once betrayed a trust or confidence . . . . The present prosperity of Western Nevada is more due to him than to any other ten men, and should his work here be stricken out, with it would go at once two-thirds of our people, improvements and wealth."

In November, 1875, after Sharon had been elected to the Senate, Daggett severed his connection with the paper and Judge Charles C. Goodwin became the editor. Daggett resumed the editorship on December 1, 1877, and in the following year was himself elected to Congress. His mantle again fell on Goodwin's shoulders, who remained as editor-in-chief until 1880, when Fred Hart succeeded him; Hart in turn gave way to Colonel Henry G. Shaw in 1881. The *Enterprise* continued independent publication until 1919, when it was merged with the *Virginia Chronicle,* only other survivor of the bonanza period.

Under a series of editors ending with Dennis E. McCarthy, who had been with Goodman on the early *Enterprise* and took it over on May 24, 1874, this paper also attained great influence until the decline of Comstock mining. The combined papers survived under different owners until 1927. Now the *Virginia City News,* printed on a hand-press, is the only paper published in Virginia City.

Over the Divide on the Comstock, in Gold Hill, Alf Doten started the *Daily News* on October 12, 1863. According to Wells Drury, who worked with Doten on the *News,* it expired in a manner that was typical of the period:

"Alf Doten was just placing the neck of the ginger-ale bottle across his thumb, as was his custom when called on to do his own pouring, when all at once his attention was attracted by a sign behind Charley Price's bar. The sign read: 'At midnight all drinks in this saloon reduced to ten cents' . . . . 'Thus passeth the glory of the world,' exclaimed Doten, forgetting to imbibe the tempting fluid which mantled the goblet.

" 'It doesn't seem to me that I can endure this humiliation,' said Alf, addressing a faithful companion who was always willing to stand by in such trying times.

"The clock showed the time to be 11:55. In a few minutes the brag of Gold Hill that it was able to support at least one first-class drinking place would be wiped out.

" 'I want to have the honor of buying the last two-bit drink in the old town,' said Alf . . . .

"The clock made that premonitory w-h-r-r-ing soung to indicate that the hour was about to be struck.

" 'Here's to the departure of Gold Hill's glory and pride,' was the toast they proposed, and they drank in silence.

" 'Not much use trying to run a nonpareil paper in a long-primer town any longer,' said Doten. 'I was willing to stick it out as long as there was a living chance, but now that there is nothing but ten-cent shebangs, the old *News* might as well suspend.' "

A notable instance of the peripatetic and transitory character of early publishing plants in Nevada is found in the perigrinations of the *Silver Age,* which succeeded the *Territorial Enterprise* when the pioneer paper left Carson City for the Comstock in 1859. The *Silver Age,* a weekly published by John C. Lewis and a partner named Sewall, was Union in politics and was favored by the legislature with the first public printing. In November, 1862, the plant was sold to John Church, S.

A. Glessner, and J. L. Laird, who moved it to Virginia City and changed the paper's name to the *Daily Union*. W. J. Forbes became its next owner, in the autumn of 1868, and promptly changed its name to the *Trespass*. Then John I. Ginn and Robert E. Lowry took over the stock and for a few months the *Trespass* was the *Safeguard*. But not for long. J. J. Ayres and C. A. V. Putnum bought the press, moved it to White Pine County to publish the *Inland Empire*—until Governor L. R. Bradley purchased the plant, only to sell it shortly afterward to Holmes C. Patrick, who took it back to California, where it originally came.

The *Evening Crescent*, which was moved in 1868 from Washoe City, where it had been the *Eastern Slope*, was the first paper in Reno. Although Carson City newspapers predicted an unfavorable existence for Reno, which had sprung to life as a freighting and distribution point on the Central Pacific Railroad, the town prospered and its newspapers have shown the same progression as its other business. Numerous publications beside the *Crescent* have come and gone. The daily *Nevada State Journal*, which started in 1870 has had a long list of editors and owners, including such persons as the former Governors Emmet D. Boyle and James G. Scrugham. The *Reno Evening Gazette* began publication in 1876 as a daily under John Alexander, then passed to the Fulton interests. The Sanford brothers published the *Gazette* from 1915 until 1939. It is now included among the Speidel interests, but Graham Sanford is still editor and publisher (1940). Other Reno publications are the *Bolletino del Nevada*, an Italian weekly and the sole foreign language publication of Nevada; the weekly *U. of N. Sagebrush*, published by the Associated Students of the University of Nevada during the school year; and the bi-weekly *Nevada Mining Press*. The adjacent town of Sparks has its semi-weekly *Tribune*.

Among the notable mining camp papers was the *Esmeralda Union*, published in Aurora from 1864 to 1868. It was obliged to cease publication when mining petered out. Belmont, in Nye County, had a one-day paper, the *Silver Age Extra*, which printed Civil War news on July 4, 1862, and also had the *Silver Bend Weekly Reporter* in 1867, the *Mountain Champion* in 1868, and the *Belmont Courier* in 1874.

Austin's *Reese River Reveille*, which first appeared in 1863 during territorial days, has followed the variable fortunes of that famous old mining camp. Now a weekly, it features reprinted articles from the first files, recalling the town's colorful past. The name of the paper, which is published in Lander County, is perpetuated in the Reveille

Mining District of central Nye County, discovered in 1866, and the Reveille Range, which includes the district. The *Reveille* is the oldest continuously published paper in the state.

Eureka, the cradle of lead-smelting industry in the United States, is unique in the Nevada newspaper field; its *Eureka Sentinel,* which has been brought out continuously since 1870, has, with the exception of six years during the 1870's, been controlled by men and women of the Archibald Skillman family. The *Sentinel* has faithfully recorded all central State news, including all the ups-and-downs of Eureka mining history, since the day when the husky oriental, "Chinaman Mike," began to turn the crank of the old hand press. It even appeared on the day in 1879 when, though the *Sentinel* building withstood a fire that swept a large part of the town, the paper's crew set up "hot" copy with wet blankets draped over their heads to ward off the heat. Another notable incident in its career occurred when one of its reporters narrowly escaped with his life after making disparaging statements concerning a citizen's legs.

In Eureka, too, was the *Cupel,* which printed its best until a cloud-burst sent a flood through the canyon town in 1784, drowning the editor and sweeping the printing-plant away. This paper's name was of especial significance to everyone in the mining town of Eureka; all the camp's ores required smelting and assayers in testing them had to use a cupel, a receptacle of bone ash. Half a dozen other papers in the Eureka section, including the *Ruby Hill Mining News,* whose editor died in a gun fight, printed their last edition before 1890.

The *White Pine News,* started in Treasure City in 1868, moved to near-by Hamilton in 1870, thence to Cherry Creek, then to Taylor, and last to Ely in 1890, when Denver S. Dickerson, later acting-governor, became its publisher. In 1923, by merger and purchase, the *News* and the *Expositor* of Ely were united into the present *Ely Daily Times,* of which Vail Pittman is editor and publisher (1940). Ely also has a weekly newspaper, the *Record.* Papers were published at Ward and Schellbourne, in the Ely vicinity, but their careers were brief.

When the Pioche mines were first worked on a large scale and a town was formed, the *Ely Record* was Johnny-on-the-spot with the news in 1870, followed by several others. The *Pioche Record* is a weekly at present. The neighboring town of Caliente still publishes the weekly *Herald.* During the years when Delamar led the State in gold production, the *Delamar Lode* served its population.

Relatively good natured quips between papers in far removed sections of the State were customary in the early days, particularly if a paper unwittingly gave its rivals a chance to exercise their caustic sense of humor. When in 1874 the *Reno Journal* advised that, "a newspaper warmed and placed inside the waistcoat will keep out the cold better than a large amount of clothing; now is the time to subscribe," the *Pioche Record* commented, "We have often wondered as to what the object was of publishing the Reno Journal; the above paragraph informs us it is to supply underclothing." Carson City's *Daily Nevada Tribune* gleefully reprinted the jibe.

Las Vegas, which did not become a town until 1905, has had several newspapers, the most persistent of which has been the *Age*, now a weekly, and the *Review-Journal*, the present daily, which also publishes a weekly *Review-Journal* for neighboring Boulder City.

In 1863, when the mining town of Unionville was the seat of Humboldt County, the *Humboldt Register* appeared, and it continued until 1869, when it moved to Winnemucca with the county courthouse but survived only briefly. Its plant was taken to Elko and used for the *Independent* of E. D. Kelly and Company. The daily *Star* of Winnemucca represents a merger of the old *Silver State*, which started in 1869 and was once owned by George S. Nixon, and the old *Star*, which began publication in 1906. Neighboring Paradise has had its *Paradise Reporter* and its *Local Messenger*: National had its *Miner*. Battle Mountain publishes a weekly *Scout* and has had several intermittent publications. Lovelock has its weekly *Review-Miner*, a merger of the old Seven Troughs *Miner* and the Lovelock *Review*. Former papers of surrounding areas are the Rochester *Weekly*, the Seven Troughs *District News*, and the *Vernon Review*.

In the northeastern part of the State is the *Elko Free Press*, which has progressed through weekly and tri-weekly stages to its present daily status. The *Elko Independent* has been a weekly, daily, tri-weekly, and again a weekly publication. The wanderings of newspapers in this area are exemplified by the adventures of the *Gold Creek News*, which moved to Elko as the *Daily Argonaut*, and ended up in Golconda as the *Golconda News*. The trade town of Wells has intermittently had a weekly paper, as typified by the late *Progress*. Before 1903 the gold camp of Tuscarora had a procession of newspapers. Most recent publication in Elko County is the weekly *Messenger*, printed in Mountain City since that town became a copper-producing center in 1935.

Similar to the many papers that mining towns have had was at least one paper of the ranching district—the *Metropolis Chronicle*, a short-lived Elko County weekly published during an ill advised campaign in 1911-13 to bring farmers into the district.

In Carson City, the State capital, where political feuds are not unknown, the rivalry that existed between the newspapers of early days was exceptionally bitter. Personal opinions, which today are couched in polite language, were formerly expressed with extreme truculence and were treated with a seriousness that can well be referred to as deadly: back in 1874 a reporter of the *New Daily Appeal* and a member of the Daily Tribune shot out their differences with the result that both men were wounded and one of them was crippled for life.

Some Carson papers were purely political campaign sheets, such as the *Daily State Democrat,* published for three months in 1864, and the *Independent,* which Adolph Sutro established in 1875 while seeking a seat in the United States Senate. At the time Sutro was digging his tunnel to tap the Comstock Lode and the paper was first printed in the settlement near the tunnel mouth. No less than twelve papers have been printed in Carson, the most persistent of which has been the daily *Appeal.* The present *Chronicle* is a weekly. Politics have probably had more than a little to do with the closing down or change of title and policy of other sheets in all the more important towns of the State.

At one time the Democratic *Carson News,* an afternoon paper, came under the managership of Anne Martin, a little spinster untrained in journalism who struggled heroically to edit the paper. Daily, a tall courtly gentleman, the editor of the *Tribune,* Republican rival of the *News,* came down the street, entered the office, bowed low to Miss Martin, walked quietly to her desk, and wrote a vituperative editorial in answer to the abusive attack that had appeared in his own sheet that morning

Editing in the early days was an adventurous undertaking at best. During that period, and for years afterwards, Sierra storms or other transportation difficulties sometimes caused a shortage of paper, much to the editors' distress. This is well illustrated by the feud between Sam P. Davis, editor of the *Carson Daily Appeal,* and Miss Martin, who, whenever they met, engaged in heated arguments on circulation. Davis claimed a preposterous figure and scoffed at Miss Martin's contentions. But one day San Francisco failed to make delivery of paper because of a freight embargo. The *News* had received the last large order. Davis was frantic. He asked to borrow enough to run off an issue. Miss Martin consented to make the loan if he would take only enough for true circulation needs. Triumph was sweet; Davis required far less paper than she.

In Douglas County, where the *Territorial Enterprise* was established, various papers followed, among them the *Nevada Prohibitionist,* which lasted only a few months in 1888. When much of the population of Genoa shifted to Gardnerville, a merger of the Genoa *Weekly Courier,* and the Gardnerville *Record* created the Gardnerville *Record-Courier,* which still appears weekly. Fallon in Churchill County has two weeklies, the *Eagle* and the *Standard,* both of which are more than thirty years old.

The *Como Sentinel* (1864), after bringing out thirteen issues in Como, moved with the county seat to Dayton and became the *Lyon County Sentinel.* When county seat and population later shifted to Yerington, the weekly *Mason Valley News* became the only paper in Lyon County.

The *Mineral County Independent and Hawthorne News,* a weekly, now supplies the news to Mineral County, where several other papers have given service in the past.

With the discovery of silver at Tonopah and gold at Goldfield in the first years of the century, the journalistic story of the Comstock was repeated. New papers appeared overnight. A survivor of the dozen or more established is the *Daily Times and Bonanza* of Tonopah; the Goldfield weekly *News* and *Weekly Tribune* have now suffered the fate of the *Daily Tribune,* which represented a merger of several papers in 1909, but disappeared in 1929.

Beatty, Rhyolite, Bullfrog, Manhattan, Tybo, Searchlight, Candaleria, Ione, Columbus, and Grantsville all had their journals, not one of which lives. The cause of the demise of these papers and of the others was best expressed in the swan song of the *Nevada Workman*: "The editorial pork chop is becoming more and more elusive. The unprincipled but necessary advertiser is becoming more unprincipled and less willing. The enthusiastic subscriber grows more enthusiastic and beautifully less . . . All these circumstances render it improbable that the *Workman* will continue to be the weekly delight of its numerous intelligent and busted constituency. Vene, Vidi, Vici; which being interpreted in this case, means, 'We came, we saw, we got it in the neck.' "

Nevada now has more than thirty newspapers, eight of them published daily, the remainder weekly or bi-weekly. All the dailies have wire-service and are illustrated; the weeklies present little outside news and give emphasis to local happenings. Both dailies and weeklies use national feature services.

THE CHURCHES

Nevada's first little settlements, made under religious leadership, had a brief existence. In the early 1850's Mormons were sent out to trade during the summer with travelers of the overland trail through Carson Valley, and their reports of the valley's fertility led Brigham Young to order several families to take up farms there. The colony was in 1855 placed under the leadership of his right-hand man, Orson Hyde, spiritually as well as politically. Other colonists were sent to the Las Vegas area. But in 1857 the Saints were ordered back to Utah to help resist the troops being sent out to establish Federal rule. The Mormon settlers held religious services regularly during their brief stay. Today the Church of Jesus Christ of Latter-day Saints, popularly known as the Mormon Church, is again becoming a strong unit. Two large churches were erected in 1940, one in Reno and one in Sparks, and there are smaller churches in many parts of the State.

After the Southwest became part of the United States the Roman Catholic Church in California was reorganized. Although uninhabited except by scattered Indian tribes, what was to become Nevada had been included in the diocese of Sonora and later in the dioceses of the two Californias. Then a new diocese, that of Monterey, was created but by 1853 the population of California had increased to such extent that the diocese of Monterey was divided and Nevada came under the direction of Archbishop Alemany of San Francisco. With a further increase in population the archdiocese of San Francisco was again divided, with Nevada north of the thirty-ninth parallel becoming part of the vicariate apostolic of Marysville; the territory south of the parallel remained under the jurisdiction of the Archbishop of San Francisco. In all, Catholic Nevada had been in the archdiocese of San Francisco, the Vicariate of Marysville, the diocese of Grass Valley, the diocese of Sacramento, the vicariate of Utah, and the diocese of Salt Lake, before 1931, when the diocese of Nevada was created. Owing to the division of the territory, the first two priests coming into it, in 1858 and 1860, were sent out by Archbishop Alemany, and Father Manogue, real founder of the church in Nevada, was sent out, in 1862, by Bishop O'Connell of Marysville.

The first Catholic church in Nevada was built after the arrival of Father H. P. Gallagher at Genoa, in the summer of 1860. Before this masses had occasionally been celebrated, confessions heard, sermons preached, and other rites of the church administered, but in unconsecrated structures. Father Manogue, first pastor of Virginia City, built three of its four successive Catholic edifices and much of the early prestige of the Church in the community was the result of the respect and affection he aroused. In addition to the churches he established, he erected an academy, an orphan asylum, and a hospital. Catholic congregations were established in many of the early mining camps of the State soon after they appeared, but only a few have survived. Some of the parishes had their own pastors, others had intermittant care. All of the large towns have their own pastors today.

Because of the scattered population, priests at times still say mass under difficult conditions. As late as 1909 mass was said in Rawhide in a saloon. After the usual Saturday night dance, which continued until dawn, the bar and pictures would be shrouded and a packing case turned into an altar, with beer bottles as candle holders.

The California Conference of the Methodist Episcopal Church was the first to send a spiritual leader into the new mining camps of Nevada; in 1859 it appointed Jesse L. Bennett as circuit rider among the settlements east of the Sierra Nevada. It is told that he preached his first sermon in Virginia City on C street in 1861 and that when he passed a hat for contributions it was filled with coin, nuggets, and dust. Soon Methodist churches were built in Dayton, Washoe, and Gold Hill.

By 1861 both the Baptists and Presbyterians were beginning systematic work. The Reverend Cyrus William Rees, a Baptist cleryman, established headquarters in Dayton and preached also at Fort Churchill, Carson City, and Virginia City. Rees remained for a number of years in the area. Aurora also had the services of a Baptist missionary, the Reverend Y. B. Saxon, who early erected a neat chapel. Under the Baptists the first negro congregation of the State was organized in Virginia City, in 1863; it built a church but had a brief existence because of a division of the congregation over the question of a minister. Later, congregations of Baptists were organized in many parts of the State.

The first Presbyterian congregation was actually an interdenominational organization. Other congregations were so widely scattered that one of the early Presbyterian clergymen had a parish half the size of Pennsylvania—as large as Massachusetts, Rhode Island, and Connecticut combined. In a tour of his district he covered thirteen hundred miles and one night he stayed with a family that had never before seen a clergyman of any denomination. It is told that in one camp he preached in a hall owned by a saloon-keeper, who obligingly closed his place of business during the church hour and appointed himself to take up the collection; anyone failing to contribute was commanded in a loud voice, "Shell out." In the remote Lamoille Valley chance visitors are surprised by the charm of a church erected many years ago by the Presbyterians under James McCombs.

In 1859 the Protestant Episcopal Church placed the Territory of Nevada in its Northwest missionary field. The first services were held in the United States district court house in Carson City and the Parish of St. Paul's was founded on September 1. On April 5, 1862, the parish was allowed a rector and church appointments. The Reverend Franklin S. Rising arrived ten days later and a small frame church was soon erected. In April, 1867, the Reverend O. W. Whitaker of Englewood, New Jersey, an educational as well as religious leader, replaced Rising, who had resigned because of failing health. After the first church had been swept away in the fire of 1875, a finer building was erected. The Virginia City parish, which soon became important, was proud of its record of support. It is told that when in 1900 the parish was in dire straits the communicants called to mind how Jim Fair had thrown handsful of gold pieces to help the church in the past, how in the early days the vestry had collected four hundred dollars on the street for Bishop Kip's expenses from the coast and back, and how when production and membership declined the congregation had valiantly refused to decrease the salary of their minister to the low figure of two hundred dollars a month. With this tradition the members refused to lower the rector's salary at the later date. Several sturdy Episcopal churches have been erected, including St. Peter's in Carson, St. George's in Austin, St. Luke's in Hamilton, and St. James' in Eureka.

The First Congregational Church of Reno was organized in 1871 and services were inaugurated in a little school house on the south side. The congregation of this church, which in later years became the Federated, originated the first anti-gambling bill, and also fostered the Young Men's Christian Association movement in the State. The church has one of the most active Young People's Leagues of Nevada.

Lutherans appeared in Gardnerville in 1877 but no church was built until 1895. Because the congregation consisted of German and English speaking people, services were conducted alternately in each language, but in general the English language has prevailed. The next community in which Lutherans settled was Reno; three-fourths of the services were in English and only one-fourth in German.

The first group of Christian Scientists to assemble in Nevada held its first meeting at Elko in the spring of 1903 in a private home. Scientists organized in Goldfield in 1905, in Reno in 1907, Ely in 1907, and Carson City in 1911. A beautiful church was completed in Reno in 1939.

Reno Negroes organized the Bethel Methodist Episcopal Church in 1939. Its choir, which is exceptionally good, has appeared on many concert platforms.

Unity and the Seven Day Adventists have strong followings in Nevada. Temple Emanu-el in Reno ministers to an orthodox Jewish congregation, from which a group is breaking away (1940) to form a new congregation.

Religious organizations of Nevada have had to contend with the problem of large, thinly populated areas, few towns of size, and rapidly shifting centers of population. The results of the United States Religious Census are therefore not surprising. This census is taken by the Government every ten years, with the cooperation of all local and national denominations. The denominations vary somewhat in turning in figures on membership, some giving only actual memberships, others including all children belonging to members of the congregations, and all people considered in the denomination's "sphere of influence"—that is, inactive members and non-members who attend or contribute occasionally. In 1926, the last year for which figures are available, the total church membership of the United States was reported as being 54,576,346, out of a total population of approximately 120,000,000. In Nevada, with a population that was probably close to the total of 91,000 found in 1930, the church population was 19,769. Of this number the Roman Catholics reported 8,447, the Latter-day Saints 4,889, Protestant Episcopalians 2,933, the Methodists 1,084, the Baptists 674, the Lutherans 497, the Presbyterians 417, the Christian Scientists 180, Jewish congregations 164, the Seventh Day Adventists 125, and the Salvation Army 68. In the total membership reported for the United States, 8,320,785 were under thirteen years of age; in the total Nevada church membership 5,046 were under thirteen years of age, 4,720 in this category being reported by the Latter-day Saints, the Roman Catholics, and the Protestant Episcopalians.

EDUCATION

Thinly scattered, tending to shift rapidly from place to place, the population of Nevada has confronted educators with problems similar to those with which religious groups have had to contend. But interest in public education has always been great, and provision for a school system supported by county taxation was made when the Territory of Nevada was organized in 1861.

The State constitution in 1864 enlarged the provisions and in 1865 school districts were set up throughout the State and county taxation for schools became compulsory. Later, district taxation was occasionally resorted to. Additional support was in time derived from the investment of permanent school funds made possible by donations of public lands, and a State tax not to exceed twenty cents on a hundred dollars assessed valuation. County superintendents were appointed and their traveling expenses were to be paid by the counties. Although these superintendents were to supervise all schools in their counties, no qualifications for the office were set up, and the amount of their salaries was left to the discretion of the county commissioners.

Good schools were soon established in the larger towns, but the rural districts fared badly. Taxes often being insufficient, they operated with deficits, if at all. But in the main, the people heartily supported education. The Buel Shoe Fund is an outstanding example of the good will shown by the people. In the fall of 1863, when the maintenance of schools was still a rather personal affair, trustees were elected in Austin, and a committee was appointed to raise funds for the first school. A collection of nine hundred and thirty dollars was made. In the following spring the Buel Shoe Fund was added. Colonel Dave Buel, a prominent and successful resident, was a man of prodigious stature; his feet were proportionately large, and he liked his shoes so loose that they always excited surprise and admiration. On May 26, 1864, the citizens, inspired by the spectacular success of the Gridley sack of flour (*see Tour 7*), brought out a pair of the colonel's shoes and put them up for auction for the benefit of the town school. Tom Wade, auctioneer, sold and re-sold them until more than one hundred dollars was realized.

Two years earlier the Carson Rowdy Fund had come into existence. Two would-be bad men swaggered down the main aisle of a Carson theatre, armed with bowie knives and six-shooters, and ordered the curtain dropped. When their command was not obeyed at once, they rushed for the stage. The actors fled in dismay, the curtain fell, and the conquerors proceeded to reduce it to ribbons with their knives. For their fun they cheerfully paid one thousand dollars, which was deposited in the town's school fund.

Teachers long received very low salaries, frequently not more than fifty-eight dollars a month, and the county superintendent did not undertake systematic work. Moreover, these superintendents were often political appointees without knowledge of pedagogy. Although there were some well-qualified and earnest teachers, and the communities where they worked had good schools, this was far from being the general rule, for no system had been devised to assist rural schools to find competent teachers. About 1887 the county superintendents were dispensed with as an economy measure and their duties were turned over to the district attorneys, who became ex-officio county superintendents. As not even a legal education was required for the district attorneys, and they also were poorly paid, in most places the school situation became very bad.

Some efforts were made to correct the early deficiencies by establishing private schools, such as the Sierra Seminary at Carson, a coeducational institution where the usual elementary courses were taught and older students could do advanced work. This institution, started in 1861, was maintained for many years. The Prisk Seminary in Austin, opened in 1863, served eastern Nevada in the same way as the Sierra served the western part of the State. Both, in addition to academic studies, taught vocal and instrumental music. There were also two well attended church schools, St. Mary's School for Girls and St. Vincent's School for Boys, established by Father Manogue at Virginia City. In 1873 Bishop C. W. Whitaker of the Protestant Episcopal Church founded the Diocesan School for Girls at Reno, which became the outstanding institution for the higher education of young women. Bishop Whitaker's School, as it was usually called, was closed in 1885 just before the University of Nevada, with its greater educational facilities, was transferred to Reno.

The University of Nevada had been opened eleven years before at Elko but had been little more than a high school. After its transfer to Reno in March, 1886, it steadily improved in academic standing and influence. That a large part of this influence is owing to its School of Mines is widely conceded; this department sends its graduates to jobs in many parts of the world.

A new district system replaced county control of public schools in

1907, when a law was passed sanctioning the appointment of a super-intendent of public instruction, with authority to supervise the deputies in charge of five big school districts then erected. Deputies, who were required to visit every school under their jurisdiction twice a year, often found it a trying experience. The travel allowance permitted them was fifteen cents a mile, and, as roads were poor, many visits had to be made on horseback. When automobiles were first available, gaso-line cost from forty-four to fifty-five cents a gallon. One deputy report-ing in 1917 said he had to travel 5,744 miles by automobile, stage, train, and teams and had had to pay twenty-five cents a mile for a car he had chartered; as his salary was $2,000 a year, he served notice that he would make fewer inspections. Another deputy reported visiting 63 schools in a district covering 18,165 square miles and of traveling 4,772 miles "over steep and dangerous grades." Supervision is still difficult. For example, in Elko county, covering 16,608 square miles, there are sixty-one scattered schools to be visited. Thus the costs re-main high, which is one of the reasons why Nevada spends more per capita than any other State on its schools. School facilities of the State range from modern, well equipped structures in the cities and towns down to adobe huts, and even old log buildings in outlying regions. Total attendance in 1933 was 21,512 with 909 teachers em-ployed. The number of grade schools of all types is 328.

Some of these schools have as few as five pupils, for the law makes it mandatory that a school be established if this minimum number of potential pupils with no educational facilities reside within a reason-able distance of one another. The average attendance for such a group must be three to insure its continuance. When a school is opened in a remote rural district for so small a group the classes may be held in a ranchhouse room—set aside for the purpose—or in a rudimentary structure especially provided. The State superintendent of schools, as well as the deputies, are sometimes hard pressed to find accommoda-tions that come up to existing requirements and it is not uncommon for schoolhouses—public property—to be moved from one place to the other, as needs change (*see Silver Peak, Tour* 5).

The State has worked hard to raise the standards of teacher qualifi-cations and to establish a reasonable scale of salaries. On the other hand it has occasionally had to curb ambitious communities that wanted to pay too much and provide facilities that were clearly beyond their means.

Since 1918 children between five and twenty years of age of one-quarter or more Indian blood have attended the public schools when this was desirable. The Federal government at first paid fifteen cents a day for each child, but later increased the payment to thirty-five cents a day.

The State maintains a teachers' employment bureau, also a teachers' retirement pension system. The State Department of Vocational Education has three divisions, supervising vocational rehabilitation, vocational home economics, and agricultural education.

The Arts

ALTHOUGH Nevada, with a small population, has made but few contributions to the arts, the drama and music has always been held in high esteem and this appreciation is spreading today to other arts, notably to painting.

DRAMA

The first entertainers to reach Nevada came in small groups of three or four men and women who, wandering from strike to strike with a small tent for a theater, reaped a fair harvest for their songs and jokes. Times have changed, the tent show has vanished, but old timers still speak of it regretfully, for it had a robust character and primitive appeal well suited to its day. There was no stage scenery, and often no stage. The music was nearly always produced by a banjo and a snare-drum, with the occasional addition of a fife or, rarely, a flute. After the male members of the troupe had regaled the audience with crude jokes and such songs as "The Days of Old, the Days of Gold, the Days of '49," and "Happy Are We Tonight, Boys, Happy Are We," the climax came when—stirring spectacle in a world of men— an actress, a real woman, a lady with a voice, appeared. Neither her looks nor her voice mattered much when she sang "Sweet Annie of the Vale" or "The Blue Juniata," and the applause, as well as the cash and the nuggets that rewarded her efforts were tributes not only to her talent but to her womanhood.

These bedraggled shows gradually moved to more isolated settlements as the camps developed into towns with good theater buildings visited by well-known stars. In the last years of the nineteenth century the tent show faded out of sight.

After the tent show period came Nevada's golden age of the theater and of music. Its history was colorful and at times brilliant, as might be expected in an area producing a quarter of a billion dollars worth of precious metals. Enthusiasm reached such heights that gold and silver were often showered at the feet of favorite players and singers.

Virginia City had the money to pay for the best and it did. For a while it vied with San Francisco as the cultural patron of the West, at times outstripping that city in quality of entertainment. The first real theater appeared about 1860 in Virginia City, when William Henry Howard, the sheriff, erected the Howard; in 1862 and 1863 Topliffe and Sutliffe, and the stalwart Tom Maguire built amusement houses. Tents still housed variety, however. At one time five companies were presenting the drama of tradition, from Shakespeare down, while six others were coining money with song and dance acts and acrobatic displays.

John Piper bought Maguire's Opera House in 1875, and after the fire of that year rebuilt it and named it Piper's Opera House. After it had again been destroyed by fire in 1883, a new theater bearing the old name was erected on B Street instead of D Street, where it stands today.

This opera house was the scene of many triumphs. David Belasco, later to find fame in New York's theatrical world, was its stage manager. Adelina Patti and other singers appeared behind its footlights. Indeed, the leading actors and actresses of the East were proud to be sought for performances at Virginia City, and few are the nationally known names of that period that cannot be found on the old theater bills of the Comstock.

Adah Isaacs Menken was a particular favorite in Virginia City. The daring Adah startled the town with *Mazeppa,* in which, clad in pink tights, she rode across the stage, lashed to the back of an unsaddled horse. The camp was so appreciative that it presented her with a bullion bar worth $2000. Edwin Booth, John McCullough, Thomas R. Keene, W. R. Sheridan, and Laurence Barret interpreted Shakespeare at the Piper Opera House; Frank Mayo, the elder, gave *Davy Crockett* and *Streets of New York,* and Joe Jefferson was there more than once in *Rip Van Winkle.* Robson and Crane, Clara Morris, Salvini the Younger, and James O'Neill also had their names on local billboards.

Gold Hill and Carson City vied with Virginia City in obtaining the most noted performers first. In Carson City in 1860 John O. A. Moore, and a Mr. Packer erected the Theater Saloon. The theater was in a wing of the main building, which was occupied by a saloon. In spite of the theater's secondary position, the reserved seats were comfortable and the curtain is said to have been particularly elaborate. In 1866-67-68 Sue Robinson Getzler and Amy Stone were star attractions and Mark Twain lectured twice. In 1868 Barret and Mc-

Cullough appeared in Shakespearian tragedies. The Pixley Sisters and Willie Edouin gave *Under the Gaslight* and *After Dark*. In 1869 J. A. Herne appeared in Carson as well as in Virginia City in *Rip Van Winkle*. Lucille Western appeared in *East Lynne*, and with Herne in *Leah, the Forsaken, Oliver Twist, Camille*, and others.

Madame Modjeska appeared here and on various other Nevada stages as did General Tom Thumb and his wife, and Rose Etynge. The list is endless.

The slump caused by decreasing production on the Comstock brought a decline of the theater in Virginia City, but Reno soon took its place as a center for high-priced theatrical attractions. Dyer's Theater, Reno's first show-house, erected in 1871, was destroyed by a cave-in. Fire wiped out both its successors, Smith's Academy of Music and Hammond and Wilson's, erected on the same site, the first in 1879, the other in 1889. The McKissick Opera House was then built and was the ranking theater of the town until its place was taken by the Majestic Theater, erected in 1910 by George S. Nixon, then a U. S. Senator.

Three years before this, Wheelman's Theater had burned. It was a home of melodrama, now remembered principally because Clara Kimball Young, of later motion picture fame, played ingenue parts there as a girl.

The Wigwam, dating from late in 1909, and the Granada, opening as the Rialto in 1915, are substantial brick structures used for motion pictures at present. Otis Skinner, Jane Cowl, Guy Bates Post, and Minnie Maddern Fiske appeared on the Granada stage; James O'Neil, Robert Mantell and Nance O'Neil were attractions at other Reno houses.

When the railroads, at about the time of the first World War, put an end to the practice of granting New York theatrical companies special stop-over privileges at Elko, Winnemucca, and Reno, they hastened the inevitable transformation of the theaters into motion picture houses.

Today Las Vegas occasionally sees a stage show and has two theaters, as well as a huge, new War Memorial Auditorium with excellent stage equipment. It is used by a little theater company of considerable talent and also for out of town attractions. Elko, Ely, and Winnemucca also have their theaters as have Tonopah and Goldfield, but they are used only for motion pictures. In the early days of Tonopah the Orpheum Circuit sent several shows a month to the Butler, and after the completion of the Hippodrome in Goldfield in 1906 such performers as Nat Goodwin and Edna Goodrich appeared for several weeks at a time. Reno now has an active and talented drama group that presents plays each year between October and May. This self-supporting amateur organization is gaining considerable support. Most of the members are native Renoites.

The University of Nevada also has an amateur group that produces several plays during the school year and the students of most of the high schools of the State present one or two plays a season.

ARCHITECTURE

The design of houses and business and public buildings aroused little interest in Nevada until very recent years. The reason is easily found. The Territory's first great influx of white immigrants was composed largely of men intent on making fortunes in the mines and going back home or to the large cities to spend them. Little or no thought was given to the erection of permanent dwellings until the Comstock and other discoveries, seemingly inexhaustible, led to the erection on the Virginia Range of substantial public buildings. Gradually a number of comfortable houses were erected; few were palatial, even though furnishings were costly. But production slowly declined, residents wandered away to new discoveries, and one by one the larger houses of the Comstock were destroyed or were moved to Reno, Carson City, and other communities. The new camps also produced fortunes for a few, then gave out, and again there was a migration to more hopeful prospects. Gradually the valuable discoveries grew fewer and the old timers either left the State or continued to move from place to place, sure that there was still treasure in the hills. Then came Tonopah, followed shortly by Goldfield. But they too, had relatively brief periods of fabulous production.

The majority of older Nevadans have lived in from one to a dozen different mining camps and have witnessed these swift booms and slow or rapid declines. They have seen the ruins of the first great mining town, Virginia City, and though they are perpetually hopeful of new bonanzas, experience has taught them to put little faith in the permanence of any town. This feeling has persisted even when they have turned from mining to other businesses—for most men who have known the excitement of a rush always remain prospectors at heart, ready to move when rumor brings a hint of possible bonanzas. They have not tended to take root easily and even when the furnishings in their houses were more than ordinarily comfortable and costly, they had one thing in common—

they could be moved. Only in communities that have survived booms and depressions do some of the dwellings look as though the builders had expected to stay. With such a widespread feeling of impermanence it was natural that design should be ignored.

Mere shelter was long a pressing problem in the Territory. Timber suitable for construction was hard to find except near the Sierra foothills. The first settlers in the western valleys had to erect log cabins of the usual frontier type until John Cary built a sawmill on Clear Creek in July, 1854. But he charged a hundred dollars for each thousand board feet and cash was scarce. Then a steam sawmill, erected in 1859, provided competition that lowered the price of lumber. The rush to the Comstock, however, created such a demand that the mill men again could get any price they chose. Lumber was needed not only for house building but for the mines, and whole forests were used to timber them.

First comers on the Comstock were happy to share space in a tent; the majority lived in dugouts, for a time at least. Some managed to get lumber enough to put fronts on their mountain-slope homes. The first sign of affluence on the part of saloon-keepers and other business-men was construction of a frame facade in front of the tents in which they served the public. By 1863, when twenty sawmills were operating in Washoe County alone, hammering could be heard night and day as stores, barracks, offices, theaters, and churches were being thrust together. But few of the early buildings survived for any great period. Fires were a frequent occurrence in the excited, happy-go-lucky community.

Although solid structures were built in time—chiefly offices for mining companies and business men—the majority had the simplest possible plan. Nearly all were cubes or rectangular blocks. The businessman or householder who wanted to make a special display gave lavish orders for jigsaw ornament, plush and leather-covered furniture, grand pianos, rose-splashed carpets, gilt and crystal chandeliers. The solid sandstone mansion erected by Sandy Bowers, one of the first Comstock millionaires, to satisfy the yearnings of his Old World wife, was an exception to the rule of jerry building. Most bonanza kings went to San Francisco, the western metropolis, to construct the palaces that would impress the world with their new-found wealth. It was these nabobs who helped give Nob Hill its name.

Stone early came into use for the larger public structures; stonecutters were few, however, and such as there were often succumbed to the prospecting fever, while not even a stone building was immune against the ravages of the ever-recurrent fires. Not many years after the first camps sprang up, good deposits of brick-clay were found and a bright red brick came into use for offices and stores—or at least for their street fronts. These red facades with wooden awnings over the sidewalks were long the hallmark of prosperity in Nevada business districts.

The psychology of the mining camp has had a marked influence upon other walks of life: stockmen, or rather the ex-miners and ex-prospectors who became cattlemen, never quite recovered from its effects, and many a ranch house today wears the impermanent look so often seen in the camps.

Adobe early came into use in the lower part of the State and even around Eureka and Austin the number of adobe structures is not small, particularly in the older camps. The adobe was often strengthened with uncut slabs and chunks of rock, with logs, or tough mahogany and juniper roots, and occasionally, with old beer and whiskey bottles. In the so-called bottle-houses the glass containers were laid horizontally, bottoms flush with the outer wall; when such walls were topped with a steep gable roof dripping jigsaw lace—as at Rhyolite—the result was bizarre, to say the least.

Much adobe was used for the older ranch houses, which, being in isolated places where skilled carpenters and other builders were rare, slowly developed along haphazard lines. Snug and quite comfortable on the whole, the rural Nevada homes sprawl in whatever form and direction the needs of the owners dictate. The typical ranch house is one story high, with at least one frame unit, painted or unpainted. Behind or beside it under sheltering cottonwoods or Lombardy poplars are the chuckhouse and outbuildings. Close by is the barn, adjoining the inevitable corral. Rural houses built in the last thirty years, particularly in the neighborhood of the larger towns, resemble those of the western Plains, though the one-story bungalow is preferred to the house of two stories.

A peculiarity along the railroad lines is the use of old railroad ties for the walls of barns and even of houses. When the cracks and joints have been chinked with cement or adobe, they provide stout shelters against the snows and winds of the northern winter.

Nevada was frontier country almost up to the time of the World War, though a few communities—notably Reno, Carson City, Elko, and Winnemucca had begun to have a more settled look. The Tonopah discovery of 1900, as well as the strikes at Goldfield and other places helped bring the State out of a long depression, and turned the older

Rothstein: Farm Security Admin.

ST. MARY'S IN THE MOUNTAINS,
VIRGINIA CITY

UNIVERSITY OF NEVADA, RENO

RESIDENTIAL STREET, RENO

THE CAPITOL, CARSON CITY

Photograph courtesy Nevada State Highway Department

NIGHT CLUB DISTRICT, LAS VEGAS *Photograph by Glenn A. Davis*

EUREKA

AIR VIEW, RENO

MANSION BUILT NEAR RENO BY SANDY BOWERS *Rothstein: Farm Security Admin.*

RENO MANSION BUILT BY GEORGE NIXON, MILLIONAIRE OF THE SECOND GREAT BOOM *Rothstein: Farm Security Admin.*

Rothstein: Farm Security Admin.   **TYPICAL ARCHITECTURAL DETAIL, RENO**

Photograph courtesy Nevada State Highway Dept.

WINNEMUCCA, STOCK AND MINING CENTER

STORES ON MAIN STREET, ELKO   *Rothstein: Farm Security Admin.*

towns into distribution centers. In these more settled communities a new generation has grown up with new habits and new standards, and its influence is becoming apparent all over the State.

Public schools and high schools are outstanding among the modern buildings in almost every town. Large handsome structures, usually of stone or brick, they embody the best ideas of design and equipment. In the county seats the courthouse is also notable for its size, if not always for its design. Churches, too, rise above the generally low roofs. New homes of conservative design are found in a few places, but the older Nevada is more apparent than the new, even in Reno and Las Vegas, which are beginning to resemble the cities of other parts of the country.

Nonetheless, there is hardly a community thirty years old that does not have at least a few houses well worth examination, for Victorian ideals were persistent here and were sometimes expressed in ornament that deserves preservation. Particularly charming are some of the small houses of Victorian Gothic design, found largely in the Reno-Carson City area and along the Humboldt. Their narrow pointed windows, steep gable ends, and delightfully frilled porch and gable decorations repay close study. Also of interest is some of the ironwork, found on balconies, roof ridges, bayed towers, and wherever else the builders fancied. Some of this ironwork came from foundries in Virginia City, but occasional bits were wrought in California.

A great deal of time can be spent in these older towns examining the intricate jigsaw work, which gave many a carpenter and mill-worker a chance to exercise his ingenuity. Column and post brackets show infinite variety. The eave brackets produced by the turning-lathes exhibit the same originality, though they are rarely as pleasing as the products of the jigsaw. One oddity, repeated quite frequently in Reno and Carson City, is a grille resembling Chinese Chippendale and used under the eaves of porches. Probably the most striking ornaments are the complicated grilles fastened under the eaves on the gable fronts of numerous structures.

In an essay that merely traces the development of Nevada's solution to the problem of providing shelter, there is no room for a description of the few buildings whose architectural features are notable. They include some modern buildings in Reno and Las Vegas, St. Mary's in the Mountains, in Virginia City, the Bowers' Mansion (*see Tour* 4), and public structures scattered here and there in the State.

MUSIC

Nevadans have never displayed any general tendency to burst into spontaneous song. Their original contributions are limited to a few ballads celebrating sentimental episodes of the cow ranges. But they have always enjoyed good music and given warm patronage to performers. In the early days music was taught only in private schools; it is now included in the curriculum of all public schools, and in the larger towns each school has one or more bands, with some members not yet nine years old, and also choral societies. This intensive teaching is showing results all over the State. Concerts by visiting artists are well attended, and those by local performers are increasing in number. The numerous women's clubs are making a place for music in their programs and some are including music appreciation courses.

To a large extent the school bands are taking the place of the town bands that were organized in almost every mining community. Without a band no camp could celebrate properly; the Comstock had at least half a dozen. But the standards of performance and repertoire have risen decidedly since that time.

The outstanding prima donna to come from the State was Emma Nevada—born Emma Wixom—whose affection for the State in which she grew up led her to adopt its name at a time when other American singers thought they had to adopt French or Italian names in order to acquire prestige. Richard Jose grew up in the Reno home of an uncle who taught him blacksmithing before tl clear beauty of his voice was recognized.

PAINTING AND SCULPTURE

The plastic arts do not flourish in pioneer communities, and although quite a bit of Comstock wealth was exchanged for paintings and sculpture it was largely spent outside the State—usually on work of transitory value. The chief demand for such products during the State's boisterous youth was for the adornment of the saloons—those clubs for homeless males in any community where the number of women is small. Some of this barroom art was not without merit, but most of it had been bought by collectors and carried out of the State—either as works of value or as curiosities—before Nevadans gauged the extent of their loss.

Here and there a primitive oil can still be found, painted by someone whose urge to preserve on canvas some of the beauty of country was greater than his skill. The Nevada Historical Society has a few of these relics, some of which show considerable freshness and vigor.

The Latimer Art Club of Reno, composed of an active group of women artists, was founded in 1921 by Lorenzo P. Latimer, California artist, and until 1939 was the only art club in Nevada. Since 1935, Nevada's interest in art has greatly increased, for that year marked the beginning of the national annual exhibitions of American art, in which every State in the Union participates. Work from all over the State is submitted for this show and is displayed at the University of Nevada. A committee appointed by the governor makes the selection of work to be sent to the exhibition in New York City.

The interest in art, awakening in the whole country, is noticeable all over Nevada, not only among artists, but in the general public as well. In 1939 a group of Carson City artists formed the Nevada Art Association, and in the same year the Reno Art Center was organized by a number of citizens who wished to sponsor free art classes conducted by the Work Projects Administration. The Art Center also holds a continuous series of art exhibits and has occasional lectures.

The Old Mint at Carson City is being converted into a museum that will contain an art gallery, and in Reno promotion of the future Nevada Art Galleries is under way. In 1938 *The Reno Evening Gazette* began a weekly column on art, conducted by Lillian Lewis Borghi, an artist.

Only one Nevadan, Pat O'Brien of Reno, has received attention outside the State for sculpture, but the paintings of several artists are attracting favorable attention. Among these Robert Cole Caples is notable. His work includes murals; one is in the lobby of the Washoe County Courthouse, and others are in the University Library. His charcoal studies of Indians are done with strength and simplicity.

Reno artists who specialize in water-color landscapes are Minerva Pierce, Dolores Samuels Young, Muriel Goodwin, Zella Kay Piersall, Lillian Lewis Borghi, Helen Joslin, Hilda Herz. Richard Guy Walton has done murals for the Washoe County Library that show an inventive mind and much talent. Hans Meyer Kassel, a portrait and landscape painter of excellent technique, who is represented in Norwegian, German, and American galleries, has lived in Reno for several years. Dan Muller, who now resides in the East, was a prolific producer of western studies in oil. A busy mural painter who has decorated several Nevada churches and business houses is Jose De Soto, a Spaniard, who lived for a while in Nevada.

Fred Forbusch, of Carson City, works in wood, principally mountain mahogany. Some of his products were exhibited at the San Francisco World's Fair. Buck Nimy of Lovelock executes pen-and-ink drawings of range subjects and Ted Drummond of Reno does woodcarving and etching. Emily Hilliard and Harriet Fairhurst of Reno stress portraiture.

Willis Church of Reno and Herbert Swinburne of Carson are architects as well as artists. Frances Broili of Reno specializes in decorative oils and china. Edwin M. Dawes gained recognition in Minnesota for his lyrical landscapes before coming to Fallon. Jonas Malm is another active artist at Fallon. Lew Hymers of Genoa works in the fine arts as well as in the newspaper and commercial field.

John Mariani and Merle Singleton, of Sparks, are talented young men who are now teaching art. Andy Huhn and Jack Cooney are versatile artists of Carson City, who were employed by the State Highway Department to do murals for the Nevada exhibit at the San Francisco Fair.

Ada Ducker and Virginia Harsh of Carson City work in oil, the former painting horses, and the latter landscapes. Minnie Price of Las Vegas is a water-colorist, and also a teacher of ceramics, who uses a new synthetic clay, one of whose ingredients is obtained at Caliente, Nevada.

Sports and Recreation

NEVADA offers a wide variety of sport and recreation. The drillers' and muckers' contests, which, with thoroughbred racing, wrestling, and fighting, were popular in the early days of settlement, have been replaced by more modern sports. The earlier favorites are revived only during mining camp celebrations.

Hunting and Fishing (for seasons and license fees see General Information): One of the chief recreations is hunting, and many out-of-state enthusiasts come in for it. Wild game is found over so wide an area that no one region can be recommended as better than another. Most areas where game abound are easily accessible from paved roads. Deer, found in nearly every county, are particularly numerous in the northern section of the State. Although the deer are fair game during proper seasons, antelope, mountain sheep, and elk—recently imported—are protected at all times. The Humboldt National Forest is a natural habitat of grouse, sagehen, and deer, which are steadily increasing in number.

Ducks, pheasants, grouse, sage grouse, quail, partridge, sagehen, snipe, prairie chickens, cottontail rabbits, and mountain hare, doves, and migratory fowl can be hunted during certain seasons. Both waterfowl and grouse are numerous in the northern part of the State.

Fishing, which vies with hunting in popularity, is more practiced each year, as Federal, State and county fish hatcheries aid in stocking the streams. Several storage reservoirs have improved fishing by regulating the flow of streams. The Humboldt River tributaries, rising high in the Ruby, Jarbidge, and Independence Mountains, afford excellent trout fishing, and the main channel harbors bass and catfish. In the same region are the headwaters of the Little Salmon, Bruneau, and Owyhee rivers, also notable trout streams. Among the well-stocked small mountain streams of east central Nevada are those of the Schell Creek and Egan ranges; they offer chiefly the rainbow and eastern brook trout. In western Nevada the Truckee, Carson, and East and West Walker rivers, with their many tributaries, are popular fishing streams.

Throughout the fishing areas are lakes of varying size, from Pyramid Lake—30 miles in length—to the minute bodies of water found in the deeper recesses of the mountains. The lakes and streams off the beaten paths sometimes contain more fish than those nearer the main-traveled roads. Pyramid Lake has gained fame for its large trout, a species of landlocked salmon weighing from twelve to forty-two pounds.

Tahoe, Walker, and Topaz Lakes are popular fishing spots where carp and lake trout are very plentiful. Lake Mead, formed by Boulder Dam on the Colorado River, has been stocked with a wide variety of fish, and white salmon have been taken in the river just below the dam. Bass and catfish, in addition to trout, are now plentiful in the river.

Camping: There are many campsites throughout the State, particularly in the national forests. Among the choice improved camp spots in the Toiyabe National Forest are Kingston and Big Creek Canyons. This forest has a number of hot springs noted for their mineral content, the most important of which are Spencer and Darrough Hot Springs in Big Smoky Valley, and the Potts Hot Springs and Diana's Punch Bowl—or the Devil's Punch Bowl—near the Potts Ranger Station in Monitor Valley (*see Tour 7*).

The chief recreational attraction in the Nevada National Forest, the Lehman Caves National Mounment, is near a Forest Service campground. An especially beautiful camping area is in the Ruby Mountains, where peaks rise nearly 12,000 feet and there are deep, rugged canyons, fishing streams, cool breezes, and lakes bearing ice until at least July.

Many excellent camping spots are in the Jarbidge region (*see Tour* 1a), a heavily wooded district in the Gold Creek Range, and in the Humboldt Forest.

Walking and Riding: Foot and horse trails are numerous throughout the State, marked chiefly in recreational areas, though many unmarked trails are in the mountains and lead to awe-inspiring views. One of the most delightful hikes (*see Tour* 6) is made from the campground near the Lehman Caves to the summit of Mount Wheeler, one of the highest peaks in Nevada; another is up Mount Rose, which overlooks Truckee Meadows and Lake Tahoe. The Ruby Mountains contain many marked trails, as do the Lake Tahoe and Charleston areas.

Horseback riding, a particularly popular diversion in Nevada, is featured in the vicinity of Reno on the dude ranches; there the traditions, costumes, and trappings of the Old West are paraded—largely the Old West of the motion picture westerns and of Buffalo Bill. There are also dude ranches with good stables in other parts of the State, and horses are everywhere available.

Swimming: Nevada is proud of its facilities for swimming because of its reputation as a State with no water at all. Most pools are out of doors. Hot springs, municipal, and privately owned pools are found from border to border. Reno, Lovelock, Winnemucca, Elko and Ely have municipally owned pools where season tickets run as low as four cents a swim and single tickets as low as twenty-five cents. In addition there are numerous privately owned pools, chiefly in the larger towns. Aside from the artificial pools, Lake Tahoe, Pyramid Lake, Walker Lake, Topaz Lake, and Lake Mead afford excellent swimming.

Boating: This has become a real sport in the Lake Mead area, where motor boat trips are one of the chief attractions. At both Lake Tahoe and Lake Mead aquaplaning and rowing are increasingly popular. Speed boat races are held annually on Lake Tahoe.

Winter Sports: Nevada, which has many accessible slopes with dry snow, is fast becoming a winter playground, and is developing excellent ski courses, the best known of which are on Mount Rose (*see Tour 4*). Mount Rose also offers tobogganing and has an up-tow, a ski jump permitting a 165-foot leap, a racing course, and a slalom course. More surprising is the Charleston area, which, though in a region with subtropical climate, provides facilities for all the sports of winter. It is a short distance from Las Vegas. Ward Mountain, near Ely, is another winter sports district where courses are being developed. There is, of course, skiing on unchartered slopes near almost every town in central and northern Nevada when the snow blankets the ranges. Some ice skating is done in various northern and central towns, though this sport is not common.

Athletic Contests: The University of Nevada participates in an extensive program of inter-collegiate sport contests, including football and basketball games, and track meets. The high schools of all the larger towns have football and basketball teams that participate in series of games for the State championship.

Horse Racing: Reno and Las Vegas hold racing meets with open betting. Races are also held in connection with various county fairs.

Baseball and Softball: Baseball has long been a major sport in Nevada, as elsewhere. The Reno Garage in Reno sponsors a club that has a good baseball park, where the club plays on Sunday, meeting various strong teams from the Pacific Coast and other points.

A State league, composed of clubs from Reno, Lovelock, Fallon, and

Smith Valley, also play Sunday baseball; and Ely, Tonopah, Manhattan, Silver Peak, Sparks, Verdi, Virginia City, and Wadsworth sponsor town teams playing on Sunday, though no regular schedule is followed.

There are softball leagues in Reno, Las Vegas, Elko, Fallon and Ely. Las Vegas won the 1939 championship at a tournament held in Fallon. The year 1939 saw the first girls' softball teams, with four organized in the Reno area and several in other parts of the State.

Golf: With the completion of an 18-hole golf course in Reno, Nevada began to attract out-of-state golfers. Winnemucca, Elko, Ely, Carson, Glenbrook (Lake Tahoe) and Las Vegas also have courses. Beside a well-conditioned 18-hole sand fairway, Las Vegas has a 9-hole grass course. The Glenbrook, Lake Tahoe course is excellent.

Motorcycling: Both Reno and Las Vegas have motorcycle clubs holding annual races that include a Hare and Hounds Chase on Thanksgiving Day, a Hill Climb on New Year's Day, and a 400-mile endurance run over varied terrain in the spring.

Boxing: Several fights notable in history of the ring have been staged in Nevada. Joe Gans, a Negro, defeated "Battling Nelson" at Goldfield, Jack Johnson defeated Jim Jeffries at Reno—winning the heavyweight title, and Bob Fitzsimmons took the crown from Jim Corbett at Carson City. Interest in amateur boxing has always been high in Nevada and several Nevada boys have gained considerable reputation. One of them, Ernie Collins, an Indian boy from Schurz, has achieved success on the coast.

Bowling: Reno has five men's bowling leagues of six teams each; these are often matched against out-of-state teams. Various other towns also have men's leagues and in Reno and Las Vegas women have leagues.

Chess: The small but efficient Nevada State Chess Association conducts an annual State tournament each year to determine the Nevada chess championship.

Part II

Touring the State

Tour 1

(Salt Lake City, Utah)—Wells—Elko—Battle Mountain—Winne-mucca—Lovelock—Reno—(Sacramento, Calif.) ; US 40.

Utah Line to California Line, 416 *m.*

Paved roadbed throughout.
Accommodations in principal towns afford choice of auto courts or hotels.
Western Pacific and Southern Pacific R. R. roughly parallel route.

US 40, the valley route between Salt Lake City and central Califor-nia, has a character unusual in Nevada in that for the most part it fol-lows a river, the winding Humboldt, which has cut deep gorges, some-times narrow and sometimes broad, in the many north-south ranges that crossed its course downward from the high north eastern section of the State. The mountains are more and more barren as the river moves west-ward, their sheer faces brilliantly stained with minerals that take on an unearthly glow at sunset. Where the river crosses the north-south val-leys, meadowlands of wild grass provide feed for part of the thousands of cattle that are the principal source of wealth in the northern part of the State. Sheep feed in summer on slopes high above the valley and in the fall add their bleat to the bellow of beef cattle herded into corrals near the railroad stations.

From one end of the State to the other, side roads lead to campsites among cedar and juniper, to tumbling trout streams, and, in the eastern and far western parts of the State, to sub-alpine meadows that are the delight of botanists seeking blooms of unusual beauty and color.

The valley route has both charm and interest at all times of the year—though travelers in July and August are often too annoyed by heat to notice them unless they adopt the only sensible procedure for all summer travel on the Great Plains, in the South, and in the West, which is the mid-day siesta. A full halt in the air-cooled hotels and auto-camps from ten to two avoids the sword-like sunbeam of mid-day, but more experienced travelers are now learning that very early and late after-noon driving not only gives them more comfort, but here in Nevada it enables them to enjoy magnificent light affects that make the ends of day memorable.

The noon-day heat of these heaviest travel months was long a re-minder of the horror tales of the days of pioneer overland journeys. Oxcart travelers, however, had difficulties unknown to the modern motorist.

If ever there was a Golden Road it was the Humboldt route. Samarkand never drew the hordes of wealth-seekers that panted and scrambled along this river on their way to the Mother Lode. For the most part utterly ignorant of wilderness travel-ways and needs, very often unsuitably and inadequately equipped, cocksure in their belief that they possessed an innate instinct on routes superior to that of experienced guides and scouts, the early emigrants formed one of the most appallingly happy-go-lucky swarms the world has ever known. Before the rush was more than half under way, old mountain-men like Jim Bridger had withdrawn advice and services to sit in cynical peace and watch the procession pass.

But this was far from being the horror trail of the storytellers. It is true that there were bad stretches—chiefly over the sinks—but people who prepared for these crossings methodically, carrying sufficient hay and water for their animals, wearing wet handkerchiefs over their noses and mouths, lightening their loads of heavy tools—including grindstones—and such frivolities as melodeons and bureaus, got through without more than temporary hardships. The danger from Indians has also been over-emphasized; the Indians were annoying, but people who followed the rule of not straying far from their trains, of keeping regular guard relays during halts, rarely suffered loss of life or animals.

For every person who died on the way there were thousands who came through safely. The trip was high adventure and those who made it were proud to have had part in it—indeed, they would not have missed it for any price. Few realize today that the emigrants looked ahead to the journey overland in part as a sight-seeing trip; they watched eagerly for the landmarks of which they had been told, covered notable eminences with their names to leave record that they had been there, took time off to climb to points noted for their views, picked up rocks and other souvenirs to remind them of this and that wonder. As they grew older they loved to find an audience that would listen to their story of the trip—and many were prone to exaggerate and spread the stories of misfortunes they themselves had not experienced. Diaries kept on the route are the best proof that tales grew with the telling in later years; the lack of perilous events and the monotony of the entries is surprising.

This country interested every newcomer; its high coloring and wierd formations were novelties. But many, accustomed to green-clad hills and lush meadow bottoms, were shocked by the gray-green sage and imagined the country a desert; they knew of only one kind of land that would produce wealth, the kind they had left behind.

Tales of the stagecoach days, the 1850's on this route, have also been the subject of much blood-and-thunder fiction. Buffalo Bill and others who have made—and make—their livings by sensational stories turned each journey down the Humboldt into a story of peril and agony. Though the rocking stages were not comfortable, most travelers accepted the discomforts philosophically. Mark Twain, try as he would in *Roughing It,* could fill in his narrative only with stories of what had happened to somebody else. Richard Burton, experienced world traveler and later translator of the *Arabian Nights,* found not a single lurid story to light up his narrative of the trip from Salt Lake City to the West Coast.

The movement westward really got under way about 1840, largely stimulated by the economic collapse of 1837. But for 30 years employees of the great fur companies, as well as independent trappers, had been exploring the West in search of the valuable furs. In 1826 and 1827 Jedediah Smith and a small band had galloped across the Great Basin; Hudson's Bay trappers were penetrating to the Humboldt from the north; and the Mexicans and Spanish were pushing up from the south. The first westward movement was directed toward the lush green valley west of the Cascade Range in Oregon. From that territory and from the Southwest, traders and mere adventurers had penetrated into Mexican California. Those who got a foothold in California began to broadcast the possibilities of settlement there in the hope of drawing enough Yankees around themselves to over-rule the natives. The first large party to make California its goal was led by John Bidwell in 1841. Bidwell's plan was to follow the well-known Oregon Trail to a point near Fort Hall on the Snake—in what is now eastern Idaho—and then cut southwestward. But the warnings of trappers frightened some of the travelers, and the party split at Soda Springs, one half going to Oregon and thence to California, and the remainder, led by Bidwell, south toward the Humboldt. The Bidwell party managed to get into the Salt Lake Desert and then made a wandering detour before reaching the Humboldt; but it reached California by November without the loss of a single member. One man in the Bidwell party returned east to waylay other westbound travelers in 1843; at Fort Hall he decided to go back to California by way of Oregon, and only a few would-be settlers, guided by the scout, Joseph Walker, who had crossed Nevada along the Humboldt route ten years before, followed the Humboldt. In the next year the Stephens-Townsend-Miller-Murphy party, waylayed by Sutter's agents, the Greenwoods (*see Tour* 2a), at Fort Hall, left the Oregon Trail and under the guidance of the old trapper came down to the Humboldt, followed it westward, and even managed to get their wagons across Truckee Pass. In 1845 several other parties followed the same course without serious misadventure, largely owing to expert guidance.

But in 1846 came the dreadful Donner misadventure that was to shed a cloud of horror over the route for many years. Lansford Hastings, a young lawyer who had gone to California in 1842 and developed dreams of a Yankee republic with himself at the head, joined an eastbound party of disgruntled immigrants led by an experienced trapper. He conceived the idea of making a short cut across the Great Salt Desert to Fort Bridger—now in southwestern Wyoming—on the Oregon Trail; the guide disapproved but the difficult crossing was made. Near this point Hastings persuaded one party to try his short route to California and started off with it, leaving an "Open Letter" to influence others The unusually well-equipped party led by George Donner was the first to fall a victim to Hasting's glowing accounts of the short-cut; Hastings left word that he had gone ahead but would be on the lookout to guide them at difficult points. One of the Donner party wagons was so large that it was called the Pioneer Palace Car and needed eight oxen to drag it; other wagons were heavily laden with the household goods of the more prosperous pioneers. The size of the wagons, as well as the inexperience of the party of eastern farmers, was responsible for painfully slow progress down rocky canyons to the Great Salt Lake. The desert crossing was made with extreme difficulty and then, by mischance, the party turned south through inviting Clover Valley, which forced them to make the circuit around the Ruby Range. By the time the travelers had crossed Humboldt Sink the journey had become an endless nightmare; quarrels had broken out, one man had gone insane, supplies were nearly gone, and the oxen and other animals were dying from exhaustion. The water and forage of the Truckee Meadows beguiled them into a delay that was fatal. Early snows overtook them in the pass and all but a small advance group was forced to stay on the heights of the mountain range. By the time relief arrived after various delays only 33 of 81 people were left alive, and three of the survivors died on their way to Sutter's Fort.

No matter what route was taken by an overland party the going was difficult beyond the Continental Divide. Rocks mangled the feet of the animals and alkali-laden dust burned faces and throats. Moreover, this high dry country was nearly always traversed at its driest and hottest period, and as the trains increased in number the ground, even on the lush prairies eastward, was churned to fine dust that enveloped the route in a perpetual cloud. By 1852, when 100,000 people had already crossed the country, the dust-cloud never had a chance to settle, watering and camping places were perpetually fouled, and within a month after it sprouted all forage was gone for a long distance on both sides of the trail. Yet another handicap of travelers during the gold-rush years was that the West was going through one of its great drought cycles; in 1922 a lake near the upper California boundary went dry, revealing wheel tracks made by oxcarts in crossing the dry lake bed nearly 100 years before.

With completion of the transcontinental railroad, which parallels US 40 in Nevada, trail travel fell off sharply though occasional wagons made the crossing until the 1880's. To stimulate business along the route the railroad company brought in settlers on cheap tickets entitling them to places in freight cars equipped with cooking stoves. This was the period in which many of the towns along US 40 came into existence, chiefly as strategic distribution and shipping points for the settlements and mining camps developing in a wide band north and south of the railroad. Some still carry on their original function but are also business centers for the many large and small ranches around them. Reno is the only town that has a census population that would classify it as more than a village in the East but the population figures are completely misleading. Several other towns are equal to Reno in business, cultural, and social development, as well as in facilities for modern comfort. At certain seasons their week-end populations are more than double the number of permanent residents.

Section a. UTAH LINE *to* WINNEMUCCA, 237 *m.*

US 40 comes into Nevada from the east across the blazing hot flats of the Salt Lake Desert, where travelers so rash as to take the shorter Hastings route, were paralyzed by mirages, heat, thirst, and the boggy terrain. These flats end at the Pilot Range, just west of the Nevada Line.

At the western edge of this vast salt plain, 75 miles in breadth, stands PILOT PEAK, about 20 miles north of the route. Immigrants, grateful that the crossing was over, camped by Pilot Creek, where they found water and grass after their appalling day-and-night journey of from 48 to 90 hours, during which their animals had waded through ashy undulations, sometimes sinking to their knees, with this landmark ahead but never seeming any closer. The peak was named by Fremont in 1845.

US 40 crosses the Utah Line in WENDOVER, 0 *m.* (4,245 alt., 9 pop.), (*see Tour 7a*), in conjunction with US 50 (*see Tour 7a*), at a point 127 miles west of Salt Lake City. Two-thirds of Wendover lies in Utah. On the slopes of the Pilot Range (R) and browner peaks to the south, are the beach marks of ancient Lake Bonneville. Since automobile racing was begun on the Salt Flats three decades ago, Wendover has been a headquarters and supply base for the meets.

At 0.5 *m.* is the junction (L) with U. S. 50 (*see Tour 7a*).

The Toano Mountains are crossed through SILVER ZONE PASS, 20.1 *m.* (5,940 alt.). This range and pass were the first in Nevada to be used by travelers coming across the Utah desert. Now the Western Pacific Railroad follows the old trail. These mountains, steep, spotted with mahogany, juniper, and pinon, and reaching far to the south, offer some feed to sheep and to cattle.

From the summit the highway drops swiftly between jagged scarps of rugged splendor into GOSHUTE VALLEY, 22.6 *m.,* beyond which are the Pequop Mountains, a backdrop of ever changing color.

At 33.5 *m.* is the junction with an unimproved dirt road.

Left on this road, which passes SHAFTER, 11.9 *m.* (5,550 alt., 10 pop.), junction point of the Western Pacific and Nevada Northern Railroads, to FLOWERY LAKE (L), 21.4 *m.,* a grass-covered, spring-fed swamp. Here the Donner Party paused long enough to cache belongings in order to lighten their wagons. Fremont, who camped here in 1845, called the place Whitton Springs, and divided his party, sending one division northwestward to follow the Humboldt River while he led the remainder southwestward to a rendezvous at Walker Lake.

OASIS, 34 *m.* (5,106 alt.), on US 40, is a service telephone and Red Cross station.

Right from Oasis on Nev. 30, a graveled road, to an unimproved road at 6.7 *m.;* L. here 1.4 *m.* to COBRE (6,921 alt., 45 pop.), northern terminal of the Nevada Northern Railroad, at the main line of the Southern Pacific. On Nev. 30 is MONTELLO, 25 *m.* (4,985 alt., 350 pop.), a repair point on the Southern Pacific and a shipping point for big cattle outfits in the Thousand Springs

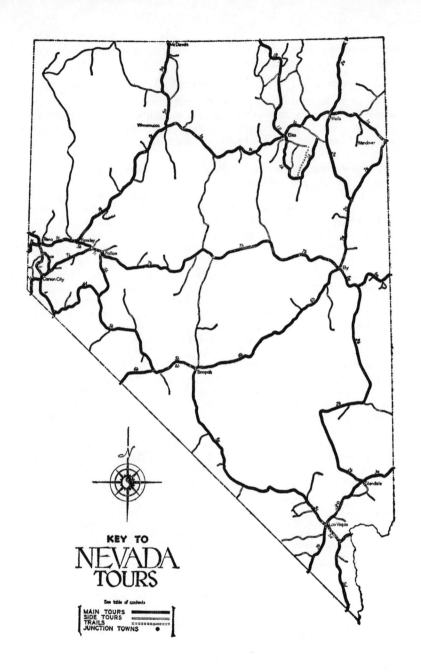

KEY TO
NEVADA
TOURS

See table of contents

MAIN TOURS
SIDE TOURS
TRAILS
JUNCTION TOWNS

country and for the Delno Mining District (L). It is also sportsmen's headquarters for sagechicken, duck, and deer hunting.

Left from Montello on a dirt road into the Valley of the Thousand Springs,
so-called by travelers over the old Fort Hall-to-California Road, who entered this
district from what is now Idaho, and found abundant water.

EMIGRANT SPRINGS, 32.7 *m.* from Montello, was a much used stopping-
point on the Fort Hall road. Right from the Springs on the early trail, which
can be followed to the northeastern corner of Nevada along Goose Creek. Nev.
30 continues northeast across the Bonneville lake-bed to the State Line, 35 *m.*,
where it joins Utah 70.

West of Oasis US 40 climbs the eastern slope of the Pequop Mountains to PEQUOP SUMMIT, 37.9 *m.* (6,980 alt.). Like the Toano
Range, the Pequops are partly covered with mahogany, pinon, and
juniper. The southern end of the range is a winter range of deer, as
well as for the few antelope that remain in this area. The northern end
bounds the Thousand Springs country. In early days this rough region
was controlled by a band of marauding Paiutes, who, it has been suspected, were incited by renegade white men to attack oxcart trains in
order to steal livestock.

After descending the western slopes of the Pequops US 40 cuts northwest across another valley, sage-covered and sweeping toward distant
violet and blue ranges. The valley is north of the Independence Mountains. Gradually the Ruby Mountains (L) come into view—snow-
patched even in summer and rising more than 11,000 feet.

WELLS, 61.3 *m.* (5,626 alt., 831 pop.), is the southern terminal of
a branch of the Union Pacific, and the junction with US 93 (*see Tour
2a*). While the present town grew up when the Central Pacific Railroad was built, the area just northwest was one of the principal camping
spots on the California Trail and the town was named for the Humboldt Wells. Dozens of springs were here, scattered over a meadow, as
in the Thousand Springs region northward. Immigrants called them
wells, apparently because they considered many of them bottomless.
Before the coming of the railroad, hundreds of wagons were here at one
time, as travelers rested and fattened their animals before starting on
the long journey down the Humboldt.

Wells has long been a supply point for the livestock growers along
the upper Humboldt, in Ruby and Clover Valleys to the south, in the
Thousand Springs area to the north, and in the vast O'Neil region east
of the Jarbidge Mountains. Local prosperity is reflected in oiled streets
and modern public facilities. On the streets are seen Paiute ranch-
hands, Mexican railroad workers, cowboys, stock buyers, miners, and
tourists, as well as ranchers and their families. For many years Wells
was virtually treeless, then experimentation by the County Farm Bureau
showed that hardy trees would grow if properly planted and tended. As
a result the town now has well-shaded residential districts, particularly
attractive in contrast with the surrounding areas.

Between 1870 and 1890 cattlemen in this region ran it in a high,
wide, and handsome manner. But in 1889 thousands of high-priced
cattle were on scant forage, a long deep winter with notable blizzards

followed, and spring found the cattle dead in the fields and on the range. Wealthy stockmen went bankrupt almost overnight, and some were forced to begin all over again as cowboys. Up and down the grapevine of the long Nevada valleys men chuckled over the story of a Negro camp cook, who looking over the dismal scene, rolled his eyes heavenward and reverently exclaimed; "Lawd, Lawd, how your snow done equalize society!"

The road turns westward across the broken slopes of the northern end of East Humboldt Mountains (L), not far from the Humboldt, which is increased by the waters of Mary's River and several smaller streams. Northeast across the valley, Bishop Creek afforded entrance to the Humboldt for the Stevens-Townsend-Murphy party, which successfully crossed to California. Murphy's son Dan was later a big cattleman with a ranch near Halleck.

Southward the Humboldt River comes into view near the road. It was a stream that excited derision in many besides Mark Twain—who said that if a man was bored and wanted to entertain himself, he could jump back and forth across the river until exhausted and thirsty, and then drink it dry. It has been a river of many names. Known to the trapping fraternity as early as 1827, it was first called the Unknown, then Mary's River, possibly for the Indian wife of Peter Skene Ogden; next Ogden's River and Paul's—the latter for one of Ogden's men who died on its bank. Mary's River is now the name of a tributary. Fremont named it Humboldt River for Alexander von Humboldt, the German explorer, and the name stuck.

Although Greenwood, piloting his train, found grass in abundance, and the river with sufficient flow to dilute its alkali content, later travelers had less happy experiences. The river zigged and zagged, every zig marking a chasm through rock, and every zag a small level area. Sand and gravel were often hub-deep on the trail, and dust smothered both men and beast. In the pools and lower reaches the water was so full of alkali that, like the whiskey in Virginia City Mark Twain described, a smell was enough to "disable a man for life."

US 40 turns abruptly north across the river at 78.8 m. On benchland (L), less than a mile away, there was a Paiute camp within the memory of people still alive. Approximately at this point during some periods of oxcart travel, many wagon trains swung along the edge of Ruby Mountains, and then westward across the South Fork, returning to the main route near Beowawe (see ahead).

At 79.9 m., just beyond a railroad overpass, is the junction with a graveled road.

Right on this road to DEETH, 0.5 m. (5,336 alt., 75 pop.), a shipping point for ranches on Mary's River, and in the Charleston and O'Neil regions northward. In horse and buggy days the town was a lively headquarters for ranchmen, and was many times larger than it is now.

North of Deeth a graded dirt road (closed in winter) skirts the west edge of Mary's River. The road turns L. at 9 m. and climbs to POLE CANYON CREEK SUMMIT, 22.8 m., (6,954 alt.), which is on the northern edge of the Great Basin. This country was once controlled by a rich outfit that introduced

Polled Angus cattle into an area of Herefords. One day the owner of the concern stopped for dinner at a small ranch where excellent T-bone steaks drew a compliment from the guest. The little daughter said proudly: "Oh, daddy never kills red and white cows. He brings nice black and white ones home." There is no record of what the guest said, or of what happened to the rustler.

At 44.7 *m.* is the graded dirt North Fork road (*see Tour 1B*).

The graveled road continues to wind and climb past several small creeks to the isolated ranching community of CHARLESTON, 49.2 *m.*, (6,008 alt.), which rests in a little valley where Bruneau River breaks northward through a deep canyon. For many years Charleston had a reputation as one of the toughest places in the State—and doubtless it was. Law and order had a difficult time growing up there. After a man-hunt in this primitive area a sheriff said: "By darn, the trip was a success. I didn't get my man, but I rode plumb through Charleston without being shot at." Today, only two caved-in log cabins on '76 Creek mark the site of the old town. Near Charleston the last stage hold-up in Nevada took place on December 4, 1916, when a lone bandit wounded the driver and looted the Jarbidge stage.

Old-timers tell of salmon runs up Bruneau River, and of the amazing number of antelope that formerly browsed on the rolling desert westward. Neither salmon nor antelope remain. The Bruneau, however, is noted for its trout fishing and the area between Charleston and Gold Creek still offers excellent sagehen hunting. The rugged Jarbidge Range is the home of mule-deer.

The road north of Charleston is often impassable from the first autumn snow until early summer. The western boundary of the Jarbidge division of the Humboldt National Forest is crossed at 53 *m.*, in the ascent of the Jarbidge Mountains to COON CREEK SUMMIT, 64 *m.* This section of mountain road is very beautiful at any season, but especially during the fall when willow, aspen, and chokecherry are aflame

Left from the summit 1 *m.* on a trail to the top of COPPER MOUNTAIN (9,911 alt.), which offers a magnificent view of the sunken gorges of southern Idaho and the dim Sawtooth Range northward.

For three miles the main road now winds through alpine county around the northern end of the range, with Bear Creek pouring down to the Bruneau. Tamarack and burnt-earth make this region resemble the Mother Lode country of California. The road crosses JARBIDGE SUMMIT, 67 *m.*, where it turns sharply R., giving for a moment the impression that it suddenly terminates in space. The road drops 2,000 feet in 5.5 miles and provides a spectacular descent, breath-taking for persons not used to mountain driving. By Jarbidge River at the foot of the grade is a Forest Service campground (R) with stoves in a beautiful grove of aspen and mountain laurel. A ranger station is a half mile beyond Jarbidge.

The whole region is in almost primitive state, with a heavy stand of timber unusual to northern Nevada. Deer and grouse are plentiful and fishermen describe the region as paradise. Coon Creek, Bear Creek, Jarbidge River, and other streams teem with trout. High above the conifers and red cedars is found the rare fox-tail pine. The wild red raspberries and black gooseberries of the thickets make delicious jellies.

The road follows the east bank of the river to JARBIDGE, 74 *m.*, (6,200 alt., 392 pop.), where mine dumps dot the canyon like ruins of ancient cliff-dwellings. Jarbidge (Indian, Ja-ha-bich, the Devil) was probably applied to this district on account of its ruggedness and the presence of hot springs. This is the most isolated of all Nevada mining camps. Exploited since 1910, for a number of years it was the chief producer of gold in the State. The total production of this area to 1921 was gold and silver ore valued at nearly four million dollars. The Elkoro Mines Company owns most of the important properties. Within recent years, new deposits have been discovered. The mines shafts on steep canyon slopes are behind and above false-front stores and log cabins, making a picturesque settlement. In heavy winters drifts as high as 30 feet cut this community from its neighbors.

North of Jarbidge at 82 *m.*, the road crosses the Idaho Line, at a point 48.5 miles south of Rogerson, Idaho.

US 40 continues to the junction, 90.5 *m.*, with Nev. 11, a graded dirt road.

Left on this road is HALLECK STATION, 0.9 *m.* (5,226 alt., 3 pop.), on the north bank of Humboldt River; it was established to serve Fort Halleck, and Starr, Pleasant, and Lamoille valleys (*see Tour 1A*). The surrounding area matches San Jacinto, to the north, as one of the coldest spots in the United States. The thermometer has officially registered 50° below zero. Down the north-south valley, paralyzing winds from Idaho spend themselves against the Ruby Mountains, concentrating their cold in this basin. Pogonip, the fog that was dreaded by Indians, occasionally puts a sheath of frost crystals on every shrub and blade of grass. It is then that the still air does strange things with sound. Small sharp sounds, such as that from an axe or from a wagon crossing the frozen earth, can be distinctly heard for many miles along the bitterly cold meadows.

Nev. 11 continues southeast, passing the entrance to the 100,000-acre 71 RANCH before curving south along the western base of the Ruby Mountains to the foot of SECRET CANYON, 11.5 *m.;* R. here 7.4 *m.* to the SITE OF FORT HALLECK, established in 1867 when Fort Ruby (*see Tour 1A*) was abandoned with the approach of the railroad. Only foundations remain as this post was closed in 1886. Troops stationed here saw no major engagements but their presence encouraged settlement of the surrounding valleys.

Nev. 11 continues eastward winding up a steep grade in narrow Secret Canyon by Secret Creek, which cascades down from lovely Secret Valley. When troops were first stationed in the vicinity they were puzzled by the sudden disappearance of marauding Indians. Later this high pocket of green meadow was discovered. At one time rustlers also frequented the hideaway with cattle stolen from pioneers on the Humboldt Road. Narrow Secret Canyon and Secret Valley divide the Ruby Mountains, to the south, from the East Humboldt Mountains on the north; both are part of the Ruby Range. The road ascends again to cross SECRET PASS in low eroded granite hills and descends to ARTHUR, 23 *m.*, in Ruby Valley. Arthur is at the junction with the Ruby Valley road (*see Tour 1A*).

In autumn the pass and the eastern valley are a gathering ground for deer forced down by the snows to the shelter of cedar and mahogany.

Nev. 11 turns south, then east around the southern edge of the East Humboldt Range to its junction with US 93, 43.6 *m.* (*see Tour 2a*), at a point about 25 miles south of Wells on US 40 (*see before*).

US 40 now crosses the North Fork of the Humboldt, a flood stream in springtime, but practically dry in late summer and fall.

It was along here that early immigrants feared the "Humboldt Ghouls", Indians whom the pioneers misnamed "Diggers". The Indians themselves also had cause for alarm. On one occasion a man from a train, using some ruse, lured an Indian girl off into the sagebrush. Discovered by her relatives, he was brought to the white camp and his life demanded. No voice was raised in protest; whereupon the immigrant was shot, scalped, and dismembered.

A low, grayish point of rock (L) looms against the burnt-red hills across the Humboldt. Here in the early 1850's stock guards of a wagon train were attacked by Indians. When the main train reached the spot the following day and found their companions dead, the men dug graves and carried large white stones from the bluffs to mark them. Between this point and Elko other relics of the westward trek are visible along the river.

The NEVADA SCHOOL OF INDUSTRY, 105 *m.*, was established in 1913 for the care of delinquent boys. Athletic and vocational training are given to help correct antisocial tendencies.

ELKO (Shoshone, White Woman), 110.5 *m.* (5,063 alt., 4,018 pop.) (*all types of accommodations, including auto-courts; auto-service and other facilities; charter airplane service; pack trips to mountains arranged through Chamber of Commerce*). This town, seat of Elko County and the largest community between Salt Lake City and Reno, is the chief trade and service center for a country as large as New Jersey, Connecticut, and Rhode Island combined. Seen from the railroad it is not impressive; the wide street bisected by the tracks is lined with buildings erected for the most part in the 1880's and 1890's, and falsefronts are still among them. But a cue to the town's true character is seen even from the train; only two lots away from a small house dripping Victorian trimmings is a cocktail bar whose bakelite and chromium elegance would fit well into upper Fifth Avenue in New York. A stroll down streets away from the railroad reveals other surprises—shops selling clothes bearing trademarks of prominent designers. fine tweeds, and even lalique glass. Shops making leather goods to satisfy the high standards of cattlemen are local developments. The library, surrounded by a lawn, is in the mansarded structure built to house the University of Nevada in its early years, but the white-columned courthouse and the modern grammar school and high school—which, together have nearly 900 pupils—are as modern and well-equipped, and as wells affed, as any in the United States. The newspapers reveal a social life that is anything but provincial; cocktail, bridge, and dancing parties with floral decorations from the coast, musicals, lectures, and study classes on current events, are as common as the club and lodge meetings that play such important parts in Nevada life.

On a bluff north of the business district are numerous substantial modern houses and even some of the older homes have interior decorations and furniture similar to those now fashionable in the metropolitan centers of the Atlantic Seaboard. Some years ago householders of Elko began to plant apple trees in their yards, front as well as back, with the result that in spring the town is half buried under fragrant pink-touched snowy blossoms.

These evidences of up-to-the-minute prosperity do not mean that Elko is not still a cattle town. In the cocktail bars with their murals the whole of Elko County mingles democratically, though the buckaroos— and often the owners of vast cattle ranches and large bands of sheep— prefer to frequent the "clubs", where the bar is merely a background for roulette wheels, faro banks, horse-keno counters, and poker tables.

Elko came into existence as a freighting point for the boom camps of the Hamilton and Eureka districts. Even before the Central Pacific Railroad construction camp was set up here in 1868, traders were on hand to serve trail travelers and real estate speculators to find choice lots. The hurly-burly of construction camp days was augumented by the yells of freighters trying to turn their wagons, each drawn by four lumbering oxen, in the crowded, dusty streets. At first supplies from the mining camps came in only from the west, and from the farms already under cultivation in Lamoille, Pleasant, and Ruby Valleys (*see Tour 1A*), but after May, 1869, when the transcontinental route was completed, machinery, foodstuffs, whiskey, champagne, and people arrived daily from both directions.

Charles Crocker, one of the Big Four building the road, gave many of the names for the stations established as the tracks progressed eastward and probably gave this one.

By the middle of 1869 the town was well established; a census showed 68 children between 6 and 18 years of age and 64 under 6. A school was opened and various other public enterprises were soon under way. Then and in later years the saloon-keeper and the inhabitants of Adobe and Piety Rows were particularly heavy contributors when collections were made to build schools and churches. By 1870 there were enough citizens who enjoyed the staider social events to produce strawberry and oyster suppers.

Still, there were enough homeless males to keep up an uproar and guns went off in the saloon districts with frequency. A favorite story of this period concerns a bully who selected Elko as a place he was going to rule. He enforced his threats and hints of troubles by prominent display of a gun. Everyone but a young clerk was fairly well intimidated; he said the bully was a faker and was publicly critical after the ully mistreated a consumptive sojourning in the town. Other people began to repeat the comments and the self-appointed boss decided to stop them by going to the source; he came into the store where the young man worked, drew his gun, and with sulphurous oaths told what he was going to do if there were any more criticisms. The clerk dropped to the floor behind the high counter. The bully made a dash around the end—and was tripped over backward by the clerk who had crawled forward to meet him. Catching the bully off-guard, the clerk was able to snatch his gun and use it as a bludgeon. Yells brought passers-by who finally separated the combatants. This public set-back infuriated the bully who told all who would listen what he was going to do to the young man when he had time to settle with him. Victory had given the clerk further confidence and after various zealous friends had reported the threats in the hope of stirring up more excitement, he walked boldly into the bully's saloon and asked for a drink. The bully glared and refused it. The clerk reminded him that his license was for serving the public and he wanted his drink. He got it, and it was apparent to the town that the bully's reign was over.

By the time the boom camps to the south had begun to decline, others had sprung up in the north. But, more important, the country was covered with herds of cattle and Elko was becoming the cattle capital it is today. By 1879 it had an Opera Hall where traveling companies were presenting *Pinafore, East Lynne,* and *A Case for Divorce, or*

Fate, Lost and Won. The latter was given by Nellie Boyd's troupe, but had such little favor it moved on to Tuscarora, where taste was less critical of acting and of female charms. This Opera Hall had certain deficiencies; in its early days the boards of the stage were not nailed down and an actor who lost himself in his role might take a fall, or a slap from a suddenly tilted plank.

For a long time the people of Elko, like those of other towns along the line, carried on a constant feud with the railroad company, which charged any rates it chose. The railroad became more reasonable when the counties began to levy heavy taxes against it. The company gained additional unpopularity by forcing sale of its sections of land—the checkerboard granted for 20 miles on both sides of the right of way. The cattlemen were carrying on their war against sheep and the company would threaten to sell to sheepmen the alternate sections of fertile bottom land, which produced the winter hay for herds. The public lands between the blocks owned by the railroad company could not be used by the cattlemen if this arrangement were carried through.

This was only part of the long fight for control of the range. Every cattleman took up land for a home-ranch, a base of operations. This home-ranch was usually near meadows, where then, as now, grew the wild hay that had to be cut for winter feed. As the number of outfits increased it became necessary for each to own its hay land. Both for the home-ranch and the meadowlands it was necessary to control water, which in time meant acquiring more land. In the first years right to certain meadows and water-rights was established by use, with each man enforcing his claims by battle if necessary. Eventually the meadows were acquired in part by claims taken up under the various land acts, but here, as elsewhere in the cattle country, physical force was long the law and a newcomer had to be agile as well as merciless to wedge his way in. Big outfits ran out small ones, by threats if possible, by gun and destruction if gentler methods did not work.

The county had its cattle barons before 1880 and the Senate Saloon of Elko had many calls on the varied skills of its bar-men, who, it advertised, could mix a "Tom and Jerry, Hot Scotch, Apple Toddy, Milk Punch, Bran Mash, Muldoon, or a Dashaway at any hour of the day or night."

The dreadful blizzards of 1888-90 wrecked local business by ruining the free-spending cattle-growers. While the town was in the doldrums it had reluctantly to perform an execution, that of the only woman ever hanged in Nevada. The woman had bigamously married a second husband while she was on vacation in California and had murdered him when he followed her to Elko County, and hidden the body under her house; shortly afterward she and her first husband left but a tenant quickly discovered the remains.

As the cattle business improved Elko began to recover prosperity, though it had no great spurt until the Western Pacific was built in 1907 and established a division point here.

The great event of the year is the Elko County Fair, usually held in late summer; this completely depopulates more than a thousand square miles of country as everyone comes in for a reunion and to witness the rodeos, agricultural and mineral displays. Round-up times are also periods of great activity, as beef is brought in for shipment on the hoof. Celebrations over the end of the long, lively period of work are prolonged, though not as violent as in the past.

Westward, and just across the river, is the MUNICIPAL SWIMMING POOL (*nominal fee*), which is the most popular recreational spot in the county. Just south of the pool is Hot Hole, a large sinter-mound about 100 feet in diameter, that holds a deep and hot mineral spring. Other sinter-cones are scattered on the adjacent hillside. On the river bank (L) numerous vents from the hot springs offer laundry facilities to migratory workers. More than one dusty, dirty group of early migrants stopped here to bathe and to wash clothes.

Elko is at junctions with Nev. 46 (*see Tour 1A*) and Nev. 11 (*see Tour 1B*).

Right from the municipal pool over a dirt road, passing an old experimental plant built to extract oil from shale. It was operated for several years. The deserted mining camp of BULLION, 27.4 *m*. (6,386 alt.), is in a district discovered in 1869 above a steep canyon and on the east slope of the Pinon Mountains. Bunker Hill (approx. 9,000 alt.) looks down on the slag dumps of smelters, and the ruins of a town that saw the production of three million dollars in ore before 1884. Activities revived in 1905, and the district again produced in 1916-1917.

The main highway now skirts the edge of ranchlands along the Humboldt into which, at 120.5 *m*., pours the South Fork. In the willow thickets bordering the sloughs live exceptionally large numbers of pelicans and cranes. Across the river (L) ruts of the Humboldt Road can be clearly seen on a steep hillside east of the South Fork. This is the point where the Donner Party reached the Humboldt after their long detour around the Ruby Range. The Greenhorn Cut-off branched from the main route here to wind up a shallow canyon (R) to the head of Susie Creek, returning to the Humboldt at Carlin. The river now enters precipitous Carlin Canyon, a gorge that was impassable for wagons until after the Central Pacific was built in 1867. Early travelers hated these detours, which prolonged the period before they would meet the dreaded Forty-Mile Desert and the Humboldt Sink. Often the need for haste was urgent; all who lingered were reminded of what had happened when the Donners reached the top of the Sierras too late for their safety.

A serious pest at present in this area is the Mormon cricket—a huge insect that crawls rather than flies; he is a menace to motorists as well as to those depending on plant life, for after a few have been crushed on the highway the road-surface is as slippery as smooth ice. Where "cricket warnings" are seen, and where there is evidence of pests on the road, cars should be driven slowly and with great caution. Eggs of the crickets are laid in the ground in late summer and in the following spring they begin to hatch. By mid-summer the insects are moving in close formation over hill, valley, and whatever is in the way. The column rarely swerves; if a stream blocks the line of march the crickets go as far out as possible on rocks and over-hanging grasses and willow branches, then drop into the water and swim. Many are lost during the water passage but streams are too rare in late summer to greatly reduce the size of the menace.

CARLIN, 135.5 m. (4,897 alt., 825 pop.), has repair shops, and an icing plant of the Southern Pacific. Shops were established here because of a large spring of pure, cold water. The town is in a small valley that runs north to the Tuscarora Mountains and east and west along Humboldt River between Carlin Canyon and Palisade Canyon. Here the Overland Trail to California returned to the river after a long detour, and here early travelers slaked their thirst and filled their jugs. Westward were two routes, one crossing the Humboldt and skirting Palisade Canyon on the south, and the other swinging into the northwest over Emigrant Pass. US 40 roughly follows the latter.

Right from Carlin over a dirt road to low foothills holding a small fossil area, the CARLIN BEDS, 2 m., between layers of diatomaceous earth. Bones of prehistoric mammals—camels and the primitive horse—have been uncovered in this area.

The road continues northward to the Lynn District, 24 m., where exceptionally fine turquoise are found.

US 40 crosses the low sage-covered foothills of Tuscarora Mountains to a junction with Nev. 20, a graded dirt road, 114.7 m.

Left on this road to PALISADE, 4.2 m. (4,821 alt., 134 dist. pop.), a village by the Humboldt that was named for the sheer walls east of it. Palisade was the northern terminal of the Eureka-Palisade Railroad, which formerly brought lead and silver bullion from the mining camps at Eureka. Near this place the Southern Pacific streamliner was wrecked late in the summer of 1939 with considerable loss of life. Federal investigators found that the accident was brought about deliberately by tampering with the rails, but the criminal has not been caught. Nev. 20 continues southward through Pine Valley, a cattle ranching country between the Cortez Mountains (R) and the Pinon Mountains (L). At 84 m. is EUREKA (see Tour 7b), on US 50 (see Tour 7b).

EMIGRANT PASS, 146.5 m. (6,121 alt.), a narrow divide between high, brush-covered hills, was a well-known concentration point on the Humboldt Road. In the narrow canyon just west of the pass is Emigrant Spring (L), a camping spot where travelers washed the alkali out of their throats and discussed probable troubles ahead. Here, too, they often took stock of their supply of cream of tartar, with which they expected to leaven Humboldt water, and of the alum they used on the noses of their beasts to prevent blisters from becoming infected. The water, the dust, and the heat did strange things to men traveling the road in those days. On one occasion, a man, observing that his companions were approaching madness, impersonated a jackass and leaped about, whinnying for grass until he fetched smiles to tired faces.

Near the spring is PRIMEAUX (5,723 alt.), a tourist and bus stop, where a collection of relics is displayed. Chief articles of interest are Chinese joss-house equipment, gold bullion molds from Tuscarora, a half-burned papoose blanket taken from the back of a slain squaw, and oxen shoes and yokes.

The canyon angles south to the river, and north to the road. Down this sandy gulch went the covered wagons, intent on returning to the river at Gravelly Ford. The old-timers had no disposition to climb the steep ridge westward where the highway now crosses TWIN SUMMIT, 151.3 *m.* (5,703 alt.). West of the summit the Shoshone Mountains rise austerely beyond the willow-thicketed Humboldt and ranches with lines of Lombardy poplars.

At 155.7 *m.* is the junction with Nev. 21, an oiled road.

Left on this road, crossing the Humboldt, to BEOWAWE (*bay-o-wah-we*), 5.6 *m.* (4,695 alt., 521 dist. pop.), a small ranch and mine railroad station in one of the most picturesque valleys in the State. The Horseshoe Ranch here is a remnant of a former vast ranching empire. Sheltered between two mountain ranges, and dotted with cottonwood groves, Beowawe was long one of the principal Paiute campsites. Antelope and deer were abundant in this area, and the Paiute maintained an all-year camp near the hot springs and geysers southward. In the fall, after the groves have turned a brilliant yellow, this village and its environs are notably beautiful. At dusk the sage-covered valley glows in purple mist, and the surrounding mountains burn softly in shades of brown and red.

Left from Beowawe 2.4 *m.* on a dirt road to EMIGRANT CEMETERY, in the sagebrush.

The dirt road continues to GRAVELLY FORD, 6.4 *m.*, a river crossing often mentioned in early travel diaries. Here tragedy overtook the harrassed and wrangling Donner Party; James A. Reed, whose Palace Car had been abandoned in the salt flats of Utah, killed John Snyder in a heated quarrel, the cause of which is uncertain. At first the immigrants were resolved to hang Reed, but after importuning by his wife, they decided to exile him, and drove him away on foot and without food to find his way to California if he could. He not only survived but helped to send the first rescue party back to the Sierra to aid the starving survivors. It was here also that an emigrant, while fording the river in a wagon, allowed his wife and two small children to float away in the wagon-box because he was intent only on saving his wagon and team. It was realized by those who rescued the woman and her babies that "alkali works into the nerves" but they were resolved, nevertheless, to hang the man or throw him into the river—and would have done so if the woman had not frantically begged for her husband's life.

South of Beowawe a desert merges into the fertile lands. At times it throws into relief the sheer beauty of every peak of the distant Cortez and Shoshone Mountains, which shimmer in distant violet mists. Auburn and purple are the predominent hues at sunset.

Nev. 21 continues southwest to THE GEYSERS, 13.4 *m.*, whose discovery is credited to A. S. Evans about 1867, during construction of the Central Pacific Railroad, though the springs must have been known long before that time for on cool mornings their steam is visible for miles. The geysers are confined to a small slope on the southeastern part of Whirlwind Valley. Their action has built a sinter terrace about a half mile long and 100 feet wide, and about 100 to 150 feet above the valley floor. Sinter mounds, or fumaroles, one to three feet high, composed of glassy opal with a faint pinkish tinge, have been formed around the active geysers. In eruption the waters of most of the geysers rise less than a foot at present (1940) though a few spout with greater force, one throwing water 12 feet. The eruptions last about a minute and the intervals between spoutings vary from 15 minutes to an hour. During the winter the geysers show increased activity, probably because of greater water surface. In some years, also, they show much greater activity than in others. Numerous hot springs and fumaroles, as well as several mud pots, occur along the terrace.

The flat valley floor here, with its sparse vegetation, sometimes serves as an emergency landing field, and the Government maintains a beacon and equipment for emergency landings.

DUNPHY, 160.7 *m.,* was headquarters of the Dunphy outfit, one of the largest stock owners ever in the State. At this point on the river, shallow and lined with dense willow growth, are two of the crossings occasionally misnamed Gravelly Ford. Between Dunphy and Battle Mountain the river affords excellent bass and catfish angling. Near here the Southern Pacific streamlined trains make their fastest time between Chicago and the Coast. The speed average is from 85 to 90 miles an hour, though greater speed can be safely attained.

ARGENTA SIDING, 174.2 *m.,* (4,544 alt.), is a rail point for a company working the large barium deposits in the Shoshone Mountains (L), and for Humboldt River hay ranches. West of Argenta the Humboldt now flows reasonably straight and free. In the 350 miles between its headwaters and the Sink, the river meanders for about 600 miles—which caused wrathful early travelers to declare it was the crookedest river in the world. West of Argenta the river bends north around the tip of the Shoshone Mesa (R), and the highway leaves the base of Shoshone Mountains (L) to make a long curve to the northwest.

BATTLE MOUNTAIN, 186.7 *m.,* (4,511 alt., 368 pop.) (*hotels and other facilities*), is another town whose appearance is deceptive. Neither its census size nor its cottonwood-shaded streets give indication of its importance as the supply center for one of the most active mining districts of modern Nevada. It receives from and ships on not only the Southern Pacific, but also the Western Pacific across the river. This divided trade is largely responsible for the scattering of business houses that makes it seem merely a pleasant village to passing travelers. It is also a trade center for ranchers and has ambition to wrest the seat of Lander County government from old Austin; the two towns are at opposite ends of the long county, so wherever the seat of government happens to be inhabitants of one center of population or the other are going to have to travel nearly 100 miles to transact legal business. Austin has an edge, however, in possessing the solid courthouse that represents a considerable investment to all the people of the county.

The town of Battle Mountain was named for the range stretching to the south and the range was so named because in 1861 it was the scene of the first of a series of skirmishes between the natives and the whites. The Indians had attacked a wagon-train at Gravelly Ford, killing several people before making off with considerable loot; ambushed among the rocks on the mountain rim, they expected to annihilate their pursuers, but suffered heavily themselves through a surprise attack from the rear. They were later pursued southward and again took punishment. This stopped the Indian attacks along the river in this region.

The town was established in 1868 as a station to serve the camps of the Battle Mountain Mining District, partly in Humboldt County and discovered in 1866; the district developed somewhat slowly until the railroad arrived but by 1870 32 mines and two smelters were in operation. The Little Giant, discovered in 1867, was near the old camp of Battle Mountain, a few miles from the present town; it produced about one million dollars worth of silver. Before 1880 an English corporation had taken more than 40,000 tons of copper-ore from Copper Canyon, 15 miles to the southwest, and had shipped it to Wales. In 1871 50 tons of antimony were shipped from deposits along Cottonwood Creek, some miles west of town, and veins near Galena, also southward, were soon to give up about five million dollars worth of silver, lead and gold.

Copper Canyon also had good gold placers, but today its copper is much more important. One of the claims became involved in litigation that stopped work for seven years. By the time the case had been settled in the supreme court the owners found that high-graders had removed nearly all the values.

For some reason—perhaps because its camps were so scattered—Battle Mountain never gained a name for outstanding deviltry and its existence seems to have been unusually quiet. The district, moreover, has shown a much better record for steady production than have others whose names flared big for a time. For about 12 years after 1885, when mining activity was low all over the west, particularly in the silver districts, the place was very quiet; since then work has been going on fairly steadily with $2,500,000 worth of gold, silver, copper, and lead mined during the first two decades of the twentieth century, and production increasing in the third decade, after new discoveries.

Freighting to Austin began early, along the course of Reese River, and added to the town's bustle and business. Austin's spectacular period, however, was nearly over in 1880 when the Nevada Central Railroad, called Farrell's Folly, was completed from Battle Mountain to Austin. Nonetheless, the road continued to carry supplies to the vast central region until its charter expired in 1938 and its business was taken over by motor trucks.

Like other old Nevada towns, Battle Mountain has a very fine school. which cost about $200,000. It also supports three churches.

Left from Battle Mountain on Nev. 8A up the long Reese River Valley where the waters of this former feeder of the Humboldt have been largely diverted for irrigation purposes, principally to increase production of hay to feed the many cattle owned by the valley ranchers. Numerous bands of sheep also graze on the low ranges along both sides of the valley. This is the road usually traveled by Battle Mountain people doing business at the county seat.

LEWIS JUNCTION, 9.5 m., is merely a crossroads; L. here 4 m. to the nearly deserted camp of BETTY O'NEAL, which grew up after a discovery of gold and silver in 1880. The Betty O'Neal was shut down in 1882 because of a serious boiler explosion, and again in 1918, when the manager died. Reopened in 1920, with a new 100-ton flotation mill, it went through a new period of prosperity in which the camp even had a paid baseball team.

Nev. 8A continues southward up Reese River and reaches US 50 (see Tour 7b) in AUSTIN, 94 m. (see Tour 7b).

VALMY, 200 m. on US 40 (cabins, water, gasoline), is also in a mining district.

At 208.7 *m.* is the junction with a dirt road.

Right on this road to the STONE HOUSE STATION RUINS, 2 *m.*, remains of an early mail station. TREATY HILL, just north of the ruins, commands a view in all directions. For generations hard battles were fought between the different Indian tribes over the springs and hunting grounds of the Battle Mountains and the Humboldt Valley. The legend is that after one battle centuries ago the chiefs decided to settle their problems by compromise. A stone wall was built on the brow of this hill, and in the peace treaty it was agreed that all land on "the side of the rising sun" belonged to one group and all on "the side of the setting sun" to the other.

North of the junction sharp peaks of the Hot Springs Mountains rise across the river valley. A prominent outcrop on the east side of the mountains was within full sight of many a forty-niner rushing on to California but not one stopped to prospect and make the discovery that has resulted in recent fortunes.

West of GOLCONDA SUMMIT, 218 *m.* (5,154 alt.), the highway winds down along the river with location posts and old prospect holes still visible on all sides.

GOLCONDA, 221 *m.* (4,392 alt., 232 pop), inhabited since 1861, has long been a shipping center for stockmen. The GOLCONDA HOT SPRINGS were once valued for therapeutic qualities. These springs were a source of considerable curiosity among early westbound travelers, who were also grateful for them as here was the beginning of a long, smothering drive. From this point onward, the light, ashy dust once stirred, went to rest only with the sun, and the air was filled "with all sorts of prismatic hues." Some of the travelers wore green goggles; and some wore bandages or little aprons over nose and mouth as protection against the dust.

Right from Golconda on a graveled road 28 *m.* to the GETCHELL MINE, in foothills on the eastern side of the Osgood Range. The large and notable producer of recent years was ignored until 1934, when Emmett Chase and Ed Knight found it. The ore was of sufficient grade to be worked, but much capital was needed for development. Major dividends have been paid since October, 1938.

Skirting the northern end of the Sonoma Range, with Sonoma Peak on the left, US 40 turns abruptly west.

Somewhere along the river between Golconda and Winnemucca is the unmarked grave of Joseph Paul, a member of Peter Skene Ogden's exploring party, and probably the first white man to die in Nevada. Paul became ill on Ogden's first trip west along the river and died on December 18, 1828. In Ogden's report of 1829 he recommended that the stream be called "Paul's River, as he must remain here till the great trumpet shall sound."

WINNEMUCCA, 230.4 *m.* (4,344 alt., 1989 pop.) (*all types of accommodations and services; hospital, golf-course; municipal swimming pool*), is at the junction (R) with US 95 (*see Tour* 5a), which unites southwestward with US 40. The first settler was a Frenchman who set up a trading post on the trail to California in 1850. People crossing the river here with their oxcarts named the place French Ford and when a bridge was built in 1865 it became French Bridge. A ferry was also operating by that time, to the bridge-builder's disgust, because the ferryman charged only half of what he did. Two years before this a primitive hostelry, later known as the Winnemucca Hotel, had been opened not far from the place where a large modern hotel now stands, and this soon became a terminal for the stage line going north into Idaho. The settlement was at a key position on the river-route in a very low saddle at the base of Winnemucca Mountain (6,740 alt.), which rises sheer without dwarfing foothills.

Long before the railroad arrived many mineral discoveries had been made in all directions around the settlement; the Winnemucca Mining District had been organized in 1863, and workings were already beginning to dot the mountain before the first mile of the Central Pacific had been laid.

In 1862 J. Gianacca, who later built the bridge, had conceived the idea of a canal along the Humboldt for 90 miles between Golconda and a projected mill city. The canal would carry ore of the district to central smelters and provide water-power to run them. By 1865 30 miles of canal had been built, but Gianacca began to have difficulty raising funds, particularly with the railroad being constructed along the same course. Moreover he was beginning to realize that the soil was too porous for the project. In all, nearly 60 miles of canal were built but water never reached Mill City. In 1872 Gianacca built a ten-stamp mill by the canal at the upper end of this town and in time it came to serve numerous mines of the district.

Winnemucca's key position was again to its advantage in 1868, when the railroad tracks reached the site; it was made the first division point west of Truckee, California. The War Department's Special Commission on the Central Pacific Railroad reported on December 3, 1868, that tracks had been completed to Carlin and the road was nearly ready for operation to that point, with only two bridges to be finished. Ties, they said, were being laid 2,400 to the mile and passenger trains could run safely and smoothly at from 15 to 30 miles an hour; heavy trains were being run daily with rails, ties, and fuel over 445 miles of track east of Sacramento; the road was being constructed "in good faith and in a substantial manner, without stint of labor, and the equipment [was] worthy of its character as a great national work. The telegraph line [was] first class."

When the first through train, with four carloads of notables, arrived on May 11, 1869, the town put on a celebration suitable to the occasion —firing guns, blowing horns and whistles, ringing bells, driving souvenir spikes, and drinking champagne—the usual drink of early Nevada when it wanted to show it could spend with kings. From then on the one regular town spree came on the day the Central Pacific pay-car came through. That night the more peacefully inclined Winnemuccans would resignedly give up all thoughts of sleep as choruses mounted in the favorite: "Oh, for a home in a big saloon, on the banks of some raging

This primitive is the work of an old prospector **LANDSCAPE**

who disappeared into the desert about 1920. It is in the Nevada Historical Museum.

Rothstein: Farm Security Admin. **NEAR VIRGINIA CITY**

STOKES CASTLE, NEAR AUSTIN

Photograph courtesy Nevada State Highway Dept.

GENOA, THE OLDEST SETTLEMENT

Rothstein: Farm Security Admin.

Rothstein: Farm Security Admin.　　　　**ON THE EDGE OF TONOPAH**

THE BOTTLE HOUSE, RHYOLITE

PIPER'S OPERA HOUSE, VIRGINIA CITY *Photograph courtesy Curtis Photo*

AUSTIN

Rothstein: Farm Security Admin.

OLD MINE OFFICE, VIRGINIA CITY

MINER'S UNION HALL, SILVER CITY

**LUNCH TIME, INDIAN SERVICE
DAY SCHOOL**

**A PROTEST FROM
THE CRADLE BOARD**

Photographs courtesy U. S. Indian Servic

HOME OF A SHOSHONE ON THE WALKER RIVER RESERVATION

BASKET MAKER. MOAPA RESERVATION

TRACTOR DRIVER—A MODERN
PAIUTE

LOST CITY MUSEUM, OVERTON   *Photograph courtesy U. S. Forest Service*

PREHISTORIC PETROGLYPHS   *Photograph courtesy Chamber of Commerce, Las Vegas*

canal." Black eyes and broken noses often identified the celebrants when the morning after broke.

Meanwhile, the town was developing rapidly. There had been the usual fights on where the town should actually be—at the ford, at Centerville—where the center now is—or at Winnemucca by the railroad.

The station had been named in 1868 by C. B. O. Bannon, a nephew of the man who had been Lincoln's Secretary of the Interior. Just why he chose the name of the Paiute chief is not clear, for old Winnemucca, though wisely advising peace with the whites, was not unwilling to lead his tribesmen if they decided to go on the war-path against the invaders who were taking their lands, killing off all game, and burning up their pinenut forests. The name has been given various translations, running from Dweller-by-the-River to One Moccasin.

By 1869 the town had a business directory listing three wholesale and retail merchants, one forwarding and commission firm, four hotel-owners, one restaurant keeper, one firm of brewers, one watchmaker, one shoe-maker, one dentist, two physician-surgeons, one owner of a "Livery, Feed & Sale Stable & Corral", one "News Depot" agent, and one "Photograph Artist." It was no wonder that the town began a fight to take the county seat from declining Unionville (*see ahead*). People of Unionville fought stoutly. The *Silver State* of Unionville—later the leading paper of Winnemucca—said "The principal production of the village [Winnemucca] consists of sand hills, vapid editorials, and a morbid hankering for the county seat. It is one of the most delightful places on the earth to move away from." But Winnemucca won in 1873.

Freighting to the outlying mines increased rapidly and nearly two dozen teams drawn by 8 to 20 mules were to be seen around the freight station at one time. In 1874 there were enough teamsters to bring on a strike with the demand for five cents a pound on freight to Silver City, Idaho.

Sheep and cattle-shipping in time became more important than ore-shipping, as the price of silver declined. All are now important. The town had the usual fires to wipe out earlier makeshift structures and gradually rebuilt itself into the stable-looking town of the present. Social institutions also developed and in 1873 the first Humboldt County Fair was held, complete even to a silver cup for the "Best Equestrienne." By that time there was also a Society of Humboldt Pioneers. Before the end of the decade the town had a Dramatic Society, which devoted part of its profits to building a boardwalk between Upper and Lower Town.

But Winnemucca was still something of a frontier settlement in 1900 when three strangers rode down the dusty main street. Hitching their horses behind the First National Bank, they hoisted a last drink in a near-by saloon, and sauntered into the bank. Within a few minutes the strangers walked out the rear door, remounted, and rode away with $32,640. Before disappearing they fired their guns to inform the town

that Butch Cassidy's boys—famous outlaw band of many western stories
—had been there.

The gang rode east along the river to a relay of fresh horses, also
stolen—and stolen at that from the president of the bank. A posse
quickly gathered, commandeered a railroad switch-engine, and went
in pursuit. News of the robbery was telephoned east to Golconda, but
Butch's boys had already passed. Later, when the robbers, though on
fresh horses, were almost overtaken, they drove off the posse with rifle
fire. In spite of the fact that three Winnemuccans followed them into
central Wyoming, the band reached its hideaway and the money was
never recovered.

Winnemucca stages an annual Nevada Rodeo (*first week in Sept.*),
for which bucking horses and wild range steers are brought in and to
which riders come from long distances, attracted by generous cash prizes.

There are numerous Basques in the neighborhood, who came in first
to herd sheep. Many are now owners of bands, some of considerable
size. The Basque restaurants serve some favorite Basque dishes, but no
matter what the menu, dinner always ends with cafe royal—black
coffee well-laced with rum.

Among the impressive buildings of the town are the HUMBOLDT
COUNTY COURTHOUSE, which replaced one destroyed by fire in 1918;
ST. PAUL'S ROMAN CATHOLIC CHURCH (1924), which shows baroque
influences in its design; and the large WINNEMUCCA GRAMMAR
SCHOOL, on which construction began in 1927. This school has a wide
reputation for its practical equipment and for the instruction it gives; it
is significant that, among the periodicals and papers in its teachers'
library, the *New York Times* and *Harper's Magazine* are particulary
well-worn. The shallow lobby, which is decorated with reproductions
of classic busts, ends at a broad staircase with lights at its corners supported by white plaster models of the Statute of Liberty.

On Baud Street (L), three blocks from US 40, is a CHINESE JOSS-
HOUSE, built in 1902 in a section that formerly held several hundred
Chinese working placer claims along the river. On a hill three blocks
in the opposite direction from US 40 is the CHINESE CEMETERY, with
a pagoda-topped brick oven in which pigs were ceremonially roasted
during burial rites. It is told that in earlier days Indians used to linger
near by until the Chinese had left after a burial and then swarmed in
to consume the funeral meats.

Left from Winnemucca on a poor dirt road that passes through Grass Valley
to the Pierce Ranch in Pleasant Valley, 44.9 *m.* from which the PLEASANT
VALLEY FAULT (L), 45.7 *m.*, can easily be approached on foot. The creation of this geological wonder occurred during the night of October 2, 1915,
when violent earthquakes destroyed or badly damaged many ranch houses in
this isolated area. The following day amazed residents saw crevices open in the
valley floor as the earth shook, saw the fissures close, and again open. A sheepherder, appalled by the violent antics of Nature, ran six miles to the nearest
settlement for help and on his way leaped a crevice; on his return he found
that it had spread to a deep chasm 18 feet wide. Along the slope of the precipitous Sonoma Mountains (7,000 to 10,000 alt.) the main fault is visible for
25 miles. It has a vertical displacement of 15 feet.

Section b. WINNEMUCCA *to* FERNLEY; 130.2 *m., US* 50-95

The Humboldt River, still paralleled by US 40, with which US 95 is united between Winnemucca and Fernley, now swings to the south in what immigrants called the Great Bend. The Eugene and Blue Mountain ranges are on the right, and on the left AULD LANG SYNE PEAK, prominent as a producer of gold and silver.

West of WINNEMUCCA, 0 *m.,* is MILL CITY, 28 *m.,* (4,225 alt., 21 pop.), an old mining center now chiefly a service station and shipping point for tungsten. It never became the industrial town Gianacca had hoped for (*see before*).

1. Right from Mill City over a graveled road to the TUNGSTEN MINE, 8.7 *m.,* one of the important tungsten producers in the United States and also one of the largest in the world. A hundred and fifty men are employed here in concentrating the metal used as a hardening alloy in the manufacture of steel.

2. Left from Mill City on Nev. 50, a graveled road, through Buena Vista Valley. The road follows an alternate of the Overland Trail to California that went south over Carson Sink to the Carson River, located at a point near the present town of Fallon (*see Tour 7c*).

STAR CITY, 12 *m.,* now only a name, was the scene of one of the wildest booms in the State after the discovery of rich silver ore in the Sheba. Star City was a town of 1,200 inhabitants by 1863, with two hotels, a Wells-Fargo Express office, a special telegraph line to Virginia City, and daily mail service. By 1868 the boom had collapsed. So sudden was the decline that in 1868 someone remarked, "The daily mail, the express office, telegraph office, are all in operation yet, but the entire population consists of a single family, the head of which is mayor, constable, postmaster, express agent, telegraph operator and I believe the sole unanimous voter!"

The Sheba and the De Soto have been idle for many years. At its peak some rich ore mined in the Sheba ran as high as $2,000 a ton and Sheba stock sold for $600 a foot on the San Francisco exchange.

At 21.5 *m.* on Nev. 50 is the junction with a dirt road; R. here 4.1 *m.* to UNIONVILLE, scattered for two miles along beautiful Buena Vista Canyon. Only a few houses and many crumbling adobe walls remain of one of the oldest mining camps in the State. The present inhabitants grow apples, peaches, plums, poultry, and vegetables, and add to their incomes by occasionally mining operations, gleaning what remained after about $3,000,000 worth of silver ore had been removed. Production began to decline in the Buena Vista District about 1870 and ceased in 1880, with minor revivals at lengthening intervals.

In May, 1861, Hugo Pfersdorff and J. C. Hannan came over the Humboldt Range from Humboldt City, founded on the western side of the mountains in the previous year. The beauty of the scene from the heights was responsible for the canyon's name, which became the name of the district, promptly organized when four other prospectors arrived from the Comstock. All but Pfersdorff soon left to buy supplies—and proclaim the wonders of the new discovery—but enough people were on hand by the Fourth of July for a celebration, and three days later the townsite was laid out on the homestead claimed by William Whitney at the head of the canyon. The new town-founders had not yet learned to mix real estate development with mining, so all that was asked for a lot was two days of work on the road and improvements on the lot to the value of fifty dollars. To this Upper Town was gradually appended Lower Town—Dixie—and Centerville; by 1863 a stage was making hourly trips from one end of town to the other.

This was shortly after W. J. Forbes began to publish the *Humboldt Register,* a sheet whose charm, patiently recovered by Roger Corbett, has preserved the life of the early camp and given it some immortality. Forbes carefully recorded the trials of town-building along the Humboldt; adobe did not endure in the well watered pocket and half the lumber imported at great expense was "just what it was cracked up to be" and the other half was "knot". As for firewood, the editor said, he had difficulty distinguishing it from hay—some of the trees were so puny and some of the hay was so coarse. Roofing was a particularly difficult problem until some immigrants from Europe taught how to do expert thatching. A visitor to the courthouse in 1863—Unionville had become the seat when the first huge Humboldt County was organized—found the clerk huddled into one corner with his records and reported that at least in that corner "the rain didn't come any thicker than it did outside." Three months later a saloon was rented for the courthouse; with the first good rain, however, the commissioners found that its boasted "concrete roof", of lime and sand laid on canvas, had little utility.

By the spring of 1863 there were about 20 new residents a day and the town had 10 stores, 6 hotels, 9 saloons, 2 express offices, 2 drugstores, 4 livery stables, and a watchmaker's shop. By August there was a brewery. Everyone was madly staking out claims and speculating in "feet", stimulated by discovery of the rich Arizona a few months before. The Branch Mint, the Universe, the Sultan, the Grand Mogul, the Golconda, and many claims were being advertised as new bonanzas. Only Editor Forbes was brutal enough to point out that it was mostly talk; he even suggested that the town needed a gymnasium to give the miners some healthful exercise and expressed apprehension on what might happen when the rainy season set in, since men who had been in the canyon two years had not yet driven "their tunnels in far enough to protect themselves from the rain." Satirizing the constitutional convention he proposed a State of Buena Vista, whose seal should show "a mountain with good croppings and float; on the mountain side, untaxable hole in the ground, six inches deep: near by, cedar tree; under its shade, two miners with pack of cards, working assessments."

But the town did settle down to work in time and conducted itself fairly sedately. Arrests were relatively few—that may be accounted for by the difficulties of building a jail stout enough to incarcerate anyone against his will. There was a Sunday school and also a public school in 1863, but no church until one was built by the Methodists in 1871—the first church in the county. Forbes' paper helped nurture the cultural life—page one was devoted to poetry and essays, page two to State and national news, page three to local items, and page four to advertisements—among them, regularly, a column devoted to magazines and newspapers, including the *Atlantic Monthly* and the *Police Gazette.* Dances, grand balls—almost any occasion was an excuse for one—parades, races, duck hunting, fishing, and jumping contests were almost daily events.

Construction of the transcontinental railroad hastened the end of the camp. With the growth of Winnemucca as a distributing and shipping center, trade and population drifted away. Winnemucca began to demand the county seat. Then a fire destroyed the courthouse at Unionville and opposition grew to rebuilding it here. Each time the question came to a vote loyal residents of Unionville managed to defeat the move; then Winnemucca unfairly carried it to the State legislature to force the removal. Unionville managed to defeat the bill once, failed the second time. Unionville sought an injunction against the county officers to keep them from removing the records, on the ground that the legislature had no right to interfere in county affairs. The suit for injunction at last reached the State supreme court, and was rejected in July, 1873.

More than a million came from the Arizona before 1878 but by 1881 only 200 people were left in town, all loyally believing that rich discoveries would again be made. Many of them remained until removed by death.

Nev. 50 turns R. to cross the Humboldt Mountains, passing south of Spring Valley District, located in 1868, relocated in 1871, and first worked systematically in 1873. Placer operations continued until about 1895, Chinese brought in to build the Central Pacific gleaning after Americans had skimmed the cream. It is estimated that $10,000,000 came out of the district. Nev. 50 continues to ROCHESTER, 34 *m.*, in a district discovered in the early 1860's by prospectors from Rochester, New York. Though some mining was done there after in a desultory manner, there was no real activity until large bodies of silver ore were found in 1911. More than $9,000,000 worth of minerals, chiefly silver, have come from it since then. To the north is the Humboldt District, where Humboldt City sprang up in 1863. It was quickly overshadowed by more important camps.

At 42 *m.* Nev. 50 meets US 40-95 at DAD LEE'S (*see ahead*).

At 49.2 *m.* on US 40 is the junction with a graded dirt road.

Right on this road to RYE PATCH DAM, 0.7 *m.*, a Federal irrigation project that impounds the waters of the Humboldt for use in the Lovelock area. Including water rights, the cost of the dam was approximately $1,000,000; it is estimated that it will furnish enough water to irrigate 30,000 acres.

DAD LEE'S STATION, 58.4 *m.*, is a desert trading post where numerous relics are shown. When Dad Lee, well-known to travelers for years, died in 1936, he—like several other men in times past— was still insisting that he was the only William F. Cody—Buffalo Bill. Dad was buried in an obscure spot on the desert.

At this point is a junction with Nev. 50 (*see before*).

Right from Dad Lee's to OREANA, 0.6 *m.* (4,179 alt., 68 pop.), which was moved from its site on the highway by the railroad company. Once it was a lively center for one of the first lead-mining districts found in the country; it is now an important tungsten producer. On the northeast is STAR PEAK, (c. 9,925 alt.), noted for its mineral deposits. One of the first smelters in the State was operated here to reduce lead-silver ores.

Visible at Dad Lee's on a slope of the Humboldt Mountains 15 miles away are extensive deposits of Middle Triassic fossils.

At 65.7 *m.* on US 40 is the junction with a graded dirt road.

Left on this road to a point where it branches, 3 *m.*, and then R. to the CHAMPION MINE, 5.5 *m.*, where dumortierite (aluminum silicate) is produced. It is used in the manufacture of spark plugs. This is the only known commercial deposit of this mineral.

One traveler at this point on the Humboldt Road, noted in his diary: "The arrival at Cold Springs, only six miles from the far-famed MEADOWS, heartens everyone. You could feel it in the air. Good water, such as few had had for three weeks, was a boon not soon forgotten. We now take practically four days' rest—in preparation for that Desert Run. . . ."

LOVELOCK, 72 *m.* (3,977 alt., 1,290 pop.) (*hotels and other modern facilities of various types*), seat of Pershing County, has had a checkered history. At the time of the great western migration the Humboldt completely disappeared as a river about two miles northeast of the present town. What was left of the water spread out thinly over a fairly good-sized area, forming a natural meadow and a tule swamp; this was the Big Meadows of travelers on the Humboldt Road who nearly always camped here for a day or two to cut hay for use on the 24-hour trip across the Sink to the southward and to rest and fatten the cattle somewhat before subjecting them to this most trying part of the journey. In the early 1860's George Lovelock, an Englishman, built a little stage station here; he had come to the Coast by way of the Horn after a shipwreck on the Sandwich Islands. When the Central Pacific was being built it was planned to make what is now Oreana the next station because of its clear, cold spring; but Lovelock by means of concessions on the right of way, to which he had laid claim, managed to have a station built here. The meadows early attracted cattlemen as a winter feeding place for their stock and before long some ranches had been established near by. Irrigation ditches were built to tap the Humboldt upstream and the water was used to enlarge the hay acreage. It was not long, however, before there were more cattle in the district than the surrounding arid ranges would support and the number of locally owned cattle had to be reduced. The ranchers then began to feed and prepare cattle from other districts for market; trails from the north and east were thick with dust as the herds came in. The comparatively mild winter climate aided this development. To add to the fattening grasses alfalfa was planted in continually larger areas. But as settlement increased upstream on the Humboldt and its tributaries, the Humboldt flow began to dwindle to the extent that in the late 1880's Dan De Quille predicted that before long no water would reach this area. In 1908 the Humboldt-Lovelock Irrigation, Light and Power Company, whose stock was owned largely by valley ranchers, built reservoirs that would irrigate about 8,000 acres of land, largely in the upper Lovelock Valley. Then, in 1934, construction of the Rye Patch Dam (*see before*) was begun by the U. S. Bureau of Reclama· tion. Since 1936, when it came into service, the entire valley has started back to the prosperity made possible by an assured and dependable water supply. Various methods of irrigation are used, according to the type of terrain. On the higher lands some wild flooding is practiced; in other places the furrow method is used; but a modified border flooding is most general. Grain and alfalfa are the principal crops, though there are some dairy and a few poultry farms, principally serving local markets.

Lovelock is the distributing and service center for a large, thinly populated area where mining as well as stock-growing is carried on. Its current prosperity is evident in the well-kept streets and public buildings, freshly painted houses, and well-stocked stores.

Basques live in this area as well as in that north of Winnemucca, because sheep can find nourishment on ranges where cattle would starve. Their attractive dark-eyed daughters are easily identified. The Basques began coming into the Northwest not long after settlement began, and many entered Nevada from Oregon. A proud, conservative, devout people who had resisted efforts to force them to use Castilian rather than their own peculiar dialect, they naturally drifted to the part of the United States that most nearly reminded them of their own Pyrennes, and to the work they had long been accustomed to—the raising of sheep.

In this district as in other parts of the cattle country the old violent division of feeling exists between cattle and sheepmen—even though they no longer carry on the old range wars. A sheepherder is as partisan as a cowhand in defense of the intelligence of his charges; on the rare occasions when he is willing to talk, he will discuss sheep and their ways in loving detail. He has names for many of his charges and knows their personal idiosyncracies; this one is an incurable granny, bound to kidnap every lamb in sight, and that one has a particularly keen sense on a coming change of weather and will begin to move restlessly toward the south long before weather forecasters predict approaching snow. The cattleman cannot bear to listen to these stories; he will, indeed, become vitriolic and apoplectic in trying to express his contempt for the sheep. "Dumb!" he will shout. "Throw one over a cliff and the rest follow. No cow would do such a thing. No independence at all—one man can herd a whole band. Haven't sense enough to eat, some of them. I've seen the puny little things starving with milk in front of them. Me! I say suck or die! Wouldn't bother with 'em."

Right from Lovelock on Nev. 48, an improved dirt road, across the Trinity Mountains (5,600 alt.), 20.7 m., to a dirt road; R. here to the SEVEN TROUGHS MINING DISTRICT, 28.4 m. From the mines, still active, on the eastern slope of Seven Troughs Peak, (7,497 alt.), $2,606,912 in gold, silver, copper, and lead have been taken.

West of Lovelock US 40 leaves the Humboldt River to skirt the southern edge of the Trinity Range and cross the old Forty-mile Desert; the highway pursues a course considerably north of the early road, one route of which went south and one just north of the Humboldt Sink. Early travelers knew that their last water before crossing the desert was to be found in the Humboldt Slough, which drained south. "Even the very wagons seem to know that we are off today for the great adventure—in sand, volcanic ash, alkali, furnace heat, and the stench of putrid flesh—We crossed along the edge of an immense baked plain with the fetid stinking slough for a guide, although the wreckage along the way almost paved our route. . . . It must have been here that one emigrant said he counted a dead animal every 106 feet."

The beasts died of various causes, among which was the poisonous water in this stretch. Of the water flowing into the Sink itself, Mark Twain wrote that he and his prospecting friends tried to drink it, but it was like drinking lye, "and not weak lye, either." They put molasses in it, they tried pickles, they made coffee of it—but as one of them said, it was "still too technical."

Before leaving the Slough to cross the Desert—crossed, if possible chiefly by night—the drivers soaked their wagon wheels, checked the tongues, axles, brakes and hounds, filled casks, and encouraged the animals to drink all they could. A few miles west of Lovelock, the Humboldt Sink is visible (L), with the dreaded Carson Sink south of it. The sinks are a remnant of ancient Lake Lahontan. For the first few miles the road was relatively smooth, of sand and clay. Then came miles of deep heavy sand; sometimes whole trains of wagons were abandoned in it and those following had to pull out and around the stalled wagons—and often found themselves bogged. Not far from Desert Wells, shallow holes filled with bad water, they made choice of routes—one led to the Truckee and the other to the Carson River. It is small wonder that men, half-maddened by heat, thirst, and fear, lost their tempers and quarreled violently over which road to take.

This route proved less and less hazardous as travelers began to listen to those who had learned how to cross the sinks safely. Much stock was actually brought over them in the 1850's with little loss. Even among the earlier trains the wisely guided and well-prepared experienced no very great hardship. There was grass in plenty to this point, and water in the Humboldt. It was only when the half-mad horde of gold seekers sought to reach California without leadership and poorly prepared for the journey that the natural resources were exhausted and mishaps multiplied.

At **88.3** *m.* is the junction with Nev. 1A, a dirt road.

Left on this road to an area known as the INDIAN HUNTING GROUNDS, 3 *m.*, because arrowheads, spearheads, and other parts of Indian weapons have been found on it in numbers. Mounds in this area await exploration, though the remains of Indians, buried with their weapons, have already been unearthed. CARSON SINK, reached at 12 *m.*, is a swampy area covering approximately 100 square miles, a catch-basin for the waters of Carson River, and the overflow of the Humboldt. Upstream reservoirs now allow very little water to reach the sinks.

At the junction the Humboldt Sink is visible (L). In the summer of 1828, Peter Skene Ogden was trapping down the river, and upon finding 37 beaver in 75 of his traps he noted, "This is tolerable. . . . The large tracks of pelicans seem to indicate a lake. If it proves salt, beaver will be at the end." The lake proved to be the muddy Sink of Humboldt River.

At **90.7** *m.* is the junction with a dirt road, marked "To Lovelock Caves."

Left on this road 4.5 *m.*, thence L. 2 *m.* across railroad tracks; here R. 4 *m.* and L. 9.2 *m.* to a trail that leads 2.3 *m.* to LOVELOCK CAVE (4,500 alt.), in the north face of a limestone hill overlooking Humboldt Sink. When the cave was first worked as a guano mine in 1911, traces were found of ancient peoples. Scientific exploration was carried on by the University of California in 1912, at the request of the Nevada State Historical Society, and in 1924 with aid from the Heye Foundation. About 10,000 artifacts were recovered, nearly all of which are now in Berkeley, California, in the Nevada State Historical Society Museum in Reno, and in the Southwest Museum at Los Angeles. These include woven fabric and various implements, as well as parts of skeletons. It is believed that the cave was inhabited 2,000 years ago, and as late as the year 1300.
Some early Nevada historians wrote of Horseshoe Cave, in this area; it can not be entirely identified today, but it may have been the Lovelock. Among the fables of the Paiute is one of an ancient tribe of cannibals, small, redhaired, and freckled. At war with them, the Paiute drove the entire tribe into Horseshoe Cave and told them that unless they promised to stop eating their neighbors the cave would be their funeral furnace. The fierce little man-eaters said they would promise nothing; whereupon piles of driftwood were heaped at the cave entrance and all the cannibals were cremated.

Southwest of the junction US 40 runs between Humboldt Sink (L) and the Ragged Top Mountains (R). Carson Sink (L), below the Stillwater Mountains, is visible when the highway tops the ridges.

HOT SPRINGS (*cabins, supplies*), 114.3 *m.*, is the Emigrant Springs of the Forty-Mile Desert; some early travelers called it the Spring of False Hope. Coming across the desert, the oxen, their mouths parched and their eyes bloodshot, would sniff the western breezes, paw at the sand, and bellow furiously; there was moisture in the wind. The beasts would rush forward and plunge into the scalding water, then run around in circles bawling from pain. The travelers, however, would fill their casks and allow the water to cool, but they did not tarry here, for there was no forage. The sun was pitilessly hot on Hot Springs Mountains (L) and Two Tips (R) and small cyclones of sand moved in twisting columns across the arid hills.

Strange tricks of light are noted in the area; the midsummer heat suspends the trees of the Fallon area to the south on the shimmering hills. Fabulous rivers seem to flow up instead of down.

FERNLEY, 130.2 *m.* (4,025 alt., 466 pop.), is a trade center in a fertile valley that is a winter feeding base for livestock. It is also the terminal of a branch of the Southern Pacific that runs north along the western shore of Pyramid Lake (*see ahead*) and thence to lumber camps in the Sierra Nevada Range. At Fernley is a trading post where curios made by the Pyramid Lake Indians are for sale.

Here US 95 (*see Tour 5b*) separates from US 40.

Section c. FERNLEY *to* RENO; 32.5 *m.* US 40

This section of US 40 follows the Truckee River, the stream that has created the fertile Truckee Meadows in which Reno and Sparks stand. Oxcart travelers reaching this stream after the long trek over alkali wastes sometimes became hysterical with joy and cattle could hardly be restrained from plunging into the river with the cart dragging behind them.

West of FERNLEY, 0 *m.*, at 2.5 *m.*, US 40 crosses a boundary of the Pyramid Lake Indian Reservation. The Truckee River, crossed at 5.8 *m.* was called the Salmon Trout by Fremont in January, 1844; but in October of the same year, the Townsend-Stevens-Murphy party, which made wheel tracks across the Forty-Mile Desert, named the river Truckee (trucky), the nickname they had given to a Paiute who had guided them across the desert. This Truckee was the father of Winnemucca, who near the banks of this same stream 16 years later gave the forces from Virginia City and Carson Valley the drubbing of their lives.

Until 1905, WADSWORTH, 3 *m.* (4,077 alt., 212 pop.), now a scattered village whose most impressive building is a large square brick school with a cupola, was the most important railroad town in the State. It was a seasonal village site of the Paiutes when Fremont camped here in 1844. Later a trading post was established. Then the Central Pacific Railroad arrived in 1869, and made it a railroad division point. In 1905 the Southern Pacific Railroad shops were moved to Sparks, and even stores and houses went along on the flat cars.

Right from Wadsworth on paved Nev. 34, 11.2 *m.* to a river gorge with a wooded basin north of it that proved to be an effective ambush on May 12, 1860, during a battle with the whites. The affair started when several men at Williams Station on the Carson River lured two Indian girls to their quarters and imprisoned them. When the tribesmen discovered where the girls were, they attacked the post, killing three men and burning two more who were inside. News of the killing reached Virginia City, and more than 100 men under divided command marched down the east side of the Truckee toward the Paiute camp on the site of Nixon. Seeing no Indians here, they rashly entered the wooded basin, and were bottled up by the gorge behind them. From every rock and tree came a storm of arrows. The retreat became a rout and then a disaster. But this fight did not end the matter.

On June 2 scouts of a larger force, reinforced by regulars, found what was left of the slain men as other scouts on ridges warned of approaching Indians. When the main force came up, the battle line reached from the east bank of the river to a conical butte from which Young Winnemucca commanded his warriors. After three hours of fighting the Indians slowly retreated, and at sunset the battle ended. On June 5 the troops again marched, but the Indians had vanished northward.

NIXON, 16 *m.,* is the Pyramid Lake Indian Agency. The reservation buildings stand among old poplars on the site of a semi-permanent Paiute village. Fremont and his "forty men and one hundred horses" visited the Indians here in January, 1844. Here also the tribes held council over problems that beset them in the spring of 1860. The winter had been severe and times had changed. White men swarmed everywhere, slashed into the pinenut forests, decimated the antelope and deer, and frightened ducks and geese from the marshes. Some of the braves wanted war, but Young Winnemucca (not related to Old Winnemucca) wanted peace; for the whites, he said, were as thick as sand on the lake shore. War was precipitated, however, by the action of a few Bannocks.

Neither trout nor cui-ui (kwee-wee) angling in Pyramid Lake was practiced by Paiutes before white men came. The Indians depended on crude rafts of bound tules, and waited for the fish to run up the river to spawn. During the run of the cui-ui, men, women, and children gathered along the stream and speared the fish as they swam through the shallows. Trout meant food for the present only, but cui-ui meant food for the winter months. The back meat of these fish was stripped, smoked, and stored, a custom that still prevails. Even the Paiute name for Pyramid Lake meant Lake Where the Cui-ui Live. Now that the flow into the lake has been curtailed by upstream storage, the fish-runs have practically ceased. Cui-ui schools circle through the shallows near the river mouth, searching in vain for spawning grounds; and pelicans step in and gorge themselves.

Paiute veneration for the dead is marked. On Memorial Day, now adopted by the Indians, women and children bring great baskets of wild flowers from the Virginia Mountains (L) and the desert hills (R) and each sandy grave in the Nixon cemetery is for a little while vivid with desert colors. Rigor mortis is prevented in deceased warriors by vigorous massage and incantations; for how could a stiff Indian hunt his game in the afterland? Tribal distinctions on the reservation are evident even among the children: a youngster will throw out his chest and proudly declare the name of his tribe, then others will chime in with force vaunting the glory of their tribes.

At the TRADING POST (L) information is available on roads, fishing, and boats. An Indian guide must accompany each boat and the Indians are in sole charge of renting out the craft. Indian buckskin garments, beadwork, and baskets are for sale at the post.

North of Nixon wild dahlias grow in profusion near the road and in every draw are pink, white, and purple-red lupines.

The eastern lake shore is practically uninhabited, except near Nixon, but there are two or three ranches on the western shore at Sutcliffe (*see ahead*) and in the draws westward. That up Hardscrabble Canyon, at the southern end of the lake not far beyond the end of the paved road, is reached by a road that winds up through thickets of wild peach to a narrow pass. The walls suddenly widen to form a very fertile meadow almost completely surrounded by very steep slopes. At one time this ranch was the home of a notable white stallion of Arabian blood. Saddle horses are bred there.

Nev. 34 continues northward through the reservation between slopes (L) of changing color and contour and Winnemucca Lake (3,875 alt.), which was called the Little Lake of the Cui-ui by the Paiute. Until 1934 it still contained many fish, and many geese and ducks lived in the bordering tule marshes. This lake, like others, has gradually receded until it is only in wet years that it contains any water. At the northern end is KUMIVA PEAK (7,240 alt.). In this area are many curious formations, called beehives.

The northern boundary of the reservation is crossed at 42 *m.*, and the road traverses low hills, and flats, and an arm of the Smoke Creek Desert. On the left is Granite Peak (8,990 alt.) at the southern end of the Granite Mountains.

EMPIRE, 78 *m.*, is owned by the Portland Cement Company, which has a gypsum plant here, one of the largest of its kind in the West.

GERLACH, 80.5 *m.* (3,933 alt., 417 pop.), is a division point of the Western Pacific Railroad and supply base for mines and the few cattle ranches in this arid area. Near the hot springs here (*bathing*) Fremont's expedition camped late in 1843.

The road proceeds across desert. At 124.5 *m.*, is a remarkable PETRIFIED TREE AREA (L) with one tree standing close to the road. Another petrified tree in the vicinity has a diameter of 15 feet, testimony to the different nature of the region in the past. The whole vast stretch has the wild colorful beauty for which Nevada deserts are notable.

Nev. 34 continues northward to a junction, 165.5 *m.*, with Nev. 8A (*see Tour 5a*) a short distance from Vya. In this region the bright blue blossoms of the camassia quassia make carpets of shimmering color in summer on some of the isolated meadows.

West of Wadsworth US 40 makes a gradual ascent through the Truckee River Canyon, the northern flank of which is the steep Virginia Mountains, geologically older than the Sierra Nevada, and colored a brilliant red and yellow by mineral deposits. When touched by the setting sun they resemble the Italian Dolomites. Green alfalfa fields lie (L) below the highway.

DERBY DAM (L), 11.9 *m.*, is a concrete and earthen structure that diverts the Truckee waters to the Lahontan Reservoir of the Newlands Reclamation Project near Fallon (*see Tour 7c*).

US 40 winds up a canyon opening into a small valley.

The COURT OF ANTIQUITY (L), 158.4 *m.*, is a flat-topped prominence between the highway and the river. Upon this ancient stage, aborigines met in council and upon the stone floor and walls left crudely chiseled records. About a dozen of these petroglyphs are still easily distinguishable, but most of them have been almost obliterated by erosion. Present-day Indians are not familiar with their meanings and even the oldest chiefs of the local tribes say they did not know of their existence until recently.

Just west of the court the Virginia Mountains abruptly end at the Truckee Meadows; beyond is seen the full sweep of the towering

Sierra Nevada. Those distant peaks were already white when the Donner Party traveled along this river.

At **162.1** *m.* is the junction with a graveled road.

Left on this to a dirt road, 2 *m.*, and again L. to the GLENDALE CROSS-ING, 3 *m.*, sometimes called the Old Stone and Gates Crossing. At this point much of the westbound travel turned south through Truckee Meadows. James Beckwourth, garrulous trapper and guide, waited here in 1851 to inform emigrants of a new pass he had discovered across the mountains to the north, and of the road he had built across it. His route is now roughly followed by US 395 (*see Tour* 4) in crossing to Susanville.

SPARKS, **162.4** *m.* (4,427 alt., 5,278 pop.), was established by the Southern Pacific, and named for John Sparks, then Governor of Nevada. When the Southern Pacific moved its shops and other property from Wadsworth (*see before*) in 1905 it brought even the houses along. Since that time many new houses have been built, for the town has become the home of many people working in Reno but seeking a place with less expensive real estate for their homes. The line of division between the towns is practically lost along US 40 and newcomers sometimes mistake Sparks for Reno itself. Sparks has its own schools, churches, and service facilities, and resents being considered a suburb of Reno.

Even the fast trains make a 20-minute halt at this division point and some westbound through-travelers on what is still called "the evening train" sometimes break their journey by transferring briefly to the "mail train," which runs between Sparks and San Francisco and leaves as soon as the *Overland* pulls in. The transfer enables them to have about 15 minutes in Reno to pull slot-machine handles and place a few roulette counters—plenty of time, as the porters explain, "to lose a lot of money." Porters keep track of the winnings and losses of businessmen who travel over the route frequently and when their charges come aboard again at Reno immediately ask for the tally. "Made up what he lost the last time," they jubilate, taking vicarious pleasure in the scores.

A growing industry of this area is the propagation of wild game for the hunting ranges of the State. Several ranches supply wildfowl, chiefly pheasant. The pheasant hen, while a prolific layer, shows little or no sense in mothering her brood, the loss sometimes reaching 100 per cent of the lay. The small operator hatches the eggs under bantam hens, but the large operator uses the mechanical incubator. After 24 days the small birds hatch. Their lives during the first two weeks are in delicate balance; the loss is often high, as wild fowl of any type are extremely difficult to raise. Some operators raise the pheasant by the Braille method in which one wing of the young bird is pinioned securely, so that it can range widely but not fly away. Others merely keep the fowl in yards with wire netting on all sides and the top. The grace and beauty of the males is indescribable when the sunlight slants across a pen, bringing out the flashing greens, purple, brown and buff of their feathers.

A *piece de resistance* in some local hotels is the stuffed bird; when the waiter removes a large silver service cover he brings into view two birds erect in a field of wild rice. The meat had been cooked and cleverly inserted into the original skin without disarranging a single feather.

A model PHEASANT FARM is at the corner of Pyramid and Prater ways.

1. Left from the eastern end of Sparks on a dirt road to the NEVADA GAME FARM, 3 *m.*, where many kinds of wild fowl, including pheasants, are propagated.

2. Right from Sparks on paved Nev. 32 to Nev. 33, 2 *m.*, Nev. 33 continues north through hills sometimes brown and deeply folded, sometimes streaked with rose and purple. Near the lake are the Rainbow Hills. PYRAMID LAKE, 32 *m.*, about 30 miles long and from 7 to 10 miles wide, is a sparkling deep blue body of water surrounded by bare, sharply-eroded hills of everchanging colors. It is the largest remnant of the great inland sea, Lake Lahontan, that once covered a large part of northwestern Nevada. Pyramid Lake is now fed by what remains of the Truckee River after its waters have been impounded for irrigation, and by brief flood streams from canyons of the surrounding mountains. It has no outlet. The diversion of the Truckee is seriously endangering this beauty spot, which is one of the outstanding lakes of the West.

Particularly striking are the tufa islands—several of which might be the pyramid that suggested the name to Fremont in 1844—and the piles of tufa near the shores. The islands jut up sharply from the water, forming one of the weirdest lake scenes in America. Discriminating people of the Truckee Meadows bring out-of-state visitors to this lake on their first trip into the environs, for its color and the color of the surrounding terrain is breath-taking. The shores are popular for steak-parties at sunset, particularly at the time of the full moon, for the gamut from red to dark purple is then complete.

Directly across the lake near the southeastern shore is ANAHO ISLAND (248 acres), a Federal bird refuge on which is the West's largest rookery of pelicans. Sometimes their number is so great that the island seems covered with snowdrifts. The southern end of the lake is a favorite fishing ground for these awkward birds, which flock to the mouth of the Truckee River during the run of the cui-ui. Rattlesnakes are also numerous on the refuge.

Just north of Anaho Island is the most remarkable pyramid, rising 475 feet above the surface. Paiute lore says the pyramid is a giant basket placed over an erring woman. Although she was turned to stone, her breath is visible—the steam from hot springs. Another legend declares the pyramid to be the home of the lake spirit, which devours persons swimming in the waters—for there is a noticeable undertow during windy weather, and bodies of the drowned are slow to return to the surface.

North of Pyramid Island on the eastern shore is a tufa formation known as the SQUAW WITH A BASKET; and a cluster of sharp stone teeth rising from the water at the northern end is called THE NEEDLES.

The mountains around the lake are deceptive, appearing under some atmospheric conditions to be low, rolling hills and under others austere and lofty. About 30 vertical feet above the waters on the shore is a dead white ribbon marking the water level of only a few years ago. It is composed of numerous bodies of minute algae. Through thousands of years of life, the same algae have formed the bulbous, calcareous shell layers that so grotesquely sheath the promontories and island. As Pyramid Lake gradually recedes its waters are becoming increasingly saline, and it is feared that if it continues to sink, within a few years fish will no longer be able to live in it, and the lake will become another Dead Sea. Its water now is hardly drinkable, but the heavy mineral content makes swimming much easier than in wholly fresh water lakes.

The principal fish in the lake, called native trout locally, but really a species of landlocked salmon, grow to unusual size. One has been caught weighing 65 pounds, and only rarely is one taken that weighs less than 3 or 4. To fish in the lake, a special permit (*good for one day only*), in addition to the state license, must be obtained from the Indians at Nixon (*see before*), or at SUTCLIFFE, 35.6 *m.*

The road northward beyond this point is in poor condition.

RENO, 32.5 *m.,* (4,491 alt., 21,500 pop.), is at a junction with US 395 (*see Tour 4*).

Railroad stations: 135 E. Commercial Row for Southern Pacific and Virginia & Truckee; 325 E. 4th St. for Western Pacific.

Airports: Off US 395, 4 *m.* SE. of city; owned by United Airlines but used also by private and other planes.

Bus stations: Union Stage Depot, 232 N. Center St., for Feather River Stage Co., Inland Stages, Mt. Lassen Transit Co., Pacific Greyhound Lines, Las Vegas-Tonopah & Reno Stage Lines, Virginia & Truckee Transit Co., Oregon, California & Nevada Co., Reno Loyalton-Calpine Stage; 246 Sierra St. for Burlington Trailways; 354 N. Virginia St. for Nevada Transit Co., Reno to Sparks, fare 10c.

Taxis: 25c within city limits; $1 for two to airport, time 15 minutes.

Traffic Regulations: Turns in either direction at intersections except where traffic sign direct otherwise; parking in business district strictly limited to one hour.

Accommodations: 89 hotels, many furnished apartments and auto courts.

Tourists Information Service: Nevada Division of California Automobile Ass'n., 237 S. Virginia St.; Reno Chamber of Commerce and Nevada State Highway Department, Washoe County Library Building, Virginia St., between Lake and Mill.

Hospitals: Washoe County General, Washoe and Mill Streets; St. Mary's, 235 W. 6th.

Golf: Municipal Course, SW. on Arlington, 18 holes, greens fees 50c from 2:30 P. M., $1.00 all day, 50c all day Fri. (ladies' day), $1.25 a day Sat., Sun., and holidays; $5.00 monthly: family ticket (2 adults, 1 minor); $7.50 monthly.

Tennis: Wingfield Park, Whitaker Park, Evans Park, Municipal, University, free.

Baseball: Idlewild Park, free; Threlkell Ball Park and Moana Hot Springs (day and night games), adm. charged.

Swimming: Idlewild Park, 10-6:30; children under 18 free, adults 25c; suits 20c, towels 5c. Lawton Springs 50c and Moana Springs 25c; suits 10c; Reno Hot Springs 35c; suits and towels rented.

Race Track and Rodeo Grounds: Alameda Ave., extreme NE. section of city.

Between the high steep slope of the Sierras and low brown eastern hills, RENO spreads far over the Truckee Meadows, dropping gently from the heights where the university stands, crossing first the railroad tracks and then, a few blocks south, the Truckee River. Beyond the river is a gentle rise leading to a broad plateau. Seen from the air at night the town looks like a Christmas tree with its strings of white light interspersed with twinkling red, blue, and green. From the railroad and the paralleling US 40, the view is far less impressive and also quite misleading. Neither highway nor railroad route gives a view of the charming tree-shaded Truckee, the large houses on landscaped grounds above the river, the comfortable Victorian cottages north of the routes, and the gracious university campus on the heights. Even main street, Virginia, is seen from the through-routes only as a broad street with its near buildings southward obscured by signboards and a sprawling iron arch proclaiming Reno as the "Biggest Little City in the World." Two blocks south of the railroad Virginia Street becomes a thoroughfare of well-appointed shops offering goods of distinction and quality. Crossing it are side streets with two or three blocks of small shops carrying similar goods. Paralled to Virginia Street, westward, is Sierra Street, where the five-and-ten, branches of large mail-order houses, and other mercantile concerns are found all the way from the railroad to the river.

Close to the river and east and west of Virginia Street are the public buildings and one of the largest hotels—though the chief older hotel, and second largest, is on Center Street, the next east of Virginia. Only the area stretching four blocks east and west and about seven blocks south of the Southern Pacific tracks is largely treeless; elsewhere practically every street is lined with cottonwoods, poplars, and other trees that resist traffic fumes.

The city does not lend itself to easy classifications for it is metropolitan in its diversity.

There are many Renos and the two acres of neon lights, night clubs, gambling houses, and drinking places near the railroad station form only one of them—and though commercially important, not a particularly representative one at that, in spite of feature articles and the news reels. Most Reno citizens visit it only occasionally and then largely with guests from out of town. It is never the Renoites who shout noisily, and boisterously toss balloons and confetti about; they are in fact, somewhat annoyed when the liberty they extend is mistaken for license. A second Reno, also not representative and to some extent overlapping the gambling-drinking Reno, is the divorce circle, composed of newcomers, the divorce lawyers, and also the lawyers' wives, who endeavor to keep their husbands' clients from growing too homesick. The divorce circle has various divisions, economic as well as mental. Women with money—and most of the newcomers are female—live in the smarter hotels, expensive furnished apartments, or on nearby ranches, and the rest live as well as their pocketbooks permit; a few even do housework or clerk in stores to maintain themselves during the necessary period. How these divorce-seekers spend their time depends in part on their means, in part on their up-bringing, and in part on their state of mind. To the majority the breaking up of their homes is a heart-breaking business and they react according to their natures; some grow reckless, gamble and drink wildly, invite attentions from any man they happen to meet, while others live quietly and are rarely seen in the cocktail rooms and night clubs. It is the former who provide a disturbing element greatly resented by Renoites, in spite of their determined tolerance for human fraility and their appreciation of the revenue brought in.

A third Reno is composed of moneyed newcomers who have visited the State for this or that reason and been fascinated by landscape and skies; they, and the people who have become residents to escape high property and income taxes in other parts of the country, have built large comfortable homes on the edge of town—chiefly on the southwest. A few enter the civic life in time but the majority lead a social life apart.

Another aloof Reno is composed of the F. F. V.'s—their Virginia is the Comstock. Long accustomed to having plenty of money, uninterested in making a show of themselves or their possessions, uninterested in current social rivalries, these cliff-dwellers rarely leave their own quiet circle, though their names are found on subscription lists of the more conservative civic organizations.

The university is almost a town in itself, with two social layers—one composed of students, the other of the faculty families. Part of the students and faculty members take some part in the life of other parts of town but most are too busy to come down from the Olympian heights except at intervals. Part of the faculty families and students support movements to bring in lecturers and musicians—or at least buy tickets when local organizations arrange for the events; faculty members also lecture to the countless fraternal and other clubs that provide the chief diversions of the vast majority of Renoites.

An important Reno is political; the number of office-holders and would-be office-holders is large. But political Reno is gregarious, so its members are found in many layers of the community. Nevadans continue to conduct their public affairs on a personal basis and the man who wants a job, or wants to keep one, must have friends who will back him.

There is also a businessmen's Reno, composed of the owners of stores and other facilities serving not only the city but most of western Nevada. The members of this circle belong to Rotary, Kiwanis, and similar organizations, and also to the Masons, Elks, Odd Fellows, and so on. Their wives form the women's affiliates of the fraternal organization—the Eastern Stars and Rebeccahs.

The Reno of the society page first column stories is composed largely of the wives of professional men—chiefly lawyers—and the professional men themselves. This group handles its visiting cards strictly according to Emily Post and keeps its eye on Washington.

Women have been particularly active in the art, musical, dramatic, and cultural clubs that have increased rapidly in number since 1930, though the leaders happen to be professional men. The cultural clubs are of various graduations, from those that have lectures because of an interest in the subjects covered to those inspired by an uneasy yearning for the prestige of cultural activities.

The religious congregations have their own social life but most of their members also participate in other town activities.

With all of its metropolitan aspects and its decidedly mixed population the essential Reno is completely democratic; bell boys and barmen call millionaires by their first names, a reminder that they shared pot luck in earlier times, and may again, and that one man has merely been luckier than the other—the assumption is accepted on both sides. Behind the surface caste system is a genuine fraternity, at its best in bad times.

Few men fail to look out for the widows and orphans of old comrades and more than one political appointment is given for the frankly expressed reason that "George has a wife and children to support," or that "Mary's father helped me out when I hadn't had a grubstake in six months." Though accustomed to entertaining the public, Renoites do not have the overflowing surface hospitality of people in some other parts of the country. But like all real Nevadans they have a deep feeling of brotherhood that comes to the surface for the stranger as well as for their own. Also like other Nevadans, they deeply love their State and nothing stirs them as much as a slur by those who do not appreciate it.

In addition to the permanent residents and the gambling-divorce visitors, there is a transient Reno composed of other Nevadans, for Reno is the metropolis of the State as well as the second largest city in the Great Basin. Nearly every Nevadan outside the Las Vegas area likes to come up to town every few months—and some come oftener. Young people of the State's smallest towns long to live in Reno—its bustle and excitement enchants them. A few Renoites, on the other hand, still have the old Comstock urge for San Francisco; but if they do establish themselves in California they are sure to come back regularly, unable to resist the desire to see their own beautiful mountains and to hear the old familiar talk of mines and cattle.

One set of out-of-state visitors does not come in to visit the slot machines and night clubs; these are the winter sport fans. From the time when the newspapers begin to report snow on Donner summit until the roads over the Sierras are clear at all times, hotel lobbies are filled each Friday and Saturday with energetic young people in sweaters and ski-pants and the streets are lined with cars having special attachments for carrying skis and other sport paraphernalia. These visitors, in sharp contrast with the whooping week-ending oldsters, are regarded locally with particular affection. The town is particularly given over to them during the intercollegiate sport contests. At that time the center of social life is on and near the university campus, as fraternity and sorority houses give house-room to part of the guests.

Reno's diversity of interests is astonishing. In addition to its Roman Catholic, Baptist, Methodist, Protestant Episcopal, Jewish, Congregational, Presbyterian, Christian, Latter-day Saint, Lutheran, Nazarene, and Christian Science congregations, it also has an African Methodist congregation composed of most of the two hundred or so Negroes of the town, an Assembly of God, a Unity Center, and supporters of the Church of the Revelation. Though the town's two newspapers pay particular attention to mining news the editorials of one daily discuss such topics as the beauty of Chinese peachblow vases, the genius of Turgenev, and the customs of the Azerbaijan Turks. A lecture by Eve Curie sells far more than one thousand tickets and the Westminister Choir has even stronger support.

The site of Reno was a very welcome camping place of overland travelers even before the gold-rush. The unfortunate Donner Party (*see Tour* 1), made its final fatal mistake of lingering in the Truckee Meadows one day too long before attempting to find the pass across the Sierras. The first man to live here was C. W. Fuller, who built a shelter, a half dug-out, half log, on the south bank of the Truckee in 1859, the year of the Comstock rush. The next year he built a toll bridge of logs that lasted until 1862, when it was washed away. Fuller rebuilt his bridge but in 1863 traded his property to M. C. Lake, who set up a trading post and also did some ranching. In time the place became known as Lake's Crossing.

In 1868 the Central Pacific crossed the Sierras and landed its end-of-the-tracks camp across the Truckee from Lake's post. Lake by this time had enough claim on the land that the railroad company had to deal with him before it could establish a town here to handle the great Comstock business, for which the Big Four had fought their winning fight against the Union Pacific backers.

In selecting a name for the town the romantic put forward Argenta in consideration of the most valuable freight the railroad would carry; but Charles Crocker, the Big Four man who took town naming as his favorite chore, selected Reno to honor General Jesse Lee Reno, of West Virginia, a Union officer killed at 39 years of age during the Battle of South Mountain. The name had been suggested by men who had served with him in the Mexican War.

Reno was officially born on May 9, 1868, with a public auction of real estate conducted by an agent of the railroad company. The event aroused the enthusiasm of a gold strike. Buyers had appeared the day before and camped on the ground all night; blankets and food were at a premium. The first lot brought $600, and 200 lots were sold that day. A hundred houses sprang up within a month and Reno's initial building boom was on its way. By 1871 the town was able to wrest the Washoe County Seat from Washoe City (*see Tour* 4).

A year after the town came into existence Lake's post burned but even though the construction camp had moved on there was enough business to justify his replacing the store with a hotel. Though his bridge was washed away twice more by spring floods, he could well afford to replace it as hundreds of head of cattle were being driven south across the Truckee to supply booming Virginia City and his toll was a dollar a head. But bridges were under charter by this time and when his charter expired in 1872 the county proposed to make the bridge free. Lake indignantly stationed armed guards on the bridge, prepared to defend what he considered his rights, and the case was carried to court; eventually he gave in. Meanwhile, he made an addition to his hotel, which he was later to replace with a yet larger structure, part frame and part brick, with turrets and arches, which he named the Riverside; the largest hotel in Reno today bears the same name and merely replaced Lake's pretentious building, which burned in 1922.

Though Lake's hotel was well-patronized from the beginning, the first business district of squat low frame structures with false fronts developed several blocks away, along the railroad tracks, the center being what is still called Commercial Row. Houses were largely north of the tracks. The first town was practically destroyed by fire in 1873, and the next in 1879; after that business structures were chiefly of brick. The town was incorporated in April, 1879.

Reno had some of the usual frontier rowdies in the early days but its "601" did not tolerate them long because it was already a family town by December, 1869, with a school that at the end of the first term was employing three teachers. First sessions had been held in the basement of a gristmill but a schoolhouse was soon built—at First and Sierra streets.

The Virginia Truckee Railroad had early replaced the freight teams bringing bullion up the valley and Reno prospered until production began to decline on the Comstock. Between 1880 and 1900 it was largely a placid distribution and shipping center for the ranchers of the valleys to the south and for scattered mining camps of the south and southeast.

The great boom came locally after the strikes at Tonopah in 1900 and at Goldfield in 1902. The nearest main line railroad approach to these busy new centers was Reno and people as well as freight passed through in quantities. With money circulating freely the town became a city in 1901. For ten years the boom continued and even with the extension of railroads to the great new camps from the south and southeast Reno remained the chief transfer point. The population doubled between 1900 and 1910.

After Tex Rickard's great triumph in staging the lightweight championship fight between Gans and Nelson at Goldfield in 1906, Reno decided to gain national attention for itself by a similar enterprise. In 1910 Reno watched Jack Johnson win from the great Jeffries, who had come from retirement to defend his world championship title. Sport fans and newspaper correspondents from many countries were present for the fight. H. Hamilton Fyfe, an English writer covering the event for the *London Daily Mail*, saw little of an uplifting nature in the fistic battle. He did, however, carry away "pleasant recollections of the little mountain town" and "the gay, impetuous stream which sparkles through it." He wrote of "the delicious morning and evening freshness . . . the snow-topped Sierras dreaming in 'the last long evening yellow' of sunset."

In later years Reno followed up with a fight between Max Baer and Paul Uzcudun, the Basque "woodchopper." Jack Dempsey also fought here and Reno was committed to a course of publicity making its appeal largely to the sporting fraternity. With the establishment of legal gambling in 1931 and discovery of Nevada's easy divorce law, the city went through another boom. It widely publicized these special attractions and for a time the rush of divorce-seekers was so great that people with very simple houses found it very lucrative to move in with relatives and rent their own abodes furnished; many returned to find that lavish tenants had completely redecorated the houses and left new expensive furnishing when they departed.

Bit by bit the permanent population increased with various service facilities developing to care for the transients and yet others coming to serve the servers of transients; the success snowball rolled bigger year by year.

An annual rodeo, underwritten by the merchants, has become a permanent feature. During this period the mayor issues an ultimatum decreeing "western dress"; it is applied to transients as well as residents and the person who ignores it finds himself hailed before a kangaroo court and must either agree to accept the edict or pay a fine. The resultant costumes are sometimes peculiar; whereas elaborate stage western costumes of leatherwork and silk are the delight of some residents and visitors, and ten gallon Stetsons and high-heeled cowboy boots are very popular, some men get by the kangaroo court with only a colored shirt and a flowing silk tie, and middle-aged women may pass with a silk handkerchief bearing bucking horses and similar symbols.

The city has become the chief banking and shopping center of the State as well as the principal distribution center. The divorce business, with more than 3,000 decrees granted in 1936, is not increasing with competition coming from Las Vegas as well as from other States. Since 1939, however, the marriage business has grown with Californians coming in to evade the three-day notice law, and also the medical examination required under State law. The gambling devices bring the city a sizeable income in licenses; slot-machines are in every hotel lobby, restaurant, and similar public place, but the clubs offering diversified gambling are practically all within the few blocks near the railroad, where the "stockade" also has its discreetly segregated place. The stockade is under close police supervision.

The police work is conducted with efficiency and dispatch and trial and sentence for crime have few delays; in cases where evidence is so strong that prisoners offer a plea of guilty, sentence is sometimes pronounced the day of arrest. Serious crime is not prevalent and the juvenile crime record is unusually low. Schools are adequate in number and well-equipped. There are two hospitals in the town, the Washoe County General Hospital and Catholic St. Mary's; on the outskirts of town is the State hospital for the mentally ill.

Reno has two garden clubs of recent origin but rapidly increasing memberships. Some members of these clubs also belong to an organization that came into existence early in 1940 to promote the intelligent care of public beauty spots and further decoration of the city with trees and plants.

Of interest in the town are numerous old houses of the Victorian period, some of them brought down from Virginia City. Moderately conservative designs predominate in the large new houses being built around Virginia Lake and the golf-course in the southwestern part of the city, but a few structures of modern International design are appearing in various sections of the city.

POINTS OF INTEREST

1. The POST OFFICE AND FEDERAL BUILDING, Mill

St. between S. Virginia and S. Center Sts., on the bank of the Truckee
River, which it faces, was completed in 1935. The three-story white
structure of steel and stone, with a foundation of granite, is of modern
design with aluminum decorations. Many of the Federal offices in
Reno are in the upper stories.

2. The WASHOE COUNTY LIBRARY BUILDING, a green,
stucco-covered structure with aluminum plaques of the State seal on the
front roof parapet, faces tree-shaded Powning Square on the east side
of Virginia Street between Mill and State Streets. This was erected
as the Nevada State Building for an exposition in 1927 celebrating the
completion of the first improved transcontinental highway. The second
floor is largely occupied by the Civic Auditorium, which seats about a
thousand people and is used for amateur theatricals of the little theater
group as well as for concerts, lectures, and celebrations of various kinds.
The Reno Chamber of Commerce, the Juvenile Probation Department,
the Nevada National Guard, a division of the Highway Department,
and the Nevada Boy Scouts have their offices here. The WASHOE
COUNTY LIBRARY (*open 9-9 weekdays, and 1-5 and 7-9 Sun.*) occupies
most of the main floor; it contains approximately 55,000 volumes and
has current magazine and newspaper reading desks. In the Children's
Room are three murals completed in 1940 by Richard Guy Walton;
they present scenes from the life of Tom Sawyer, whose creator did
his first literary work in early Virginia City.

In the southwestern corner of the basement is the NEVADA STATE
HISTORICAL SOCIETY MUSEUM AND LIBRARY (*open daily except Sun.
9-12 and 1-4; on Sat. 9-12*). The exceptionally fine collection, crowded
into a very limited space, gives an understanding of early Nevada.
Among the exhibits are articles used at Genoa in the Territory's first post
office, including a sand shaker—the early blotter; a leather mail-bag used
by a Pony Express rider; an old stagecoach whip; a bathtub used at
Candelaria in the days when all the camp's water was hauled from
a spring nine miles away and cost a dollar a gallon; the doll-buggy of
Persia Bowers, adopted daughter of Mr. and Mrs. Sandy Bowers
(*see Tour* 4); unusual home-made musical instruments used occasionally at early dances and entertainments in Carson and Eagle valleys
—one was made from a child's bath-tub, one from a five-gallon coal-
oil can, and another from a very old Seth Thomas clock; a huge old
Swiss music box of very sweet tone that stood at one time in the Elko
Depot Hotel lobby; a beautiful little melodeon from the Presbyterian
Church of early Virginia City; old fire helmets and buckets. Of great
interest are the bells, among them one from the fire house at Divide,
the western end of Virginia City, for which Mackay, Fair, and others
gave several hundred of dollars in bullion. Another bell came from the
early Methodist church at Unionville; it was later used on a ranch
to summon the hands at mealtime. A third bell, of the table type, was
used in the Maguire Opera House at Virginia City to ring the curtain
up and down on many notable actors. There are also numerous articles
of domestic interest, including china, lace, and embroidery brought

POINTS OF INTEREST IN RENO

1. Post Office and Federal Bldg.
2. Washoe County Library Bldg.
3. Washoe County Court House
4. Nixon House
5. Newland's Circle
6. Mark Twain Cabin
7. California Building
8. Biltz Building

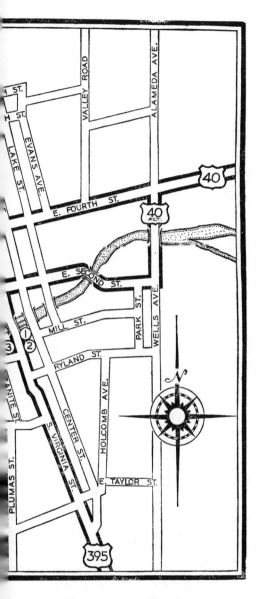

across the Plains. Among the old etchings, drawings, photographs, and oils are several paintings made about 1900 by an old prospector who had no technical training but a genius for putting down what he saw in the landscape; one, reminiscent of Rosseau in its naive charm, has birds in the foreground larger than the stagecoach in the background, but manages to convey the atmosphere of the southern deserts. The old artist started off one day in winter with paints and a fresh grub-stake and was never seen again. The championship trophies of the old Reno Wheelmen's Club are here. The museum also has numerous relics of early and modern Indians of Nevada, including artifacts from Love-lock Cave and Lost City.

The Historical Society Library has the finest collection of old Nevada newspapers and other publications in existence, though, unfortunately, it was partly destroyed during a period when the State lost interest in the museum and library.

The Nevada State Historical Society had its beginning early in the twentieth century when Jeanne Elizabeth Wier came from Stanford University to take charge of the history department of the University of Nevada. Interested in preserving historical relics and the reminiscences of the still-living pioneers, she began to collect them and to stir attention to Nevada history, and soon gathered about herself a group that organized the Historical Society.

3. The WASHOE COUNTY COURTHOUSE, corner S. Virginia and Court Sts., is the place where many famous divorces have been granted. It is of light gray limestone with a shallow portico and central dome. Details are classical but suggest French Renaissance influence. Murals by Robert Caples are on the walls of both floors. Other murals are by Hans Mayer Kassel. Two divisions of the District Court sit here, and handle criminal and civil cases as well as divorces. It is told that some divorcees, elated by their freedom, pause on leaving the court-house to kiss a front pillar, or even walk to the Truckee to hurl their wedding rings into the river; but boys who recover the rings declare they are of the dime-store variety, and accuse the throwers of fradulent practices.

West of the Virginia Street bridge along the Truckee is delightful WINGFIELD PARK, which also includes a landscaped island that is linked with the mainland by two bridges and bisected by Belmont Road. Among the trees and flowering plants are tennis courts and a playground. The landscaping is extended along the north bank of the river to the western edge of town.

The south bank of the Truckee abruptly becomes a bluff occupied by large widely spaced houses on landscaped lawns. Many of the houses were built in the Tonopah-Goldfield days and are of designs usual in prosperous communities about the time of the World War.

4. The NIXON HOUSE (*visited by appointment*), 631 California Ave., a broad low-roofed structure built shortly after the Goldfield boom, which helped pay for it, was one of the first to be erected in what was at the time practically a suburban area. After the death of George

S. Nixon, who was serving at the time in the United States Senate, it came into possession of Dr. and Mrs. William B. Johnston, who offer it freely for meetings of groups interested in chamber music and other cultural activities. Doctor Johnston, who is himself an artist working in pastels, chiefly landscapes, does research work in physics with Dr. R. A. Watters in the basement of this extraordinary house, which is reminiscent of legation buildings in Washington. It was built quite frankly for the giving of large parties. A broad hall flanked by two parlors, one of which (R) is now the family living-room, leads to a cross-hall giving access to large rooms beyond the parlors. The room flanking the present living-room is a state dining room, still containing elaborately carved furnishings that were made to order by a German cabinet maker. Tile insets as well as the workmanship are of interest. At the other end of the house is the music room. The end rooms are extended to form rear sun-parlors. Between them is a paved patio overlooking the river and a distant horizon of low brown mountains.

California Avenue continues westward, curving to pass modern estates. Near the end of the plateau is (5) NEWLANDS CIRCLE, named for Francis G. Newlands, who as United States Senator worked for the establishment of the Newlands Irrigation Project—first called the Truckee-Carson. This gracious small park has evergreens and birches framing views of distant mountains.

California Avenue descends to a street crossing a bridge and extending to Riverside Avenue on the north bank of the Truckee. Westward near the bridge is IDLEWILD PARK (L), covering 48 acres along the river and containing a swimming pool, a fish hatchery, and a few deer, buffalo, bear, monkeys, aquatic birds and other animal life. In the park is a MARK TWAIN CABIN (6), brought from Aurora in 1927. The forlorn, dilapidated structure may well have been the humorist's home during his brief stay in that town; it certainly accords with the condition of his pocketbook at the time. There is no record of the many other derelicts it must have sheltered at one time or another. Surrounding it is a low paneled wall, each panel representing a county and containing ore specimens from that county.

7. Also in the park is the CALIFORNIA BUILDING, constructed for the highway exposition in 1927. It is occasionally used for exhibitions and recreational purposes. In 1939 it became the home of the Reno Art Center, which sponsors WPA classes. The center, which arranges art exhibitions (*see newspapers for announcements*), will eventually be housed in its own building.

VIRGINIA LAKE, 42 acres, including a 30 acre man-made lake, lawns, landscaped grounds, a fine bridle path, and an island, adjacent to the southwestern division of the city, offers scenic and recreational opportunity to resident and tourist alike. This park and lake were constructed by the WPA and Washoe County. It offers excellent angling in season, affords a cool spot for canoeing and row-boating and is a favorite swimming spot. In the winter, it is a prime favorite with ice skating groups and others interested in winter sports.

West of Virginia Lake in the same section of the city is the MUNICIPAL GOLF COURSE, constructed by the WPA under the auspices of the county, a first grade, standard municipal course, that draws golf enthusiasts from great distances. One hundred and eighty acres of beautiful greens, sand traps, roughs, parked area, and all that makes a good course, is an extremely interesting lure to the sport enthusiast as well as a beauty spot of the city.

8. In the BILTZ BUILDING, at 19 Sierra St., just north of the river, are photographic murals (*viewed by permission*) of Reno scenes, the work of James Greil.

9. The FIRST METHODIST CHURCH, on the northwestern corner of First and West Sts., is an attractive structure of Gothic design. A square arcaded belfry rises from the center of the roof.

10. ST. THOMAS AQUINAS CATHEDRAL, on the corner of Second and Chestnut Sts., was dedicated in 1908. Its design shows Spanish baroque influences. The red brick walls rest on a heavy foundation of granite and entrance is through three arched doorways. At each of the front corners rises an elaborate tower with open stages.

11. Northward on Maple St., on a low rise at the head of Chestnut St., are the RENO ART CENTER GROUNDS, already being landscaped though funds are not yet available (1940) for construction of the galleries and studios.

12. The CUTTS HOUSE (*open by appointment*), at 643 Ralston St., contains the fine art and book collection of Charles Cutts. It consists of fine paintings and prints, rare porcelain and pottery, old ivory, exquisite glass, rugs, textiles, embroideries, pine baskets, rare books, and other articles.

13. On the little steep-gabled SMITH HOUSE, 621 Washington St., is a small balcony in front of a window with pointed arch; the supports are of cast iron but the balustrade is the most delicate and beautiful piece of wrought-iron in the city. Nothing is known of its origin though the tradition is that it was brought up from California in the early days of the city.

14. The CHURCH OF JESUS CHRIST OF THE LATTER-DAY SAINTS (1940), 1309 Buena Vista St., is one of the striking structures of the town. Its gleaming white walls are broken by sections of glass brick and the mass is decidedly irregular, with an unusual clerestory and spire.

The main entrance of the UNIVERSITY OF NEVADA is on Ninth Street at the head of University Avenue, the northern extension of Center Street. The hilltop campus covers more than 100 acres on a plateau affording a view of the Truckee Meadows and the distant Sierra Nevada and the Virginia Mountains. The buildings, nearly a score in number, with many of the newer ones of Neo-Colonial or collegiate renaissance design, are among green lawns, flower beds, elms. and near a clear tree-shaded lake.

The second State in the Union to provide in its constitution for an institution of higher learning, with the aid of the Morrill Act of 1862, Nevada established a State university that should teach the mechanic arts, mining, and agriculture, as well as academic subjects. Two years after the State constitution was accepted in 1864, Congress set aside 90,000 acres of land to provide income on which the institution should operate. The university was opened in Elko on October 12, 1874, but was moved to Reno and reopened on March 31, 1886. President LeRoy D. Brown was the first administrator in Reno and, having 50 students, he was assisted by Professor Hannah K. Clapp. There was only one building, Morrill Hall, at that time. The buildings number 26 and the instructional, research, and extension staff about 200. Student enrollment averages 1,200.

The institution has had several gifts of importance: Mrs. John W. Mackay and her son Clarence founded the Mackay School of Mines and provided for the Mackay Athletic Field, the Mackay Training Quarters, Mackay Quadrangle, Mackay Science Hall, and a bronze statute of John W. Mackay. They also contributed valuable newspaper files, early pictures, and material of the Comstock days. The library building, commemorating Alice McManus Clark, a native of Virginia City, was presented by her husband. Various scholarships of from $50 to $500 have been established by private donors.

The university, which is fully accredited by the American Association of Universities, concerns itself not only with education of the youth of the State but also with service to all people of Nevada. How well the young people are educated is best shown by the exceedingly large number of Nevadans attending—one out of every 95 inhabitants of the State is enrolled. The College of Agriculture, the Agricultural Experiment Station, and the Agricultural Extension Service rank high in accomplishment, carrying scientific and economic advances to rural people, and also training their sons and daughters in 4-H clubs. The Mackay School of Mines and the local U. S. Bureau of Mines staff have done far-reaching work for the leading State industry. A university professor of Latin who was an enthusiastic mountaineer decided about 1910 that the snow, source of waters essential to the rancher, should be measured annually for water content as a public service; he evolved a method of snow survey that is used the world over today. The controlling serum for the dreaded red water disease that attacks cattle was evolved by the veterinary department.

One of the popular annual events is Engineering Day, held on a Saturday in March. The engineering colleges outdo themselves to present displays for visitors; electricity is generated, a photo-electric eye is demonstrated, and anyone may have his eyes tested for color blindness and affinity. There are also chemical and mining displays. All the males on the campus wear whatever fuzz of whiskers they can produce.

Mackay Day, the first Saturday following Easter, is traditional clean-up day. Every male student appears in old clothes to give the campus all necessary attention, while the girls prepare a substantial lunch for the hungry males, which is served on long tables in the gymnasium. After the meal awards for various athletic events are made—the rifle team awards, Women's Athletic Association awards, and so on—a track meet and a football game are held in the afternoon, and at night a dance with the participants in special costumes.

The students issue a weekly newspaper, the *University of Nevada Sagebrush,* which maintains a high standard of journalism. They also publish a year book, *The Artemisia,* to chronicle the student year in pictures.

Visits on the campus are made afoot from Monday through Friday (8:30-4:30) as the university streets are then blocked off, except during summer holidays. Nearest the gate is (L) the ALICE McMANUS CLARK LIBRARY (*open during university year* 7:30 *a.m. to* 9:30 *p.m. Mon. to Thurs. inc.;* 7:30 *to* 6:00 *p.m. Fri.;* 7:30 *to* 12:30 *Sat.;* 1:30 *to* 5:30 *p.m. Sun.; during summer vacation* 9:00 *to* 12:00 *a.m.*). The library contains about 62,000 volumes, excluding 12,000 Federal documents and several thousand pamphlets. Of great interest are the murals and charcoal drawings of Robert Cole Caples, and the Cardinal Rampolla collection of Italian and other marbles presented by Mrs. Ludovica D. Graham of Reno.

The AGRICULTURE BUILDING (L), straight ahead beyond the library, is an ivy-covered brick structure well back on a green lawn and among flower beds. It houses the Biological Museum and various collections, including economic insect life histories and mounts of birds and animals of economic importance. Courses in animal husbandry, home economics, and agriculture are given here.

The EDUCATION BUILDING (L) contains an auditorium where lecturers appear, plays are presented, and meetings held. The hospital cottage (L) is on the same drive, which continues north to the street, dividing to swing (L) past the barracks where rifle practice is held, and (R) behind Mackay Field, scene of football and track meets, with Mackay Training Quarters across the turf. The barracks are sometimes used for agricultural and stock shows.

A street runs (L) from the hospital to pass in front of Lincoln Hall, the men's dormitory. Down Virginia Street are (L) Artemisia Hall—a new dormitory for women, the dining hall, and Manzanita Hall—the older women's dormitory. Beyond Manzanita is a wooden tramway, picturesque between a long sweep of lawn and the end of MAN-ZANITA LAKE a shallow cup set in green banks with weeping willows sweeping the edges. The walk turns left to return to the Clark Library. From there it leads (R) to Stewart Hall, one of the three oldest buildings; foreign language and history are taught here. An elm-shaded brick walk leads along the west side of a lovely green quadrangle, passing (R) the Hall of English, housing journalism and English classes, and the agricultural Extension Service Building, from which non-resident agricultural teaching is directed. This path also divides, at the upper end of the quadrangle, paths going (L) to the Education Building, straight ahead to the gymnasium, and (R) behind a bronze

STATUE OF JOHN W. MACKAY, by Gutzon Borglum. Back of the statute is the MACKAY SCHOOL OF MINES, a brick structure with formal white Doric portico, the design of Stanford L. White. It contains the Mackay Museum, mining, metallurgical, geological, and mineralogical collections. The exhibits illustrate mining and its history in the State. On the east side of the mezzanine floor are cases containing fossil specimens. In the basement is a seismograph, upon which quakes even thousands of miles away are recorded. A small stamp mill, originally given by Fair to his small son, has been set up in the building to give students practical knowledge of milling. In the rear is the entrance to a building where the United States Bureau of Mines carries on research.

Down the eastern side of the quad are (L) the electrical and the mechanical engineering buildings and Mackay Science Hall. A number of chemical specimens are in the latter. Back of the Science Hall are a green house and several small buildings.

The walk turns left, completing the quadrangle, and gives a view (L) of the president's house. The oldest building, Morrill Hall, has steps rising from the sidewalk; administrative offices are still in this early building, the wooden steps of which have been worn by the many feet of students in the past. The Agricultural Experiment Station, one of three early buildings, was moved to North Virginia Street to make way for the Clark Library. Its herbarium contains 15,750 mounted sheets, all of western species, and more than half native to Nevada. A large number of photographic negatives of native plants are also here. In the building is the office of Dr. J. E. Church's snow survey.

Section d. RENO *to* CALIFORNIA LINE; 14 *m.*

This brief section of US 40 runs through a curving valley that grows rapidly narrower as it nears the Sierra Nevada.

West of RENO, 0 *m.,* US 40 follows the Truckee River. Small farms are along the stream between foothills of Peavine Mountain (R) and of towering snow-capped Mount Rose (L).

LAWTON'S HOT SPRINGS (L), 5.7 *m.,* is a popular resort with a large swimming pool. Prize-fighters who engage in bouts in Reno usually choose this as their training quarters.

West of VERDI, 10 *m.* (4,908 alt., 257 pop.), formerly a lumber camp, US 40 enters heavily wooded country where evergreens predominate.

At 14 *m.* the highway crosses the CALIFORNIA LINE at a point 23 miles east of Truckee, California.

Tour 1A

Elko—Jiggs—Harrison Pass—Ruby Valley—Arthur; 93.9 m., Nev. 46 and unnumbered improved roads.

This loop route is for the most part in valleys along the west and east sides of the Ruby Mountain, which are in a division of the Humboldt National Forest. But between the valleys a high pass is crossed and side roads and trails on both sides of the mountain lead to high camps, and alpine lakes and meadows in one of the most beautiful wooded sections of the State.

Nev. 46 goes south from ELKO, 0 m., crosses the Humboldt River, and winds up a shallow gulch in the Elko Hills, covered with second-growth juniper and cedar. ELKO SUMMIT, 4.2 m. (approx. 6,000 alt.), affords a broad view including Elko, which, after dark takes on a metropolitan look with its neon signs, street lights, and airport and radio towers. Eastward is the broad sweep of the towering Ruby Mountains. Nev. 46 roughly parallels the Hill-Beechey Road, also called the Old Telegraph Road, developed in the late 1860's by stage and freight companies shuttling south with food, machinery and other supplies and bringing north great loads of bullion from the boom camps of Hamilton and Eureka.

At 12 m. is the junction with a graded dirt road.

Left on this road toward the mountains, following Ten Mile Creek, where within the memory of living men Indians fished with horse-hair snares and cooked their catch with fires lit from fire-coals, which were carried wrapped in bark. The stream has cut deep below the surface, and the former meadows are covered with sagebrush.

In the spring of 1875, when restlessness among the Indians led all Nevada to fear trouble, some cowboys on their way to Elko camped by this creek. Except for one young giant fresh from the East, who boasted endlessly of his physical prowess and his experiences, they were men who had grown up with the country. All were well armed. Around the sagebrush fire that evening the smoke became sulphurous with horrible stories of Indian massacres of the past. At the fire sank to embers the leader rose and said, "Boys, we'd better post a horse-guard tonight. I seen fresh Injun tracks on the trail down the river. We can't let them varmints steal our horses." So a guard was posted, and the other men rolled in for the night, all, cowboy fashion, with their clothes on, except the tenderfoot who put on a flowing white nightgown.

The cold of an early spring night closed around. Just before dawn a volley of shots broke the silence. The greenhorn leapt up in his white robe, eager to prove himself as bold as bold men anywhere—and could not find his gun! At the same moment into camp staggered the horse-guard, a feathered arrow dangling from his coat, "They got our horses!" he shouted. "There's hundreds of them! Scatter for the fort before they get us!" Into darkness raced the cowboys and the greenhorn in his white gown, followed by shots and terrible war cries. It was barely daylight when the shoeless and lacerated easterner

DESERT THISTLE

JOSHUA TREES

THE RARE FOXTAIL PINE, IN CHARLESTON MOUNTAIN

Photographs by S. B. Doten

BITTER ROOT

DOUGLAS PHLOX

SAGEBRUSH *Photograph courtesy U. S. Forest Service*

This variety, notable for its height, is found in several
sections of the state. It was sometimes used in the early
stamp mills for fuel until wood could be carted in.

TIMBERLINE

CREOSOATE BUSH IN THE CLARK COUNTY DUNES

RUBY LAKE (10,000 Altitude) *Photograph by H. B. Lukey*

ASPENS ON CHARLESTON MOUNTAIN

Photograph by H. B. Lukey   JUNE SNOWDRIFT IN JARBIDGE ROAD

POGONIP (HOAR-FROST)

Photograph courtesy Office of Indian Affairs

Photograph courtesy H. B. Lukey
SPRINGTIME

staggered into Fort Halleck, his night shirt hanging in bloody ribbons from his shoulders. Hysterically, he told of the attack, and of how he had been trailed and fired at as he fled. Bugles sounded and out dashed a troop of cavalry to Ten Mile Creek, where it deployed in skirmish formation to scour high sagebrush for hidden warriors. Carefully, furtively they approached the spot where the cowboys had made camp—and saw them squatting around a campfire, a coffee pot steaming on the coals. Horses fed at the creek banks. In amazement they listened to the tale the greenhorn had told. "We wondered where that hombre went to. He must a-had a nightmare."

A few days later a settler was talking with the commandant of the fort. "By gum," he said, "sumpun queer happened the other mornun when I was a-wranglun my hosses. It was pitch dark but I swear to God I seen a ghost a-runnun like hell acrosst the hills. I drawed a bead on the critter, but I guess I plumb missed him."

The graded dirt road continues to a Forest Service road, 17 m.; L. here 0.5 m. to LAMOILLE, (5,887 alt., 68 pop.) (hotel), a charming little trading center of a cultivated valley settled in the late 1860's.

Right on the Forest Service road, which leads into the V of glacier-worn Lamoille Canyon, forming a crescent in the heart of the most rugged section of the Ruby Mountains. The northern boundary of Humboldt National Forest is crossed at 2 m. Lamoille Creek (trout fishing) is a cold, clear, and tumultous stream that feeds from snow covered cragged reefs and peaks rising as high as 11,000 feet. Mountain mahogany and aspen blend into patches of pine and stunted willow and a wide variety of wild flowers bloom on the canyon floor. Mountain sheep formerly ranged in the high peaks above, but they were ruthlessly exterminated 25 years ago. The road crosses numerous pegmatite dikes in the granite. In these are found garnets, beryl crystals, mica, and many other minerals. Among them are some very fine gem stones.

At 5 m. on the Forest Service Road the barracks of a former C.C.C. camp are passed. The road continues to climb along the edge of the canyon— through masses of flowers in summer. At 6 m. from the Lamoille junction is a fork; L. here about 200 yds. to THOMAS CANYON CAMP (toilets, stoves, tables, rock fire bowls, wood, and water), beautifully situated in a bowl formed by eroded cliffs and the high peaks of the Rubies. The campsites are around a circular area filled with tall aspens; the road encircles the grove and each of the campsites, also among aspens, has privacy. The campgrounds were named for one of a party of teachers who lost his life when caught here in a blizzard.

On the southwest corner of the camp is a trail that leads about 0.4 m. through gnarled mahogany and sub-alpine blooms to a roaring cascade. The trail goes on to a beautiful meadow, 0.7 m., a mountain flower-garden.

The forest road continues up the slope to a ranger station, 9 m., built of logs. Lamoille Creek for about 2 miles above the ranger station is a natural spawning ground for trout, and no fishing is permitted. The road winds on to a parking space at 12 m. Here a trail starts zigzagging upward among increasingly beautiful beds of blue elephant's head, lupines, paintbrush, and countless other flowers.

The trail passes several large shallow lakes, rimmed with pines. The water trickling from them is cold and crystal clear. As the trail rises, the lakes grow deeper. Crossing the summit (10,407 alt.), the route soon winds along LIBERTY LAKE—3 m. from the parking point—so deep and clear that the trout—rainbow and native—can be seen far below the surface. The trail drops rapidly along the creek that flows from Liberty Lake to FAVRE LAKE, 4 m., which offers very fine fishing and in the early morning reflects the peaks as though it were beveled glass. A meadow sloping down to the shore is frequented by grazing sheep in the summer. This is a particularly desirable campsite with plenty of firewood.

Left from the ridge 15 m. on the ranger trail (open July 3) along the backbone southward to Harrison Pass (see ahead). High and cool, some lakes of the Rubies retain small icebergs throughout the summer. RUBY DOME (11,358 alt.) is the highest peak in this range. From its summit the vista is magnificient.

Early travelers left the Lamoille Valley and turned westward across the South Fork of the Humboldt River to go through Dixie Pass at the northern end of Bullion Mountains. Close to Lamoille is a junction with the old Jiggs road; R. here 17.9 m. through Pleasant Valley to LEE (5,730 alt., 70 pop.), another trade center, surrounded by broad fields of hay and grain that reach to the west flank of the Rubies. A number of streams come down in this area to form the South Fork of the Humboldt. Left from Lee on an 8-mile trail following the main creek up Long Canyon, where lupine, larkspur, paintbrush, sego lily, and sunflower bloom all summer long. On bare rocky points dwarf moonflowers spread white petals to the evening. Blue grouse find covert in the gulches, and in high patches of tamarack, Franklin grouse—fool hens—gawk stupidly at visitors. From these areas a cougar now and then stalks a band of sheep or the fat colts of ranch horses, or seeks fawns in the aspen and choke-cherry thickets.

The mountains eastward were prized hunting grounds of Indians who built rock and brush barriers in walled canyons and then drove deer and antelope into their traps. Old burns on the high mountain slopes are the result of fires started by lightning.

The Jiggs Road goes on south to a junction with Nev. 46 in JIGGS, 30.7 m. (see ahead).

Nev. 46 continues southward from the Lamoille road junction, paralleling the Pleasant Valley route.

JIGGS, 33 m. on Nev. 46, is at the southern end of the Pleasant Valley road (see above). The place seems to have been ironically named: it was in turn Mound Valley, Skelton, and Hilton. When local ranchers fell into a wordy and fruitless feud over a permanent name, some unusual federal authority was reminded of a comic strip in which an endless feud was the most characteristic feature, and Jiggs was adopted as the post office name.

Jiggs is in Mound Valley, named for the low hills that resemble ruined pyramids. Because pinon hills westward offered nut harvests, Indians formerly had a year-round camp here. This valley was settled by Texans in the late 1860's, but has since been distinguished as the headquarters of "King Fisher", an infamous outlaw who has figured in Zane Grey novels.

Left from Jiggs on a trail up along the north branch of Toyn Creek to OVERLAND LAKE, 7 m. (approx. 9,000 alt.), which rests below the rough scarp of Ruby summits and drains into Ruby Valley. In spite of its alpine setting, its surface waters are strangely tepid. Trout in it are exceptionally slim-bodied.

At 36.3 m. on Nev. 46 is the junction with a graded dirt road, now the main route; L. on this into the Rubies along a beautiful meadow-flanked stream. The winding ascent reaches Harrison Pass, 49.5 m. (7,247 alt.), where a small granite arch (L) has been eroded. Eastward is a long view across Ruby Valley, and the Goshute, Pequop and Toano Mountains.

At the summit is a junction with the forest ranger trail (see before). The road now zigzags steeply down the eastern slope of the mountains to Ruby Valley. The eastern boundary of the Humboldt Forest is crossed at 54.2 m.

At 54.6 m. is the junction with a graded dirt road.

Right on this road to CAVE CREEK (R), 9.1 m., where a stream of icy water flows from the eastern base of almost perpendicular Pearl Peak (11,000 alt.). An underground stream, about four feet wide and of unknown length, extends far back under the mountain. Preliminary exploration in 1865 by soldiers from Camp Ruby proved disastrous, for the explorers were lost. It is said that beautiful stalactites hang from the roof of the entrance chambers, reflecting in mirrored perfection by the black waters.

Drainage from the eastern slope is used to irrigate a small strip of Ruby Valley but most of the water flows into Ruby and Franklin Lakes, shallow bodies that vary in size and offer broad expanses of tule and marsh for the nesting of wild ducks and geese. The lakes are now a Federal game refuge. A traveler's journal of 1861 declared: "Such swarms of ducks and geese as I saw in and around the little lakes up and down the middle of the valley I never expect to see again!"

When Richard Burton, later the translator of the *Arabian Nights,* made his trip westward by stage in the early 1860's on his way from the City of the Saints, he wrote—"About two miles from the station (Ruby Valley) there is a lake with water-fowl, from the wild swan to the rail." He did not visit it. "I preferred, however, to correct my Shoshone vocabulary under the inspection of Morse Wright, an express rider from a neighboring station. One of your 'one horse' interpreters, he had learned the difficult dialect in his youth, and he had acquired all the intonation of an Indian. Educated beyond the reach of civilization, he was in these days an oddity; he was convicted of having mistaken a billiard cue for a whip-handle, and was accused of having mounted the post supporting the electric telegraph wire in order to ban what it was saying."

The Cave Creek Road continues south to the SITE OF CAMP RUBY, 17.1 m. (6,015 alt.), sometimes called Fort Ruby, now on the Togininni Ranch. Fort Ruby became a military headquarters along the Overland Stage route in the fall of 1862. Troops stationed here engaged in several lively skirmishes before the end of the Goshute War in 1863, for both Goshute and Paiute were on the warpath. Their attacks were directed chiefly against the stations of Overland Stage, these representing the most dangerous invasion of their traditional hunting grounds.

Before the establishment of the post Uncle Billy Rogers had a trading post here, serving passing travelers as early as 1859. An old scout, he had been sent to this valley to investigate the area as a possible Indian reservation. When he reported favorably and the reservation was not set aside he was so disgruntled that he remained to ranch and employed Indian laborers to show the land was fertile.

Camp Ruby was a stage station of the Overland Mail Company, a change station for the Pony Express, and eventually a relay station for telegraph messages. The early stage stations were very primitive affairs, as the English Burton and many others testified. Of the station east of Camp Ruby he wrote: "While the Shoshone is tracking and driving the old mare, we glance around at 'Robber's Roost', which will answer for a study of the Western man's home. It is about as civilized as a Galway shanty, or the normal dwelling place in central Equatorial Africa. A cabin fronting east and west, long walls thirty feet, with port holes for windows, short ditto fifteen; material, sandstone and bag limestone slabs compacted with mud, the whole roofed with split cedar trunks, reposing on horizontals which rested on perpendiculars. Behind the house a corral of rails planted in the ground, the inclosed space a mass of earth, and a mere shed in one corner the only shelter. Outside the door the hingeless and lockless backboard of a wagon, bearing the wound of bullets—and resting on lentels and staples, which also had formed parts of locomotives, a slab acting as stepping stones over a mass of soppy black soil strewed with orkes of meat, offals, and other delicacies. On the right hand a load of wood; on the left a tank formed by damming a dirty pool which had flowed through a corral behind the 'Roost'. . . .

"The inside reflected the outside. The length was divided by two perpendiculars, the southernmost of which, assisted by a halfway canvas partition, cut the hut into unequal parts. Behind it were two bunks for four men; standing bedsteads of poles planted in the ground, as in Australia and Unyamenezi, and covered with piles of ragged blankets. Beneath the framework were heaps of rubbish, saddles, cloths, harness and straps, sacks of wheat, oats, meal and potatoes, defended from the ground by underlying logs; and dogs nestled where they found room. The floor, which also frequently represented the bedstead, was rough, uneven earth neither tamped nor swept, and the fine end of a spring oozing through the western wall kept it in a state of eternal mud. A redeeming point was the fireplace, which occupied half of the northern short wall; it might have belonged to Guy of Warwick's great hall; its ingle nooks boasted dimensions which one connects with an idea of hospitality and jollity; while a long hook hanging down it spoke of the bouillon-pot and the iron oven of hot rolls. Nothing could be more simple than the furniture. The chairs were either posts mounted on four legs spread out for a base, or three legged stools with seniform seats. The tables were rough dressed planks, two feet by two, and rickety trestles; one stood in the center for feeding purposes, the other was placed as a buffet in the corner near the fire, with eating apparatus, tin coffee pot and gammelles, rough knives, 'pitchforks', and pewter spoons. The walls were pegged to support spurs and pistols, whips, knives and leggins. Over the door, in a niche, stood a broken coffee mill, for which a flat stone did duty. Near the entrance, on a broad shelf raised about a foot from the ground, lay a tin skillet and its 'dipper'. Soap was supplied by a handful of gravel and evaporation was expected to act as a towel. Under the board was a pail of water with a floating can, which enabled the inmates to supply the drainage of everlasting chores. There was no sign of Bible, Shakespeare, or Milton; a Holywell-Street romance or two was the only attempt at literature. En revanche, weapons of the flesh, rifles, guns and pistols, lay and hung all about the house, carelessly stowed as usual, and tools were not wanting—hammers, large borers, axe, saw and chisel. An almost invariable figure in these huts is an Indian standing cross-legged at the door or squatting uncomfortably close to the fire. He devils the whites for their wastefulness, preferring to crowd in parties of three or four over a little bit of fuel than to sit before a blazing log. These savages act as hunters bringing home rabbits and birds, we tried our revolvers against one of them and beat him easily; yet they were said to put, three times out of four, an arrow through a keyhole forty paces off. In shooting they place the thumb and forefinger of the right hand upon the notch, and strengthen the pull by means of the second finger stretched along the bowstring. The left hand holds the whipped handle, and the shaft rests upon the knuckle of the index."

By 1865 the Overland Stage Line Company, tired of paying high prices for grain and farm produce in Salt Lake Valley, had established the Overland Ranch in Ruby Valley, several miles north of here.

Ruby Valley Indians were a peaceful group. In 1861 Sho-kup, their chief, sent a message to Uncle Billy to ask him to come to the chief. During this visit Sho-kup told the scout: "In the mountains is a very cold lake. Sometimes ice stays there all summer. Here lives a big fish who is a very evil spirit. When he rises from the water and looks at an Indian, the Indian dies in a few days. I was at the lake and I saw the evil spirit. Now I am a very sick man. I have told my people I want Buck to be chief after me for he is a good man." The next morning Sho-kup was dead.

For his burial, members of the tribe killed Sho-kup's horses and laid them beside their master; but when they also moved to kill his wife she ran to the white man for protection. Buck sent word if she was not sent back at once his warriors would attack every white man in the valley. She was not returned— but an accident saved the situation. In the Indian camp, the chief medicine

man was accidentally killed by a rifle discharged while the braves were pre-
paring for battle. The dead man was accepted as a sacrificial substitute to accompany Sho-kup's spirit in the hereafter.

The lake of the evil spirit, commonly supposed to be Overland Lake (*see
above*), is more likely Peak Lake (10,025 alt.), an isolated and inaccessible
body northwest of Cave Creek.

Though Ruby Valley remained quiet, the station keepers were more than
once disturbed when Pony riders rushed in across the sage crying, "Deep Creek
station keeper was scalped last night!", "Buildings burned at Butte Valley!"
or "Egan Canyon raided!", "Shell Creek station keeper killed!"

From the junction below Harrison Pass the loop road goes north
along the eastern base of the Rubies, passing broad fields from which
cattle are shipped each fall. Under protection of Fort Ruby, the OVER-
LAND STAGE RANCH, 60.2 *m.*, in 1865, produced 8,745 bushels of oats,
8, 575 bushels of barley, besides 1,655 bushels of potatoes, 1,854 bushels
of turnips, 1,000 bushels of carrots, and 78 bushels of beets.

Left here on a trail along Overland Creek, which rushes down the mountains:
the trail leads up steep ridges to OVERLAND LAKE.

RUBY VALLEY, 65 *m.* (6,048 alt., 62 pop.), is a community center. Ranches in this area use Indians in the hay fields or as cowboys
when the cattle are turned out on the range. Around the Indian camps
fences and brush are seasonally laden with strips of "jerky" (deer flesh),
being dried for winter use.

At 86.6 *m.* is the junction with a dirt road.

Left on this road to a Forest Ranger Station, 0.9 *m.* where fishing and trail
information are available.

The road crosses the Woodhouse Ranch, where at 91.7 *m.* is an old
Indian campground (L). Plowing here sometimes turns up Indian
artifacts.

The ARTHUR POST OFFICE, 93.9 *m.* (6,075 alt.), serving the
ranchers in the northern end of the valley, is at the junction with Nev.
11 (*see Tour 1a*), at a point about 23 miles southeast of Halleck on
US 40.

⁙⁙

Tour 1B

Elko—Dinner Station—North Fork—Rio Tinto—Mountain City—
Owyhee; Nev. 11, 43, 11A.
Elko to Owyhee, 98.3 *m.*

Asphalt paved for 26 *m.*, graveled elsewhere.
Hotel in Mountain City, excellent campsites throughout.

This route north to Idaho traverses mountains and valleys, passes through the Duck Valley Indian Reservation, and through old mining towns. There are many beautiful vistas.

Nev. 11 branches north from US 40 (*see Tour 1a*) at ELKO, 0 *m.*, passing the MUNICIPAL AIRPORT (L), 0.2 *m.,* a graveled field, illuminated at night, where United Airline, Government, and private planes break their 600-mile journey between Salt Lake City and Reno. The airport is equipped with a short-wave radio station and has Weather Bureau service.

North of Elko Nev. 11 immediately begins the ascent of brown hills through Dobe Canyon, probably named by stagecoach drivers and early freighters who had many a difficult time after rains had soaked the heavy clay. Through this canyon moved the mighty stampedes to Tuscarora, Mountain City, and other early mining towns, after outfitting at Elko. Highway construction has unearthed innumerable fossils in shale beds that are a prominent geological feature of the hills around Elko.

From DOBE SUMMIT, 9.4 *m.* (6,880 alt.), early Humboldt travel returned to the Humboldt River through a wide canyon (L) to Carlin. North of Dobe Summit Nev. 11 traverses low rolling country and passes meadows where range cattle browse through spring and early summer. When sheep from southern deserts are on the trails here, the hills at dusk are warm with yellow fires as herdsmen gather the flocks to protect them from coyotes.

DINNER STATION, 22.5 *m.* (5,955 alt.), at a crossroads containing only a handful of people, is a bleak, two-story stone structure flanked by ranch buildings. Formerly, as its name declares, it was a stop for meals on the route to the ranches and mines of northern Elko County. At this station in the 1870's, weary oxen rested under their yokes, and the lathered teams of the stagecoaches were relieved by fresh beasts, while inside the fort-like walls drivers and travelers ate. In the surrounding area drainage from Lone Mountain (L) has made hay fields and meadows possible.

Near Dinner Station is the junction with Nev. 43, which has the better roadbed northward. Nev. 11 becomes the alternate route to Owyhee.

Left on Nev. 11, climbing to a low pass in the Independence Range, where there is a junction with a wide trail, 11.5 *m.; L.* here about 4 *m.* along a jagged ridge to the summit of LONE MOUNTAIN (9,046 alt.), the most distinctive feature of this region. Grass and sagebrush blanket the ridges, but aspen groves declare the presence of water in the canyons. Approach to the summit is not difficult and the view is memorable. When frosty nights or west winds have clarified the atmosphere, and neither the smoke pall of forest fires nor desert haze obscures the vast stretches, the view westward seems to have no limit. Between the foothills of the Cascades and Lone Mountain, the tumultuous unrest of the earth in ancient days is etched in stupendous waves across the Humboldt ranges on the Black Rock Desert. Around the horizon spreads a land that is fabulous in magnitude and in its record of mighty upheavals long ago. In the southwest the distant Humboldt Sink is a dirty gray patch; in the blue southeast are the snow-patched peaks of the Rubies. Low and close in the northwest are the white lines of roads that enter a smudge of green trees on the grey slope of a sagebrush hill, the site where gold and silver fortunes were taken from the earth, the old camp of Tuscarora.

On the western slope of Lone Mountain is a private road leading (L) to the Sleepy Hollow and Rip Van Winkle mines—the latter usually called The Rip. The Merrimac District was organized in 1870 but production was low until 1908, when recovery of more than $42,000 worth of gold ore began. Later silver lead was discovered and operations have continued at intervals.

Nev. 11 descends the western side of the range through steep Taylor Canyon to a junction with Nev. 18, 20.4 m.; L. here 7 m. to TUSCARORA (6,200 alt., 127 pop.), chief camp of a mining district on the eastern slope of Mount Blitzen that produced from 25 to 40 million dollars worth of ore, chiefly silver. During its heyday—in the 1870's and 1880's—several thousand people were here, including about two thousand Chinese who had been imported to build the Central Pacific, and remained to glean after the whites had moved to richer spots. Elko, which handled the vast freighting business for this district, considered Tuscarora a particularly tough camp and was fond of telling one story as an illustration of Tuscarora's fondness for a personal settling of its troubles even after law enforcement agencies had been established. A man named Rockafellow had been using such violent and profane language in public against Major John Dennis that the zealous sheriff arrested him; but Dennis went to the justice of the peace and bailed him out for the pleasure of beating the tar out of him. And he was thoroughly flogged himself for his pains.

Through the first years after the Beard brothers began to operate placers here they had very little company; after 1871, when W. O. Weed found the first silver lode, a rush began that insured 14 years of high prosperity. During this time the Dexter gold mine was located and it continued to operate until 1898. Several mills were built and even after one mine and then another ceased to yield profit, faith continued that the district would come back; about once a decade, still, someone makes a serious attempt to explore new levels. The first water for the camp had to be piped nine miles from the Independence Mountains, and valley and hillsides were denuded of sagebrush for miles in an attempt to provide fuel for the mills and pumps. Collection of the sage required almost as many men as operation of the mines, but the profits were great enough to bear the expense. The pumping was constant and heavy because water was struck before the shafts were much below the ground. In later years the mining companies were much in litigation over claims and the final blow came when a fire stopped the pumps and flooded the workings

In spite of its reputation Tuscarora like any other mining camp had its peaceful social circles with dances and dinners of high quality, and summer evenings found most of the householders sitting in chairs along the sidewalks under the wooden awnings to exchange the news with passing neighbors.

The MASONIC TEMPLE still has the expensive wall-paper and flower-covered carpets of the boom days and its roster contains the names of people later scattered to all parts of the world—from Alaska to South Africa.

In Tuscarora a dirt road (R) forms a short-cut back to Nev. 11 northward.

At the junction with Nev. 18, Nev. 11 makes a right turn and at 29 m. meets the short-cut from Tuscarora. Continuing north along the western base of the high Independence Range, which is sparsely timbered, Nev. 11 passes ranches from which thousands of cattle and sheep are annually marketed. By fall the valley is dotted with huge stacks of wild hay, used for winter feeding. Here the road passes out of the Great Basin and streams drain toward the Snake River in Idaho.

At 40.1 m. is the junction with a dirt road (open only in summer); R. here into the Independence Mountains, by Forest Service campsites in beautiful Jacks Creek Canyon. Above the narrow canyon are peaks that wear white coronets the year round. Close to the never-melting snowfields on the crest are great patches of blue, red, yellow, and white sub-alpine flowers. Does are also seen near the road. The view from the pass is breathtaking. Far, far away mountains shadowed by the sun are amethyst and sapphire; nearer ranges are burnt umber. Travelers crossing the pass (7,833 alt.) in mid-summer sometimes believe they are seeing lakes on the eastern slopes, so thick and brilliantly blue are the wild irises in the mountain meadows. The Forest Road continues to a junction with Nev. 43 (*see ahead*), 19.5 *m.*, at a point three miles south of Penrod Bridge.

Nev. 11 crosses a low rise and goes down through another canyon and is in the Humboldt Game Preserve.

DEEP CREEK, 45.6 *m.*, is an old stage station below Lime Mountain, where gold mines are producing quantities of gold ore. The Bull Run Mountains, westward, are also covered with mining claims; the name of the range is a reminder of the partisan sentiments of many of the early prospectors. In the range, about six miles away, is the Cornucopia District where a discovery of gold in 1872 brought a rush, temporarily depopulating Tuscarora. But though the mines produced about a million the camp had a brief existence. The windowless, sagging walls of a two-story hotel blink across the great Owyhee valley. Bending gently the road runs through Deep Creek Canyon.

At 45.6 *m.* is the junction with Nev. 11A, a dirt road; R. here 5 *m.* to the old Edgemont District, where gold was discovered in the middle 1890's. Two mines have produced more than a million dollars' worth of ore. Bull Run Creek, farther upstream, offers many trout to fishermen. Nev. 11A proceeds northeastward across the range passing the MOUNTAIN CITY RANGER STATION, 29 *m.*, to a junction with Nev. 43 (*see ahead*), close to Mountain City.

WHITE ROCK, 64.5 *m.* (5,789 alt.), is a supply center on Nev. 11 for scattered ranchers. Nev. 11 continues northward over a level plain, one of the few places in Nevada where on at least one side—northwestward—the far horizon is not formed by mountains. This remote country of deceptive distances is cut by deep tributaries of the Owyhee and is inhabited by antelope, deer, and wild horses.

OWHYEE, 84.8 *m.*, is at the junction with Nev. 11A (*see ahead*), the main route.

North of its junction with Nev. 11, Nev. 43, the main route to the north, runs through the upper valley of the North Fork of the Humboldt and into the Humboldt Game Preserve, created for the protection of sage chickens and waterfowl.

On the principal northern branch of Humboldt River is NORTH FORK, 50.6 *m.* (6,500 alt., 138 district pop.), a community center with post office, general store, and service station. During haying season Indians come from the Duck Valley Reservation (*see ahead*) to work here and live in primitive wickiups. The river swings down from its countless sources in the Independence (Jack Creek) Mountains across the valley westward (*fish, duck, sagehens, grouse, deer*).

At 55.1 *m.* is the junction with a graded dirt road.

Right here to the Deeth-Jarbidge road, 28 *m.*, reached at a point 4 miles south of Charleston.

Slightly south of this junction on Nev. 43 a distinct change takes place in the physical aspect of the country. It is on the divide, with drainage to the north creating a branch of the Owyhee River, which enters the Columbia, and drainage to the south eventually losing itself in the Great Basin. This east-west divide, running irregularly across northern Nevada, forms the northern boundary of the Great Basin.

At 62.6 *m.* is the junction with the unpaved Jacks Creek Canyon Road (*see before*).

An artifical lake (L), 63 *m.*, has replaced hay fields along tributaries of the Owyhee River, which plunges northwest through a gorge in the Independence Mountains. This lake, created primarily for upstream storage, provides fishing, boating, and duck hunting.

OLD PENROD BRIDGE, 65.2 *m.*, was named for "Manny" Penrod, one of several claim-holders of Virginia City fame, who, having no notion of the fabulous wealth under their feet, sold Virginia short. Unlike some, he was not so chagrined that he blew his brains out, but he did spend his last years in this isolated area.

At 65.3 *m.* is the junction with a graded dirt road.

Right on this road along Gold Creek to the abandoned camp of GOLD CREEK, 3.6 *m.* (6,700 alt.), which sprang up on the theory that every sagehen in the region had gold nuggets in its craw from feeding on gravel in the stream—according to the theory of an early Elko editor. The town disappeared when it was found that the wild chickens had plenty of gravel in their craws but no gold. Today a lone fire plug in the sagebrush marks the spot where an incredible notion led men to build a town before they learned whether they had anything to build it for. Since Gold Creek died there has been no mining town in this valley, but, from 1873 on, there has been minor production of placer and lode gold and silver. The surrounding hills provide some of the best grazing in Elko County.

At 8.5 *m.*, by a junction with another dirt road, the main side road turns L. and becomes a dirt road leading to a Forest Service Ranger Station and the GOLD CREEK PUBLIC CAMPGROUNDS, 9 *m.* (7,064 alt.), in Martin Canyon, an area where wild flowers make pastel loveliness on the hills throughout the summer. WATERLOG SUMMIT (c 7,600 alt.), 15.4 *m.*, is at the head of a long canyon descending with Meadow Creek to Bruneau River. Meadow Creek is locally famous for both its trout and its rattlesnakes, the latter of which, say all bad anglers, predominate. The MEADOW CREEK CAMPGROUND (R), 17.5 *m.*, is used chiefly by fishermen and prospectors.

North of the junction of Meadow Creek with the river the canyon broadens into a ranching valley, walled in on all sides by great mountains. ROWLAND, 25.5 *m.* (5,662 alt., 7 pop.), is the community center of this backwoods district. Two thousand feet below the surrounding mountains, it has a year round climate sharply different from that in the remainder of northern Elko County.

At 64 *m.* on Nev. 43 is the junction with a dirt road.

Left here to the WILD HORSE DAM, 4.1 *m.* (6,189 alt.), built in 1937-38 to retain flood waters from Owyhee River tributaries for use on the Duck Valley Indian Reservation.

The main road now climbs through broken hill country on whose slopes are acres of wild flowers, including lupine, Indian paintbrush, and the sunflower for which was named SUNFLOWER SUMMIT, 72.5 *m.* (6,563 alt.). In side canyons dense thickets of mountain mahogany, aspen and chokecherry border the streams and provide a natural home for deer. The road winds down along Allegheny and California creeks to the fields bordering the Owyhee, where at 83 *m.* it becomes Nev. 11A. (*for Nev. 11A southward to Bull Run Basin, see before*). On both sides of the road the workings of gold-silver mines, operated since 1870, speak of the Mountain City mining discoveries that led to a permanent settlement.

Left on Nev. 11A is RIO TINTO (L), 3 *m.*, by the great copper mine of the same name that came into operation in 1935. Over these brown-stained hills on the west side of Owyhee River prospectors passed for years unaware of the minerals under their feet. Deep under the surface was found one of the largest deposits of high-grade copper yet discovered. The Rio Tinto is now controlled and operated by the Anaconda Copper Company. The comany's neat and modern houses and streets are quite different from those of the old gold and silver camps.

Nev. 11A northward passes ranches along Owyhee River (L) and comes to MOUNTAIN CITY, 85 m. (5,641 alt., 1,500 district pop.), whose log cabins built when the place was settled in 1869 stand side by side with new business structures. Following a production of more than $1,000,000, prior to 1881, principally in silver, mining in this area declined, though it had periodic revivals, until discovery of the immense Rio Tinto copper deposits brought unprecedented prosperity to the district. For many years the town was only a post office and store serving ranchers, but now it is the center of business and play for ranchers, miners, prospectors, and promoters.

North of Mountain City the road crosses the western boundary of the Humboldt National Forest, and the eastern boundary of the Duck Valley Indian Reservation.

OWYHEE, 98.3 m., headquarters of the Duck Valley Indian Reservation, is in a broad fertile river valley at the northern end of Bull Run Mountains. Stores, a hospital, and a school, serve about 400 Indians, who cultivate small farms along the river. These Indians retain many of their old customs and native crafts. Along with deerskin gloves, moccasins, and other customary articles, an occasional fine robe made from the prime white fur of the snowshoe rabbit is offered for sale at the trading-post.

South of Owyhee 0.5 m., is the junction with Nev. 11, the alternate (*see before*).

Tour 2

(Twin Falls, Idaho)—Wells—East Ely—Pioche—Glendale; US 93. Idaho Line to Glendale, 460.4 m.

Paved throughout.
An Oregon Short Line branch parallels route between Idaho Line and Wells, the N. N. Ry. between Currie and East Ely.
Accommodations in Wells, Ely, Pioche, Caliente; long stretches between towns and service stations.

US 93, crossing eastern Nevada from north to south, is fairly straight, with easy grades. It passes through several long valleys between mountain ranges of various types and constantly changing colors. Near it are some of the most remarkable formations in America.

Section a. IDAHO LINE *to* EAST ELY; 207.4 *m.*

US 93 crosses the IDAHO LINE, 0 *m.*, at a point 47 miles south of Twin Falls, and continues across rolling country. The old immigrant road, the Fort Hall Cut-Off used by many forty-niners, is separated from the highway by mountains, the road from Fort Hall, Idaho, following Goose Creek, and the modern highway a branch of Salmon River. About 43 miles south of the Idaho boundary US 93 crosses the early road, which followed Bishop Creek to a point just west of the present town of Wells.

Caleb Greenwood, that amazing frontiersman, is credited with being the first to have charted this course to California, though there is strong support for the contention that the honor should be given to Joseph Walker. Walker guided a group to California the year before Greenwood made his trek (1843). Although no record has yet been found to prove that Walker followed the Humboldt, it is highly improbable that he would have done anything else as he had used that route a number of years before. His train traveled through Owens Valley in California with the wagons, the first to cross the Sierras to California. Greenwood returned to waylay other immigrants on the Oregon Trail and induce them to cross to Sutter's Fort—where Sutter hoped to build up a Yankee colony to support him against the Mexicans —advertised the route, and made it a much traveled way between Fort Hall and Fort Sutter. Greenwood used the Truckee Canyon route over what became Donner Pass. Sutter's diary speaks of John Greenwood as the man he had employed to attract settlers to California; John was the name of Old Greenwood's son. Another enterprising man, Hastings (*see Tour 1a*), had the same plans as Sutter for stimulating California immigration, but unfortunately chose a course that crossed the vast salt flats of Utah.

Through this area and westward along the Humboldt, Greenwood, who had lived among the Crow and understood the Indian viewpoint, negotiated with the tribes for safe passage, and by his wisdom avoided trouble. Later travelers were not as wise, shooting the natives with slight provocation, or without any, and holding their lives of no more worth than those of the jackrabbits along the way. Always a just man, Greenwood was as sternly set on doing his own son to death for the wanton murder of an Indian as he would have been had any other member of the train transgressed his orders. Young John had shot the Indian when the Greenwoods were guiding their second train to Fort Sutter. John escaped, riding ahead on an excellent animal, but fell in with a Mexican and was killed in a card dispute.

For approximately 30 miles the highway parallels the Salmon River, which flows north to the Snake and is one of the few Nevada streams to send waters into the ocean. The Salmon affords good trout fishing.

CONTACT, 15.5 *m.* (5,375 alt., 146 pop.), a trading center in a stock-raising area, was first a mining camp established in 1895. It was so named by miners because it is on the "contact" of limestone and granite.

US 93 crosses a broad valley west of Independence Range, in which are Thousand Spring and Rock Spring Creeks, along which the Fort Hall Cut-Off took its way. In spring and summer great herds range over this terrain. The vegetation is luxuriant and the forested mountains contrast with the stark beauty of ranges farther south.

WELLS, 67.7 *m.* (5,626 alt., 831 pop.), (*see Tour 1a*), is at the junction with US 40 (*see Tour 1a*).

South of Wells US 93 passes through Clover Valley, a slightly more humid region along the East Humboldt Range. This valley was a favorite of eastern Nevada Indians. Along here are large ranches typical of those throughout the eastern part of the State. Many cattle graze on the hills and valley floor. Forming an 80-mile crescent between Wells and Ely is one great valley, bearing different names. It is progressively more level toward the south and also more attractive.

East of the highway at 82.4 *m.* is a boggy area, where gravel pits dug during road construction revealed quantities of well-preserved teeth identified as belonging to huge prehistoric mammals that roamed this broad valley below the towering Ruby Mountains.

WARM CREEK RANCH is at 92 *m.* The ranch house, like all others in the valley, is far from the road. The ranch gives its name to a junction with Nev. 11 (*see Tour 1a*). Westward is a division of the Humboldt National Forest, and eastward is Spruce Mountain (11,041 alt.), a mining district in the East Humboldt Range.

The highway crosses a low divide, Goshute Pass, which was probably used by Fremont in 1844, when he swung south from his earlier camp at Flowery Lake to travel around the southern end of the Ruby Range. It is believed that Hastings took his train over it in 1846. The Donner party acting on his advice and trying to overtake him, also used it. Some historians gather from his notes that Bidwell crossed the route of the modern highway further north and used Secret Pass; but from his description of where he reached the Humboldt it seems more likely that he, too, crossed the valley at about this point in 1841.

The road now enters a broad and less productive valley, with Mount Taylor to the west, and the northernmost peaks of Antelope Range to the east.

CURRIE, 130 *m.* (5,885 alt., 52 pop.), named for an early settler, is a shipping point on the Nevada Northern Railroad for sheep and cattle men.

US 93 skirts Goshute Lake, a large dry alkali flat between the northern tip of the Egan and Schell Creek ranges.

At 146.8 *m.* is the junction with US 50 (*see Tour 7a*), with which US 93 unites between this point and East Ely (*see Tour 7a*).

EAST ELY, 207.4 *m.* (6,415 alt., 791 pop.), (*see Tour 7a*), is at

the southern junction with US 50 (*see Tour 7a*) and at a junction
with US 6 (*see Tour 6b*).

Section b. EAST ELY to GLENDALE, 253 m.

The eastern section of US 6 unites with US 93 between East Ely
and Conner's Station.

Southeast of EAST ELY, 0 *m.,* US 93-6 passes between two divisions of the Nevada National Forest, first winding up a canyon of picturesque rock formations and then crossing low hills heavily timbered
with juniper.

From the western end, 17.4 *m.,* of CONNERS PASS (6,997 alt.),
is a far reaching view to the north; snow-capped WHEELER PEAK
(13,058 alt.), the second highest in the State, is seen (L). The highway now descends a wooded canyon and enters the huge Spring Valley.

At 25 *m.,* by the southern junction with US 6 (*see Tour 6a*), is a
gasoline station.

US 93 skirts the eastern base of the Schell Creek Range, crosses a
low divide in Fortification Mountains, and heads due south across the
broad Lake Valley floor, making a chalkline course as far as eye can
reach. This grand valley is chiefly covered with sage and juniper, the
latter occasionally in dense clusters close to the highway. Among the
properties along here is GEYSER RANCH, 54 *m.,* one of the largest
in eastern Nevada.

PONY SPRINGS, 78.5 *m.,* was a watering hole for early ranchers
of the district.

The highway now enters a region heavily wooded with juniper,
passing between Wilson Creek Range (L) and the Ely Range (R).
There is a noticeable change in topography: flat-topped mountains with
abrupt eroded sides and deep canyons are more frequent. These cliffs
are brighter in mineral coloring than those farther north. In summer
the roadsides are yellow with waving wild sunflowers.

To climb up through PIOCHE, 108 *m.* (6,100 alt., 400 pop.), seat
of Lincoln County, US 93 makes a wide S. The town, once center of
one of the State's most important mining districts, has spread down
from a narrow canyon high on the eastern side of the Highland Range.
Dry Valley, a broad flood channel, lies below.

Paiutes led William Hamblin into the Pioche district in 1863. His
discovery precipitated a boom and the Meadow Valley District was organized in 1864. But there was no real development until F. L. A.
Pioche, a French banker from San Francisco, became interested. In all,
the district has produced more than $40,000,000 worth of ore.

By 1870 the camp, far from administrative centers and the much
traveled trails, was considered—and not without reason—the wildest
and toughest camp in the West. Guns were the only law. They accounted for 75 deaths before anyone in the town died of natural
causes. It was not only a matter of the badmen who came in to bully
the town and shoot the timid; according to pioneer yarn spinners, mine

owners imported thugs at the rate of 20 a day to fight one another's encroachments. The cemetery on the lower hillside became the pride of Pioche; they told far and wide of its Murderers' Row, and more significantly of Boot's Row, where several dozen of the hired assassins were laid after they died with their boots on.

Old-timers were fond of recalling the days when nobody knew whether he would live to see the next morning. An arrival of 1871 was a young Illinois lawyer, William W. Bishop, who later defended John D. Lee in the notorious Mountain Meadows case in southern Utah. With him was his young bride. It happened that a deputy sheriff shot and killed three desperadoes on three different street corners while the bride was leaving the stage and entering the hotel. This display of frontier spirit was too much for the gentlewoman from Illinois; within a few minutes she was headed back toward civilization.

Another story often told is of two desperadoes convicted by public opinion of the wanton slaying of an aged prospector. They were forced to dig their own graves, and then were ordered to stand by the pits and be shot. It was a tidy way, in the absence of courts, of dispatching an unpleasant job with clean hands.

During this early period a small smelter had been built to reduce the complex silver-gold, lead-zinc ores. Fire bricks for the smelter had been packed in from the construction camp of the uncompleted Central Pacific Railroad in the vicinity of Elko. The bricks had been made in Scotland and had journeyed by sailboat half way round the world to San Francisco. Bullion from the smelters went out on pack mules over the route to Elko.

Before a post office was established in 1870 mail was carried by private carrier at the rate of 25 cents a letter and then forwarded by coach from Hamilton to Elko. In 1871 when Pioche was credited with a population of around 2,000 people the frame shacks of the town were swept away by the usual fire, which also exploded 300 kegs of powder. The explosion raked the crowded street with debris, leaving 13 dead and 47 wounded. By 1874 there were 6,000 people, including gunmen, gamblers, dance hall girls, saloon keepers, and speculators, as well as prospectors, mine operators, miners, and business men.

During the Fourth of July celebration in 1876 the town bell was cracked by incessant ringing. Citizens thereupon decided they would have a bell worthy of their town and threw hundreds of dollars in silver into a molten mass, for their enthusiasm getting a bell that was long noted for its sweet and resonant tone.

Pioche, unlike many another camp, has had almost uninterrupted production of metals, and there are huge proven ore bodies still to be mined. The camp is still active—though socially far quieter than in the past—with several mines and plants operating. The cheap power now obtained from Boulder Dam is expected to make this town a leading lead and zinc producer.

Of interest is the OLD LINCOLN COUNTY COURTHOUSE, built of brick in the late 1870's at a cost of more than a half a million—though the actual cost of construction was only a fraction of that amount. Compound interest on bonds and refinancing had made it the most costly courthouse in Nevada—and it was condemned in 1933, three years before it was paid for. But in early days Lincoln County thought nothing of spending huge sums. If a sheriff made a journey of two or three hundred miles and turned in an expense account of $15,000, it was paid.

All around Pioche, and even on the dump at the foot of the town grow clouds of pink and white wild peas.

US 93 winds up from Pioche to cross the rolling foothills of the Highland Range toward a sage-covered plateau flanked by picturesque CATHEDRAL GORGE (R). This great chasm, deeply and beautifully eroded, has marked trails.

At 114 m. is a junction with a graveled road.

Right here 1 m. to an observation tower overlooking Upper Cathedral Gorge. It is particularly visited at sunset, when the coloring of the formations is dramatic.

At 118 m. on US 93 is the junction with graveled Nev. 54.

Right here to CATHEDRAL GORGE STATE PARK AND GAME REFUGE (picnic grounds), 2 m. Pageants and Easter ceremonies are held in the park annually. The gorge is remarkable for its coloring and for the formations eroded by wind and rain in a soft chalky clay. Arches and spires are everywhere; at dusk in particular some of the formations resemble architects' models of European cathedrals, and of lower Manhattan's skyscrapers. One near the picnic ground looks like a huge and elaborate wedding cake. A stupendous mass, at about 3 m., is especially remarkable for its purity of line, its great columns, and its innumerable spires. There are also many weird shapes, resembling contorted human figures and animals.

At 119 m. on US 93 is the junction with an improved road.

Left on this road to PANACA, 1 m., a small ranching center close to a low mesa with sides of curious green-grey. Founded in 1864 by Mormons led by Francis Lee, it is an excellent example of the results of Mormon pioneering. The town has the county high school, serving Pioche as well as smaller communities. The name is of Indian origin and refers to ore.

US 93 continues south down an immense flood channel, the Meadow Valley Wash, where the highway is built on an embankment to avoid the danger of spring inundations. In places rock cliffs are near the route, with strange formations shaped by countless centuries of erosion; even today occasional cloudbursts change the contours. In this section an abrupt change in the type of vegetation is seen—at the division line between the sagebrush and creosote bush zones.

At 125.2 m. is the junction with a dirt road.

Left on this road to BEAVER DAM STATE PARK, 34.2 m. (camp sites), near the Utah line, at the edge of the Nevada National Forest. It is a hunting base and affords excellent fishing.

As the road nears Caliente it swerves west to avoid the narrower lower section of Meadow Valley Wash, where floods are sometimes torrential. The Union Pacific tracks still run through the canyon southward though much money and engineering skill have been expended to prevent a repetition of the disaster of 1910, when more than 100 miles of track were carried away. Just as the highway enters a side canyon the long, low, modern LINCOLN COUNTY HOSPITAL (R) is seen in the shadow of cliffs some distance off the route.

Charming CALIENTE, 133.9 m. (4,398 alt., 1,696 pop.), is at the bottom of the narrow crooked side canyon. Its very wide main street is bisected by rails of the Union Pacific, for which it is a division point. Before the highway turns onto this main street it passes a long row of comfortable company houses, painted the familiar bright yellow, behind neat fences and very tall poplars. The stores, of cement block painted white or grey, have the air of prosperity inseparable from a community that has long had a steady source of moderate income. Conspicuous in the center of the main street, by the station, is the solid hotel owned by the railroad company.

Left at the lower end of town to KERSHAW CANYON-RYAN STATE PARK, 3.9 m. a popular camping and picnicking spot.

US 93 climbs quickly out of the canyon through the Highland Range and onto a rolling plateau between distant ranges. Joshua trees are seen here and there, increasing in number to the southward. The thick short branches rise above cacti and creosote bush. In the spring the joshua tree with cream clusters of flowers is one of the loveliest things on the Nevada deserts. In this rolling country reptiles are occasionally seen, among them the deadly sidewinder, a small rattlesnake whose venom is extremely poisonous. It is seldom dangerous, however, unless cornered.

The highway reaches the upper end of Delamar Valley, which is one of the most striking in the State because of its broad clean sweep, its mountainous background, and its flora. The whole valley looks as if it were under cultivation, with crops in various stages of growth. One patch may be a foot in height, while next to it is another where the plants are no more than two or three inches high, suggesting that this crop was planted much later than the other. Close to the ranges eastward are forests of joshua trees, whose large yellowish white flowers look like overgrown hyacinths. The obstinate Manly party of 1849, after breaking away from the experienced leader, Jefferson Hunt, to find a quicker route to California, followed the approximate course of US 93 across this valley, unknowingly laboring toward the tortures of Death Valley, far to the west.

At 146 m. is the junction with a dirt road.

Right on this road, which runs across a gently rolling valley where joshuas rapidly increase in number and size as the mountains are neared. In late spring the carpet flowers in this joshua forest include pink sand verbena, white primrose, and several other flowers of a delicate pink and lavender. Following the line of the range are the great cables carrying power northward from Boulder Dam. Close to the foot of the mountain, 16 m. is a large enclosed cemetery, reminder of early Delamar's reputation as a maker of widows; three months in the mines were sufficient to produce the fatal silicosis. The narrow road climbs steeply, curving up a bare slope, rounds a low peak and reveals DELAMAR, 18 *m.*. jammed half way up a shallow rocky canyon above enormous piles of light tan tailings. The discovery here, in the Ferguson District, was made in 1892 and the principal claim was purchased by Captain John De Lamar in the following year. By 1895 a barrel chlorination plant had been established. Until 1900 this camp was the principal gold producer of the generally inactive State, and operations were continued until 1909. There was some activity in 1920 and 1921, and in 1939 about 25 men were at work on small claims or on the tailings. Most of the houses and stores are now merely stone shells and the single narrow street is largely peopled by dogs and frisking children. But smoke rises from one of the mills below and the residents are sure that the deposits will provide a comfortable living for some years to come. Total production of the Delamar Mine up to 1908 was estimated at twenty-five million dollars.

The Roman Catholic Parish of Pioche had been established in 1870 by the Reverend Lawrence Scanlan, but had irregular pastoral care. Father Scanlan became first Bishop of Salt Lake in 1891. Late in 1895, soon after the boom was on at Delamar, an urgent sick call came to Salt Lake from the camp. Since no other priest was available the bishop himself answered the plea, traveling by train, stage, and horseback to reach this remote spot. Seeing the missionary field at hand he set about organizing a congregation and by Christmas had a small chapel and quarters for a priest erected. He stayed until April, preaching and celebrating mass.

Pahroc Valley, reached at 148 *m.,* is another of the high valleys so typical of Nevada. It is remarkable for the evenness and uniformity with which it flows in a gentle slope southward for many miles. The plant life here is chiefly creosote bush, so thick and so strangely even in height that the whole floor looks as if it had been mowed. A few miles southward the creosote bush yields to greasewood and in springtime to sheets of wild flowers.

US 93 goes down a slope where piles of huge boulders are seen at intervals. Dotting the smooth expanse of brush, they look as though some neat giant had tidied up his dooryard. Then the road turns south between the jagged Pahranagat Mountains on the east, and the Hiko Range on the west.

At 173 *m.* is the junction with an improved road.

Right on this road across Pahranagat Valley to HIKO (Shoshone, White Man) 4 *m.* (3,681 alt., 29 pop.), the second seat of Lincoln County and founded as a mining camp with high expectations in 1866. But little ore was found here at the base of Hiko Range, and in 1871 the county seat was moved to the new boom town of Pioche. Deserted buildings that once housed several thousand people remain, though weather-beaten and tumbling into ruins.

CRYSTAL SPRINGS, 177 *m.,* once a stage-coach station, and the first seat of Lincoln County, is today only a ranch. The station was established during the brief flurry at Hiko. In contrast with the brush plain roundabout are green meadows and old cottonwood trees. Here US 93 goes southward through the fertile Pahranagat Valley, an extensive stock-raising district that had a grim early history. Once a mecca for horse thieves, it is said that at least one man has been shot and killed on every ranch, and that on a few several died violent deaths. As late as 1875 it was customary for horse thieves and rustlers operating in southern Nevada, Utah, and Arizona to drive their stolen herds to the Pahranagat Valley for fattening. It is declared that at one time as many as 350 different brands were to be found in this region, a circumstance suggesting how widely the thieves had operated. Occasionally an attempt was made by law-abiding ranchers to rid the area of the outlaws but their efforts were long in vain.

It is also told that one horse-thief was followed to the valley by owners of beasts he had stolen. Pleased to have reinforcements, the settlers quickly organized, caught the thief, and prepared to hang him in one of the ranch stables. A noose was placed around his neck, but as word of hoist away was given a double-barreled shotgun was thrust through the door and a voice commanded a halt. The vigilantes were forced to free the scoundrel, who thereupon joined the other "horse fatteners", and rode away to Hiko for a celebration. Their insolence so enraged the settlers that a permanent vigilance committee was formed, a branch of the 601's already operating further north. Whenever the settlers were successful in their raids, they too held celebrations, sometimes lasting two or three days.

Traveling westward with his wife and child in a poor outfit, a man named Hancock received aid in this valley from Billy Edmonson and Doc Engstrom. At night Hancock murdered his benefactors, stole their belongings, and continued to the coast. But ten years later, when he was imprisoned in California for another crime, his wife, long intimidated, told Lincoln County officials of the early murder. After serving ten years in California, Hancock was returned to Nevada, found guilty, and sentenced to hanging. Illustrating the casual spirit of the frontier is the tale that after being sentenced Hancock turned politely and said: "I thank you, gentlemen of the jury," to which the foreman responded, "You are entirely welcome."

The Pahranagat Valley is a long plain divided for 25 miles by a thread of green. It is largely owned by the Mormon church, which has divided the fertile areas into small ranches to be purchased by its homesteaders. The valley is walled in by bleak and denuded ranges with clearly marked strata, so tipped and faulted that some of the hills look as if they have been pushed over and now rest on their haunches. The color is striking. There are many warm springs in the valley and even in Indian days this was a popular year-round campsite where the natives produced melons, among other foodstuffs.

ALAMO, 189 m. (4,600 alt., 150 pop.), an old Mormon settlement, is a prosperous community in the valley. The cottonwoods for which it was named, and the tall poplars, make it a shady oasis during the summer heat. As usual in tiny Nevada communities, the school stands out above the scattered houses. The big yellow busses before the door during the winter week days are indication of how large an area the schoolhouse serves. Nothing is more surprising to easterners than a visit to one of the remote Nevada schools. The high standard of education is apparent after only a brief conversation with the staff. No colloquialisms are heard and the lack of provincialism in interest is notable.

The highway skirts shallow Pahranagat and Maynard Lakes, where ducks, geese, and snipe are plentiful and draw sportsmen from considerable distances.

Passing COYOTE SPRINGS (L), 209 *m.,* US 93 crosses low hills where the flora is chiefly cactus and mesquite. During springs when the plants are in full bloom this section is very beautiful. For countless miles yellow flowers cover the lowlands, with brilliant red cactus blooms standing out conspicuously above the rest.

The rocky color-splashed flanks of the Sheep Range are westward, then the majestic Arrow Canyon Mountains, the sides of which have been deeply eroded. The Arrow Canyon Range, in which slender peaks alternate with flat-topped mesas, is one of the most rugged of the State. As the highway crosses a deeply eroded desert the Mormon Range is eastward across Muddy River Valley. The country through here looks as if an imprisoned cyclone had spent a century of frantic effort trying to get out of the mountains. The Moapa Indian Reservation is visible (R) below sandstone peaks.

At 247 *m.* is the junction with a graveled road.

Right on this road to the MOAPA VALLEY INDIAN AGENCY, 1.5 *m.,* center of ranches where some 250 Paiute force a scanty living from the soil, aided by Federal grants. Here in the shade of numerous cottonwoods on the banks of Muddy River are their cabins. Old Indian women are occasionally seen squatting on the ground before doors, weaving baskets of reeds and grasses. Garbed in bright-colored clothes and usually barefoot, the women dry pumpkin seeds and deer meat in the fall for winter food. The younger men work in the fields on the small individual acreages.

MOAPA (R), 248 *m.* (1,700 alt., 200 pop.), is a Union Pacific station in a region where several gypsum plants operate. Until automobile trucking began, this place, now little but a water tank, freight station, small store, and small school, was a distributing and shipping point where dozens of mule teams were seen at all times. The little cafe is the sole survivor of several that did large businesses.

GLENDALE, 253 *m.* (4,453 alt., 27 pop.), is at the junction with US 91 (*see Tour 3a*). Between Glendale and Las Vegas US 93 is united with US 91 (*see Tour 3a*).

Tour 3

(St. George, Utah)—Glendale—Las Vegas—(Baker, California); US 91.
Arizona Line to California Line, 128.3 *m.*

Paved roadbed throughout.

Union Pacific Ry. parallels route between a point just west of Glendale and the California Line.

Accommodations limited except in Las Vegas.

It is well to carry drinking water in case of motor trouble, particularly if leaving main route though as a general rule water can be obtained along the main highway at about 20-mile intervals.

US 91 crosses the extreme southern tip of Nevada, where some ranching areas are hidden behind starkly eroded foot hills, and beyond stretches of rolling desert. Weird, beautiful formations of the kind characteristic of the Grand Canyon country are seen throughout. The highway follows the Virgin River for ten miles, crosses Muddy River just west of Glendale, and continues through awe-inspiring terrain. High, rugged mountains are visible on both sides above a valley floor with vegetation including cacti, joshua trees, and Spanish bayonet. US 91 roughly follows the old Spanish Trail, which in this section became part of the Mormon Road to Southern California.

Section a. UTAH LINE to LAS VEGAS, 85.5 m.

US 91 crosses the ARIZONA LINE, 0 m., at a point 46 miles southwest of St. George, Utah.

MESQUITE, 1.7 m. (1,700 alt., 512 pop.), is a trade center of a ranching country settled by Mormons in 1880 on the bank of the Virgin River. It was abandoned a few years later, but resettled by Mormons in 1895.

On the opposite side of the Virgin River is BUNKERVILLE, 7 m. (2,500 alt., 287 pop.), one of the oldest community centers of ranchers producing vegetables, melons, and grapes. It has been subject to occasional river floods and in the summer of 1936 was struck by a cloudburst that caused considerable damage. The grapevines are off-shoots of stock from France and Spain.

At Bunkerville, as in many other Mormon colonies in the early days, the community operated under the United Order, wherein every person contributed according to his capacity, shared according to his needs, and participated in mutual ownership and management of all community properties. This form of economic organization was adopted so that the struggling colony could bring irrigation waters from the river to the high bench.

Southwest of RIVERSIDE, 11.5 m. (2,250 alt.), which is merely a gas station, the road continues along the high benchland of Virgin Valley to a junction with paved Nev. 12, at 36 m.

Left on Nev. 12, through the lower Moapa Valley, from which come turkeys, cantaloupe, watermelons, and vegetables. This valley was the center of the tax controversy that led to a Mormon exodus in 1871.

The early settlers in this region had paid their taxes in kind—in cotton, grain, livestock, and so on—to Arizona. But after a Federal survey in 1869 these lands were allocated to Nevada and Lincoln County demanded the back taxes and insisted that they be paid in gold. As a result Brigham Young ordered all the colonists home to Utah though they had already spent considerable money and effort on irrigation systems and homes. For many years thereafter the land the colonists had cleared remained idle; later many of the original settlers returned and bought the land back from the State.

The exodus and the demonetization of silver in 1873 left Lincoln County, then one of the largest counties in the West, in dire financial trouble.

OVERTON, 12 m. (1,360 alt., 603 pop.), another old Mormon settlement is the valley's community center. Formerly it was part of the Patterson Ranch, which was purchased by a Utah woman when the settlers returned in 1881. The early Mormon communities of the valley were such models of thrift and industry that more than one traveler, Frederick Dellenbaugh, wrote: "As pioneers the Mormons were superior to any class I have ever come in contact with, their idea being homemaking and not skimming the cream off the country with a six-shooter and a whiskey bottle." Because of the valley's isolation the pioneer family names are in a majority here. With the fall in agricultural prices many of the little ranches have been saved only through Farm Security loans.

The OVERTON MUSEUM (R), 13 m., erected by the C.C.C. and under control of the National Park Service, is of adobe. It houses relics found in the ruins of Lost City, an ancient Indian village now covered by Mead Lake (*see First Nevadans*). Lost City, about 5 miles south of Overton, is sometimes called Pueblo Grande de Nevada; it belonged to the third Pueblo period. Among the artifacts and other relics is a skeleton, preserved as when it was found. By the museum is a reconstruction of a kiva and ceremonial place of the kind indicated by the remains of Lost City.

Nev. 12 curves eastward above the canyon of the Muddy River, which is now an arm of Lake Mead, to the junction with the unpaved Valley of Fire road (R), 15 m. (*Though this approach from a paved road is shorter, the approach from Crystal—see ahead—is much more spectacular.*)

Nev. 12 continues down to the shore of LAKE MEAD, 19 m., where recreational facilities are being developed. Near this point was the Mormon village of St. Thomas, which has been inundated. While creation of the lake covered some of the fertile land on which the Moapa Valley people depended, the loss will be far more than compensated by the growing tourist business.

Slightly southwest of GLENDALE, 37 m. (4,453 alt.), chiefly a large service station on US 91, is the junction with US 93 (*see Tour 2b*), which unites with US 91 between this point and Las Vegas.

US 91-93 crosses the Muddy River and then rolling country that would be bleak were it not for many-colored strata. When these are bathed in a misty purple light late in the afternoon they have the awe-inspiring grandeur of all Colorado Basin formations. The rock, highly eroded, has been so sharply tilted in many places that formerly horizontal strata are now vertical.

CRYSTAL, 52.5 m., is merely a name on the map at the junction with the unpaved Valley of Fire Road.

Left on this gently wandering route, which gradually climbs through greasewood to a low ridge at 16 m., where a casually home-made sign indicates that the edge of the VALLEY OF FIRE STATE PARK has been reached. The road curves (R) to swing around the shallow head of a canyon whose coloring resembles the deep rose in the heart of a large sea-shell. Travelers at this point give conventional murmurs of praise, mingled with slight disappointment. The road again curves (L) and begins its descent between walls that rapidly become higher and redder. Far ahead for a moment appears a deep-blue strip of Lake Mead. The road continues its leisurely way. At 20 m., where the canyon is widest and makes a sharp turn (R), is a campsite and shelter of stone. It does not seem possible that any place could be surrounded by more vivid color. Yet as the road winds ahead the red of the walls increases in intensity and even the ground assumes the same intense hue. A final twist and an ascent begins. Here great masses of rock are piled into fantastic figures; the walls have been eroded into pillars, elephants, camels. At one point the road swerves to avoid a gigantic stone false-face leering diabolically. In this section the vegetation along the roadside is a bright blue-green dusted with white and caves and windows have been sandblasted into the fiery walls. The climax of color and eerie formations is reached in a very narrow pass, 24 *m.*, high above the northern arm of Lake Mead. In this valley of flame, which more than earns its name when the sun is low, are petroglyphs carved by long forgotten people, and also the petrified remains of ancient forest trees.

The road descends rapidly from the pass on a rocky slope that gives little hint of the flaming pocket southward. At 25 *m.* is the junction with Nev. 12 (*see before*), at a point 3 miles east of Overton.

Southwest of Crystal US 91-93 crosses rocky desert sparsely covered with greasewood, cactus, and an occasional yucca. Passing a dry lake bed (R), it skirts a spur of the Las Vegas Range to reach the long, straight, comparatively level stretch with Las Vegas a toy city in the distance.

At 75.4 *m.* is the junction with a dirt road.

Left here (*carry water and candles if exploring cave; guide advisable*) to GYPSUM CAVE, 7.6 *m.,* which was discovered by early settlers. Unaware of deposits here of great scientific importance the chief interest of early visitors was in the gypsum deposits, which were later exploited to some extent under a mineral claim. Only in very recent years was it discovered that deep in the cave, which extends inward about 300 feet and has six rooms, were layer after layer of excrement of the prehistoric giant sloth covering and preserving the bones of the early sloth and other prehistoric animals, and, far more important, evidence that man was one of the sloth's contemporaries. Stone points that capped primitive javelins, fragments of charcoal, and painted dart shafts were found (*see Early Nevadans and Plants and Animals*). Inside the entrance, which is 70 feet wide but only 15 feet high, the ground slopes sharply downward 50 feet to the first room.

At 78.5 *m.* on US 91-93 is the junction with an improved road.

Left here sharply to the LAS VEGAS AIRPORT, 1 *m.,* where the bleached skulls of cattle have been used to border the field.

In LAS VEGAS, 85.5 *m.* (2,033 alt., 10,000 pop.), are junctions with US 95 (*see Tour 5c*) and US 466-93 (*see Tour 5A*).

Railroad Station: W. end of Fremont St., for Union Pacific Co.

Bus Stations: Burlington Lines, Las Vegas-Needles Lines, Central Bus Station, 9 Fremont St.; Union Pacific Bus Depot, 2 Fremont St.; Las Vegas-Tonopah-Reno Stage Line, Overland Hotel.

Airport: Municipal, 8 m. N. E. (*see before*) for Western Air Express & T. W. A.

Accommodations: Hotels, boarding houses, inns, auto courts, and trailer campgrounds.

Tourist Information Service: Chamber of Commerce, 113 South Third St.

Motion Picture Houses: Two.

Golf: 9-hole sand course at Country Club, S. Main St. (US 91), and a 9-hole grass course 3.2 mi. N. W. of US 95.

Swimming: Lorenzi's Pool, 2 m. NW of city; Mermaid Pool, 113 N. Fifth St.

LAS VEGAS—The Meadows of Mexico travelers on the old trail between Santa Fe and Southern California—is seat of Clark County and distributing center for a very large but thinly populated mining and ranching country. It is also developing into one of the chief travel and recreation centers of the Southwest. In part this new role is a matter of accident, the result of a key position in an area with widely varying natural attractions plus the man-made wonder, Boulder Dam. A sound and far-sighted public policy, however, has taken advantage of national interest in the dam to make the city and the area around it attractive enough to bring visitors back repeatedly. Attractive public buildings and houses are under construction all over town, the rows of catalpas and of poplars planted during the early days of the town, are being protected and lengthened. Relatively little emphasis is placed on the gambling clubs and divorce facilities—though they are attractions to many visitors—and much effort is being made to build up cultural attractions. No cheap and easily parodied slogans have been adopted to publicize the city, no attempt has been made to introduce pseudo-romantic architectural themes, or to give artificial glamor and gaiety. Las Vegas is itself—natural and therefore very appealing to people with a very wide variety of interests.

All the world meets on the broad sunny streets—eastern businessmen interested in studying the amazing powerhouse 20 miles away on the river, and in playing a bit of roulette in the evenings, health-seekers basking in the brilliant sunshine, an occasional Paiute woman with baby cradled on her back, toothless prospectors in town for a new grubstake, cowboys rolling along in elaborate high-heeled boots, ranchers and their wives buying supplies and seeing the movies, young people rushing down to Lake Mead to swim or up to camp to ski in the Charleston Mountains, men and women of any age on their way to the stables for horses, local men and women going to rehearsals of the little theater group.

The townsite covers 12 square miles on a plain with distant mountains in view on every side—the many colored Charleston Range particularly conspicuous on the west. Within the city, whose business center is close to a new and very modern Union Pacific station at the head of Fremont Street, are Old Town—West Las Vegas—where many of the simpler houses stand; North Las Vegas, a suburb where large houses have been built; and an inner residential district with many modern homes. Beyond this fringe, on all sides, is the desert.

The town is particularly lively at night. Neon lights call attention to the bars, gambling and night clubs, in which Hollywood celebrities, miners, prospectors, divorcees, corporation presidents, cowboys, and little old maids bent on seeing life at last, add to the stacks of silver dollars and watch the whirl of roulette wheels, or splash ink over the horse keno slips. Some restaurants are crowded till dawn.

An annual event, Heldorado, staged in the spring, celebrates the Old West, with four days of whiskers, bustles, hoops and boisterous fun. The women wear the long full skirts, basques, and bonnets of frontier days; and the men, half lost in beards, flaunt jeans, boots, gay shirts, and huge hats. Parades, a rodeo, street dances, and other events intended to recreate the early spirit turn Las Vegas into a rollicking hybrid of two vastly different eras.

The natural meadows and the springs on the Old Spanish Trail, which curved north from Sante Fe and west around the Colorado River to Southern California, were known soon after 1776, when the Escalante party made the first attempt to establish a trail between Sante Fe, New Mexico, and the missions in California, to promote trade in donkeys and mules. Although this expedition advanced no farther than the valleys of central Utah and apparently returned to Sante Fe without traversing the Las Vegas area, others later extended the route they had started to explore. By 1830 caravans of traders were using the trail regularly and the big springs and meadows of the Las Vegas valley were a welcome camping place on this circuitous desert route. Whether the old mine workings found in the area south of Las Vegas (particularly Eldorado Canyon) belong to the Spanish or Mexican periods is unknown. Possibly they predate the Escalante expedition.

Captain John C. Fremont in reporting his visit here in 1844 wrote of "a camping ground called Las Vegas. . . . Two narrow streams of water, four or five feet deep, gush suddenly, with a quick current, from two singularly large springs . . . the taste of the water is good but rather too warm to be agreeable."

Jefferson Hunt, sent late in 1847 from Salt Lake by the Church of the Latter Day Saints to obtain seed and foodstuffs in California, camped at this spot and reported favorably on it when he returned. Soon the springs were a stopping-place for people traveling from Salt Lake City to California by the southern route. The springs today are in a basin from 20 to 30 feet in diameter; the powerful upward rush of water flowing from them makes a stream from 6 to 8 feet in width. They are slightly northwest of the city and a resort has been established near by. The first American occupation of Las Vegas came in 1855, when William Bringhurst of the City of Great Salt Lake, arrived with a band of 30 young men detailed by Brigham Young, "to go to Las Vegas, build a fort there to protect immigrants and the United States mail from the Indians, and to teach the latter how to raise corn, wheat, potatoes, squash, and melons."

The settlers cleared the mesquite away; built an adobe stockade 14 feet high and 150 feet long; hauled logs from the Charleston Mountains to the west; built cabins, fences, a dam and bridges; and planted crops. The enclosure was referred to as The Fort. Some of the orchards and vineyards started then, still bear. On January 10, 1856, a post office was opened and named Bringhurst for the president of the mission.

Families followed the men and a school was built inside The Fort. Meetings were also held in this building. The Mormon gospel was preached with typical zeal, and it is related that "many Indians were converted and baptized."

The history of Las Vegas Mission records one of the few instances in which mining was practiced by Mormon pioneers. When the existence of extensive lead deposits in a district some 18 miles southwest of the little colony was reported to Brigham Young, he at once dispatched Nathaniel V. Jones to the area, investing Jones with authority to call the settlers and missionaries to his aid in "mining and manufacturing" lead. The first ore was smelted in December, 1856, and 9,000 pounds were run off, but the metal was found to be "very hard to smelt," as Jones reported. He also said that attempts to cast the metal in bullet molds had given poor results.

On January 28, 1857, the mines were abandoned, though it was not until 1861 that the reason for the poor luck in bullet-making was brought to light. In that year miners more familiar with their business discovered that the "lead" of the Mormons was a galena ore carrying silver.

But it was not this bullet-making fiasco alone that brought an end to the Las Vegas colony. Despite conscientious attempts to teach the Indians the rudiments of agriculture and the presentation of generous gifts, the Paiutes could never quite overcome their natural habit of helping themselves to whatever unguarded livestock, provisions, or crops they saw. The venture simply was not profitable; and with trouble from the Federal government reaching a peak, Young called for a concentration of Mormons near the Great Salt Lake. On February 23, 1857, the settlers were "released" from the mission. To those few who remained to harvest the crop a final blow came when the "remnants of Israel," as the Indians were called, descended and carried away the entire crop.

Though Las Vegas was entirely abandoned, the cabins and the stockades the Mormons built remained. Carriers of the overland mail were glad to break their trips at the protected spot near Vegas Springs.

Following the Mormon abdication, O. D. Gass acquired the land and water rights. During the Civil War, three companies of cavalry and one company of infantry were stationed by the spring for the protection of the travel route to southern California and the post was called Fort Baker. Mining began in the surrounding regions and Eldorado Canyon was an important gold and silver producer.

About the time Gass acquired the ranch—and until 1869—it was in the Territory of Arizona and Gass sat in the legislature of that territory. He operated the ranch with Indian labor. One day a recalcitrant native was killed and Gass hastily fled with his family to Barstow. When post riders and other travelers brought no reports of an uprising or of signs of devastation, Gass made a hesitant reconnaissance. Approaching the old stockade he was amazed to find water running in the irrigation ditches and his place as well cared for as if he had never left it. Looking cautiously around he discovered Qua-ech, a wily old Indian who had long lingered about but never done any work; the Paiute was sitting on top of a hay-mow directing operations in his favorite costume—a bright red blanket and a high top hat some miners had given to him. Inclining his head gravely he gave the long-absent owner a full account of affairs on the estate, acting as though he had been the duly appointed superintendent. Gass' mystification apparently showed in his face because after the report had been given, Qua-ech, with twinkling eye, said abruptly, "Why you no ask squaw how much for brave?" It had not occurred to Gass that his dilemma might be settled in this simple manner. The squaw felt her strong position and bargained long but the affair was eventually settled. The price of peace for Las Vegas was $18.

In 1882 the ranch and water rights were acquired by Archibald Stewart, a forty-niner who had made his stake in Angel's Camp and later established a cattle ranch about 100 miles north of Las Vegas. Stewart's wife was induced to come to Las Vegas with her small children on what was to have been a visit lasting a single season, but this became the home of the delicately bred young woman until her death in 1929. Three other children were born in the following years, two of them in her mother's home in California. For many years neighbors were far away and the children had to be taught at home; eventually they were sent to school in California. Under such conditions social life developed along unusual lines; a single dance meant a party lasting nearly a week. News and mail came in by pony rider. Chief diversions of the flock of children were horseback riding and hunting. Stewart was killed during a quarrel by the owner of the Kyle Ranch—now the Taylor Ranch. When word was brought to Mrs. Stewart that her husband was dead she immediately set off on horseback to bring back his body. Lacking wood, she had to take the doors of her house to make a coffin. Later Mrs. Stewart married again; but in the meantime she had increased her holdings and ranching activities.

In 1903 when the San Pedro, Los Angeles and Salt Lake Railroad was projected, the ranch was bought for a townsite and division point by W. A. Clark, former senator from Montana, acting for the company. Before the railroad's townsite was opened another townsite beside it—now Old Town—was acquired by J. T. McWilliams. People flooded in, in part because of the boom in the newly discovered Bullfrog and Greenwater Districts. Known as McWilliamstown then, the camp was prosperous and busy by reason of the immense freighting business to the mines.

On May 15, 1905, Las Vegas was really born. Around a platform erected under a spreading mesquite tree near the present freight depot, nearly 3,000 people gathered to hear C. O. Wittemore, representing the railroad company, explain guarantees of future development contained in the bills of sales for lots. These included a water system that would place water under pressure on every lot, the improvement of all the streets, the building of a handsome depot and other railroad structures, and, finally the erection of railroad shops to employ several hundred men. The sale of lots lasted two days, and during that time 1,200 were sold at a total price of $265,000. The promises of the company were taken seriously—and they were all fulfilled.

On the morning of the 17th, tents and lumber and other building materials were being enthusiastically hauled to the site. Because the streets had not yet been cleared, eager men and women had to search among the greasewood for the stakes marking their lot corners. Before darkness came the town had appeared—a grotesque assortment of buildings in all possible stages of completion. In tents were a post office, saloons, and gambling houses, as well as hotels and a bank. The hotel was a huge canvas structure 140 feet long, with large additions for dining room and kitchen. Until the following winter this great ungainly tent was the center of all social activities.

But within 30 days Las Vegas was more than a tent town. Stores and houses were taking shape everywhere. During the summer, the Las Vegas Land and Water Company, a subsidiary of the railroad company, graded and oiled 10 miles of city streets, built concrete or wooden curbs throughout the town, and brought water to every lot.

With the completion of the railroad from Salt Lake in June, 1905, and the construction of the Las Vegas & Tonopah Railroad in 1906, Las Vegas rode into commercial and political importance. In 1908 more substantial buildings were erected; and to protect them a volunteer fire department was organized. In 1909 the town became the seat of the newly organized Clark County.

In January, 1910, however, a phenomenal rainstorm wrecked 110 miles of railroad track in the Muddy Valley Wash south of Caliente (*see Tour 2b*), and more than five months elapsed before train service was resumed. Las Vegas was largely deserted and hard times ensued. In October of the same year fire of incendiary origin destroyed the school.

But the town revived; in 1911 the legislature passed a bill creating the City of Las Vegas. In 1925, after the water from Las Vegas Springs was found to be inadequate for city needs, an artesian well was sunk that brought up three and a half million gallons every 24 hours. In 1937, after the Boulder Dam construction boom, the city, looking forward to continued growth, sank another, which produced a larger flow than the first. During dam construction days the town was the scene of much shipping and had a greatly augmented population. Few people, however, then realized the possibilities of the city as a resort center. When realization came the residents extended their activities to development of the region as well as the city, sure that whatever brought business to Clark County would benefit its railroad center and county seat.

POINTS OF INTEREST

1. The UNION PACIFIC STATION, completed in 1940, stands in a shaded park squarely across the head of Fremont Street. Its long horizontal planes and great windows make it a satisfying example of the modern International design.

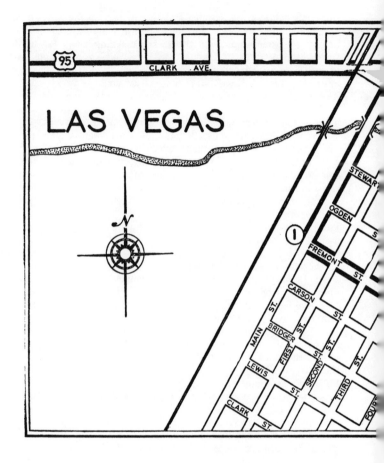

POINTS OF INTEREST IN LAS VEGAS

1. Union Pacific Station
2. Chamber of Commerce

3. Federal Building.
4. War Memorial Building.
5. Las Vegas Racetrack and Ball Park
6. Heldorado Park
7. Stewart Ranchhouse

2. The CHAMBER OF COMMERCE (*open weekdays* 9-5), 113 S. 3rd St., is a one-story stuccoed structure housing a tourist bureau, a small collection of frontier relics, and the Rockwell collection of arrowheads. During rush seasons the bureau is sometimes open far into the night to assist visitors in finding places in hotels and auto courts. The policy and practice of this Chamber of Commerce are worth study by those interested in publicity techniques.

The LAS VEGAS CITY PARK, an area bisected by cross-streets and lying between 2nd and 5th, Stewart and Linden Sts., is being developed as a civic center.

3. The FEDERAL BUILDING, in the park on Stewart St., between 2nd and 5th, is of the standard Government design. Above a first story faced with limestone is a second story of brick accented by limestone pilasters with Ionic caps. A balustraded parapet crowns the eaves. This structure houses the post office and Federal court.

4. The WAR MEMORIAL BUILDING, also in the park, on Stewart St., between 4th and 5th, is a huge brick building striking in its simplicity. The central third of the facade is stepped forward and further accented by four very narrow vertical piers. The tiers of windows on the other thirds are recessed and separated by shallower piers. The only ornament at the roofline is provided by a slight rise in the central third and its piers. The interior is equally simple. The ends of the foyer are occupied by offices and stairways and over the foyer are rooms rented to the American Legion. In the large auditorium, which has a hardwood floor, are movable seats, as the hall is used for dances and prizefights as well as for lectures, concerts, and the performances of the competent little theater group. The stage, one of the largest in the Southwest, has full equipment for professional productions and also elaborate lighting devices. The construction was done entirely with WPA labor.

5. The LAS VEGAS RACETRACK AND BALL PARK, on 5th St., between Stewart and Linden, is used for rodeos, baseball, races of various kinds, and for the popular softball, which is played in the evening under flood lighting. The grandstand seats 700 and bleachers hold twice as many.

6. HELDORADO PARK, on 5th St., opposite the sports park, is a stockaded area controlled by the Elks. This is the center of the annual celebration. The fraternal organization has been making a collection of old vehicles and other relics for use in the parades. These are kept in the park and the plan is to make them the nucleus of a museum. In addition to stagecoaches, oxcarts, early automobiles, ore carts, and the like, is a much prized relic, a one-room iron jail.

7. By 5th St., on the bank of Las Vegas Creek, a short distance north of Heldorado Park, are the remnants of the Mormon stockade about the STEWART RANCHHOUSE. Very tall old cottonwoods shade these relics of early Las Vegas, which have seen Mormon missionaries, Union troops, stage drivers, untamed Paiutes, horseback mail-carriers,

Photograph by H. B. Lukey   **ELKO BEEF**

Photograph courtesy Shell Oil Company   **SHEEP**

Rothstein: Farm Security Admin.

SHEEPHERDER PACKING TO LEAVE SIERRA CAMP

The ewe is following her
new-born twins from the
lambing field.

LAMBING TIME

BUCKAROO

Rothstein: Farm Security Admin.

THE REMUDA

ON PYRAMID LAKE RESERVATION

A PRIZE 4-H CALF

FALLON TURKEYS
Photographs courtesy Extension Service, Dept. of Agri.

Photograph courtesy Office of Indian Affairs   **WASHOE INDIANS BALING HAY**

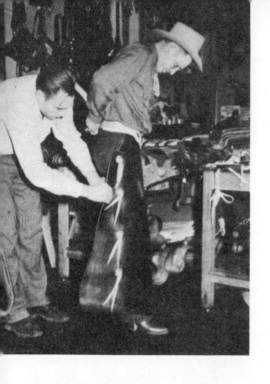

BUYING CHAPS FOR
USE ON RANGE

A CRITICAL CUSTOMER

Rothstein: Farm Security Admin.

pioneer homesteaders, and construction workers on Boulder Dam—one of the mightiest works ever undertaken by man. By the gate is a memorial plaque erected by Desert Holly Camp of the Daughters of Utah Pioneers.

Section b. LAS VEGAS *to* CALIFORNIA LINE, 42.8 *m.*

South of LAS VEGAS, 0 *m.*, US 91 continues over rolling desert studded with creosote bush and cactus.

At 11.5 *m.* is the junction with a dirt road.

Right on this road and across the Spring Mountain Range, at 23 *m.*, to the fertile Pahrump Valley, a stock-raising area bordered by mining districts. In the heart of the valley is MANSE, once part of the ranch holdings of Eugene Cazerung, a land baron who was shot and killed in a quarrel with his Mexican ranch foreman. This valley was early settled by a man named Younts, who brought horses south with a partner. They were attacked by Indians on the Amargosa Desert and lost most of their livestock but decided to settle anyway.

SLOAN, 19.5 *m.*, a way station, is below Black Mountain (5,042 alt.), which rises at the northern end of the McCullough Range.

Right from Sloan to the BLUE DIAMOND, 3 *m.*, a large deposit of limestone worked throughout the year.

The country now traversed by US 91, dotted with low hills and dry lake beds, has long seen mining activity. In spite of its barrenness it has great beauty when its colors are heightened under the burning red clouds at sunset or in the tranquil blue light of the early hours. Far north is snow-capped Charleston Peak, towering above La Madre Mountain.

JEAN, 30.2 *m.* (2,865 alt., 50 pop.), a railroad station on the Union Pacific, has an emergency landing field.

Right from Jean on paved Nev. 53 to GOODSPRINGS, 7 *m.*, an old mining district at the eastern base of the Spring Mountain Range. The camp is a producer of gold, silver, platinum, and vanadium. Many motion pictures have been filmed in the vicinity because within a radius of a few miles is practically every type of scenery needed for typical "westerns"—mountains, rolling desert, dried water holes, and primitive mining activities.

The region is sparsely covered with cactus and joshua trees. Also here is a rare member of the catalpa family whose appearance is that of a willow except in early summer when it is covered with a fluttering mass of pink and white flowers resembling those of the snapdragon. East of Goodsprings, Nev. 53 crosses the Spring Mountain Range to the California Line, 22 *m.*, at a point 25 miles north of Valley Wells.

Continuing its gradual ascent from Jean, US 91 skirts a dry lake bed and crosses rolling country in the shadow of Devil Peak (5,865 alt.), a mountain that was a landmark for early travelers. At its base five men on their way to Las Vegas from San Bernardino disagreed over the division of some ore they had gathered. In a gun fight all were killed outright or received wounds from which they died. When their bodies were found several days later, their gold and silver ore, said to have assayed $1,000 to the ton, was piled around them. Even today "desert rats" of southern Nevada from time to time try to find the source of that rich ore.

US 91 crosses the CALIFORNIA LINE, 42.8 *m.,* at a point .50 miles northeast of Baker, California.

▟▟▟

Tour 4

(Susanville, Calif.) — Reno—Carson City—Minden—Gardnerville—
(Mono Lake, Calif.); US 395.
California Line to California Line, 84.4 m.

Paved roadbed; no difficult grades.
A branch of the W. P. R. R. parallels route north of Reno, and the V. & T. R. R. between Reno and Minden.
Accommodations in Reno, Carson City, Minden and Gardnerville.

US 395 makes an 84-mile loop through Nevada along the foothills of the Sierra. Throughout its course in Nevada it runs between high ranges, crossing the fertile Truckee and Carson Valleys, climbing to low passes, and running through canyons. It traverses the country that was the heart of early Nevada, the country of its first wild mining booms and its first permanent settlements. For miles the route is lined in the spring with the beautiful pale pink blossoms of Nevada wild peach.

US 395 crosses the NEVADA LINE, 0 *m.,* at a point 70 miles southeast of Susanville, California. Between the State Line and Reno US 395 loosely follows a route to California established by James Beckwourth, the mulatto trapper and scout; it was known as the Beckwourth Road. This route crosses Beckwourth Pass (Chilcoot) into Sierra Valley, where a trading station was established in 1852.

Close to the California Line US 395 skirts Dry Lake (L), a catch basin for the spring run-off from Peavine Mountains (R). In late summer, when the lake is dry, the hard baked surface is used as a speedway for try-outs of new motorcycles and automobiles. Running northward is Dry Lake Valley, a grazing area.

The HEINZ RANCH, 2.3 *m.,* is one of the oldest in this part of the State. As the highway climbs out of Dry Lake Valley, Rattlesnake Hill, a red butte, is visible to the rear. On it is a former Indian burial ground where artifacts are still discovered. In 1867, when a small band of Pitt River (California) Indians had been raiding the cattle of Long Valley ranchers, Pyramid Lake Paiute received the blame for the depredations. Matters became so complicated that the old chief decided to vindicate his people and took to the war trail. Aided by a dozen whites his warriors finally surrounded the Pitts and exterminated all but one. Rattlesnake Hill is considered the site of this inter-tribal battle.

The COPPERFIELD MINE (L), 3 *m.*, is now inactive.

US 395 crosses PEAVINE SUMMIT, 4.2 *m.*, a low pass between Granite Mountain and Peavine, then drops to Black Spring Valley. The old BLACK SPRING PLACE, 8 *m.*, a tumbled-down shack that was moved to its present site from the Black Spring, a mile south. The Black Spring was named for John Black, who operated the station on the Beckwourth Road, and who with John Poe, a cousin of Edgar Allen Poe, and others established Poeville, a mining camp now deserted in one of the rugged canyons on the east side of Peavine.

The highway climbs gradually out of Black Spring Valley to a divide that offers a broad vista of Truckee Valley and Reno. The approach to Reno is foretold by signs along the road, advertising "Love Blessed" wedding rings, and the Dog House, a "haven for divorcees"—also "Harold's, the place to rattle your bones and win some dough." All highways approaching Reno are lined with signs announcing wedding rings designed to insure wedded happiness, retreats for the brokenhearted, and gay night spots for those whose disillusionment is more devil-may care.

RENO, 16 *m.* (4,491 alt., 21,500 pop.), (*see Tour 1d*), is at the junction with US 40 (*see Tour 1*).

US 395 goes south through the fertile Truckee Valley with signs on both sides of the road advertising "Guest Ranches" for divorce-seekers who prefer the moonlight and tree toads and the smell of the countryside to the gay night spots of The Biggest Little City in the World. The impressive Sierra range (R) is still wooded on its higher flanks. On the valley floors are green fields, chicken ranches, grainfields, and produce gardens. Great poplars surround modern ranch houses as well as those that bear the unmistakable architectural stamp of earlier days.

At 25.4 *m.* is the junction with Nev. 17, the Geiger Grade (*see Tour 8*).

From the junction clouds of steam are seen southward in the depression below the highway and on a low plateau (R). At one point (L) close to the junction hot water is bubbling up a few yards from the road. At present these hot springs, which have high mineral content, do not erupt more than a few inches and some merely ripple the surface of the pool, but about 1928 the water was thrown several feet in the air at intervals and there have been other periods when spouting was violent. The reason for the variations is unknown though it has been noticed that the pressure is much greater when earthquakes are prevalent in California. These springs are considered among the geological wonders of the world because here it is possible to study the formation of precious mineral deposits in rock. On both sides of the road are small resorts offering swimming in warm water pools.

At 26.1 *m.* is the junction with Nev. 27, the Mount Rose Road.

Right on this paved route, which enters a division of the Nevada National Forest (*campsites, trails*) and rises 4,000 feet in about 20 miles, though this is not particularly noticeable. Broad, magnificent vistas are revealed on every curve—far across the lowland meadows, over the Virginia Range, to ranges with glistening peaks. The road offers a route to the Ski Club and is often crowded on winter week-ends, particularly during the sport programs.

GALENA, 7 *m.*, at the foot of the skiing area, has shelters and a variety of runs. It also has a very fine summer picnicking spot in GALENA COUNTY PARK.

At 14 *m.* is the MOUNT ROSE SUMMIT (8,933 alt.) between (R) Mount Rose and Slide Mountain. GRASS VALLEY (R), an alpine meadow with a small lake, below the top of Mount Rose has particularly wide variety in its slides, which are 5 feet to one mile wide and from 5 to 17 miles long. There is one jump of 125 feet and a ski lift.

At 23 *m.* is the junction with Nev. 26; R. here 5 *m.* along the shore of Lake Tahoe to the California Line, where the route around the lake shore becomes Calif. 39 and leads in 11 miles to Tahoe City, a lake resort.

At the junction Nev. 28 southward becomes the main side route; here along the shore of LAKE TAHOE (6,225 alt.), one of the most popular resort areas in the region. The lake, 21 miles long and 12 miles across at its widest point, has a delightfully irregular rocky shoreline that is thickly forested with evergreens. With the peaks of the high Sierras in view above the trees, the lake is a brilliant green-blue, owing to its great depth—1,776 feet at one point. In spite of the number of resorts and private homes on its shores, the forest gives it an unspoiled look.

First recorded knowledge of the lake is in the report of Fremont's expeditions. When he was encamped at Pyramid Lake near the mouth of the Truckee River in 1844, Indians "made a drawing of the Truckee River, which they represented as issuing from another lake in the mountains three or four days distant, in a direction a little west of south; beyond which they drew a mountain, and farther still two rivers, on one side of which, the Indians said, people like ourselves traveled." Fremont then crossed the Sierras over Carson Pass and saw Lake Tahoe, of which he wrote—"We had a beautiful view of a mountain lake about 15 *m.* in length." It was not named in his report but later on his map of 1845 it was called Mountain Lake. Writing from Prescott, Arizona, in 1881, Fremont said that he gave it the name of Bonpland for the French scientist and explorer, Aime-Jacques Alexander Bonpland, and on a strip map covering his explorations that name appears. The California legislature named it Lake Bigler in 1853, for John Bigler, the State Governor. Popularly it was known as Tahoe from 1863. Neither Bonpland nor Bigler ever came into general use, nor did Tula Tulia, a name proposed in 1861. Nevada did recognize the name Bigler by inference in a legislative act of December 19, 1862, but William Henry Knight, in charge of the first general mapping of the Pacific Coast, later said that when his map was ready for the engraver in 1862, he instructed that the name be omitted. John S. Hittell, historian and editor, and Dr. Henry De Groot, journalist and publicist, who had compiled a list of Washoe words, were called into conference and De Groot produced the word "Tahoe", which was immediately approved. On Knight's advice, the U. S. Land Office approved this name.

This lake basin was formed long after the disturbances that lifted the granite core of the Sierras to their present height. It is probable the lake was created by repeated slipping of large masses of earth along a fault, which uplifted the surrounding rocks, and also by volcanic action, still evident in dormant MOUNT PLUTO, at the northwestern end. Today the huge bowl is practically closed in by mountains planed down and softened by erosion.

Formerly the Indians assembled each spring along the northern end because the water abounded with trout and because they were fond of water sports. Opposite their camping grounds is a big cavern; at certain times of the year, according to their tradition, the rock sent forth a hoarse and awful voice. They called this grotto the Spirit Lodge. Anciently, their legends say, the lake was a part of the great river Tro-ko-nene, which emptied its water into the sea. In those years, the country roundabout was more level, and covered with trees and vines that bore fruit. Then came the time when the mountains were lifted and the mighty river was swallowed; and since then the country has become barren, and the smaller Truckee River, denied egress to the sea, has had to cut a gorge and find its way to Lake Pyramid.

Tahoe is a lake of many moods. When untroubled, it lies under a full sun like an enormous pavement of colors, with long slender paths of silver across the broad belts of green and blue. In early morning it is so soft and shimmering that it looks unreal; and under a low western sun burning in cloudbands, it is a mighty plateau streaked with gold.

The water has extraordinary transparency. On a sunny day objects 65 feet down are sharp and distinct. At more than 200 feet white objects are clearly visible, and in winter some objects can be seen at even greater depth.

There are numerous camping spots and trails in this area. Among wild flowers are the snowplants, red and white heather, gentian, water lilies, wild marigold, Indian paintbrush, pennyroyal, and primrose. Smaller trees include the ash, laurel, and holly; and among the more conspicuous trees are yellow, sugar, lodgepole, white, and digger pines; red, white and Shasta firs; and alpine spruce as well as cedar and tamarack. There is a great variety of songbirds. Many smaller lakes nearby are reached by roads and trails.

Nev. 28 goes south along the eastern shore, passing private estates. One privately owned cove and beach provides the owner with a landing bay for his hydroplane.

At 38.7 *m.* is the junction with US 50 (*see Tour 7c*).

The Steamboat Hot Springs on US 395 and a resort by them were very popular in the early days, and a pretentious hotel served tourists as well as invalids seeking relief by "drinking the waters". Steamboat Springs was a terminus of the Virginia & Truckee Railroad for nearly a year, after 1871.

The highway passes over the toe of a hill and through narrow, fertile Pleasant Valley, whose lands were first tilled by Mormon settlers in 1856. On a bare hilltop (L) the brush grown lines indicating old roads leading up to Virginia City are almost the sole reminders that Pleasant Valley held a very busy mill town at one time. This lumber town, Galena, was founded as a mining camp in 1860 on the edge of the mountains westward and was so called because of the large amount of galena occurring in the ore. The mining did not pan out so the camp was moved further up the creek (*see before*) and became a short lived lumber camp supplying the Comstock. It was only one of many towns of the area founded to supply timber and fire-wood to the mills and mining camps.

At the southern end of Pleasant Valley a low summit is crossed, and the highway follows the shore of Little Washoe Lake, which with Washoe Lake to the south, divides Washoe Valley.

Close to the road and almost hidden by trees, at 35 *m.,* is (L) a brown ranchhouse that provides a particularly charming example of Victorian Gothic design. Tall prim gables and tall gabled dormers provide spaces for tall narrow windows with pointed arches and pointed panes of clear glass bordered by narrow strips of red and blue glass. This ranch first belonged to a Mormon, William Jennings, reputed to be the wealthiest man of his clan. It later passed into the hands of Theodore Winters, who maintained racing stables here and raised two Derby winners from his blooded stock; one was El Rio Rey, a magnificient animal. South of the house was a mile-track where races were held frequently in the 1880's and 1890's. North of the house were a half-mile track and the racing stables.

Hay from these valleys was so prized that some was shipped to New York, where it brought high prices, and part was even shipped to England for racing stock. The bulk of the apple crop from the nearb-by ranch of Ross Lewers, an early fruit grower, also found a market in England.

Hidden behind formal plantings of Lombardy poplars and Scotch broom, is the BOWERS MANSION (R), 36.4 m., a reminder of the first Comstock millionaires, Lemuel Bowers and his wife. The square, two-story sandstone structure is still impressive and with its two rear wings, mansard roofs covered with pale-blue and white checkerboarded slate and broken by long narrow rounded dormers roofed with rusted tin, is strongly reminiscent of Mediterranean villas. Only a high platform remains of the ornate balustraded front porch that was an incongruous note on this otherwise well-designed structure. Inside, remnants of early glory are found in the carved white marble mantelpieces and plaster ornaments on the ceilings. In one wing is a bar for the service of picnickers and visitors to the two, small, warm water swimming pools. These pools have modern concrete rims but they were first dammed in the days when the mansion was built. Both the pools and the basin around a formal fountain in front of the house then teemed with goldfish and after the mansion became a picnicking resort it was the delight of children to catch these fish with their hands.

Between the wings is a stone-paved court, shaded in summer by the leaves of an enormous grapevine. A path behind the house zigzags a few hundred feet up the steep rocky hillside among pine and manzanita to the tiny hollow where "Sandy" Bowers, his wife, and their adopted daughter, Persia, were buried.

The building of this costly mansion in the early days when no one expected to stay in Nevada roused widespread attention, and the later eccentricities of Mrs. Bowers turned her into a legendary figure. Eilley Orrum—who became plain Ella when signing documents in America—was a Mormon convert who left Scotland when 15 years old, with the Mormon missionary, Stephen Hunter, who married her. When Hunter took another wife in Deseret after the revelation on polygamy, his Scottish wife left him. Later she married Alexander Cowan and they were among the settlers sent to these valleys in 1855 by Brigham Young. When Young called the settlers back to Deseret to strengthen his forces on the approach of Federal troops, Mrs. Cowan refused to go with her husband. During their first winter in the valley, when cash was desperately needed, Mrs. Cowan kept a boardinghouse near Carson City. Later she opened one in Gold Canyon, serving the prospectors and miners who were beginning to work there (*see Tour* 8).

Among Mrs. Cowan's boarders in 1859 was Bowers, 14 years younger than she and usually called Sandy. He was among the first claim holders on the lode and he gave her a strip adjoining his, possibly in payment of his board bill. While other claim-holders sold their "feet" for prices that were to prove ridiculous Mrs. Cowan, like a good Scot, held onto her claim and persuaded Sandy to do likewise. Later they united their claims as well as their lives. Their ore was among the first mined from the lode and the daily profits began to run into thousands of dollars. As income mounted Mrs. Bowers planned for a mansion in this place, which had particularly taken her fancy, and for a trip to Europe on which she would show her Scottish relatives that they had been wrong in opposing her departure for America with the poor Mormon. Her plans even included a call on Queen Victoria—but this was made impossible by her divorces; court etiquette was even stricter then than now on this subject. Plans for the mansion were approved and good stone-cutters were found—the blocks of granite were so true that practically no mortar was used.

Then the Grand Tour, which lasted two years, was begun. It became largely a buying expedition, with the Bowers' being rooked right and left by dealers of the Continent. A steady stream of marble mantels, French furniture, and household odds and ends began to cross the Atlantic, pass round the Horn, and up the Pacific, to be freighted in across the high Sierras. On their return Sandy was too busy on the Comstock to enjoy the mansion; besides, he probably felt more at home in the saloons with his friends, and his wife did not find the elegant society she had hoped to gather around her. Sandy died suddenly in 1868, leaving cash and claims of much value, but in a very muddled condition. Mrs. Bowers' former shrewdness had forsaken her; she became entangled in litigation and speculation that soon left her destitute. With the house heavily mortgaged she endeavored to run it as a resort, on instructions from a crystal she had begun to depend on. Even that could not support her for long and, that being the great period in which spiritualism, mesmerism, and the like were the vogue, tried her hand at crystal reading for fees. For a while she had numerous clients asking her advice on stocks and places to locate claims, then the applicants fell off. When she eventually died, an old, old lonely woman, she had become a fantastic figure.

Just above the mansion in the early days was Ophir, where a stamp mill crushed ore from a Comstock claim of the same name. The mansion itself was at the upper end of what is still called FRANKTOWN, laid out by the first Mormon settlers in Washoe Valley. Founded before the discovery of the Comstock, it, like the other towns of the valley declined with the exhaustion of timber on the Sierra slopes in the vicinity. In 1872, when the town became a station on the Virginia and Truckee Railroad, it had a large hotel, two stores, a market, a blacksmith shop, and a number of neat dwelling houses. In its heyday, Franktown also furnished produce to Virginia City from its farms, and had a 60-stamp mill costing approximately a quarter of a million dollars.

In June, 1854, a company of Mormons headed by Orson Hyde had come to Carson Valley and then migrated to Washoe Valley. Hyde was pleased with this site and erected the first sawmill here. When Brigham Young recalled his followers, his settlers sold everything hastily for whatever they could get. The fact that he was paid so little for his very valuable sawmill caused Orson Hyde to send a letter calling a curse before the Lord on the people here who had treated him so unjustly; he "placed his suit in the Chancery of Heaven," he said. Later events, which included a flood, would seem to indicate that some of his invoked punishments arrived.

Franktown built the first school-house in Nevada but when the settlers left that fall the building was sold to "Lucky Bill" who moved it to Genoa for a horse stable.

US 395 proceeds through Washoe Valley, with Big Washoe Lake in the distance. Against the mountain (R) is the landscaped estate and white house of C. A. Wellesley—Earl of Cowley—who has made it his permanent home. LAKEVIEW SUMMIT, 42.1 m., is a low pass between Washoe and Eagle Valleys. Under the pavement here are pipe lines leading water from high in the Sierra to Virginia City (L); this inverted siphon was the engineering wonder of its day, for never before had water been piped to a vertical depth of some 1700 feet and then raised by its own pressure almost to its intake height.

CARSON CITY, 45.8 m. (4,660 alt., 2,474 pop.), is at a junction with US 50 (see Tour 7c).

N. Carson St., for Virginia and Truckee Ry. and also for the Virginia and Truckee Transit Company Stages; hotels, boarding houses, auto courts; information at State Department of Highways, Memorial Building, on Carson St.

CARSON CITY, smallest capital in the United States and seat of Nevada's smallest county, is near the bottom of the forested eastern slope of the Sierra Nevada in Eagle Valley.

From the early days westbound travelers, weary of the wastelands, have looked with pleasure on this fertile spot near the Carson River. With plentiful water from springs on the mountains above, the settlers planted cottonwood, balm of Gilead, poplars, locust, black walnut, maple, and many other trees to such extent that from the heights in summer the little city seems to be a park surrounding the white dome of the capitol. The long main street is wide and paved, but many of the trees along it have been sacrificed to clear parking space. Repeated fires have destroyed many of the old-time buildings and others have been torn down to make way for modern structures, but enough remain to indicate unmistakably the period in which the capital developed. The sensible wooden awnings over the sidewalks have been removed for the most part, and where the awnings formed upstairs porches doorways now open onto air. In the neighborhood of the capitol are a number of Victorian houses, with jigsaw, lathe, and iron decorations. The predominating building material for the older public structures is sandstone, usually rough-hewn from the quarry at the nearby penitentiary.

Though the great majority of people living in Carson are employees of the State, a few are employed by the Federal government—more Federal employees are in Reno—others work in the shops of the little Virginia and Truckee Railroad, in the local brewery, and in the stores and other service businesses depending on valley trade.

The town has all the clubs and fraternal organizations so prevalent in Nevada towns and every two years has a round of festivity when the legislature is in session—though the majority of the legislators come down daily from Reno.

Carson City came into existence with the backwash of gold-seekers from California. On November 7, 1851, a party that had crossed the Sierra Nevada from Brent's Bar decided to seek gold in this region. When prospecting gave poor results they decided to open a trading post here on the Overland route. While they were building a log cabin that later became the Overland Stage station, one of the men shot an eagle and nailed its skin on the cabin wall. This gave the place its name of Eagle Station; it was later called Eagle Ranch, and the meadows roundabout became Eagle Valley. Eagle Ranch on the great travel route became the social center of the scattered settlements that grew up in time, and here dances were held and the first marriage in Eagle Valley took place, by civil contract. Many of these early settlers were Mormons. When in 1857 Brigham Young recalled his cohorts to the City of Great Salt Lake, most of them responded, selling their holdings to John Mankin for a nominal amount, paid in wheat. Mankin later laid claim to the entire lower valley. For a short while he and his four sons and one daughter were the only occupants of his large tract of land, which was later sub-divided and sold.

In September, 1858, Abraham V. Z. Curry had the present townsite surveyed because he expected the western part of Utah to be separated from the eastern part and soon become a State. To induce settlement he gave a lot to anyone who would erect a building on it. Major William M. Ormsby then became an enthusiastic promoter of a town that was still chiefly on paper, and named it for Kit Carson. The rush to the Comstock Lode in 1859 stimulated the infant community and it began to look as if Abe Curry were a man of foresight. The *Territorial Enterprise,* attracted by what looked like an imminent boom, moved over from Genoa, but a few months later packed up and went on to Virginia City.

As early as 1859 Curry began to more energetically make Carson City instead of Genoa the territorial capital, and he was ably abetted by others who had caught his speculative fervor. The town's principal advantage, it was claimed, was that it was closer to the lines of travel. One of the first acts of Territorial Governor Nye in 1861 was a proclamation summoning the legislature to Carson City on October 1.

On November 25, Carson City was declared the permanent capital by the legislature and a plaza was set aside for public buildings.

In 1860 the town had only 701 inhabitants but in a year the population more than doubled; Carson had become a station on the Pony Express in 1860, and also the eastern terminus of a telegraph line from San Francisco. April 12, 1860, was a great day here; the pony rider dashed in with mail and dispatches relayed from St. Joseph, on the Missouri River, and Carson was able to telegraph the latest national and international news to the Coast—only nine days old. Carson became the Ormsby County seat in 1861. Before long it was a freighting and supply point for many mining and ranching communities in central and southern Nevada. At one time between 1865 and 1875 its population was established at more than 8,000, but it did not receive a city charter until the end of the period, when the population had begun to decline rapidly.

With the silver stampede and the development of freighting the whole territory as well as Carson had serious troubles with hoodlums of every kind. The territorial legislature in its first session, in 1861, passed various laws designed to establish order, including a Sunday blue-law making gambling and "noisy amusements on the first day of the week, commonly called the Lord's Day" unlawful. But it took more than statutes to control the wild, propertyless throng and on at least one occaasion—after many incendiary fires (*see ahead*) the "601" put in appearance.

When the legislature found no building large enough to accommodate it, Curry offered the use of his primitive Hot Springs Hotel, which was near the river. In addition he built a horse-railroad from the town limits to the temporary capitol and hauled the legislators free. Orion Clemens, Territorial Secretary and brother of Samuel, separated the senate from the assembly with a canvas curtain to carry out the provisions that a chamber should be provided for each; but the Federal government, indifferent to his resourcefulness, refused to pay for it, and subtracted the cost, $3.40, from his salary.

One of the first acts of the assembly was to divide the territory into counties and they named the smallest (in which was the capital) for Major Ormsby, Curry's friend who had been killed during the Paiute trouble of 1860. When a courthouse was needed, Curry was ready with another hotel, the Great Basin, which he sold instead of lending, convinced that the time had come to collect dividends on his foresight. This hotel-courthouse was used by the legislature until 1869. It and its successor could have told many stories of vote-buying, vote-trading, and general political corruption. As contemporary papers show, the tales would have been embellished with accounts of fistfights, hot-headed tempers, resounding oaths, and many a juicy bit of highhanded legerdemain, particularly during those years when legislators chose United States Senators.

Politics all over the country was a wild game at the time, with corruption so rampant from the Atlantic to the Pacific that it is not surprising that vigorous Washoe should have had its share of what only in later years was called scandal. With the United States Senate gaining the reputation it held for several decades as the club of new millionaires, it is inconceivable that the Comstock should not have produced several candidates for seats in the Chamber and that they should not have resorted to the widely current practice of buying their way in—and resorting to kidnapping and intimidation if that served their purpose. Not all the men who wanted to go to Washington had prestige alone in their minds. They were men of big interests and they felt that the best way to protect them was to have a hand in the legislation touching them.

A familiar figure at the legislative sessions was Charles C. Wallace, usually called Black Wallace because of his coal-black hair and because he was hand-in-glove with the "Black Republicans". A trusted political henchman of the Central Pacific Railroad, he held the inside track on legislative manipulation in Nevada. Under his direction caucuses were held, candidates were chosen, and bills were passed or carried out in the waste baskets, it has been said. Black Wallace liked a good stand-up-and-knockdown fight with the winner take all—and he usually took it.

Matt Cannavan, sent to the assembly from Storey County, was also busy. A shrewd Comstocker, he framed a bill that would have forced the stock brokers of Virginia City to pay for a quarterly license. The indignant broker pooled $5,000 and gave that sum in bills to Peter Burke, who set out to save the situation. Soon after arriving in Carson City he was lured into a resort and was soon completely intoxicated and snoring. Cannavan quietly extracted the bills from his pocket, marked them, took the serial numbers, and returned them. The two met the next day and Cannavan offered to wager Burke that he could tell him the number of every bill he possessed. Burke was too inexperienced in politics to scent a plot; he took the wager, and lost, realized what had happened, and frightened, rushed back to the brokers and cursed them for scoundrels who were trying to land him in jail. Before the brokers could collect their wits, the Cannavan bill was passed.

In 1861 John Q. A. Moore erected the first opera house, a big wooden building with a square false front; it seated about 400 people and there was a convenient saloon under the same roof. The Carson Opera House, a larger structure, was built in 1878. For money to buy scenery, equipment and furnishings, a benefit ball was given on July 4, 1878. Formally opened by Henry Ward Beecher, the house occupied the site where the post office now stands, but was later moved to the corner of Plaza and Spear Streets where it was destroyed by fire on Easter Sunday in 1932.

Carson soon outgrew its freight-team and oxcart days. In February of 1869, construction was begun on the Virginia & Truckee Railroad, which was to connect Carson City with Virginia City. On September 28, 1869, Colonel H. M. Yerington, the superintendent, drove a silver spike to secure the first rail laid in this town, and three hours later a locomotive was puffing over a short section of track. It had been hauled from Reno by teams; two others were similarly transported to Virginia City—such being the impatience of the citizens to see their railroad in action. On November 7, 1871, the line reached Steamboat Springs; and on August 24, 1872, the last link was finished in the 52-mile railroad. Though the principal office was originally at Virginia City, it was moved to Carson City in 1900; and in 1905 a branch road was constructed from Carson City to Minden.

For many residents, the most exciting event that has ever taken place in the capital was the world heavyweight championship fight on March 17, 1897, between Bob Fitzsimmons and Jim Corbett. Fitzsimmons won with a solar plexus punch. Sport fans and newspaper men from all over the world thronged the town for many days before the fight took place. The gate receipts were only $8,000 but more than $1,000,000 was grossed from the moving pictures. These, the first films of the kind ever made, were of bluish tint and flickered and shifted without warning; but they were considered marvelous at the time.

POINTS OF INTEREST

1. Construction of the STATE CAPITOL (*open 9-4 weekdays*), N. Carson St., was begun in 1870 and though it was used by the fifth legislature in 1871 it was not completed until the following year. The big square stone structure has hewn logs of great length for its rafters. Peter Cavanaugh was the builder. In 1907 an octagon-shaped, two-story sandstone structure was added on the east side and connected to the main building by an open corridor on the first floor and by an enclosed bridge supported by Doric columns on the second. North and south wings were added in 1915. On the lower floor are offices of the governor, secretary of state, treasurer, attorney general, and of numerous departments; the senate chamber, assembly chamber, and offices of the superintendent of public instruction and other State officials occupy the upper floor. In the lower corridors is the S. L. Lee collection of mineral specimens and Indian and pioneer relics, presented to the State by Dr. Lee's widow in 1934. In the chamber at the north end of the building on the second floor is an excellent oil portrait of Abraham Lincoln by Chas. W. Shean.

The shady capitol grounds cover four city blocks, first called The Plaza. Elms almost hide the capitol in summer; near each of the four corners of the ground grows a tall pine. Along the old iron fence surrounding the area are many flowers in summer.

2. The NATIONAL HUMAN ALLIANCE FOUNTAIN, N. Carson Street, opposite the capitol, is a fountain constructed of polished granite, with a drinking bowl about six feet in diameter for horses and base cups for dogs. A round column rises about four feet above the larger bowl.

3. The MEMORIAL BUILDING, N. Carson St., facing the

southern end of The Plaza, was designed by F. D. Delongchamps of Reno and houses the State Highway Department. The two-story sandstone structure, entered through a portico, was erected in 1920 to honor Nevada's World War troops.

4. The SUPREME COURT AND STATE LIBRARY BUILDING (*open weekdays* 10-12, 1-5, 7-9), on Carson St. just north of the Memorial Building, is a modern three-story structure of reinforced concrete faced with stone; it was constructed in 1936. The supreme court room is especially impressive. The collection consists of 45,000 volumes in the general library, with the same number in law, and in law reference. The collection of statutes is unusually complete. The library also has unusually complete files of Nevada newspapers. Books are sent on request and without charge to any resident of the State but the borrower must pay the postage for their return.

5. The ABE CURRY HOUSE, on the northwest corner of Nevada and Telegraph Sts., is the core of old Carson, for it was built by the first man to believe firmly in Nevada's future and determine in advance where its capital was to be. The house, with the old-fashioned elegance of its period, was constructed of stone taken from the quarry at the penitentiary (*see ahead*).

6. MATT WRINKLE'S HOUSE is an old-fashioned structure on the N. W. corner of King and Curry Sts.

7. The WARREN ENGINE COMPANY FIREHOUSE, corner of Mussey and Curry Sts., is a little stone structure with a semifalse front that rises to a bell-tower. Warren Company Number 1 was organized by 20 young men on June 17, 1863, and soon collected $2,000 for equipment. They immediately bought an engine from the Warren Engine Company Number 4 of Marysville, California—both had been named for the Revolutionary War commander who fell at Bunker Hill. In ordering the engine and also 300 feet of hose from San Francisco the company specified that the equipment had to be on hand before the Fourth of July, for one of the pleasures of being a volunteer fireman was the chance to parade in uniform and give demonstrations. At their first ball, on July 3, all members appeared in uniform, which included a bright red shirt; tickets for the event cost $6 though "the ladies" contributed the supper.

The Warrens' first fire came in August; two buildings burned and one had to be torn down. By October members were tired waiting for more fires and determined to put on a public show at The Plaza. The climax of events came when the little engine threw a stream straight up 155 feet. Later the company purchased a steam engine and the Warrens planned another show, boasting that the engine would shoot a stream over the big pavillion that then stood on The Plaza. They were utterly humiliated when only feeble pressure was achieved; but the day was saved when a resourceful member dashed to a store across the street, bought several pounds of bacon, and threw them on the smouldering fuel.

Rules of the company were very strict; members were fined $1 for

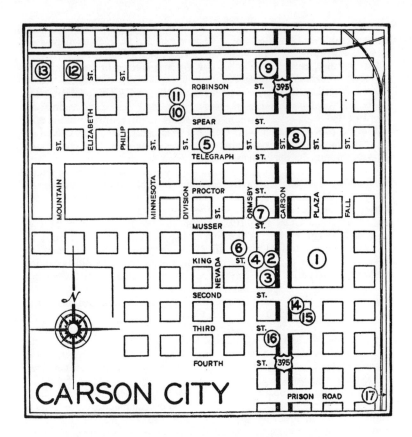

POINTS OF INTEREST IN CARSON

1. State Capitol
2. National Human Alliance Fountain
3. Memorial Building
4. Supreme Court and State Library Building
5. Abe Curry House
6. Matt Wrinkle's House
7. Warren Engine Co., Firehouse
8. Post Office and Federal Bldg.
9. Old Mint
10. Mark Twain House
11. H. M. Yerington House
12. D. L. Bliss House
13. Governor's Mansion
14. Carson City *Daily Appeal* Office
15. Benton Livery Stable
16. Ormsby House
17. Nevada State Penitentiary

being absent from meetings and $5 if absent from a fire. Moreover, they paid monthly dues of $2.50 for the privilege of membership. The parades and fire-fighting were far from being the only attractions to membership. Rival companies had been formed in 1864—the Curry Engine Company Number 2 and the S. T. Swift Company No. 3. Abe Curry had provided the engine house for the first of these. Competition was very keen on equipment and its merits, and also on fire-fighting prowess. Citizens complained that the companies were sometimes so busy fighting one another for places at the tanks from which they pumped the water that they sometimes forgot to put out the fires.

Between 1865 and 1870 there was a wave of incendiarism and blame for the fires was put on six temporary residents who had been sleeping in the Curry firehouse. Angry townspeople ordered the six out of town. Five left and after the sixth had refused to go he was found hanging from the cemetery gate with "601" on his chest. The incendiarism ceased.

The city's worst experience with fire came in September, 1926, when flames swept down King Canyon and burned ranchhouses and everything in the way. All business places and public buldings were closed to enable every able-bodied man to join the fight and even trusties from the State penitentiary were sent out to join them. Five men were killed before the flames were under control. Of the three companies, only the Warrens had survived and they had taken over the Curry engine house in 1908. They are still in service though the city now pays a few salaries.

The engine house is a museum as well as center of firefighting service. High on the walls are pictures of the Currier and Ives series "The Life of a Fireman," including among others the one in which a helmeted figure dashes from flames with the drooping body of a woman in nightclothes. Many valuable old photographs line the walls and half a dozen metal fire trumpets are displayed; one of these is the Marysville, California, trumpet of 1854. A particular treasure is a piece of early firehose, made of buffalo hide and riveted with brass.

8. The turretted red brick POST OFFICE AND FEDERAL BUILDING, North Carson St., between Telegraph and Spear Sts., has a high mansard roof typical of the period of its construction—1888. The granite steps were part of the old Ophir Mill, which cared for the ore from the great Ophir Mine on the Comstock (*see Tour 8*).

9. The OLD MINT, on the northwest corner of North Carson and Robinson Sts., is being transformed into a State museum. Ground for the great bleak square stone structure was broken with great ceremony at eight in the morning of July 18, 1866. Gold and silver were minted here with one interruption until 1893, when production of precious metals had dropped so low that the building was turned into a State assay office. Rooms are small—almost cell-like.

10. The so-called MARK TWAIN HOUSE (*private*), Division and Spear Sts., is a two-story frame structure with peaked roof and

gables. A legend inscribed in the cement sidewalk before it, proclaims that this was once the home of America's Samuel Clemens—though it must have undergone many changes if his description in *Roughing It* was accurate. Mark Twain was private secretary to his brother, Orion Clemens, first Territorial Secretary. This is only one of several places where the brothers are said to have lived.

11. The H. M. YERINGTON HOUSE, on the corner of Minnesota and Robinson Sts., is another of the Victorian structures of the period when Carson's hopes of becoming a metropolis were high. Visitors were always escorted to see it as one of the impressive show places of the town.

12. Another early show-place was the D. L. BLISS HOUSE, on the corner of Elizabeth and Mountain Sts. Festivities in some of these early houses were occasionally as formal as Emily Post could have desired.

13. The GOVERNOR'S MANSION, west side of Mountain St. at the corner of Robinson St., was built in 1905. It is a low spreading house with broad verandas, and a white-columned portico to give it a touch of proper formality.

14. On the southeast corner of South Carson St. and Second St., is the CARSON CITY DAILY APPEAL office, from which a newspaper has been issued ever since 1865, when H. R. Mighels edited the first issue of the *Morning Appeal*. Bob Davis, the journalist and magazine writer, had his first newspaper experience here.

15. The garage at the northwest corner of South Carson and Third Sts. is the FORMER BENTON LIVERY STABLE, which was the leading transportation center of the early town. One of Benton's drivers was Hank Monk, whose reputation as a devil driver made him a valued Jehu in time of need but a terror to people who were unacquainted with his skill.

16. A grocery store now occupies what is left of the ORMSBY HOUSE, on the west side of South Carson St., between Second and Third Sts. This hotel, named for Abe Curry's friend, was the leading hotel of early Carson. The story of smoky back-room sessions held here by politicians of the 1860's and later will be stirring when told—which will be when the heirs of participants have reached a philosophical and detached attitude on the practice of those days.

THE ORMSBY HOME, on the southwest corner of Third and Minnesota Sts., is the place from which Major Ormsby set out with his volunteers in 1860, to teach the "red devils" a lesson after they had burned William's trading-post and killed four men in retaliation for the kidnapping of two Bannock squaws. Ormsby, one of the 64 men killed in the battle near Pyramid Lake (*see Tour 1*), was an enthusiastic believer in Carson's destiny and had aided Curry in his plans for making the town the capital.

Left from Carson City over an improved road to the NEVADA STATE PENITENTIARY (*visitors* 9 *A. M. to* 10:45 *and* 12 *to* 2:45 *P. M.*), 2 *m.*, which has the first lethal gas chamber constructed for execution of the death penalty. Here also is the old execution chair, its back to a stone cliff, with gun-rests before it. For years the State allowed a condemned person to make a choice between shooting and hanging. Only one man ever chose to be shot. The site, close to Abe Curry's Warm Springs Hotel, was rented from him in 1862, then purchased two years later. The first buildings were burned in 1867.

A very important archeological discovery was made within the walls of the prison. Skeletons of prehistoric animals, and footprints of birds, horses, lions, wolves, and the giant sloth have been unearthed. The first discovery was made in the late 1870's when fossil remains were uncovered by a blast used in excavating for a prison workshop. The tracks and skeletons have been found at a depth of from 20 to 25 feet on what apparently was the shore of an ancient lake.

For a few miles south of Carson City, US 50 (*see Tour* 7) unites with US 395. At 48.9 *m*. is the junction with paved Nev. 36.

Left on this road 1 *m*. to STEWART, composed of the CARSON INDIAN AGENCY, established in 1890 through the offorts of William M. Stewart, then a U. S. Senator from Nevada. Here, on the banks of Clear Creek at the southern end of Eagle Valley, are 30 modern buildings, including a school, chiefly of local stone, surrounded by orchards and tilled fields. In addition to the usual subjects, the Indian children are taught agriculture, horticulture, stockraising, and home economics. The students are not only from Nevada, but also from California, Utah, Arizona, and Oregon. The agency here has jurisdiction over certain reservations within the State, and those in Inyo and Mono Counties, California. There is a trading post selling souvenirs to visitors. Pageants are annually presented, usually in June.

At 49.4 *m*. is the junction with US 50 (*see Tour* 7c).

US 395 proceeds southward over rolling sage-covered hills to drop into Carson Valley, one of the most productive areas in the State. In the blue distance is the mighty backdrop of the Sierras.

Wild flowers are scattered in spring over the valley floor and the surrounding foothills. Lupine, both blue and white, and a variety of mullein having yellow blossoms resembling sunflowers are prolific. A riot of fragrant pink petals from the wild peach line the road. Thickets of wild rose bloom along the small streams. Indian pinks, sego lilies, sand lilies, larkspur, and wild pansies bloom early on the hillsides. In late summer and fall the vivid yellow-orange blossoms of rabbit brush brighten wide areas.

At 58.1 *m*. is the junction with paved Nev. 57.

Right on this road to GENOA, 3 *m*. (4,750 alt., 150 pop.), now a scattered community but the oldest permanent settlement in Nevada, made when this area was in Western Utah. There is some controversy over the date when Genoa was really settled. The first structure, a roofless stockade, was built in 1849 by H. S. Beattie, who had come over to trade with travelers on the road to California. Robert Lyon wrote that when he stopped in, 1850 at Mormon Station, as it was then called, he found two or three women, and several children among those apparently living here. The people had a band of fat cattle brought from Salt Lake, which they were killing for meat; it sold at 75c a pound. But in the spring of 1851, when John Reese and Jacob A. Dinsey chose this site for a trading post, they found only the remains of one building. On July 4, 1851, Kinsey took possession of Mormon Station, which name it retained until 1855, when, after a survey, Judge Orson Hyde renamed it Genoa. The traders immediately erected a log cabin, which when finished was possibly the only house in Nevada. A stockade enclosing more than an acre of ground was erected at a cost of $2,000 as a protection against Indians in case of need—and also to protect the post against the numerous marauding whites. A fine crop of turnips was reaped in 1851 and these were sold to travelers for as much as a dollar a bunch.

After the influx of more people, a squatter government was formed at a meeting held November 12, 1851. Four years later, Genoa became the seat of Carson County, Utah Territory. In 1861 it became the seat of Douglas County, which position it retained until 1916. Its early prosperity was owing to the rush of California miners back to Virginia City, and the mining there, which created an immense amount of freighting and stage travel across the Sierra.

Genoa early had a newspaper, a telegraph line, and an Overland Stage station. Before long a gristmill and a sawmill were in operation and two stores supplied residents with all necessities.

In May, 1852, Israel Mott settled four miles from Mormon Station. His wife was the first woman to make her home in Carson Valley.

It was while Genoa was the seat of Douglas County that half-mad "Fighting" Sam Brown, who boasted that he had filled a graveyard, met a little more than his match. This bully of Virginia City came down to attend a court session for the purpose of intimidating the judge, jury, and witnesses into freeing one of his henchmen, who was on trial for murder. He was met by young Bill Stewart, then a district attorney and later U. S. Senator from Nevada, whose contempt for the courage of bad men was one of his outstanding traits. He pointed a gun at Brown and took his testimony.

When Brown left Genoa he was as furious as any bully could be. Looking for vengeance, on his way back to the Comstock he committed the deadly mistake of taking a few pot-shots at a peace-loving Dutchman named Henry Van Sickle. The shots went wild—for Brown was not dangerous except at close range; but they did awaken something in that Dutchman. He got his shotgun and started in pursuit, and before many hours had passed he had the terror of Washoe fleeing for his life.

When at last the furious Dutchman cornered the bully, the fight was soon over, and a long breath of relief ran throughout the area. The jury's verdict was that Brown had "come to his end from a just dispensation of an all-wise Providence." Van Sickle seems to have been indifferent to the fact that he was a public hero. He did not like to have men come along and shoot at him for fun, and so far as he was concerned, that was the whole story.

At 60.9 *m.* on US 395 is the junction with oiled Nev. 37.

Right on this road which approximately follows the route Fremont and his party took in 1844. Right on Nev. 19, a dirt road. At 13 *m.* is a junction with US 50 (*see Tour* 7) by Lake Tahoe at a point one mile from the California Line.

MINDEN, 61.4 *m.* (4,700 alt., 200 pop.), seat of Douglas County and terminal of the Carson Valley branch of the Virginia & Truckee Railroad, achieved a measure of publicity when Mary Pickford of motion picture fame chose the little courthouse here to divorce Owen Moore.

In 1855 a German immigrant, Henry Fred Dangberg, crossed the Plains and, ignoring the silver lodes on the surrounding heights, took up a ranch in this valley. Knowing what the Mormons were doing with irrigation in Utah he labored hard until he had ditched his fields and was growing hay on his ranch; with the rush for Washoe and the great demand for feed he was able to get $300 a ton. In 1864 he obtained a small supply of seed from a ship-captain who had been in Chile and planted it at places where he believed the mineral content of the soil would permit its growth; this was probably the first alfalfa grown in the State. Gradually his ranch expanded and when he died in 1904 his property extended from Twelve Mile House to Carson—36,000 acres. In 1864 he married Margaret Ferris, sister of the man who was to build the Ferris wheel at the first great Chicago Fair, and they trained their children to share their father's interests. Two years before Dangberg's death he organized the H. F. Dangberg Land & Livestock Company, which passed to the hands of his sons—John, Henry Fred Jr., and George. The company established Minden in 1905 and it at once become the county seat.

The ranch today provides the best example of diversified agriculture in the State; it has both cattle and sheep of registered stock and produces grain and potatoes as well as hay. An allied business is a creamery, and many of Minden enterprises, such as the bank and the hotel, were Dangberg-initiated. The town itself as well as its public buildings have the neat trim look associated with the old-fashioned German villages.

GARDNERVILLE, 62.7 m. (4,710 alt., 400 pop.), which like its near neighbor is a trade town of Carson Valley as well as for mountainous areas westward in California. Also like Minden, this is a town with solid buildings and shaded streets.

US 395 proceeds southeast through Carson Valley with its fertile ranches, large herds of cattle, and thousands of haystacks. The snowcapped peaks of the Sierras (R) run in a north-south line as far as the eye can see. The road leaves the valley at 66.7 m. and takes a winding course over low hills covered with sage and dotted with dwarf pine. Within a few miles the air is redolent with the smell of evergreens.

At 81.4 m. is the junction with Nev. 3 (see Tour 4A).

US 395 turns south to climb a low pass. TOPAZ LAKE (L), 83 m., is an artificial body of water lying partly in Nevada and partly in California. It impounds the waters of West Walker River for irrigation use in Lyon County. The lake has a treeless shoreline on which are many campsites. The water is well stocked with trout; boats can be rented at CARSON'S FISHING LODGE, 84.1 m.

US 395 crosses the CALIFORNIA LINE, 84.4 m., at a point 132 miles north of Bishop, California.

Tour 4A

Junction with US 395—Yerington—Junction US 95; 59.7 m., Nev. 3.

Paved roadbed throughout.
Good accommodations in Yerington.

This beautiful route, which connects two of the important highways of the State, makes a rough S to swing around the Black Mountains.

Nev. 3 stretches east from its junction with US 395 (*see Tour* 4), 0 *m.,* at a point 19 miles south of Gardnerville, and crosses a valley floor covered with sage and greasewood. The mountains to the south are in the Mono National Forest, which like most of such areas in the Southwest is less a forest than a controlled grazing area. The valley also provides excellent cattle and sheep forage. Skirting the southern edge of the Pine Nut Mountains, a favorite resort of the early Indians, the highway crosses windswept hills to enter SMITH VALLEY at 9.5 *m.* Here irrigation with the waters of the West Walker River makes possible the dairy and produce ranches whose houses can be discovered at a distance by the windbreaks of Lombardy poplars. These graceful trees are something of a nuisance in irrigated districts because their roots spread greedily toward the ditches and sometimes choke them. They also take more than their fair share of the waters needed to produce the hay that makes these ranches valuable. The 16-mile valley has about 60,000 acres of ranch land.

In August, 1859, R. B. Smith, T. B. Smith, S. Baldwin, and J. A. Rogers, of Stanislaus County, California, brought cattle across the mountains by the Big Tree route. Immigrants there had advised them that this was a good place to winter stock. Pitching camp in the valley near the banks of the West Walker River, they built a tule house. The winter proved severe and the nearest supply point was Genoa, 40 miles away, where flour was twenty cents a pound. To add to their troubles the tule houses burned in the spring. In spite of these difficulties they decided to remain and in the following year L. B. Lobel joined them and put in a crop of barley and vegetables, watering his field from a mountain stream called Desert Creek. In time others came and the valley's produce was in great demand when the camp of Aurora was booming.

Named for a Major Wellington, WELLINGTON, 10.4 *m.* (4,675 alt., 75 pop.), is the supply center of Smith Valley. In early times there was a stage station here. The Pine Nut Mountains are on the north the Mono National Forest (*camp sites*) on the south.

Left from Wellington on a dirt road to LUDWIG, 17 *m.,* the best-preserved abandoned town in Nevada. The once prosperous camp looks much as it did when it was deserted. Houses, buildings in the business area, and reduction plants still stand intact, giving the impression that the inhabitants, temporarily absent, will soon return

For some distance Nev. 3 follows the West Walker River, which tumbles through narrow WILSON CANYON, whose walls, picturesquely eroded, run a gamut of color from pale lemon yellow to deep scarlet. Through this canyon Fremont made reconnaissance in 1845, seeking the mythical Buena Ventura River, which on old maps flowed through the Sierras and reached the sea. Other early explorers spent arduous months seeking legendary rivers in Nevada and learned only after bitter experiences that not a single stream in the vast area penetrated the mountains westward on its way to the ocean. Eagerly following each new-found water course, hoping to discover an easy passage across the Sierras to California, they were soon disappointed by discovery that all flowed into lakes or vanished into sinks.

When highway engineers were surveying the route in this area they planned to carry the road on a detour to avoid the difficulties of cutting their way through rock. One county commissioner objected, insisting that Wilson Canyon was too beautiful to be left inaccessible, and in the end his will prevailed.

The road emerges from the canyon whose brilliantly stained walls sharply contrast in summer with the beauty of deep blue-green alfalfa fields stretching far eastward in Mason Valley. In season, flowers add their beauty to the scene. Indian paintbrush daubs the valley floor and hills with flaming red. Green willows line the banks of the feeder creeks, rabbit brush, greasewood, and buckbrush cover the hillsides. Cottonwoods meet overhead to form a tunnel of cool green through the valley, past prosperous ranches.

YERINGTON, 37 *m.* (4,380 alt., 1,005 pop.), is sprawled in the center of a valley whose wealth is forced from the sandy wastes by the life-giving waters of the East and West Walker Rivers. Clustered along the main highway, the business section covers about three blocks. The town supports a grammar school, a large high school, a movie, and two hotels. The Nevada Copper Belt Railroad, a branch of the Southern Pacific, provides a tie with transcontinental routes.

There has been considerable copper mining in the adjacent hills and this town, which is the seat of Lyon County and trading center of Mason Valley, is the shipping and distribution center of the camps. The valley was settled in 1860, during the first rush to Aurora. It was first called Pizen Switch, renamed Greenfield in 1861, and still later named for H. M. Yerington, an official of the Virginia & Truckee Railroad. Stories differ in regard to the origin of the first name; one is that the place was called Pizen Switch because of the number of desperate men who flocked here and another is that it was named for a saloon. It has also been told—the story is probably not true—that outraged members of the community organized a Committee of Vengeance and swore they would murder and scalp anyone who continued to call their town by its first name.

In this area in 1890 was a Paiute known as Jack Wilson because he had grown up in the home of David Wilson. He listened attentively to family readings of the Bible, making interpretations to suit himself, and soon came to believe himself the Indian Messiah. Jack was a sincere, kindly, full-blooded Paiute, but he taught his tribesmen that the white men would suddenly disappear from the face of the earth and that all the land would again belong to the Indians. The Ghost Dance was the climax of ceremonies that would bring this to pass. So much faith was placed in these prophecies that tribal leaders from far and near came to offer gifts, which he accepted gravely and in profound silence. Restlessness among the tribes spread east of the Rocky Mountains and climaxed in trouble when the white men did not disappear on schedule. The outbreak of the Sioux in 1890, which resulted in the killing of Sitting Bull and the massacre of Wounded Knee in South Dakota, are directly attributed to Wilson's teachings.

The highway leaves Mason Valley at 46 m. to enter another area of barren hills that turn an unearthly pink at sunset.

The Bidwell party of 1841 came up the west bank of the Walker River, after getting off the trail to the south. The Indians here gave them pinenuts and fish, a fare that made them ill. But they were glad to reach the Walker, which they called the "Balm" and tried to follow it to California.

At 59.7 m. is the junction with US 95 (see Tour 5), at a point 1 mile north of Schurz.

Tour 5

(Ontario, Ore.) — McDermitt — Winnemucca — Lovelock — Fernley — Fallon — Hawthorne — Tonopah — Goldfield — Las Vegas — Searchlight — (Needles, Calif.). Oregon Line to California Line, 597.2 miles.

Paved roadbed throughout.
Limited accommodations in McDermitt, all types of accommodations in larger towns.

US 95, the longest route in Nevada, for the most part runs through very little known country. But no other route in the West provides a wider variety of landscape, a better cross-section of the interests of the State in which it lies, nor more continuously arresting views. North of Fallon it runs through country where interest is divided between stock-growing and mining. North of Winnemucca short side roads lead into valleys so beautiful that one is called Paradise and into mountains where the sub-alpine flora is breath-taking. Between Winnemucca and Lovelock are both very active mining and very concentrated cattle activities. Between Lovelock and Fallon are the great alkali sinks, rimmed by brilliant colored mountains and transformed by mysterious mirages. South of Fallon the reds and purples of barren mountains grow more vivid and the route swings for more than 20 miles high above narrow, deep, blue Walker Lake. Turning gradually toward the southeastern corner of the State, US 95 passes through the great mining centers where discoveries of gold and silver started one of the last, great booms and brought the mining West to life again. Near

Las Vegas is the Charleston Range, being developed as a recreational area, where in less than half an hour a motor car moves from sandy cactus-covered desert to timberline, passing through five life zones with their characteristic fauna and flora. South of Las Vegas, at a corner of the Boulder Dam Recreational Area, US 95 turns straight south through a valley below one of the awesome ranges bordering the lower Colorado River.

Section a. OREGON LINE to WINNEMUCCA; 73.9 m.

This section of US 95 runs through the broad, treeless Quinn River Valley, west of the Santa Rosa Mountains, which are crossed about 20 miles north of Winnemucca. Side roads on the east lead up into sparsely wooded, craggy Humboldt National Forest and lovely Paradise Valley, while roads westward lead far out over lava beds and alkali flats of Black Rock and Granite Creek deserts and to some game refuges.

US 95 crosses the OREGON LINE, 0 m., at point 180 miles south of Ontario, Oregon, which is on US 30.

McDERMITT, 2 m. (4,400 alt., 559 dist. pop.), is the community center of people on very large cattle, sheep, and horse ranches. Formerly there were numbers of antelope in the area, and a few still roam the mountains (L).

Left from McDermitt on a dirt road to the McDERMITT INDIAN RESERVATION AGENCY, 5 m., where the headquarters buildings are the reconditioned structures of old Fort McDermitt—the second "t" is a map-maker's addition. Cavalry and infantry were stationed here to protect settlers, and also travelers on the Nevada-Idaho road. Before 1865 it had been Quinn River Station, a stage-coach stop. After the Paradise Valley and other Indian troubles in this isolated region (see ahead), Colonel Charles McDermit, commander of the Nevada Military District (1864-65) led a troop of cavalry to the place. Soon after, on August 7, 1865, while out scouting, he was shot from ambush. His body was brought to the station and sent to Fort Churchill, the base near Carson, where it was buried with military honors. Immediately thereafter the post was established, on a reserve of more than 2,000 acres. It had three buildings for officers, a very large barrack, a three-room hospital, and large storehouses and stables. On Dec. 1, 1886, the ground and buildings were turned over to the Department of Interior for an Indian reservation.

Indians here make a living by stock raising. Some are very old. Buffalo Missouri is an old woman who as a young girl washed clothes for the soldiers. Several others including Sally and Joe Ox Sam, Race Horse Bob, and Johnny Stay Behind, can look back across nearly a century. An occasional argument among the Indians turns a page of history and gives sidelights on the past.

One day a group of listening tribesmen surrounded two oldsters who were engaged in a lengthy pow-wow on the days when the army was in command here. "Big school here!" one declared emphatically, and pointed at a building. "No, little school here!" said the other. "Big school there!"—and pointed toward another building. The two old men for an hour or more paced back and forth between the two buildings, while personal adherents of each trailed behind. Short declarations in English were interpolated by long-winded and gesticulating argument in the Paiute tongue. After a while both men turned away, each convinced that he alone was right and that the loss of memory of the other was appalling. The explanation of the argument was that when the soldiers were here the Indian children attended school for a longer time each day than they did after the soldiers left. Too, the classes were then held in a different building from that used later. However ineffectual the educational program of the early agency had been, it had not allowed these two old warriors to forget that classes had been shorter—hence "little school!"—after the soldiers moved from the scene.

This country was once at the northern end of ancient Lake Lahontan. Upon entering the area Peter Skene Ogden and his men came to Quinn River, which heads in the northern end of Santa Rosa Mountains (L), and follows it southward, eventually reaching the excellent but short-lived trapping grounds of the Humboldt River. Ogden and his men were the first white men these Indians had ever seen.

At 14 *m.* on US 95 is the junction with the Forest Service Canyon Creek Road (*see ahead*).

At 15.1 *m.* is the junction with a dirt road.

Left on this road to NATIONAL, 10.9 *m.* (approx. 6,100 alt.), a very rich gold mining district in the Humboldt National Forest. The National Mine alone has produced $8,000,000 and is still active. This region, overlooked or ignored by early prospectors, remained for an "automobile prospector" to discover in 1907. The transition from the "desert rat" with his burro to the modern goldseeker with his car is evident in certain local place-names, such as Auto and Radiator hills.

Blocks of ground were leased, and in 1909 two men found the National vein at a depth of 40 feet. The richest ore taken out assayed $75 a pound. Shipped ore brought $24 a pound, but 'second grade' rock was worth only $2 a pound. Ore so rich gave sticky fingers to some of the miners, and highgrading flourished. Adventurers of every description flocked to the camp, and for several years the population roistered without stint and gave little thought to the morrow. At one time the National workings were protected by armed guards, and searchlights played over the mine entrance all night.

There is trout fishing in the many small streams of the area; and during the fall the country is invaded by hundreds of deer hunters who find conditions ideal in the hills where open areas are only occasionally interrupted by clumps of aspen, scrub pine, and cedar.

OROVADA, 30.2 *m.* (4,348 alt., 180 dist. pop.), is a supply and Red Cross First Aid Station.

Quinn River (R) is still what Ogden called it, "not a large stream but certainly a long one." As more and more water is diverted to irrigate hay fields, less and less of Quinn River reaches its sink in the Black Rock Desert. US 95 goes south along the western edge of Quinn River Valley, with the Santa Rosa Mountains on the eastern horizon. It roughly follows the stagecoach road over which thousands rushed between 1865 and 1880 to seek fortunes in the Idaho mining camps of the Boise Basin.

At 44.2 *m.* is the junction with graded Nev. 8A.

Right on this road which goes across a country where miles are long and houses few and far between. Quinn River Valley, long and lean, extends westward to the Black Rock Desert

AMOS, 3 *m.*, is a mail stop at the junction with a graded dirt road; L. here 13 *m.* to the AWAKENING MINING DISTRICT, in the Slumbering Hills. The JUMBO GOLD MINE, discovered in 1935, attracted national attention. It was sold for $10,000,000, purchase to be completed at any time the lessee cared to buy the mine outright, but with a down payment of $250,000 in cash with a royalty of not less than $100,000 to be paid each year thereafter.

On Nev. 8A is SOD HOUSE, 14.1 *m.*, a road station (*water; no gasoline*) where a primitive early structure built entirely of sod still stands. It has seen dusty stagecoaches hauled by sweating teams, Indians skulking through the tall sage, and has heard the bugles of cavalry on reconnaissance.

Just west of Sod House, Quinn River (R) becomes sluggish for a moment in a swamp area. Narrow Kings Valley opens from the north, cut by Kings River, which seeps into Quinn River. Here Ogden's trappers talked with Indians, and left the beaverless Quinn to seek the little Humboldt eastward. The Jackson Creek Mountains (L) separate the desert valley from the Black Rock Desert west of the range. Distantly in the valley southward, an isolated hill called Donna Schee (5,100 alt.) seems to hang suspended in the shimmering heat of summer sun but stands out boldly again in the shadows of evening.

HAPPY CREEK STATION, 30 *m.* (approx. 4,050 alt.), is another mail station. It rests on the north toe of Buff Peak (7,200 alt.) in the Jackson Mountains (L), against the margin of a large alkali flat. At sunset in this silent land, light changes so swiftly that one evening may be filled with 100 variations of color and pattern. Occasional quivering mirages project themselves against the hills.

QUINN RIVER CROSSING, 38.4 *m.*, is a mail stop that serves scattered ranches as well as mining districts tucked away in a corner of the Black Rock and Pine Forest Mountains some 20 miles westward. Mesa-like Sentinel Peak (7,000 alt.) is a southern spire of the Pine Forest Mountains. All that is left of Quinn River at this point now changes its direction and trickles southward to vanish into the long Black Rock Desert.

Nev. 8A turns northward at Quinn River Crossing toward the narrow rise between the Pine Forest Mountains (L) and Trident Peak (8,400 alt.) in the Trident Mountains (R). VIRGIN STATION (*gasoline*), 54.4 *m.* (4,700 alt.), is a county road maintenance station, and also a mail stop serving the Virgin Creek mines and ranches. North of the rise the road gently drops into a broader valley. High in the Pine Forest Mountains (L) at 64 *m.*, is the ASHDOWN MINE, which was sold in the 1930's for $500,000. DENIO, 69 *m.*, is a desert outpost almost on the Oregon Line. Here Nev. 8A turns abruptly southwestward, then west, traversing the extreme northwestern corner of the State. In the 100 miles between Denio and the California Line no supplies are available except in emergencies.

Nev. 8A follows the south bank of Thousand Creek at 83 *m.*, and soon crosses the eastern boundary of the CHARLES SHELDON ANTELOPE WILD LIFE REFUGE, established in 1931 for the protection of antelope, sage hens, and mule deer. By the end of 1936 the refuge had been enlarged until it embraced more than 500,000 acres. Here is the junction with a dirt road.

Left on this road 31.5 *m.* to the isolated PAIUTE AND SHOSHONE INDIAN RESERVATION (202 pop.). The ruins of FORT McGARRY remain on the shores of Summit Lake within the reservation. This post was established on the Applegate Cut-off, an early road to Oregon, on Sept. 9, 1867. A few soldiers had been sent here earlier and were living in tents. Stone buildings were erected and the fort was put on a more permanent basis. It was abandoned on March 25, 1871. The reservation has a very small winter population, but during the summer many Indians from Pyramid Lake come here to graze stock, living the while a more primitive and less disciplined life than they are accustomed to on the larger reservations.

An elderly Indian woman explained why the Indians like the place. "Here (Pyramid Lake) cannot see far, nothing here. Summit Lake much better to sit. There can sit long time, can see very far." She can sit and see the blazing Black Rock Desert running southward, and the ragged outline of eroded hills reaching westward to the Sierras. It has been suggested that the older Indians like to come to this remote region to engage in certain old ceremonies far from the curious eyes of the whites.

By Nev. 8A is the THOUSAND CREEK RANCH, 96.8 *m.* (*water; emergency gaso-*

line and food), where inquiry can be made on best approach to the THOUSAND CREEK FOSSIL BEDS, northward, and the VIRGIN VALLEY OPAL FIELDS on the south. The beds are gravel deposits where the fossilized bones of camels, sabre-toothed tigers, mastodons, and other mammals have been recovered. In the opal fields, discovered in 1908, stones generally occur as casts of limbs or twigs and as crack-fillings in petrified trees. In 1919 a 17-ounce black opal was found, valued by the owners at $250,000; it is now on display in the Smithsonian Institution. Generally of the fire variety, the best stones are unexcelled in color and brilliance.

West of Thousand Creek Ranch Nev. 8A winds up a stiff grade through a maze of buttes and deeply eroded walls. Occasionally the white flags of startled antelope can be seen vanishing over a hill.

COYOTE SPRINGS (L), 139 *m.*, usually affords drinking water. A little further on are the MASSACRE LAKES (R), dry sinks. In 1850, a large and well-equipped train elected to take the Applegate Cut-off into northern California. In this area, reached by way of High Rock Canyon (L), they were attacked by Indians. Rashly leaving the shelter of their wagons the immigrants charged on their foe and though they vanquished the Indians, 40 men were killed. In fearful haste the dead were gathered and interred in a common grave. Then oxen drew wagons back and forth over the spot in an attempt to disguise it and save it from desecration.

At 156.7 *m.* is the junction with Nev. 34.

Right here 1 *m.* to VYA, a service station and store. The road continues to the HEADQUARTERS OF THE CHARLES SHELDON WILD LIFE REFUGE, 18 *m.*

Nev. 8A at 162.4 *m.* enters '49 CANYON. Here at the eastern base of the Cascades is the site of a '49 camp (R); the stone wall of the canyon is covered with names and dates chiseled by travelers anxious to prove to others that they had preceded them over the Applegate Cut-off.

Close to this point Nev. 8A meets the northern section of Nev. 34 (*see Tour 1c*).

At 50.5 *m.* on US 95 is a junction with oiled Nev. 8B.

Left on Nev. 8B to PARADISE VALLEY, 18 *m.* (4,308 alt., 400 dist. pop.), the community center of an area of the same name that was settled before 1865. Prospectors visiting the valley named it and no one who has ever seen it denies its right to the praise implied. On April 4, 1865, two friendly Indians warned one of the newcomers that members of another tribe were on the warpath. Even before all of the scattered settlers could be warned, distant smoke from fired cabins rose in columns. Ten men, three women, one older boy, and four children barricaded themselves in a corral and were besieged for several hours before help arrived. Two of the men were killed. After other murders, as well as the destruction of homes and the theft of livestock, the Indians were driven away by cavalry from Fort Churchill.

Paradise Valley is hemmed on three sides by mountains. A thin arm of the Santa Rosa Mountains, topped by Santa Rosa Peak (9,300 alt.), bars the west and circles the north end to Spring Peak (9,300 alt.) and Thimble Mountain (8,000 alt.). The creeks coming down from the latter feed Martin Creek, which enters from northern watersheds. In late spring the encircling Santa Rosas are carpeted with blue, red, and yellow flowers.

The road continues along Indian Creek and up out of Paradise Valley to the MARTIN CREEK RANGER STATION AND CAMPGROUND, 32 *m.*, a base for sportsmen fishing for trout and hunting deer in the Santa Rosa Mountains. The Little Humboldt and Martin Creek tributaries are particularly popular with fishermen.

Everywhere along this route are fields of brilliant wild flowers—scarlet Indian paintbrush, purple lupines, little yellow wild sunflowers. The Forest. Road crosses HINKEY SUMMIT (c. 8,050 alt.), 31 *m.*, where the view is notable. The road winds northward through a division of the Humboldt National Forest then westward down along Canyon Creek to a junction with US 95, 20 *m.*, at a point 16.5 miles north of Orovada (*see before*).

US 95 proceeds southward with Bloody Run Peak (c. 7,400 alt.), southern end of the Santa Rosa Mountains, on the left; in the valley of the Little Humboldt the route follows a stage road over which California miners entered Idaho in the boom of the 1860's. After skirting the eastern slope of the Winnemucca Mountains (6,600 alt.) and hay fields of the Humboldt, US 95 enters WINNEMUCCA, 73.9 *m.* (*see Tour 1a*), which is on US 40, with which US 95 unites between this point and Fernley (*see Tour 1b*).

Section b. FERNLEY *to* TONOPAH, 205 *m.*

This section of US 95 is particularly beautiful, winding through sagebrush covered valleys and across alkali flats between eroded ranges whose bare red-streaked faces give hint of the great mineral wealth deposited in them. On every slope can be seen old workings and even the hillocks bear prospectors' location monuments—piles of stone covering the inevitable baking powder or tobacco can that bears the record of ownership. Wheel tracks lead off in all directions, particularly toward the draws and canyons, indications of the number of men who have done claim development work at likely spots.

At FERNLEY, 0 *m.*, US 95 abruptly changes direction, going eastward to HAZEN, 11 *m.*, (4,015 alt., c. 129 pop.), a small trading center of ranchers at a railroad junction whence a branch of the Southern Pacific starts south to Mina, to make connection with the Tonopah & Goldfield Railroad.

At 19 *m.*, in LEETEVILLE (*see Tour 7c*), US 95 meets US 50, with which it unites briefly eastward (*see Tour 7c*) to FALLON, 30 *m.* (3,749 alt., 1758 pop.) (*see Tour 7b*). Here US 50 continues eastward (*see Tour 7b*), and US 95 turns south, running through ranchlands irrigated by the Newlands Project.

The Carson River is crossed at 35 *m.*, its flow a mere trickle at times since the waters have been impounded for irrigation purposes. The road ascends gradually to a low pass in the wierdly beautiful Desert Mountain Range, and descends gently with few twists or curves, passing through the Walker River Indian Reservation to a junction with Nev. 3 (*see Tour 4A*), 69 *m.*

SCHURZ, 70.4 *m.*, is the agency of the Walker Lake Indian Reservation. Here is a trading post where baskets, beadwork, blankets and souvenirs are sold. This hamlet with its cottonwood trees stands out in the arid region around it.

Paiute predominate among the three or four hundred Indians here. Sober and industrious, they make their livelihood raising stock. The group has about 150 votes at general election, and takes its politics very seriously. An old Indian, John Cleveland, is the judge of the tribe under native law and fills his position with dignity and pomp. Impressive in the main, he dresses well, and carries out the idea of the reverence due the law in his bearing. He informs all office seekers that it is not in keeping with his position as judge to mix in politics, though he could if he wished be a man of great influence.

There are many famous names, such as Cleveland, Vorhees, and Greeley, among the Indians. In addition to the usual staff-house, hospital, and other agency buildings, there are three stores, and a meeting house in which the Indians gamble and dance.

WALKER LAKE, in view (L) at 72 m., is 30 miles long, from 3 to 8 miles wide, and has a maximum depth of 1,000 feet. The principal feeder of this beautiful remnant of ancient Lake Lahontan is Walker River, from the north; the lake has no outlet. Perch and lake trout are abundant and ducks are numerous on the high shores. At the northern end are numerous pelicans.

Fremont made his way from Smoky Valley to the eastern shore of Walker Lake, where in November, 1845, he camped to await his rendevous with the Walker division of his party. It was at this time that he honored Joseph Walker, the trapper-scout and guide, by naming the lake, river, and a pass for him.

Distances are so deceptive in the clear air here that at night the lights of Hawthorne seem only seven or eight miles away when seen from the lake's upper end.

In the steadfast intensity of its color and the beauty of its setting Walker Lake is one of the most impressive lakes in the West. As deeply and opaquely blue as the Mediterranean, under bright sunlight it looks like a field of heavy liquid of unfathomable depth. The highway is high up on its shore for 16 miles. At the lower end is Mount Grant (11,303 alt.), the highest peak in the Wassuk Range. For a short distance along the rocky base of this range, the highway runs through open cuts. Workmen, materials, and equipment had to be transported by boat. Across the lake (L) are terraces marking the many water levels of former ages.

The lake, impressive in its wild setting, has been the subject of numerous tall tales and people are occasionally met who swear that they have glimpsed the fabulous monster supposed to live in its blue depths.

The Indians here say that at first the world was all water. Then the water began to go down and at last Kurangwa (Mount Grant) emerged. There was fire on its top and when the wind blew hard the water from the lake dashed high and would have extinguished the fire had the sagehen not nestled down over it and fanned away the water with her wings. But the heat scorched the feathers on her breast; they remain black to this day. Afterward the Paiute got their first fire from the mountain through the help of the rabbit, who is a great wonderworker. As the water subsided other mountains appeared and at last the earth was left as it now is.

Then the great ancestor of the Paiute, whom they call Muninea— Our Father—came from the south and journeyed across to the mountains east of Carson Sink, where he made his home. A woman, Ibidsii —Our Mother—, followed him from the same direction and she became his wife. They dressed themselves in skins, and lived on the meat of deer and mountain sheep, for there was plenty of game in those days. They had children—two boys and two girls. Their father made bows and arrows for the boys, and the mother fashioned sticks for the girls with which to dig roots. When the children grew up each boy married his sister, but the two new families quarreled so much their father told them to separate. So one family went to Walker Lake and became the fish-eaters and the other went farther north into Idaho and became the buffalo eaters—the Bannock.

At 95 *m.* is the junction with the Cottonwood Creek Road.

Right on this unpaved but safe and well constructed road, which is under control of the Navy Department. It winds up the Wassuk Range (*second gear in most sections; water piped to roadside at intervals*) to a junction with the Mount Grant Road, 11.5 *m.* Left on this road 6 *m.* to a parking spot (11,000 alt.) 303 feet below the topmost pinnacle of MOUNT GRANT. The view from the mountain top, the highest in a vast region, is spectacular. Far below between brilliantly tinted ranges is indigo blue Walker Lake; beyond the Naval Ammunition Station at the base of Mount Grant is the stark, barren Gillis Range; southward is the narrow black thread of US 95, winding its way to Tonopah; and westward rises the long snow-capped Sierra Nevada.

At its junction with the Mount Grant Road the Cottonwood Creek Road becomes the Cory Creek Road, which continues southward and eastward to the Lucky Boy Grade, 26.5 *m.* (*see ahead*), at a point 3 miles from the town of Hawthorne. The southern approach to the Mount Grant Road provides a much used circular route, though the Cory Creek Road is not maintained as well as the Cottonwood Creek Road.

The U. S. NAVAL AMMUNITION DEPOT, whose entrance is at 102.7 *m.,* covers more than three hundred square miles. The reservation contains 28 brick residences for officers and civilians, and all the facilities usual to a military base, including an auditorium, motion picture theater, bowling alley, and baseball park. The sight of sailors and marines among the barren mountains here is startling.

HAWTHORNE, 106 *m.* (4,375 alt., 929 pop.) (*hotels and other facilities*), seat of Mineral County, spreads out from one broad main street on a sunny plain in view of distant high ranges. It is the trade center of scattered ranch families and also the outfitting point of prospectors and miners who in 1939 were cheered by promising discoveries. Here as in every other town in Nevada—and especially along this route —every little restaurant, drinking-gambling club, and store has at least a few specimens of ore on display and the owners will talk for hours of the probable assay value of the different pieces.

The presence of the naval depot has given a certain air of prosperity to the small town and facilities are in keeping with the number of visitors to the depot. From the main street small, low buildings housing the ammunition are visible, widely separated and far from habitations of any kind.

Hawthorne is truly the West in its scorn for small change; a 35c breakfast will be given for 30c if the unfortunate traveler must complete his payment with five pennies.

As elsewhere in the State, a school is one of the most impressive buildings—in this case a school for the lower grades. The low building of very modern design is up to date even to the Venetian shades at its windows. The townspeople love to tell of the young teacher who came here from the North where "fish" mean small mountain trout—and ordered half a dozen fish from Walker Lake for her biology lesson; nothing would hold the catch but the tank in which the fire company stores water for emergencies.

Right from Hawthorne on an improved road that climbs 7,441 feet, over Lucky Boy Grade, to AURORA, 28 *m.*, which in 1864 had a population of 10,000. In less than ten years it produced at least $30,000,000 in bullion. In 1860 valuable ore was discovered in this area by E. R. Hicks, and the town was named for the goddess of dawn by J. M. Corey. In early days Aurora was aggressively claimed by both Nevada and California and for election put up a full ticket for Esmeralda County in Nevada and another for Mono County, California. Nevada won the boundary decision by four miles in 1864, but until that time Aurora was the seat of Mono County.

Near by Bodie was a notoriously tough camp, where "a man for breakfast" was so frequent an occurrence that the phrase "bad man from Bodie" was coined to describe those residents who were still in the land of the living. So impressive was its reputation for wickedness that once when an Aurora family considered moving to the town, the young daughter of the family finished her evening prayers with a tearful, "Goodbye, God, we're going to Bodie." Aurora ruffled whatever virtuous feathers it could muster and pointed scornfully. Bodie resentfully charged that the child has been deliberately misquoted—that what she had actually said was "Good! By God, we're going to Bodie"!

Not quite so obstreperous as its neighbor, Aurora was scarcely a quiet community. More than once the substantial element applied drastic measures to guntoters and a hastily organized "601" committee strung up a few of the worst offenders for salutary effect. Aurora considered itself a Union town, and when the "Sescesh" element became noisy in 1862, the town became an armed camp with the Esmeralda Rifles forcing ring leaders to swear allegiance to the Union flag.

It was here that Milton Sharp, prince of all Nevada's highway bandits, dug his way out of jail. Sharp was a polite and handsome Robin Hood who preyed chiefly on Wells Fargo stages and was said to give money to the poor. After one of his jail escapes he had wandered for several days in the snow without food before returning to surrender; when asked why he had not robbed a rancher, Sharp stiffened with amazement.

Mark Twain lived here for several months while investigating some mining claims that he and his brother, Orion Clemens, Territorial Secretary of Nevada, had purchased. Failing to find the golden harvest that he sought with zeal, Twain "abandoned mining and went to milling," working a few days as a laborer in a quartz mill for $10 a week and board. While here he received an offer of $25 a week to work as a reporter on the Virginia City *Territorial Enterprise,* to which he had written letters for publication.

Aurora shows signs of returning to life, maintaining "a remarkable resistance to complete abandonment."

US 95 goes east from Hawthorne through rolling desert between sweeps of jagged mountains. North, east, and south, there is not a tree in sight or anything that resembles a tree, but the valley is broken by abrupt hillocks and mesas and no two ranges are alike in shape or color. At 118 *m.* the highway crosses a sandy lakebed and heads for the distant Gabbs Valley Range. The brush covering the

Photograph by Glenn A. Davis

BULL-DOGGING, HELLDORADO RODEO, LAS VEGAS

RIDING IN THE CHARLESTON RANGE   *Photograph by Glenn A. Davis*

DUDES   *Photograph by courtesy Ullom, Las Vegas*

Photograph by Truman D. Vencill

BUCKING CONTEST, RENO

AQUAPLANING

A DAY'S CATCH, LAKE MEAD

SKIING ON MOUNT ROSE

Photographs courtesy Transcontinental and Western Air, Inc.

TOBOGGANNING

IN THE FIREHOUSE, CARSON CITY   *Rothstein: Farm Security Admin.*

CALIFORNIA BEER HALL, TONOPAH (c. 1902)

DANCE HALL, LAS VEGAS

WATCHING A PRIZE FIGHT, NEAR RENO (c. 1904)

AN EARLY TONOPAH BANQUET

Photographs courtesy of Art Langan

floor is beautiful at all times of the year; in summer it has small creamy blossoms and in winter is faintly brown against the sun.

LUNING, 129.6 m. (4,605 alt., 36 pop.), is a railroad stop and small trading center. In 1879 silver, lead, and copper properties were located a few miles east and northeast of town. The silver mines were worked until 1893 but copper-lead mining did not begin until 1906. During the World War the district was an active copper producer. At present the town seems little more than a store and service station, but it is a supply center and shipping point for the Nevada Brucite quarry 35 miles to the north.

Left from Luning on a dirt road to RAWHIDE, 40 m. a spectacular camp inspired by the Goldfield boom and the financial slump of 1907—plus one of the most amazing publicity build-ups in the history of mining. The hysteria of Goldfield had passed its zenith and the mines had settled down to rich production; but everyone who had missed out at Goldfield and Tonopah was sure that there were better fields yet for the seeking. Tex Rickard (see ahead) had just begun to learn the tricks of showmanship; Riley Grannan, the racetrack plunger and gambler of nation-wide reputation was ready for fresh excitement; Nat Goodwin, the most popular comedian of the day, who with his wife had been brought to Goldfield to inaugurate the elegant new theater, had caught the gold fever. A strike in this district in 1906 had brought a few prospectors and later strikes had assayed so spectacularly that someone decided it was another Goldfield. Rickard led the rush from Goldfield—though others were there before him, for in the Goldfield Review's special Rawhide number, brought out early in 1908, it was told that Rickard had paid $10,000 for the Rawhide lot on which he was building a duplicate of his Goldfield Northern saloon. The paper also reported that the only post office as yet in the new camp was a tobacco-box on a post bearing a cow's tail, though the camp already had three banks that kept open till midnight. Goodwin joined the hullaballoo and the newspaper wires carried word that Grannan had scented good pickings and joined the crowd. Sober authorities say that in the course of three months 4,000 people rushed in, but the old-timers give the number as 10,000. Within another three months the trampled sagebrush was beginning to raise its head again. The camp did continue, however, and some $1,500,000 worth of gold, silver, copper, and lead were to come out of it in the course of 15 years.

During the high days of promotion, Elinor Glyn, whose book, Three Weeks, had recently been suppressed as immoral and become a best seller, arrived in Rawhide to seek more material on life in the raw. Though the decline had already begun, Rickard and others hastily put on an evening in Rawhide's Stingaree Gulch that was to surpass the lady's expectations and, through her accounts of it, bring a temporary rush of sensation seekers.

Another event of the brief ecstatic period was the death of Grannan—or rather his funeral. W. H. Knickerbocker, a former clergyman recently from California, was the only man on hand to conduct the funeral services. Knickerbocker's grandiloquent periods, his lush stock of poetical quotations, and his flare for oratory, united to produce a sermon that reduced the camp to maudlin tears. Riley himself formed only one of the subjects—Nature shared honors:

"God flings the auroral beauties 'round the cold shoulders of the north'; hangs the quivering picture of the mirage above the palpitating heart of the desert; scatters the sunbeams like lamellated gold upon the bosoms of myriad lakes that gem the verdant robe of nature; spangles the canopy of night with star-jewels and silvers the world with the reflected beams from Cynthia's mellow face; hangs the gorgeous crimson curtain of the occident across the sleeping room of the sun; wakes the Coy Maid of Dawn to step timidly from her boudoir to climb the steps of the orient and fling wide-open the gates of the morning."

From MINA, 128 *m.* (4,552 alt., 400 pop.), (*hotels, stores, service stations*), roads radiate in all directions to mines in the rugged Pilot Mountains. This is the junction of the Southern Pacific Railroad's Hazen Branch and the Tonopah & Goldfield Railroad and until 1938 it was a terminal of the Southern Pacific narrow gauge branch line from California.

In this region severe earthquakes have been intermittently recorded for many years and 12 miles from the town is an earth fault with a ridge 2 feet high, created in 1932.

RHODES, 136 *m.,* is now chiefly a map name at the junction with a dirt road.

Right from Rhodes to CANDELARIA, 7 *m.,* in a district where silver ore was discovered in 1864 by Mexicans. A year later its largest deposit was claimed but the discoverer did not develop it, and it was rediscovered 15 years later; this was the Northern Belle, which was to produce three-fourths of the $20,000,-000 that came out of the district in the early years. This camp never died entirely; in the first two decades of the twentieth century it was to produce another $1,000,000 worth of ore—gold, lead, and copper, as well as silver.

Germans and Slavonians, well mixed with Americans, were the principal boomers here and soon replaced most of the Mexicans. The boom stirred intensive prospecting of the near by country and resulted in the organization of the Belleville, Sodaville, Garfield, and Pamlico Districts, with some others of minor importance. The area was eventually served by the Carson & Colorado Railroad, a standard line, running between Mound House, near Virginia City and Mina, and a narrow gauge between Mina and Keeler, in Inyo County, California. Railroad construction brought many Chinese into the section, particularly around Sodaville. After a fire consumed one of their opium dens, incidentally roasting several drug-steeped Shoshone braves, whites, in the interests of peace, managed to spirit the proprietor out of town.

The highway proceeds south through treeless country in which borax deposits look like fields of flour. The most important of these borax fields is Columbus Marsh, located by "Borax" Smith and Eaton in 1864; the town of Columbus, now gone, was founded in 1865. In 1871 William Troop discovered ulescite here and soon four borax companies were at work. When the Pacific Borax Company moved to Fish Lake Valley in 1875, the town faded. Ten miles north of Columbus Marsh is Fish Lake Marsh, which drains into it. In this district Mott and Piper produced borax as early as 1873. In 1920 some development and prospecting work was done in an effort to find petroleum, but without success.

Teel's Marsh, also in the vicinity, has a salt deposit that was worked as early as 1867; the salt was shipped to the Comstock by camel train, and to the silver mills in Aurora on mule back. After borax was found there in 1873 a large plant was built; it was in operation for many years.

SODAVILLE, 147 *m.* (*hot mineral baths*), once the most important town between Reno and Tonopah, is now almost deserted. Before the railroad was carried to Tonopah, this was the point at which all freight for the town was unloaded—and also the place where most of the boomers transferred to stages for the slow, dusty trip across the desert. One man said it was necessary to take a shovel at the end of the trip to discover which of his fellow-passengers was his wife. Night and day the railroad and stage officers here were besieged by frantic people—mine owners trying to discover where machinery was, restaurant-keepers imploring priority for their perishable shipments. Swearing, sweating freight agents threatened to disappear forever.

Once in Sodaville an unthinking store-keeper suddenly appeared behind his counter garbed in a Hallowe'en mask and costume that had been ordered for the daughter of one of the prominent mining men of the area. It was Saturday night, pay day, and the store was jammed with Indians. What was intended as an innocuous joke proved to be the merchant's undoing. The terrified Indians fled in panic, not bothering to seek the door but plunged headlong through the window glass. Convinced that the Devil had appeared among them, they refused thereafter to enter the store.

Here, too, in 1904, "Two-Gun" Mike Kennedy, self-styled the toughest man that ever came out of the East, met his death. According to old-timers, Kennedy had bullied the camp for weeks; and on Saturday night he was cutting it wide and handsome when he ran into a quiet and peaceable miner named James Lund, in from his diggings for a little drinking and fun. Lund, unarmed, called the braggart's bluff, and Kennedy, inviting him to shoot it out, offered him one of his guns. The two men squared off in the center of the main street with the residents lined along the walks, and blazed away. The toughest man ever to emerge from the East fell with six bullets in his body, and the miner, unscratched, walked into a saloon for another drink.

COALDALE (gasoline), 166.2 m., is at the western junction with US 6 (see Tour 6b), which is united with US 95 between this point and a junction near Tonopah. Highly colored mountains (R) turn fiery at the end of day. The station was so named because of deposits of low grade coal in this area, discovered by William Groezinger, who mined 150 tons which he sold to the Columbia Borax works in 1894. The coal was mined again in 1911-12. Some turquoise were discovered in the district in 1909, and agate and chalcedony in 1910. About 1938 many placer claims were located, the land in the vicinity was taken up, and high hopes were held of extracting gold and quicksilver from the mud flats. For a time after mining experts had visited the discoveries it was believed there would be another boom, but little activity followed.

At 169.2 m. is the junction with an improved road.

Right here across the desert is SILVER PEAK, 20 m. (4,307 alt.), whose population has been increasing since about 1938 when new operations began. The town is on the edge of a sink in Clayton Valley on the eastern side of Silver Peak Range. The camp has an air of bustling activity. Values were discovered here in 1864 and a 10-stamp mill was soon at work; then a 30-stamp mill was built in 1867, but the camp died within two years. In 1907 the Pittsburgh Silver Peak Gold Mining Company bought several properties, built a branch line down from the Tonopah and Goldfield Railroad, erected a 100-stamp and cyanide mill at Blair, the northern terminal, and the district was on its way to being one of the principal producers of low-grade ores in the State. Then for 10 years after 1915 there were practically no operations. But another revival came. To 1926 about $8,500,000 had been gleaned here.

With the last revival Silver Peak wanted better school facilities, including a high school. Since both State and county contribute to support the local schools it was necessary to get consent from State authorities. According to the law, the State will not contribute to more than one high school within a radius of 40 miles—and the lot set aside for the high school site was 38¾ miles from the high school in Goldfield. Very reluctantly the Silver Peak board agreed to put the school 1¼ miles beyond their town—if that was the only way they could get it. And State authorities hastily looked around for a frame school building in some deserted camp to be moved in here. School opened, but in October a determined group went out one night and hauled the building to the central site previously selected, bringing it within the forbidden zone. Under pressure local authorities reluctantly fined the school movers—and then used the funds to stage a community Hallowe'en party.

At MILLERS, 191 m. (4,728 alt., 74 pop.), was the largest re-duction plant (R) of the Tonopah Mining Company. Once one of the districts leading mills, it has been idle for a number of years except for lease operations on its tailings.

North of the highway east and west of Millers is the Monte Cristo Range, of a pink so fiery that it glows even at mid-day. It resembles the Dolomites of northern Italy—which have long attracted visitors from far countries—but in this land of wonderful color it receives very little attention.

US 95 climbs up into long, narrow TONOPAH, 205 m. (6,063 alt., 2,449 pop.), (hotels and other modern facilities), which has had to spread out along the road and build tall buildings to keep out of the way of the mining operations on the flanks of steep Mount Butler (R) and equally steep Mount Oddie (L). This main street slants sharply. It is true there are some few parallel streets but they go only short distances before being blocked by workings. Tonopah has been saved from the fate of other great camps when production declined by its development as distributing center for a very large region; gasoline, machinery, blasting powder, whiskey, and foodstuffs are freighted out in all directions. It is also the seat of Nye County, by grace of its superior population and a very few miles of territory.

Tonopah is not merely a town and not merely the producer of $125,000,000. To almost every living Nevadan more than 40 years of age, Tonopah—with its lusty son Goldfield (see ahead)—stands for modern Nevada, for youth, excitement, hope, and the great adventure of a lifetime. It came into existence at a time when the mining West had long been going through hard times, when the population of the State was dwindling, when State finances were in a desperate condi-tion, and hope was leaving all but those who remembered the days before 1880 and were sure they would return. When the great boom began here the whole State—and half of the West besides, as well as part of the East—came flocking in, driving over hot dusty miles of desert.

No great boom ever got under way in a more lackadaisical manner. It all began with a semi-literate rancher born in the mining country of California during the Mother Lode boom. Such a man would naturally start out to look over any new strike in his neighborhood and was bound to chip off bits of rock wherever he happened to sit down. Jim Butler wandered down to look over the Southern Klondyke, which was discovered in 1899 at a point 14 miles south of this place. After camping overnight in this vicinity near what the Indians called Tonopah (Little Water), he had to spend some time hunting his burro. When he found the beast Butler sat down to rest before returning to pick up his kit. Near by was an outcrop; true to form, he examined it and hammered off a few likely looking pieces, as he had done thousands of times before. This was May 17, 1900. That evening he reached the Southern Klondyke where several men were doing development work with poor results. Butler was not interested. Before he left the diggings he asked Frank Hicks, a miner who knew how to do assays, to test his ore, offering him an interest in the future claim if it turned out well. Hicks threw it aside when Butler left; he was tired of doing free assays. When Butler went back to his home near Belmont (*see Tour 6b*), he carried a few samples with him. Still having no money for an assay he took them to Tasker L. Oddie, a young New Jersey lawyer who had become Butler's successor as prosecuting attorney during his absence; Butler said the ore looked promising to him and offered Oddie a share if he could get the assay done. Oddie was new to the mining country, and Butler, as an old-timer, impressed him. He sent the sample to a friend he had made in Austin—the school superintendent who used his knowledge of chemistry to eke out a living by assaying, for rich old Austin had also fallen into bad times. The school-teacher, who was offered a share of Oddie's hypothetical share, did a conscientious job. He could not believe his eyes when he saw the size of the silver button, and thought that someone had been playing a trick on the greenhorn lawyer. Testing other samples, he found them even better than the first. The report went off by stage to Oddie, who sent a messenger to Butler.

The story is that Butler was too indifferent to do anything about the report; he was in the midst of haying. Perhaps, also, he had seen too many wild hopes based on a single assay. But Oddie talked and the assayer talked and soon there was a minor rush of prospectors—including the men of the Southern Klondyke—to stake out claims. Nobody knew exactly where to look; Jim had said he had camped at the spring and had walked some distance to find his burro. And he had not put up a location monument, which was fortunate as the time had already elapsed for doing the required development work to hold it. So the prospectors wandered about aimlessly.

In August Mrs. Butler managed to prod her husband to action, and to make sure that he really would establish his claim she drove down the hot valley with him. Oddie was too busy on legal work to go with them but one of the eight claims they staked was in his name; Mrs. Butler happened to stake the Mizpah, which was to be the richest producer of all the discovery claims. The problem then was to get enough money together for supplies to feed the claimants during development work and to get another team to help carry the ore for shipment to a smelter. They were ready to start work in early October, with $25 worth of food; with them was one of the Southern Klondykers, Wilson Brougher, taken into the expedition for the sake of his wagon and mules.

The story is that Oddie and Brougher did the digging, with stout black-mustached Butler giving advice and Mrs. Butler doing the cooking. The first ore had to be hauled north to Austin for shipment but no one minded that after the smelter sent back $800 on the first ton. Other prospectors and miners had begun to gather and the Austin school superintendent, Walter Gayhart, laid out a town. Those who had tents were fortunate; those who did not slept in dugouts, under wagons, or on the ground. Within three months a mining man from Reno offered to lease the Mizpah for 10 months on a 25 per cent royalty basis. Butler liked the idea and when others appeared they were offered leases on near by claims, 112 in all. Among those who arrived—with demand for one-fourth interest, in the discovery claims —was Hicks, the Southern Klondyker who had refused to do the assay until after he had heard of the rich strike. Butler amiably gave him one-thirty-second share on the discovery claim. The leases were made verbally and the only book-keeping was the record of returns Oddie jotted down in a little note-book. It is doubtful whether any other industrial enterprise in history involving $4,000,000 was carried through purely on oral agreement—and without litigation.

By mid-summer of 1901 the town was developing rapidly but the problem of getting supplies in and ore out was becoming acute. Provisions often sold at fantastic prices and water, freighted four miles, sold for 25c a bucket. The only supplies that never seemed to fail were liquor; everyone started a saloon, even Butler. At the end of 1901 there was a lull, as leases ended at the beginning of the new year, and many who expected to renew them went away for vacations in places where they could spend their new wealth. About that time came what was called the Tonopah Sickness, apparently, since only the men were affected, a lung congestion induced by the high silicate content of the rock. Men died on all sides after a brief period of gasping, and those not yet ill fled from the place.

In the fall of 1901 Philadelphia interests bought the eight discovery claims for about $350,000, organized the Tonopah Mining Company, and made Oddie manager. A little later the Tonopah-Belmont Company, the Jim Butler, the North Star, the Montana-Tonopah, and the Tonopah Extension were organized, and regular freight and stage service to Sodaville was established.

The real rush to Tonopah came in 1902. The town grew fast. And quite as many people came to view the phenomenal new town as had business interests or work in it. There was even an Opera House by the spring of 1903.

That year came the Goldfield boom (see ahead) and by winter the whole world seemed to be rushing to the camps—eastern industrialists and financiers, miners and prospectors from Alaska, South Africa, and all places in between; actors, journalists, engineers, and a fine assortment of speculators, gamblers, and other camp followers. Even Wyatt Earp, Tombstone's notable sheriff, arrived to start a saloon. The Tonopah & Goldfield Railroad began to lay tracks across the desert from Sodaville, reaching Tonopah on July 24, 1904.

All Goldfield—as well as the governor and his wife—came down to welcome the first train and help Tonopah celebrate in style, with a white-robed beauty queen christening the first locomotive with champagne. The queen and her court rode in the parade on a float provided by the Elks and were followed by the Tonopah Volunteer Firemen in full regalia. Drilling contests, long and noisy, were held and everyone drank to Tonopah, the greatest camp on earth—except the Goldfielders, who had their own candidate for the position.

Tonopah was an unusually orderly camp; prospectors had made it and prospectors ran it. Spirits were high but order was maintained. Indeed, residents had some difficulty satisfying the yearning of visitors who had been brought up on Buffalo Bill and Nick Carter; the visitors expected a shooting daily on every street corner and were bitterly disappointed when none took place. Otherwise honest residents were driven to magnifying minor disturbances, and when a surface blast went off at a mine would agree that there had been "a shooting".

Long before this the Crystal Water Company had brought plenty of water to the town and the old sign in a saloon that had a small washtub—"First chance $1, second chance $.50, all others $.25"—had gone. Moreover, society was organized. Young men arriving to work in banks and mining offices with clothes they considered suitable to a remote camp, hastily wired or wrote for formal attire; dinners and dances in such clothes were nightly events. Tables were decorated with flowers sent in from California and no banquet was complete without oysters, quail, and champagne.

Great rendezvous of the men was the Tonopah Club, a saloon and also a gathering place where news was exchanged; there was always plenty of excitement in the form of play for big stakes. At first the gambling was merely at stud poker and faro without a license. Then a cowboy from Oregon persuaded the club's proprietor to let him regularize the game and under his license set a limit, so there was no danger of the bank's being broken. By the time Tonopah had become a city the club had extensive quarters, complete with mahogany bar and the usual art.

Production reached its all-time high of $9,500,000 in 1913; the next year it was $500,000 less. In 1921 it was down to $5,500,000, but at that it had four mines listed among the 25 largest silver producers in the country. Gradually one mine after the other closed or was turned over to leasers, and by 1930 the population had decreased to a little more than 2,000. In 1940 all operations were on leases. A fire in the timbering of one of the mines put 75 men out of work but the residents are strong in the belief that explorations will soon find new wealth.

Close to the edge of the main street at the western end of town is the KIRCHEN CAIRN (R), holding the ashes of John Kirchen, who was general manager of the Tonopah Extension and predicted a rich find near this spot.

The yellow, stone NYE COUNTY COURTHOUSE (L), high on a bluff at the eastern end of town, contains many valuable records, including those from early Belmont.

The TONOPAH CLUB (R), in the center of town, is still in business; part of its quarters is now occupied by a restaurant and stakes are no longer spectacular.

Tonopah is at a junction with US 6 (*see Tour 6b*).

Section c. TONOPAH *to* LAS VEGAS; 207 *m.*

This section of US 95 cuts sharply south, then west to the southeastern corner of the State, crossing no high passes. Gradually, as the route proceeds southward, it comes into desert with flora typical of the Southwest, particularly beautiful in the spring of a wet year; then the vivid orange and red of desert blooms cover the valleys. Even on the hottest summer days snow-capped peaks along the California boundary are visible most of the distance.

US 95 continues the climb started in TONOPAH, 0 *m.,* to a low divide where it turns southward with vast plains and high-ranges in view.

At about 14 *m.* a distinct change in the vegetation is noted; northward is the sagebrush zone, southward the creosote bush. Occasional cacti and joshua trees appear, odd sentinels of the desert. The line of demarcation between the zones is so sharp that in this area not a single piece of sagebrush is found within a few hundred feet south of it and not a creosote bush a hundred feet north.

GOLDFIELD 26 *m.* (5,689 alt., 513 pop.), (*tourist-camp, gasoline, restaurant*), sits high on one side of a broad saddle between bare brown peaks. Seen from the highway, this fabulous town is drearier than a graveyard—for no one expects anything of the dead and Goldfield is not a ghost. Fifty-two city blocks of the lower part of the city are covered with brush, crumbling, windowless walls, tilted fireplugs, bits of scrap iron—the results of a fire in 1923. Above this waste on a plateau are remnants of the old city, the 200-room hotel now boarded up—the big stone crenellated courthouse, the two stone schools—one boarded up—low comfortable houses with stiff joshua-trees before their doors, and a few of the older business buildings where stock-brokers formerly did business all night long and fortunes were made and lost daily. Outside county and civic officials, most of the remaining people are householders who live on their savings, positive that Goldfield will come back again. It is impossible, they say, that the limited operations exhausted the vast supply of jewelry ore; that a tunnel driven just a little farther will not unlock new deposits of the kind that turned half of America to hysterical speculation. More people than live here share this belief; they refused to sell their Goldfield homes when it was still possible to do so at a profit, and they continue to maintain their property and protect it by having an elderly relative or pensioner live in it.

Goldfield was the lusty son of Tonopah. Without Tonopah and the crowds it brought in, the Shoshone, Tom Fisherman, might have found no one to pay attention to the specimen he had found a few miles to the south of the great silver camp; and without Tonopah and the money it had given him, Tom Kendall, proprietor of the Tonopah Club, would not have been able to grub-stake Billy Marsh and Harry Stimler—a half-breed who later became the professional "Indian prospector"—to look for the place from which Fisherman had taken his rock. Nor without Tonopah and the crowds it had brought would there have been many people to take an interest in this place where the first ore assayed only $12.60 to the ton. Marsh and Stimler staked their first claim on December 4, 1902. In spite of the low assay value, the discoverers were interested from the first, for they had found gold in a silver State; this was going to beat Tonopah and so, with a mining camp pun on the relationship of the two camps, they named this the Grandpa. It happened that at this time Tonopah was experiencing the usual let-down after the first excited boom; too many mining companies with over-capitilization had been set up and some of the later claims were not developing well. More men had arrived than the mines needed for work. Marsh and Stimler's next ore was a little better than the first and with a new grubstake from Tonopah they did development on the 19 claims they had staked. Other grub stakers joined them in the late spring of 1903—as sure as two men do hard work on any set of claims, some others are sure to prospect in their vicinity. Among the newcomers were Al Myers and a man named Murphy; Myers had both practical and theoretical knowledge of minerals and after looking around he selected what was to be the Combination—richest of all. A few more men arrived and Marsh and Stimler, who had to let some of the claims lapse for lack of a further grubstake, obligingly pointed out likely spots to the late comers. Charles Taylor accepted the advice and claimed the Jumbo, one of the first claims Marsh and Stimler had located; it was to give him $1,250,000.

Then rich ore was found here in October and the shipment made in December fired the fuse. Next a claim was sold for $10,000 to influential George S. Nixon and everyone who was not already in on the big money at Tonopah, and also some who were, set out for these slopes —riding, walking, limping. Stimler had sold his half over Marsh's protest but Marsh sold his share for $25,000 within a few weeks— and gave up mining forever. Taylor had tried to sell his Jumbo and another claim for $150 and had only hung on because he could not sell.

Eleven men who were early on the spot contributed $10 each to survey a townsite on the level section where the remaining large buildings now stand. The story of the sensational real estate boom of the next few months rivals anything Florida ever produced. Some lots at one time sold for $45,000 apiece.

With the arrival of experts retained by important eastern interests excitement became hysteria; claims covered the country for miles and presses could hardly keep up with the issues of stock. Soon ore was being uncovered of such richness that men who had not been able to get in on rich claims were willing to work at any wage in order to go underground and walk off with a few chunks daily. One man with luck could secrete several hundred dollars worth on a single shift. This practice, never before particularly prevalent in Nevada camps, which mostly mined silver or gold in combination with other metals, had been developed to a high degree in Colorado camps, and large numbers of experienced Coloradans had joined the stampede to Goldfield.

Numerous fences appeared to take over the purloined ore and it was the miners with plenty of money who gave Goldfield its reputation as a great spending town.

High-grading was to bring on one of the sensational incidents of Goldfield history. As the interests and work became better organized the big producers determined to put an end to the high-grading and ordered change-rooms established where all workers should leave their work clothes. The miners were indignant and talk ran high. The town's labor was highly organized but unions could not very well call a strike to maintain the right to steal. I.W.W. organizers—Wobblies— were on hand to stir up threats of violence. The miners, however, had some legitimate grievances. The panic of 1907 had suspended specie payments and the men were being paid in script—a particular insult when they were bringing up gold in quantities beyond imagination. Moreover, not all miners were high-graders and prices of commodities had not fallen much below those of the boom days. Feeling was running so high that some of the owners became frightened and persuaded the governor to ask President Theodore Roosevelt for troops. General Funston came up immediately from California and set up a camp overlooking the mines. After a few days he reported that the town was quiet and he was not needed. A Federal commission arrived to investigate on December 15, 1907. In the meantime the operators had set a wage scale at $3.50 a day for unskilled labor and up to $5 for skilled, ordered a 20 per cent reduction in commodity prices in the town and threatened that it would set up commissaries if the cuts were not made by the retailers. The railroad had reached Goldfield two years earlier so prices should have dropped long before. The commission confirmed Funston's report that troops were not needed and the President ordered their recall; after violent protests by the mine operators two companies were left until a State police force could be organized. With the troops in town and plenty of men out of work as a result of the stock market panic, it was easy to find strike breakers. Following various concessions on both sides of the controversy the troops left on March 7, 1908, but their place was taken by the Nevada State Police.

With the mines operating in three shifts, production reached its peak in 1910, paying more than $11,000,000.

Long before this, however, the town had developed stable social circles. The elegance of Tonopah was quite out-distanced; parties of all kinds were frequent and lavish and when the new theater was opened the town engaged Nat Goodwin and Edna Goodrich, most popular comedy team of the day, for its opening. For lustier souls there was the Northern Saloon, run by Tex Rickard, who had made a fortune in a Klondyke saloon, lost it in California, and came here with the gold strike. The length of the bar and the number of tenders —80 of the latter, the tale is—are still spoken of with pride by old-timers.

In 1906 someone had conceived the idea that a major prizefight would focus attention on the town and the Gans-Nelson fight was arranged. Rickard, who had been studying publicity technique, had charge. "The Battle of the Century" took place on September 6, with all the bally-hoo imaginable. The town of 20,000 held several times as many people for a few days before the 42-round fight from which Gans emerged as world lightweight champion.

In 1910 the town had reached such a metropolitan peak that it was determined to build a hotel worthy of its position; the result was the building that still stands. But at the end of that year production began to decline from its all-time high of more than $11,000,000. By 1912 it had dropped off nearly $5,000,000. Insiders were beginning to pull out though most of the people did not recognize the signs. In 1918 the mines did not produce $1,500,000 and the following year there was a 40 per cent decrease. Within three years less than $150,000 came from the mills.

This town, in a high bare saddle, has the intense sunlight that quickly gives some kinds of glass the righ purple tinge frequently seen in the Southwest; even the headlights of old motor cars have a lavender cast.

The GOLDFIELD HOTEL is a high brick structure with an ornate recessed entrance. Woodwork in the lobby is of mahogany and behind the desk is a series of strong-boxes befitting a jewelry ore town. Thick flowered carpets still cover the floors of suites that rented in the first year, when the town had several thousand transients at a time, for $20 a day. Brass beds, heavy leathered-covered chairs, and lambrequined shades on lamps remain as reminders of the past. Champagne corks by the dozens still cover the shelf above the great mirror in the bar. Champagne ran across the lobby and down the steps the night the hotel was opened.

The grim, greenish-yellow ESMERALDA COUNTY COURTHOUSE holds records of great interest to patient researchers.

As US 95 sweeps down from Goldfield joshuas are seen in large numbers, bushier and taller with each mile toward the south. Their creamy blossoms among the sharp, dark spines in spring always provide a surprise.

The vista at about 30 *m.* is memorable. The road is a sharp line across a vast undulating plain that sweeps to tawny foothills, and ranges blue in the distance. Yet not a mile of the way affords a view precisely like that before or ahead. One range with rounded peaks is deep brown, patched with purple where washes have been cut; another is sharply peaked and streaked with rose, green, and deep red. Even in the winter the brush covering has a tinge of yellow and low running plants with red stems near the road look like a planted border.

US 95 continues southeastward with the snow-capped ranges gleaming to the south. Remote and austere, they seem to belong to another world.

Right on this road into the GRAPEVINE MOUNTAINS, crossing the California Line, 15 *m.*, and a boundary of Death Valley National Monument, 4.5 miles north of Scotty's Castle.

Not far south of the junction the highway dips and the far blue mountains, with their summits looking like piles of blue fog on the horizon, drop behind brown ranges. The desert flora becomes steadily greener, the mountains less barren, though there is still no sign of trees in any direction. Paiute Mesa (L) is a roughly eroded and brightly tinted tableland.

BEATTY, 92.4 *m.* (3,392 alt., 200 pop.), catering to Death Valley visitors, is the terminus of the Tonopah & Tidewater Railroad, and a supply base for mining camps. On the banks of the Amargosa River which flows mostly underground, Beatty is one of the delightful small centers of the State. The white limbs of cottonwoods and sun-bleached sheen of old timbers blend into the wide dusty side streets. Wooden awnings hang far out over side walks and provide shelter from the brilliant sun. In 1906 Beatty became a freighting point for the Bullfrog Mining District, first explored in 1904 by Frank Harris and Ernest Cross. Although the center of mining activity was at Rhyolite, 5 miles west, Beatty handled most of the freight and traffic and proudly called itself "the Chicago of Nevada".

At the O'BRIEN HOUSE is a fine collection of ore specimens gathered from many parts of the world. Behind and around the house are old vines that bear delicious grapes. North of town is the Panhandle ranch, owned by Lawrence P. Kimball, a grandson of Heber C. Kimball, Brigham Young's right-hand man. This ranch is one of the largest in this part of the State.

Right from Beatty over paved Nev. 58 to a junction, 5 *m.;* R. here 2 *m.* to RHYOLITE, from 1905 to 1908 a city of 8,000. So promising were the first assays on the ore, so loud was the publicity on Nevada bonanzas following the Goldfield stampede, that many who bought land and stock here believed that Rhyolite would be another Virginia City. Though the mines produced approximately $3,000,000, it was discovered that the rich veins and ledges were superficial and many of the substantial buildings, of brick and concrete, erected in the belief of a long future, were soon torn down or left to disintegration. Though at the height of the boom two railroads entered the town, the only evidence of them today is the ruins of one elaborate depot, now open at intervals

as a casino to attract visitors from Death Valley. Notable among the ruins is the BOTTLE HOUSE, whose walls were built of quart beer bottles, laid horizontally, and integrated with adobe. Victorian jigsaw frills hang from the eaves of the gabled roof, and a dried coyote from one gable end. Since 1939 this has been a free museum of desert relics whose owner depends on the sale of curios for support. Around the house is an amazing garden; among pieces of glass purpled by the strong sunshine, bits of unusual rock, old cart wheels, figures from toyshops, old mortars, and what-not are many kinds of cactus and small delicate desert flowers.

Nev. 58 continues into a tiny corner of Death Valley National Monument and crosses the California Line, 13 *m.*, at a point 14 miles north of Furnace Creek Junction.

At Beatty, US 95 turns L. and skirts the western base of Bare Mountains, a stratified and faulted range, of solid stone from base to summit. In its richness and variety of colors this range is one of the most impressive in the State. The route lies along the Amargosa Desert, in view of high mountains hemming Death Valley. The highway again takes a straight line across a vast desert floor where creosote bush, cactus, and yucca grow. Against a great blue range, (R) at 110 *m.*, is a group of cream-colored hills that look like piles of shifting sand; and on the opposite side of the highway is an alkali expanse blindingly white.

CARRARA (L), 101.9 *m.*, is a camp once supported by Carrara marble quarried on the southwest flank of Bear Mountain, about 3 miles to the north. The town was formerly a station on the Tonopah & Tidewater Railroad. Large quantities of white, gray, black, and blue marble of fine quality have been found—some of the white marble of the statuary grade.

At 118.4 *m.* is the junction with paved Nev. 29.

Right here to cross the California Line, 17 *m.*, at a point 7.2 miles north of Death Valley Junction.

INDIAN SPRINGS, 163.5 *m.* (3,100 alt.), was for many years a stage stop, an oasis by warm springs in the desert. Today it is a gasoline station and an unusually attractive tourist camp near a large dude ranch.

South of Indian Springs US 95 crosses a broad valley. After passing the Pintwater and Desert Ranges (L), the highway goes down a long valley that heads straight for Las Vegas. Directly across the valley (R) is Charleston Peak (11,910 alt.) in the Nevada National Forest.

At 178 *m.* is the junction with paved Nev. 52, part of a loop route through the Charleston Mountain section of the Nevada National Forest (*best followed from lower junction for sake of views; particularly spectacular vistas toward end of day*).

Right on this road, which begins among cacti, yucca, creosote bush, and other desert flora, and within a few miles is in the upper plant and animal zones. At 17 *m.*, among conifers, is the junction with an improved road; R. (*straight ahead*) at this point 0.3 *m.* to the McWILLIAMS CAMPGROUND (*simple facilities*) and CAMP PITTMAN (L) in Lee Canyon. Here among evergreens and aspens are dormitories and other facilities providing not only a summer camping place for the children of Las Vegas but also a lodge for winter sportsmen. Ski slopes of all kinds and a ski-jump are near by. Even when the temperature at Las Vegas goes above 100° during the mid-day, three blankets are needed here at night. The public campsites are above Camp Pittman and there is plenty of room for parking cars and trailers. Only a caretaker is at the children's camp in winter, but bunks and stoves are available to visitors. The road is being extended across the Charleston Range into Pahrump Valley.

The road branching L. at 17 *m.* becomes the main side route, crossing the mountain side with many views of the desert and of the distant bare Sheep Mountains through low hanging evergreens. The variety of the flora and fauna on this mountain makes the range a happy hunting ground for zoologists and botanists, professional as well as amateur. Mule deer, mountain sheep, bobcats, lynx, foxes, badgers, porcupines, and other animals are native, and elk, antelope, sage hens, and blue grouse are being introduced. Birds are particularly numerous, and more than 400 plant species have been counted, some of them hitherto unknown. Above the ponderosa pine belt are pure stands of the rare foxtail pine, some of them seven feet in diameter. Toward timberline the trees are bent and gnarled from their long battle with the winds. At about 24 *m.* is DEER CREEK CAMPGROUND, by a short stream for which it was named; this is the only year-round stream on the range, though there are numerous springs.

At 27 *m.* is a fork; R. here 4.5 *m.* into KYLE CANYON, where a delightful lodge provides meals and rooms. The lodge is slightly beyond a ranger station (*information*) and public campsites. This is also a popular winter sports center, with various types of runs below Cathedral Rock. Many summer cottages are in the neighborhood.

Left from the lodge on a 3-mile trail that circles Cathedral rock and ascends the bare face of CHARLESTON PEAK (11,910 alt.).

At the fork the circular route bears L., becoming Nev. 39, and descends to the valley and the junction with US 95, 41 *m.* (*see ahead*).

South of its junction with Nev. 52, US 95 continues through the broad valley between the Charleston and Sheep Ranges. Bare and uninhabited as most of the ranges in this region seem to be, there are not many that do not show at least a few monuments of prospectors. Hundreds of men have sweated up and down hunting for promising ledges, though very few of them have ever made much profit, even when they had a lucky strike. Usually they are so much in need of a few dollars that they are willing to sell to the first person who is interested. Only a rare man has money enough for more than first development, and, curiously, though they are always enthusiastic about their strikes, few have enough faith in them to choose to sell on a royalty basis, rather than outright, for cash. Just the same they have a deep contempt for the men who bring their discoveries to success. A hoary but ever popular story among prospectors concerns a geologist, a mining engineer, and a mining promoter who were out hunting. According to the story, they eventually reached tracks; then the party divided, the geologist back-tracking to find where the game had come from, the engineer following the tracks forward, and the promoter going back to town for a truck to carry out the animal after it was shot.

At 186.6 *m.* is the junction with an improved road.

Left on this road into the bare Sheep Mountains; the road winds in and out among canyons, and brown slopes sparsely covered with vegetation, if with any at all. A sudden turn brings the unimproved road to the HIDDEN FOREST, 27 *m.,* a stand of beautiful evergreens.

By a cactus garden at 192 *m.* is the junction with Nev. 39 (*see before*). With eroded cliffs on the Charleston Range, mottled a brilliant red, continually nearer, US 95 is suddenly among ranchlands, where cottonwoods indicate the lines of irrigation ditches.

LAS VEGAS, 207 *m.* (2,033 alt., 10,000 pop.) (*see Tour 3a*), is at junctions with US 91 (*see Tour 3*) and US 93-466 (*see Tour 5A*).

Section d. JUNCTION US 93-466 *to* CALIFORNIA LINE; 61.5 *m.*

US 95, which is united with US 93-466 (*see Tour 5A*) southeast of Las Vegas, swings away from the other routes, 0 *m.*, at a point 4.9 miles southwest of Boulder City and on the edge of the Boulder Dam Recreational Area. US 95 crosses a vast dry lake and an area sparsely covered with cactus, creosote bush, and yucca, running parallel to the Colorado River but separated from it by the Eldorado Range.

At 6 *m.* is the junction with a dirt road.

Left on this road to ELDORADO, 10 *m.*, sometimes called Nelson. Spaniards are said to have discovered valuable minerals in this part of Eldorado Canyon about 1775, but 100 years passed before an expedition came up from Mexico to develop the discovery—only to find it already being worked by the Eldorado Mining Company. The Mexicans had a map, which they said the discoverers had drawn, exactly designating the TECHATTICUP MINE, richest producer in the camp. The district had been rediscovered in 1857, and organized as the Colorado in 1861. The district has produced two to five million in gold, silver, copper and lead.

According to one of several conflicting stories, in the summer of 1874 John Nash, organizer of the Eldorado Company, decided to jump the adjacent Queen City claim and employed three desperados to help him. He promised them $5,000 each if they would hold it for a certain period of time. Nash's plan was to hire the gunmen, make a secret arrangement with one of them to kill the others after he had acquired the claim, then kill off this man himself to cover up the transaction. When the owner of the Queen City sent a man to do the annual development work required to keep the claim, the fellow was frightened out of the country. One of the three desperadoes was a Jim Harrington, who had at least three dead men on his record; the second was a murderer known as William Piette; the third was a half-breed, Jim Jones. Early one morning, while Jones was washing his face and had soap in his eyes, Piette stepped up quietly and shot him in the back. Jones seized the heavy powder-keg serving as a wash-basin and knocked Piette down. Then running to his bunk he grabbed a gun and shot Piette, who had followed him to complete the job. Thereupon Jones fled to Piette's cabin and took his Winchester rifle; leaving a trail of blood as he ran, he fled into the hills. The word that reached Eldorado insinuated that Jones had attacked Piette and a posse went after him. Jones hid in a prospect hole about four feet deep but was discovered by the trail of blood.

Everybody in camp joined the chase and mining operations were suspended. All day under a hot and blinding sun, Jones held the posse off—and all that night. The next morning he resolved to carry the fight to his enemies but was too weak to climb out of the hole; another day and night passed before he put his handkerchief on his gun as a sign of surrender. A man named Tom Johnson was the first to reach the hole. There was the unconquerable Jones, his eyes blood-shot, his lips swollen and cracked by thirst, his clothes matted with blood. He begged for water but Johnson sent a bullet into the half-breed's forehead and the rest of the men covered the body with earth.

Nash got the Queen City, but it bore a bad reputation, and Nash himself was afraid to be caught near it after dark; he once swore that the ghost of Jim

Jones had come up to him and walked by his side. The time came when no man would enter the underground workings and many of the miners left the camp. As for Piette, he lived to poison Old Man Davis, one of the owners of the Bridal Chamber claim, and a man named Fuller, one of Nash's partners. He was also blamed for the murder of a man named Warren, who mysteriously vanished.

Not far from Eldorado, early in 1940, a prospector noticed a man-made barricade in front of a shallow cave in the face of a high canyon wall. Investigating, he discovered the skeleton of an Indian; near by were a loaded shotgun, a bow, steel-tipped arrows, bullet-moulds, and other odds and ends. Las Vegans summoned to take charge of the bones easily identified them as the remains of an Indian named Quejo who for more than 10 years was the terror of Clark County people living in remote places. There are contradictory stories about Quejo's origin and early years; one is that he was a Paiute and the other that he belonged to an Arizona tribe l t lived for a time among the Paiute near Las Vegas. There are also contradictory stories about when his career as a public enemy began. One tale is that his first victim was a Paiute who was murdered in some intra-tribal row over the methods used by a medicine man; shortly thereafter Quejo attacked Hi Bohn of Las Vegas and broke both his arms with a pole-pick. After this affair he fled into the mountains southwest of Las Vegas. Another tale blames his blood-thirsty career on the fact that he had been ordered by authorities to track down one of his brothers who was a killer and bring back his head as proof of the punishment.

At any event his known history begins in 1910 when he killed a wood-cutter for his supplies; shortly afterward he killed the guard of the Gold Bug mine near Eldorado. During his public career he was definitely linked to certain crimes by his tracks, which had unusual characteristics. For some years after these initial killings his trail was obscured, though he was blamed for the disappearance of several lone prospectors and miners. Then in 1919 Quejo attempted to steal food from the home of Ned Douglas near Eldorado and shot the miner's wife when she walked into the kitchen. This killing of a woman roused high feeling and the men who had trailed him in 1910 took up the chase again. The trail led up the Colorado to St. Thomas, now buried by the northern arm of Lake Mead, across to the Arizona side of the river, and back down the Nevada side to this region. Near St. Thomas two prospectors had been killed in savage style; two days later two men and two boys were found murdered on the opposite side of the river near Black Canyon. Seven killings in all took place in this period with Quejo's footprints showing quite clearly on the ground near the bodies. Some people said the Indian killed for food, some for other supplies; but a man who knew him said that Quejo was too expert in the capture of game to kill from hunger. Sometimes he took the shoes of his victims.

Numbers of men from Arizona as well as Nevada spent months following his tracks; the sheriff of Clark County was close to him on several occasions, once or twice finding camp-fires not yet cold. One evening when there was evidence that the killer was near, the sheriff found himself in a box canyon as night fell; and the chance seemed so good that the Indian would be the winner rather than the loser in the game of hide-and-seek that the sheriff carefully wrote his name on the cliff above the spot where he lay down to spend the night, to enable easy identification of his body if he should not see the light of day again. But the Indian disappeared and there was no clue on what had happened to him until his bones were found.

US 95 proceeds to SEARCHLIGHT, 37 m. (3,560 alt., 192 pop.), near the Opal Mountains and surrounded by a desert of mesquite and cactus. According to legend, this camp was named by two brothers who, lighting a fire here in 1898, took inspiration from the name of their box of matches. In that year a camp grew up on what is now the Searchlight claim of the Duplex Mine. In the early period one claim, later producing more than $1,000,000 was sold for $1,500, a team of mules, a buckboard, and a double-barreled shotgun. Another that produced $150,000 changed hands for a pint of whiskey. The district has produced nearly $2,000,000 worth of ores, principally gold, and at least one lump of turquoise weighing 320 carats.

Searchlight reached its height in 1906 but was active for another 14 years, and some work still goes on. It had 38 saloons on its principal street during its boom days. Like Eldorado, it was a lawless camp, though now and then gun-fights gave way to gentler pastimes. On July 4, 1902, for instance, there was a burro fight. Two jack burros, noted for their courage, were brought in; thousands of dollars besides various mining claims were wagered on the outcome of their scrap. One of the burros, the property of a "desert rat," was named Thunder, the other, a lean, lanky beast, was Hornet. Thunder and Hornet squared off on a level area below the camp and raised a dust cloud visible for miles. Thunder had the best of it in the early going, but after Hornet got his second wind he plied his heels and teeth so well that he chased Thunder into the desert. Thereupon the men collected their wagers and went to the saloons for the usual celebration.

Right from Searchlight into McCullough Range passing through an extensive joshua forest. At 7 m. is the elaborately equipped ranch of Rex Bell, former cowboy actor, and his wife, Clara Bow. Above the ranch rises Crescent Peak (6,016 alt.). CRESCENT, 24 m., is in a mining district where turquoise was discovered in 1894 by an Indian known as Prospector Johnnie. A year later a New Yorker began operations as the Toltec Gem Company. Two other turquoise discoveries have been made in the neighborhood and small amounts of silver, lead, copper, and other metals have been produced. Prehistoric workings were found during development with ancient stone hammers still lying about.

US 95 continues southward through Paiute Valley and crosses the CALIFORNIA LINE, 61.5 m., at a point about 30 miles north of Needles, Calif.

Tour 5A

Las Vegas—Boulder City—Boulder Dam; 32 m. US 93-466.

Paved roadbed throughout.
Accommodations at Las Vegas and Boulder City.

US 93-466 runs southeast from LAS VEGAS, 0 m. (see Tour 3), which is on US 91 (see Tour 3). It is united with US 95 as it leaves the rapidly expanding city through a fringe of tourist camps and passes into a dry valley with the Black Mountains, a volcanic formation that truly deserves its name, ahead on the rim of the Colorado River. In this seemingly arid area numerous wild flowers are seen in May and June, particularly brilliant after a winter with considerable rain or snow. A yellow poppy similar to the California is prominent. Among the blooms is one so rare and lovely that botanists refuse to point out its habitat lest collectors, eager to build up their herbariums by exchange, exterminate it in making up their collections. This delicate flower is the hairy white poppy, which sways lightly in the breeze. The hairs on the stem and leaves are Nature's protection against unnecessary evaporation in this land of little water.

At 18.5 *m*. is the southern junction with US 95 (*see Tour 5d*). US 93-466 begins its short climb into the Black Mountains to the divide, where sits BOULDER CITY (R), 23 *m*. (2,500 alt., 2,500 est. pop.).

Accommodations: Hotel, camps.

Transportation facilities: Union Pacific Railroad branch line from point 7 m. south of Las Vegas; also interstate busses, taxi service to Las Vegas, and planes for air trips.

Sightseeing and information services: Boulder Dam Service Bureau, in Boulder Theater, provides full information on construction, administration, places where Park Service guide and naturalist services are available, and shows free motion-pictures of area and construction; Grand Canyon-Boulder Dam Tours, concessionaire of the government in the Boulder Dam National Recreational Area, also has offices in Boulder Theater and conducts all-expense tours on Lake Mead and up the Colorado River, rents motor and sailboats for private use, and operates other recreational facilities such as bathhouses by the lake, lunchrooms, a camp at Pierce's Ferry Landing—end of two-day all-expense trip up Colorado—and so on. Rates for trips vary from approximately $4 for four hours—morning, afternoon, or evening—to approximately $25 for two-day trip. It is well to make arrangements a day in advance for longer trips though near by trips can be made on short notice; some types of trips are conducted only three or four times a week.

BOULDER CITY—Was built by the Government in 1932 as construction headquarters during work on Boulder Dam and also as permanent administrative headquarters for the Reclamation and National Park Service forces in charge of operations in the area; it is as spick and span as though it were in charge of Dutch housewives. Above the wide streets, which follow the curves of the hills, are houses of varying designs on delightfully landscaped terraces. The whole city was planned in advance of construction with the idea of making it a pleasant dwelling place as well as a point from which the area and its man-made facilities could be administered efficiently. While Las Vegas residents readily acknoweldged the need for a town for people employed at the new powerhouse and dam they were bitterly opposed to its development as a recreational center as well. Their answer has been to develop their own city and points of interest near it as a counter attraction. To the present the new city has cost about two million dollars; there is no private ownership and property leases can not be taken for more than ten years. A city-manager is in charge of civic administration. No gambling permits have as yet (1940) been issued.

The temperature at Boulder City has an annual range between 20 degrees above zero and 120, with a mean temperature of 45 degrees in January and 92 in July. The average summer temperature is only slightly cooler than at Las Vegas, but is 7 degrees cooler than by Lake Mead. There is a marked drop in temperature after sundown.

US 93-466 skirts the northwestern edge of the new town and starts a circuitous descent through black canyons to the river. Great long-legged steel towers are everywhere, carrying power up from the generating station below Boulder Dam. At 24 *m.* is the junction with another paved road.

Left here 5.5 *m.* to broad HEMENWAY WASH (*bathhouses, wharves, boats, surfboards, campgrounds*), chief sports center on LAKE MEAD, which was named for Elwood Mead, chief of the Reclamation Service when the project was put forward. The indigo-blue waters of the wide man-made lake, extending more than a hundred miles upstream and spreading into several canyons, are surrounded on all sides by steep rocky cliffs and ranges, some of them brilliantly streaked with red, green, yellow, and blue.

The main highway continues its curving course, descending more than a thousand feet in the few miles to BOULDER DAM (1,232 alt. at road level), 32 *m.*, braced across one of the narrowest parts of Black Canyon.

Close to the Nevada end of the dam is the BOULDER DAM MEMORIAL, two stylized seated figures with tall upraised wings on a large slightly raised platform with terazzo paving. Set in the pavement is a bronze diagram of the stars and planets and their courses, the positions of the stars and planets being as they were at the time the dam was dedicated.

The road crosses the top of the dam into Arizona at a point 70.6 miles northwest of Kingman, Arizona. Upstream is Lake Mead with only the tops of four round white intake towers showing above the waters. These towers, 375 feet high and 75 feet in diameter, are deceptively small when seen from the dam, to which they are connected by narrow concrete roadways. On the brink of the downstream side of the dam are four small towers providing access to the powerplants below, where the gigantic turbines are at work.

The immensity of the dam and of the powerhouses at the base of its slanting concave apron cannot be appreciated from the roadway. Seen from above, the powerplants look like stores in a toy village though one alone is nearly a third of a mile long. The interiors of the power-houses and their approaches have carefully worked out decorations in color. Both color and designs are of southwestern inspiration; the stylized Indian patterns have been admirably adapted.

Construction of the project, which was approved by President Coolidge on December 21, 1928, had long been promoted by southwestern interests, particularly by manufacturers wanting cheap power in the Los Angeles area, and by farm corporations as well as private ranchers interested in Imperial Valley and surrounding areas. It was first proposed to build the dam several miles upstream in Boulder Canyon but the present site was decided on after extensive exploration. The first appropriation for construction was made in 1930 and for a time the structure was called Hoover Dam for President Herbert Hoover, in office at the time. Total cost of the whole project, including the All-American Canal to carry water into the California deserts, will probably approach $200,000,000. The power is being divided between Arizona, Nevada, and California, with the first two being permitted slightly more than a third and California nearly two thirds. Most of the drinking and irrigation water also goes to southern California. At one time there were plans for settling migrants on small ranches in the irrigated district, but this plan has been abandoned because of the size of the tracts and the capital needed for efficient farming. So far navigation, one of the objects written into the Swing-Johnson Bill under which work was authorized, has been developed only to a limited extent; this may increase if the volume of products of the district along the river make it desirable. A major industry resulting from the construction, though not seriously considered when the project was proposed, is catering to tourists and vacationists. This business is being administered by the National Park Service in an area extending eastward toward Grand Canyon National Park; the two sections together form one of the largest publicly controlled playgrounds in the world.

The first contracts on the project were signed in 1930, the first concrete for the dam was poured on June 6, 1933, and the last on May 29, 1935. The gates in the diversion tunnels were closed on February 1, 1935 and the lake rose quickly to its permanent level. The first generator was placed in operation in September, 1936, and the fourth a few months later; the present units have a generative capacity of 515,000 horsepower.

The Colorado River and its deep canyons have long been a land of mystery. The upper river was first known to white men in 1540 or 1541 when Garcia Lopez de Gardenas with twelve other Spaniards made their way to the brink of the Grand Canyon and gazed awestricken into that abyss. They had come from Zuni in New Mexico, where the Indians told them of the canyon's wonders.

Major John W. Powell in 1869 with a party of five men underwent tremendous hardships in making the descent of the Colorado. So terrifying was the trip that three of his men deserted at Separation Canyon, on the north rim in Arizona, and attempted to scale the canyon walls. They did get out of the canyon, but on the great mesa above Indians killed them. Powell with two other men successfully navigated the remainder of the river.

In 1857, before Major Powell made his expedition, boats ascended the river for 500 miles under command of Lieutenant J. C. Ives. Ives' steamer reached Black Canyon, where the boat almost foundered on hidden rocks.

About 1859 Mormons of the Moapa Valley established a landing on the river, some 20 miles north of Black Canyon, under direction of Anson Call. For several years, Fort Callville, now submerged, was a loading station for boats carrying on trade with San Francisco. Samuel Adams did a regular business between these points in the *Esmeralda,* a boat 125 feet long. In 1868 Adams reported to the Secretary of War: "Three years ago two steamers could do the trade of the Colorado, now, seven are employed and are insufficient. Thirty-seven ships and one ocean steamer have gone to the mouth of the river within the last six months while the trade with San Francisco has increased in that same time to over $1,500,000. These are but a few of the results following the enterprise of navigating the Colorado."

The harnessing of this long, turbulent stream in its extraordinary bed has stirred imaginations everywhere. Anyone can now travel northeastward through the chasm that until 1936 had been traversed by little more than a handful of very adventurous men.

‖‖‖‖‖‖‖⊠‖‖‖‖‖‖‖⊠‖‖‖‖‖‖‖⊠‖‖‖‖‖‖‖⊠‖‖‖‖‖‖‖⊠‖‖‖‖‖‖‖⊠‖‖‖‖‖‖‖⊠‖‖‖‖‖‖‖⊠‖‖‖‖‖‖‖⊠‖‖‖‖‖‖‖⊠‖‖‖‖‖‖‖⊠‖‖‖‖‖‖‖⊠‖‖‖‖‖‖

Tour 6

(Delta, Utah)—Ely—Tonopah—Coaldale—(Bishop, Calif.) ; US 6. Utah State Line to California Line, 315.5 m.

Paved roadbed except east of US 93; this short graveled section will be paved by 1941.
Tonopah & Goldfield R. R. parallels route between Tonopah and Coaldale.
All types of accommodations in Ely and Tonopah; very limited in Coaldale.
Tourist cabins at a few points along route.

US 6, the Cape-Cod-Los Angeles road—longest road bearing the same number—crosses south-central Nevada diagonally, for the most part through mountainous country and desert. It passes close to Mount Wheeler, second highest peak in Nevada, through four national forests, through the Ely copper districts, and through the Tonopah area, scene of the State's second great mining boom. At many points ranges and abrupt outcroppings of rock are brilliantly banded with color, particularly striking when the sun is low.

Section a. UTAH LINE *to* CONNER'S STATION ; 42.5 *m.*

US 6 crosses the UTAH LINE, 0 *m.,* at a point 94 miles west of Delta, Utah, and proceeds southwest toward mountains in eastern divisions of the Nevada National Forest.

At 11.1 *m.* is the junction with a graded dirt road.

Left on this road to BAKER (*gasoline*), 1.6 *m.;* R. (*straight ahead*) here 8 *m.* on a Forest Service road to small STELLA LAKE, in a deep round basin. Cars are parked here near a marked trail that circles R. around the lake and climbs steeply for about 8 *m.* (4 *hrs.*) to the summit of MOUNT WHEELER (13,058 alt.), whose bare rocky top is the second highest point in the State. The trail to the summit rises rapidly through three life zones of plant and animal life. In summer sections of the trail are almost obscured by Indian paint brush, lupines, and other bright blooms.

At Baker the main side road turns R. to LEHMAN CAVES NATIONAL MONUMENT (*lunchroom, cabins, camp sites*), 7.7 *m.,* under jurisdiction of the National Park Service since 1922. The caverns, amid pine, spruce, fir, juniper, and mountain mahogany, are in limestone, among high peaks and deep glaciated canyons of the Snake Range. A large variety of birds nest near the streams and fishing and game hunting are popular sports in the region for which this is a base.

The caves, all deep underground were discovered about 1878 when a horse driven by Abe Lehman, who was hauling logs down the mountainside, broke through the earth's crust, revealing the cavity. In some degree Lehman explored the chambers, though they were not fully known until much later. The caverns extend 1,400 feet from the entrance, go down 200 feet, and have no natural entrance.

The chambers and galleries contain innumerable stalactites and stalagmites of remarkable color and beauty, and are exceptionally clean, as bats have never inhabited them. Some of the stalactites meet stalagmites built up from the floor, forming columns 15 to 60 feet high. No two formations are alike. Often the limestone drippings have taken the shape of strange figures, of ribbons, of folded draperies. Begun in the pre-ice age, this gradual transformation continues still, wet and dry cycles influencing the development. It is estimated that stalactites and stalagmites here increase no more than an inch in 1000 years.

Tiny needle crystals adorn the labyrinth of corridors, which are lined with fluted columns. Small winding tunnels connect chambers of chocolate, cream and buff. Some formations have been named, the more prominent being the Pearly Gates, St. Peter, the Little Church Around the Corner, the Angel's Wing, Cathedral Spires, the Parachute, and Peter Pan. Exquisite is the interior of the Grand Palace with its multitude of pendulous "icicles" resembling an inverted garden. Below them, heaped on the floor, are terraced stalagmites, countless filaments resembling cascades of Spanish combs. Some of the columns when struck give off deep musical tones. At the tips of many stalactites hang transparent, jeweled drops of water. The Hall of Music, with high arched ceiling splashed with color, is one of the most beautiful rooms.

The road to the caves continues northward to a junction with the Forest Service road up Mount Wheeler (*see above*).

US 6 turns northwest to a junction at 19 *m.*

Left here to OSCEOLA, 6 *m.* (6,800 alt.), where gold lodes were discovered in 1872 and placer mines in 1877. The ore was first worked in the primitive arrastras, but a small stamp mill was built in 1878. This is one of the few places in Nevada where hydraulic mining was done, with extensive operations beginning in 1880 and lasting for 20 years. No exact figures on the value of production are available, but estimates range from two to five million, most of it from the placers. There have been several revivals of activity in the district, and some tungsten was mined after 1916.

US 6 continues between divisions of the Nevada National Forest and crosses SACRAMENTO PASS (7,163 alt.), which affords an impressive sweep of mountain and plateau. Broad flanks are mantled with evergreen and threaded by clear mountain streams, country unlike any other crossed in Nevada by this route. The road descends southwestward to a junction with US 93, 42.5 *m. (see Tour 2b)*, at CONNERS STATION. Between this junction and East Ely, US 6 unites with paved US 93 *(see Tour 2b)*.

Section b. EAST ELY *to* CALIFORNIA LINE; 247 *m.*

This section of US 6 cuts diagonally across the State, for 170 miles passing through thinly inhabited country where filling-stations and other facilities—as well as water—are rare. The route is beautiful, however, and many connoisseurs of southwestern landscapes pick it as one of their favorites. Barren brown mountains are deeply fissured with purple; others, streaked with rose, green, and mauve, contrast with darker volcanic formations. One whole range, of salmon pink, becomes fiery red in the late afternoon.

In EAST ELY, 0 *m.*, is a junction with US 50 *(see Tour 7a)*, which unites with US 6 into ELY 1 *m.* (6,433 alt., 3,045 pop.) (*see Tour 7b*). Here US 50 continues westward *(see Tour 7b)* and US 6 turns sharply L. through a side canyon, passing through one of the most comfortable residential districts of Ely before the canyon narrows and the highway begins its climb.

At 3 *m.* is the junction with a trail.

Left here up Powderhouse Canyon in Ward Mountain. This leisurely trail is particularly rich in flowers all summer long.

On US 6 at MURRAY SUMMIT, 4 *m.*, is the junction with a dirt road.

Left here 4 *m.*, winding along a high slope and through mountain mahogany and juniper to a ski-hut at the foot of a power-driven ski-lift (15c *a ride*, $1 *a day*), operated by the Ely Ski Club. The slopes are being cleared to provide a wide variety of runs.

For 50 miles US 6 crosses rolling country dotted with dwarf pine and stained with iron oxides. At 10 *m.* snow-tipped Ward Mountain is visible (L). In this area bands of sheep are seen in the spring and fall crossing between winter and summer ranges.

At 23 *m.* is the junction with Nev. 38, paved for 13 miles and then unimproved.

Left on Nev. 38 to PRESTON, 7 *m.*, and LUND, 13 *m.*, Mormon settlements in an area where livestock raising is the leading activity but some small-scale mining is carried on. At 38 *m.* is the junction with a dirt road; L. here 4 *m.* to WHIPPLE CAVE, whose chief attraction is a room one hundred feet in width and height and five times as long. In the center of this immense room is one massive column ten feet in diameter and reaching from floor to roof. Many bats have lived here, covering the floor with guano. The cave, reached with difficulty, has no caretaker.

On US 6 Grant Range is crossed at 38 *m.* through the southernmost tip of a division of the Nevada National Forest.

Vegetation grows less as the route proceeds westward. West of CURRANT CREEK CAMPGROUND *(firewood and water)*,

43 *m.,* a shaded spot on the banks of a stream, near a ranger station (L), US 6 winds through a narrow pass.

CURRANT (*store, lunchroom, gasoline station*), 52 *m.,* known also as Callaway Ranch, is at the western base of the Grant Range. This is a trading center for stock ranches along the range.

Right from Currant on Nev. 20, a dirt road, to DUCKWATER, 22 *m.,* a ranch house that sometimes serves as a base for hunters seeking mule deer in the mountains eastward.

US 6 skirts the northern end of the GRANT STATE GAME REFUGE, and crosses a dry lake bed.

From the low Pancake Range, 89 *m.* large black deposits of volcanic rock are seen, extending for many miles on both sides of the highway. Many large and small cinder cones of recent origin are visible, remnants of the time when the earth opened wide to eject mighty flows of molten rock.

Another valley is crossed where cattle often graze. Springs and wells dot its reaches.

WARM SPRINGS (*cabins, bathing, limited supplies, horses, guides*), 120 *m.,* on the eastern side of the Hot Creek Range, is another base of deer hunters. Not far away is a small rock house built in 1866 as a shelter for travelers. For many years it was a stopping-place for stagecoaches and freight teams on the Tonopah-Ely route.

After passing through a low divide in the Hot Creek Range, US 6 crosses Kawich Valley, used for grazing cattle and sheep.

At FIVE-MILE STATION, 141 *m.,* known also as Clark's Station, limited supplies and accommodations are available. This was another stage-station stop by a spring. For 100 miles westward US 6 now passes through one of the richest mineral areas in the United States. The barren and rocky mountains are continually brighter in color and more irregular in formation. Flat-topped hills mingle with conical peaks. Sometimes a coyote or jackrabbit darts off into the brush.

North of Five-Mile Station is a section of the Toiyabe National Forest, the southern tip of which the highway crosses. Although the large area is called a "forest," there are trees only on slopes far north. The "forest" is largely regulated grazing land, and a wild life preserve. Crossing Monitor Range in the reservation, US 6 traverses a wide dry valley, with the San Antonio Range on the western skyline. Late in the day the mountains, deeply stained with iron oxide and other minerals, look like a reef afire above the purple desert haze.

At 165 *m.* is the junction with Nev. 8A (*see Tour 7b.*).

TONOPAH, 171 *m.,* (6,063 alt., 2,116 pop.) (*see Tour 5b*), is at a junction with US 95 (*see Tour 5b*), with which US 6 unites westward between Tonopah and Coaldale (*see Tour 5b*).

COALDALE, 213 *m.* (4,600 alt., 4 est. pop.) (*see Tour 5b*), is at the western junction with US 95 (*see Tour 5b*).

US 6 turns west at Coaldale, through desert with the snow-capped mountains of the Inyo National Forest visible in the west upon the California-Nevada Line.

BASALT, 235 *m.* (6,224 alt., 6 est. pop.), is chiefly a minor supply center for prospectors. US 6 continues southwest and crosses Montgomery Pass, 238 *m.* (7,123 alt.), where MONTGOMERY, a store, service station, and bar provides another oasis. BOUNDARY PEAK (13,145 alt.), the highest elevation in Nevada, is L. This rugged, sparsely wooded country is visited by deer hunters and trout fishermen.

US 6 crosses the CALIFORNIA LINE, 247 *m.,* at a point 41 miles north of Bishop, California.

Tour 7

(Salt Lake City, Utah) — Ely — Eureka — Austin — Fallon — Carson City — (Sacramento, California) ; US 50.
Utah Line to California Line, 467.8 *m.*

Paved roadbed throughout; all-year traffic E. of Lake Tahoe. Lake Tahoe westward closed by snow during winter; may be open in winter after 1941.
Water and gasoline can be obtained at 30 to 40-mile intervals.
Accommodations of all types in larger towns.

Except in the extreme eastern part, where it strikes sharply southward, US 50 bisects Nevada from east to west, crossing range after range and valley after valley. It is one of the State's most beautiful long routes, providing a series of panoramas of mountain and valley with everchanging color. Each ridge and gully is boldly outlined in violets and blues that become rich purple at twilight; distant ranges merge in a broad sweep of blue and lavender. The presence of occasional streams is indicated in summer by the rippling green of willows and cottonwoods, in winter by tangles of white, orange, and red-barked branches. On each side of the meadow bottoms in the gray-green and yellow of sage and rabbitbrush, with juniper, scrub pine, and aspen on the rising slopes. Many ranges are splashed with red, green, yellow, and brown by mineral deposits. Always in Nevada and especially on this route late afternoon travel is an adventure. The red and orange of the declining sun throws a veil of unearthly light over mountain and valley—never the same for many minutes at a time—and clouds pile into blazing masses.

Occasional herds of cattle and bands of sheep are seen on the valley floors and on mountain slopes. Hawks and buzzards swim overhead, and long-tailed, black-and-white magpies are along the roadway. Now and then an eagle soars above a lofty peak. In early morning or late afternoon a solitary coyote may cross the road and then trot off to a hummock from which he can watch the traveler pass.

US 50 traverses a thinly populated area that has at one time or another supported populous mining camps; for miles it closely follows trails broken by early mail carriers.

Section a. UTAH LINE *to* ELY, 119.8 *m.*

US 50 crosses the Utah Line in WENDOVER, 0 *m.* (*see Tour 1a*), in conjunction with US 40 (*see Tour 1a*), at a point 127 miles west of Salt Lake City.

The two routes separate at 0.5 *m.,* US 50 turning southwest to cross flat desert country and rolling hills, gradually drawing farther away from the western edge of the Great Salt Lake Desert of Utah. Close to the Utah Line the vegetation is very sparse and consists chiefly of white sage. As US 50 enters rolling hills, terraces are visible on the slopes, the ancient water levels of receding Bonneville Lake.

FERGUSON'S SPRINGS (*water*), 25 *m.* (5,800 alt.), is a highway-maintenance camp. For years it has served as a stopping place for Idaho and Utah cattlemen trailing herds south to the Ely district for winter feeding.

Passing between the Toano and Goshute ranges, and through canyons that provide excellent forage, US 50 reaches WHITE HORSE PASS, 34 *m.* (6,595 alt.).

BECKY'S SPRINGS, 60 *m.,* is at the junction with US 93 (*see Tour 2a*), which is united with US 50 between this point and East Ely.

The united roads run through Steptoe Valley, one of the broadest and most impressive in the State. Its great sweep of level floor stretches southward as far as the eye can see, always in sight of the lightly wooded Schell Creek Range (L) where grouse, sage hens, and mule deer abound and trout are abundant in the many small streams; countless dirt roads lead off to camp sites with plenty of water and firewood.

In September the floor of the valley looks as though it were covered with a dark red carpet; shadscale, evenly spaced, produces the effect.

At 74.6 *m.* is the junction with a graveled road.

Right here 9 *m.* across Steptoe Valley to a graded road running north and south along the base of the Egan Range.

Right on this road 2.8 *m.* to CHERRY CREEK (5,800 alt., 247 pop.), named for the chokecherries in Cherry Creek Canyon. Between 1872 and 1883 this mining camp had a population of nearly 6,000 and was the center of a district whose production value has never been accurately estimated—guesses range from $6,000,000 to $20,000,000. By 1893 there was hardly a leaser at work here but later there was minor activity. Copper and lead as well as gold and silver have been taken out. As mining increased here most of the buildings from the camps at Schellbourne and Egan Canyon were moved to this place, among them a store that is still in use.

The road leading to and crossing the north-south road continues westward as an unimproved road through EGAN CANYON, named for Howard E. Egan, who rode for Chorpenning's pioneer mail service between Salt Lake City and Sacramento in the early 1850's and who demonstrated the practicability of this more direct route as a substitute for the roundabout Humboldt route previously used in carrying the mail. In 1855 Chorpenning made the transfer. The first discovery of values in this district was made by soldiers in 1863 and the Gilligan silver mine was at work in the following year, feeding ore into a five-stamp mill. The road climbs through the narrow canyon to a mountain meadow, on the far side of which are ruins marking the SITE OF THE EGAN CANYON PONY EXPRESS STATION. This section of the Pony Express route was particularly difficult and its isolation encouraged the Indians to bold forays. Rumor had it that these Indians used golden bullets and later discoveries in the district seemed to confirm the tale.

At 79.9 *m.* on US 50 is the junction with graveled Nev. 2.

Left on this old road, used by the Pony Express riders of 1860-61, who more or less followed the route blazed by Egan. SCHELLBOURNE, 3.4 *m.* (6,200 alt., 3 pop.), was called Schell Creek in the days when it was a relay station for the mail riders and Fort Schellbourne after troops camped here in the 1860's to protect the mail and travelers. Though now part of a ranch, it was a mining camp for a short time after silver ore was discovered in the surrounding hills. But development showed poor results and the few buildings were moved across to the richer Cherry Creek district (*see above*).

MAGNUSON'S RANCH, 80.2 *m.* on US 50, can provide emergency water and gasoline.

Right here on an improved road and right again to MONTE NEVA WARM SPRINGS, 4.3 *m.*, a resort with an outdoor pool filled by warm mineral springs in the lower part of the Egan Range. The surrounding area is delightfully wooded and trails and campsites bring many visitors.

On US 50-93 at 101.3 *m.* is the junction with a dirt road.

Left here through Gallagher's Gap on the F-S Ranch to Duck Creek, which is followed in summer through clumps of flowers to DUCK CREEK PLAY-GROUND, 7 *m.;* campsites here among juniper, aspen, and manzanita are popular with deer hunters and trout fishermen. The forest trail continues to Timber Creek and over the Duck Creek Range divide to a private hunting lodge at 10 *m.* Crossing another ridge the trail circles past the old Success mine and a natural amphitheater at Success Summit and down into Steptoe Valley.

McGILL, 105.8 *m.* (6,375 alt., 3,000 pop.), is a trim, well-built town owned by the Nevada Consolidated Copper Company, whose smelter (*visitors admitted on pass from office*) is the largest in the State. The huge reduction plant daily treats 14,000 tons of ore, most of it brought in by company-owned railroad from Ruth and Kimberly, 20 miles away. The copper matt is shipped east to refineries, which extract the gold and silver, and forward the copper to manufacturing plants. This smelter, erected in 1906 and employing 1,500 men, has operated continuously except during two depression years.

Water for the smelter and the town is obtained from springs formerly owned by the Adams McGill Ranch, 9 miles northeast of the town, and is brought through a pipe that parallels the highway for several miles. In the valley below the smelter are large tailing ponds in which the residue from the reduction plant is deposited.

EAST ELY, 118.8 *m.* (6,415 alt., 600 pop.), is chief maintenance depot of the Nevada Northern Railroad, owned and operated by the Nevada Consolidated Copper Company. Here are roundhouses and shops, the company commissary, and the Steptoe Hospital, likewise company-owned. This town, on the higher level of a broad valley, is a suburb of Ely, but when William Boyce Thompson bought the site in the period when the smelter was being constructed, it was to have been the trade and fine residential center of the mining and smelting area.

Moved by a desire to avoid the social and labor difficulties caused by mixed groups in Montana copper towns, the organizers of the mining and smelting corporations agreed to Colonel Thompson's plan of establishing a central city at this place. It was agreed that a townsite company organized by Thompson should erect substantial homes for the technical employees of the two corporations and try to induce outsiders to buy homesites. This plan did not please old Ely residents in the least. They saw no reason why their property along the road through the canyon one mile to the east should be ignored. Forestalling attempts to build up the old town, the townsite company took options on all unoccupied land in Ely, and then set up a company that obtained water rights for the spring, east of the town, on which Ely depended. Excursion groups of homeseekers were brought from Salt Lake City on the Southern Pacific and down over the new company railroad to view the place and a few large houses were built to demonstrate what a fine modern community this was to be. There was gala air for a while, and loud were the prophecies of a metropolis. But the promoters, more experienced in the sale of mining stock than in selling city real estate, began to raise the prices of lots weekly to produce an artificial boom, and set such high standards of design and fireproof construction for the houses to be erected that would-be purchasers were discouraged. It was estimated that a lot and house would cost nearly $10,000.

Further trouble came from Elyites determined to block the use of the spring that would give the rival city water. More than rivalry was behind the protest—the Elyites felt that they would get only as much water as the new town did not need. Men with shotguns camped on the hillsides to prevent construction of the waterpipe through Ely. General economic conditions favored the Elyites, for the depression of 1907 cut off funds for development of the model town. When technical employees arriving to man the new smelter came to claim the comfortable houses promised in their contracts, most found themselves placed in barracks built for construction workers. That marked the end of the plan for a central copper city. Both mining and smelter towns were built near their respective plants.

East Ely is at junction with US 93-6 (*see Tour 2b*), and US 6 (*see Tour 6b*).

1. Left from East Ely across Steptoe Valley on a beautiful horse trail that leads up Mosier Canyon in the Schell Creek Range, a game preserve, and circle north to meet Duck Creek (*see above*). The trail is particularly attractive in the summer when the flowers give brilliant color to the slopes.

2. Right from East Ely on a trail that winds southward and up Brown's Canyon, 4 *m.*, to a cabin occupied by a man who works a small claim. The trail continues to the top of OLD BALDY, 6 *m.*, in the Ward Range. This unusually delightful trail runs through pinon pine and cedar. Early in June the ground is covered with scarlet Indian paintbrush, cardinal flower, and half a dozen kinds of early yellow asters. Among them is the moonflower, a delicate white bloom resembling the sego lily. Later come digitalis, blue bells, wild phlox, and wild roses.

Section b. EAST ELY to FALLON, 260 m.

In EAST ELY, 0 *m.*, US 50, briefly united with US 6, makes its sharp turn to press due westward over central Nevada's corrugated terrain. This route, though crossing numerous ranges, presents no driving difficulties and is a particular favorite of the many Nevadans whose passion is the heady panoramas of mountain and valley with their breath-taking color changes.

US 50, with US 6, heads into a canyon in the Egan Range where ELY, 1 *m.* (6,433 alt., 3,045 pop.), sits protected from the storms that sometimes tear down broad Steptoe Valley.

Transportation: Nevada Northern to Western Pacific at Shafter and to Southern Pacific at Cobre; full bus service on all main routes.
Accommodations: Several hotels, adequate garage and other services.
Recreational facilities: Municipal swimming pool and golf course; saddle horses rented and pack trips into near-by National Forests can be arranged—consult U. S. Forest Supervisor.

Craggy cliffs force ELY to build upward instead of outward to house its business offices, so this most important town in the east central part of the State has a somewhat metropolitan aspect, surprising when met after traveling over endless uninhabited miles of mountains and valley. The little city is also assuming the air of stability uncommon in Nevada mining towns. This is because, even after 34 years of almost continuous operation, the mines are assured of a copper supply that can be mined profitably for another 50 years—provided the price does not drop below 9 cents a pound.

Ely came into existence as the usual gold-mining camp in 1868, a year after Indian John had guided prospectors to what he believed were likely deposits. In 1869 a 10-ton lead blast furnace was built to serve the new Robinson District and a 10-stamp mill in the following year. But production was poor and neither these mills nor others erected in the later years had much profit. The camp began to assume further importance in 1886, when the courthouse of White Pine County was moved to it from declining Hamilton (*see ahead*). Three years later another stamp mill was built to care for ore from the Chainman gold mine—but there was nothing phenomenal about the output and Ely remained a town with a single wagon-rutted street.

By this time it had acquired its present name, given by A. J. Underhill, who had borrowed $5,000 from John Ely of Pioche to buy and lay out the townsite. Ely was a typical western mining man; he had come to Pioche from Montana—where, according to rumor, he had been an associate of Jack Slade, the former superintendent of the Julesburg section of the Overland Stage Company, who had been dismissed because of his ungovernable temper when drunk and was later hanged by Montana vigilantes for his dangerous gun-waving. In Nevada Ely paid $3,500 for a mine that was to produce more than $20,000,000, then sold it for only a third of a million. On this he lived in high state for a while, then went to Paris, where he lost what remained—and also his wife. He tried to drown his grief in whiskey, but recovered to make and lose several other fortunes before he died.

One evening in the summer of 1900 two young miners from Shasta County, California, arrived for work in mines near Ely. Dave Bartley and Edwin Gray, like most men from the mining States, were prospectors at heart and decided to look about before turning their services to other men's profit. Among the claims they inspected was the Ruth, owned by D. C. McDonald, local justice of the peace, who had named it for his daughter. With the true prospector's willingness to gamble on a hunch, the two decided to take a lease with an option to buy the Ruth and one other claim for $3,500. Bartley, who had been working in a copper district, believed there might be valuable copper deposits. W. B. Graham, owner of Ely's general store, agreed to grubstake the newcomers. Though after two years Bartley began to worry about the debt they were running up, Graham continued his subsidy.

Working steadily and methodically, the miners slowly dug a tunnel 300 feet back into a hill, then went down 200 feet. As they progressed the values were constantly better; the only trouble was that the mine was 150 miles from any railroad and promoters who looked over the claims shook their heads. Gold and silver ore can be crushed and its values recovered with comparatively simple equipment and very valuable quantities of bullion have small bulk; a single mule train could take out a fortune in gold or silver for shipment to the Mint. Copper ore, on the other hand, only produces from 10 to 20 pounds to the ton, has small value to the ton, its smelting requires considerable equipment, and the copper matt is costly to transport in pay loads.

The enthusiasm of Bartley and Gray drew Joe Bray of Austin to look over the Copper Flat claims a mile east of the Ruth, and he organized a company to exploit them. Then late in 1902 a stranger came to town, went straight to Bartley and Gray to ask their price on an option. When they said "$150,000" he invited them to go down to Ely and sign the papers; this was Mark L. Requa, whose scout, posing as an inquisitive old Comstocker, had given a very favorable report on the prospects. The deal was closed that night, though only after long argument because Gray insisted that all equipment installed should remain if the option were dropped. Requa had been manager of the little Eureka & Palisades Railroad, built by his father, Darius Ogden Mills, and other former Comstockers. He had decided that the old north-south road could be extended over three ranges to close the 85 miles between Eureka and Ely. Requa organized the White Pine Copper Company with eastern backing and then, as the great costs of development became apparent, and a chance to acquire the Copper Flat holdings appeared, managed to enlist further help, with the result that all holdings were consolidated as the Nevada Consolidated late in 1904, with Requa as vice-president and manager and Colonel William Boyce Thompson as a director. By this time it had been decided that the extension of the old railroad was impractical and plans were made for immediate construction of the Nevada Northern down Steptoe Valley; the first train reached Ely in the fall of 1906 with a load of celebrities, including Tex Rickard, always on hand for a boom.

Thompson had been told of Ely prospects by George E. Gunn, who had made a small fortune at Tonopah and Goldfield and was ready to retire and enjoy the world. Thompson had asked Gunn to delay his world tour long enough to look over the Ely district thoroughly and report on it; Gunn came and stayed for eight years. He had taken options on several claims and also on the McGill Ranch, which controlled the water rights to Duck Creek in the Steptoe Valley. Thompson had then organized the Cumberland-Ely Copper Company to take up the options, acting as agent for the Guggenheims. In time the Cumberland-Ely Company managed to buy 40 per cent of Nevada Con's shares and Thompson pushed plans for amalgamation of the two companies. Requa and others opposed the merger; they had planned to build their own smelter near Ely, using the waters of Murray Creek. Thompson himself had divided interests; as part owner of the McGill Ranch, he wanted the smelter built there but as developer of East Ely he favored the southern site. By this time financiers, developers, and smelting experts from all over the country were passing in and out of town to examine prospects. Experts favored McGill for the smelter and advised against construction of two; work on the smelter began in 1907 and the first ore was milled a year later. In 1910 the Cumberland-Ely was absorbed by Nevada Consolidated, which in turn is largely controlled by the Guggenheim's Utah Copper Company. By 1926 distributed profits of Nevada Copper had reached approximately $47,000,000.

Ely's CITY PARK, which parallels US 50-6, the main street, is a long, narrow, shady oasis in summer; like the town it has been drawn out thin by constricting canyon walls. Facing it are the courthouse, county hospital, and other public buildings and places of business.

The MILLARD MUSEUM (*open during business hours*), 614 High St., is owned by an assayer and his son; it contains a large collection of mineral specimens, all carefully labeled, and many other articles, chiefly relics, photographs, and pictures of old mining camps. A particularly gruesome relic is the petrified shoe and foot of a miner who was caught in a Eureka mine by a blast. Years later, in 1930, when the mine was reopened, this was all that remained of the man, whose name had been forgotten among the hordes in the booming camp district.

In Ely is the junction with US 6 (*see Tour 6b*). US 50 continues westward through the narrowing canyon whose brightly stained walls have been worn into arches, caves, and columns. At the end of the canyon the route turns (R) passing an old stage station (L) now used as a ranchhouse.

At 5.3 *m.* is the junction with paved Nev. 44.

Left on Nev. 44 to a junction at 0.7 *m.;* R. here 2 *m.*, passing the edge of RIEPETOWN (L), a collection of gambling, drinking and dance halls patronized largely by Mexicans and immigrants from eastern Europe.

Some years ago various interests insisted that Riepetown conduct its affairs more discreetly and the embarrassed county sheriff was told he must see that the dance hall girls don Mother Hubbards when parading the street. Knifings and fist fights are still almost weekly events. This tiny settlement grew up to supply facilities forbidden in the adjacent Consolidated Copper town of KIMBERLY, 4 *m.* Here are the second largest copper mines in the State, worked far underground. Kimberly itself is attractive and barracks as well as houses are white-painted and neat.

Nev. 44 continues to RUTH, 4 *m.*, (7,200 alt., 2,281 pop.), mine headquarters of Nevada Consolidated. Houses here are scattered over hillsides. Some have been moved one or more times as operations have spread. About 150 Japanese have worked here for a number of years; their pay checks are all made out to one man who settles the bills they run at company stores and acts as banker for the group. There is some opposition to the Japanese, native miners insisting that they help to lower the wage scale.

The center of Ruth is the vast COPPER PIT, more than a mile in diameter and nearly 1,000 feet deep in the shell of a mountain. Rock removed from the hole and from the constantly receding terraces forms mesas around the shell. From the rim the huge shovels, locomotives, and lines of dump cars are so small as to be nearly invisible. The open-face workings are stained with many hues, chiefly bluish-green. The pit is still being worked but deep mining operations may be necessary in the future through shafts now being opened at several points. Enough gold and silver is taken out with the copper to pay for the cost of field operations. The pit is most spectacular at sunset.

US 50 crosses ROBINSON SUMMIT 17.4 *m.* (7,606 alt.), at the head of Robinson Canyon in the Egan Mountains, and descends to cross White Sage Valley, overgrown with dwarfed sage offering winter forage to sheep. The White Pine Mountains ahead were once covered with trees that gave the district its name but all disappeared to provide charcoal for the mills of the early mining camps.

The MOORMAN RANCH (*water*), 33.7 *m.*, named for Clarence Moorman, was a stage station from 1869 to 1885 on the route to Hamilton. Today the ranch is headquarters of a large cattle outfit. From this point the stage road turned north through White Sage Valley to Wells (*see Tour 1a*).

The highway follows the stage road westward along Illipah Creek and skirts the northern boundary of the White Pine Division of the Nevada National Forest.

At 37.1 *m.* is the junction with the graded Hamilton Road.

Left on this road to HAMILTON, 11.7 *m.* (8,003 alt.), completely deserted but once the abode of 10,000 and the community center of 15,000 more along the White Pine Range.

Austin prospectors, including A. J. Leathers, made discoveries on the slope of White Pine (10,792 alt.) in 1865 and formed the Monte Cristo Mining Company to exploit them. Though a mill was in operation by 1867 there was not much interest in the place. Then an Indian brought Leathers such a rich chunk of silver chloride that he let a few friends share his excitement and join him when the Indian undertook to show where he had found it. On January 4, 1868, the jubilant men laid claim to the great Hidden Treasure on the bleak upper slope of Treasure Hill (9,239), south of the embryo camp. Shortly afterward T. E. Eberhardt claimed other remarkable deposits. Values were here in chunks and lumps; a couple of men who had joined the great rush when news of the discoveries leaked out threw up a little rock house to shelter them from the bitter winds only to find their walls held $75,000 worth of ore.

In no time the White Pine Mining District had been formed and a town had been laid out, named for W. H. Hamilton, a promoter. As the rush mounted in spite of a smallpox epidemic, 25,000 people were on hand and claims were staked right and left in every likely and unlikely place—13,000 of them in two years. Swaps, sales, and purchases went on night and day; this was another Comstock that would last forever. White Pine stocks with a total list value of $70,000,000 were on the stock exchange and excitement spread as far as New York, where one company hired a seeress to telegraph orders on what spots were to be worked. Townsites were laid out everywhere and a speculation in real estate shared interest with stock gambling. The seat of new White Pine County was Hamilton and a courthouse was hastily run up to shelter a recording office and a court, where litigation began to mount as claims lapped and overlapped.

The problem of food, shelter, and water was difficult to solve. With the only available spring some miles away, water sold at 25c a bucket. Miners sent to dig an artesian well struck an ore body and threw up their jobs. Even a handful of crackers at one time brought $2, but few minded because most of the camp was sure that the fabulous surface deposits were harbingers of bonanzas. A few experts predicted that the current production—worth about $350,000 a month in 1870—would not last and that no ledge or bonanza lay beneath; but nobody listened and money was poured into development, mills, and to some extent into public and business buildings.

As soon as the rush was on, freight and stage lines were organized to carry bullion to Elko and Wells on the first transcontinental railroad line, completed in 1869. So rich were the loads going northward that the stages were robbed on an average of twice a week between 1869 and 1871 by men who preferred to have others do their hard work for them. Not a gambler or highwayman in the West could resist a visit to the new camp. The bitter discomfort of the exposed town was compensated by the hot excitement of the day. A mere walk through the crowded streets was adventure punctuated by the curses of sweating freighters trying to force passage for their teams.

But by 1873 production had begun to decline and after a fire many began to listen to the prophecies of doom; though mining continued till 1887 the total output was only $22,000,000. The decline was so far advanced by 1886, when another fire wiped out most of the remaining buildings, that the county seat was moved to Ely. The fire of 1873 had not been an accident; a man who wanted to collect insurance—and later served time for his act—had set fire to the back of his store at five in the morning after turning off a valve in the water-main at a point where it entered town.

Among the large buildings erected was the WITHINGTON HOTEL (L). Built of sandstone and imported Oregon pine, this costly structure stands today as a warning of the ephemeral existence of mining towns. Old timers met in the neighborhood are sure to tell of a hanging that took place in one of the rooms; details are obscure. Stone foundations and crumbling walls of other buildings remain, their windows shattered and roofs fallen in. Structures that housed boisterous gambling clubs are now the homes of kangaroo rats. The Wells Fargo Express building, once the pride of the city, is now desolate, its iron shutters awry and its huge iron vaults open to the winds. In the rear room of one of the abandoned music halls are the remains of an English upright piano, shipped to San Francisco by way of Cape Horn.

Foundations of mills and smelters are also reminders of the glory that was once Hamilton. West of the town is the more modern plant of the Tonopah-Belmont Mining Company, a silver producer that abandoned operations in 1930.

From the Eberhardt Mine on TREASURE HILL, 13.7 *m.,* 3,200 tons of ore netting more than $3,000,000 were taken from a hole 70 feet across and at no point more than 28 feet deep. Glory holes, tunnels, and shafts have caved in, and the only burrowing is now done by ground squirrels.

MOURNERS POINT, on the northern outskirts, is an old cemetery, with head-stones still standing though the epitaphs have been almost erased by wind and time. How many who lie here died of violence is unknown but the number must be high.

US 50 goes westward across rolling country, an expansive plateau covered with white sage, mingled in summer with the pink penstemon. Along the highways are occasional ranches with stacks of wild hay for winter feeding, and green hay fields. At evening these valleys glow with soft colors, and sunsets above the western hills are impressive.

At LITTLE ANTELOPE SUMMIT (7,432 alt.), 42.8 *m.,* also called Illipah, are campsites, firewood, and water.

US 50 now crosses the southern end of the long, narrow Newark Valley.

At 46.2 *m.* is a primitive dirt road.

Right on this dirt road, the old route between Hamilton and Elko. THE RUINS OF ANTELOPE SPRINGS STAGE STATION are at 1.5 *m.* It is told that news of the fabulous wealth in the White Pine District lured a Dutchman who, after finding no mines and losing all his funds at the Hamilton gaming tables, set out afoot on this road to Elko. Long lines of freighters with jingling bells passed in the heat; stages with their six lathered horses rolled along in clouds of dust. At last one driver stopped. "Got an empty space here, stranger. Want a ride?" The Dutchman threw his hat to the earth and stamped on it. "By golly, no!" he roared. "I valk! I learn this damn old Dutchman somet'ing! I learn him he should go not to Hamilton!"

PANCAKE SUMMIT (6,517), 56.2 *m.,* marks the crossing of another range.

EUREKA, 78 *m.* (6,837 alt., 707 pop.), came into existence in September, 1864, when men from Austin found a very rich ore body. Legend has it that one of the discoverers exclaimed "Eureka," giving name to the future camp. Its growth, however, was neither sensational nor immediate, because no one knew how to smelt the Eureka ores— the first important lead-silver deposits discovered in the United States. The first smelter, erected in 1869, was unsuccessful but another, erected the same year, showed better results. After Albert Arentz in 1870 intro-duced the siphon tap in discharging bullion the first furnace was leased to Colonel David Buel and his partners, who formed the Bateman Association to build a large smelter. This company in turn was merged to form the Eureka Consolidated Mining Company, which was to be-come the big producer of the district. The Richmond Consolidated built a refinery in 1874 and D. O. Mills and others who had made fortunes on the Comstock completed a railroad from Palisade on the Central Pacific in the following year. This railroad saved Eureka when its production began to fall off about 1883, for the town had become a railhead serving the whole central part of the State.

The population of that period, about 10,000, gradually declined. Trouble had actually begun before the railroad arrived; law suits were rife and water had been encountered in the Eureka Consolidated shaft, forcing installation of pumping machinery. By 1885 most of the production was carried on by leasers and in 1890 and 1891 the smelters were closed. But like the Comstock, Eureka has continued to have periods of activity, first in 1905, when production was valued at nearly $500,000, again during the World War—though the output did not touch $200,000 annually and again in 1930's. But there is a belief here, as in most of the great mining districts of the past, that new deposits will revive the glories of the 14-year period when $40,000,000 in silver, $20,000,000 in gold, and 225,000 pounds of lead were credited to the district.

Eureka's history is similar to that of many other great boom towns all over the State. First came the rush of prospectors, middlemen, gamblers, outlaws, and nondescripts who could not resist the rush to new centers of excitement; Eureka, however, with its difficult ores did not go through the long period of mad speculation and lawlessness peculiar to camps in the jewelry ore districts. Yet it was not a tame place as records of 1878 show; in that year the sheriff gave licenses to 25 gambling establishments, 15 tent-shows and theaters, and 125 saloons—not a large number, considering the day and conditions but enough to avoid the charge of unnatural sedateness. Only 102 arrests and 100 deaths were reported—the latter figure low considering the amount of lead poisoning inevitable in a district where lead bars were stacked like cordwood in smelter yards.

The usual fires swept the town, the greatest on April 19, 1879, when the only buildings to escape in the business district were the fireproof *Sentinel* building and the Paxton Bank. The *Sentinel* went to press as usual, though its printers had to work under blankets soaked in water. Floods were an additional disaster less common in Nevada. Heavy rains and cloudbursts washed out the town several times. But business went on. During the worst flood a crazed woman who dashed into the torrent was rescued by a gallant man who relinquished a barrel of whiskey he had been endeavoring to carry to safety.

Eureka's early importance caused Lander County to be divided, with Eureka as the seat of a county named for the town.

By 1880 all the trees for 40 miles in every direction had been cut down to produce charcoal for the smelters that were using 200,000 bushels annually. A cord of pinenut wood produced 30 bushels of charcoal, which would smelt approximately a ton of crude ore.

The Charcoal War, sometimes called the Fish Creek War, took place in 1879. During August of that year the Charcoal Burners' Association, which employed several hundred men, came into conflict with the smelter interests, which wanted to reduce the price of 30 cents a bushel to 27½ cents. The association stopped delivery and on August 11 took possession of the town and of numerous charcoal pits. The militia was sent in and order was soon restored. But after the troops had left, on August 18, a band of miners led by a deputy sheriff attacked workers at the Fish Creek charcoal ranch south of the town. Five men were killed, six seriously wounded, and many taken prisoners. After this incident, which stirred up much popular indignation, the affair was settled.

In 1910 more than 30 miles of the railroad were washed out by an early spring thaw, depriving the town of its widespread trade. Bank failures added to the debacle and a drop in lead and silver prices led to the abandonment of so many large holdings that miners scattered to more prosperous centers.

Foundations and stone structures dating back as far as 1869 are visible for miles around the present center. Smelters still stand, as well as many deserted houses; but the inhabitants of the well-kept cemeteries far outnumber the living. The older buildings of the business district still wear the gray produced by soot that poured from stacks of smelters in the heyday.

The stone PROTESTANT EPISCOPAL CHURCH, on Spring Street, was the first religious structure erected, slightly before a frame Roman Catholic church on Nob Hill, now replaced by one of brick. The brick EUREKA COUNTY COURTHOUSE, in the center of town, was considered a fine building in its day, sharing importance with the COLONNADE HOTEL, the JACKSON HOUSE, and the OPERA HOUSE, all still standing.

Around Eureka and as far west as Eastgate purple stinkweed is abundant; in spite of its name it is a thing of beauty, except when handled.

US 50 goes north out of Eureka to turn west and cross a broad expanse in which the most conspicuous plant is the white sage. This area is a sheep and cattle range during the spring and summer.

The HAY RANCH, 88 m., was for many years one of the largest in the region. Since the days when it cared for stage and freighting livestock, it has been a stopping-place for stockmen. In the past this ranch had 2,500 acres of fenced bottom lands on which 1,000 tons of hay were cut annually to feed the 300 to 400 mules of the lines operating between various mining camps.

West of the ranch the highway runs for 23 miles without a turn. On both sides are mountain ranges, those on the south running across the western division of the Toiyabe National Forest. Lone Mountain (7,942 alt.) is the nearest peak (R).

At 109 m. is the junction with a dirt road.

Left on this road to the base of ANTELOPE PEAK (10,207 alt.), 6 m., in the Toiyabe National Forest, which extends for 100 miles south in three long narrow rectangles separated by equally slender valleys.

HICKERSON SUMMIT (6,594 alt.) is crossed at 125.1 m. Before the modern highway was built the road up this range was known locally as Ford's Defeat; an enterprising gentleman made quite

a few extra dollars by towing old "Model T's" to the top with his team.
US 50 meets Nev. 8A, a dirt road, at 128 *m.*

Left on Nev. 8A to a graded road, 8 *m.; L.* here 1.8 *m.* to SPENCERS'
HOT SPRINGS, in early boom days the leading resort of central Nevada. The
springs are on the edge of the western division of the Toiyabe Forest and
though there are no accommodations at present, many people picnic and camp
here to sample the waters, and to bathe in the waters and mud.

Nev. 8A continues down the Great Smoky Valley, passing cattle ranches
in the shadow of the Toiyable Range (R) and the Toquima (L). Many unimproved side roads run up into the mountains, which are in divisions of the
Toiyabe National Forest and provide campsites. About a third of the way
south is a vast alkali flat where the waters of Birch Creek and other small
streams lose themselves, depositing their salts and increasing the size of this
apparent wasteland. Fremont came down through this valley in 1845.

At 45 *m.* is the junction with a dirt road; L. here 0.2 *m.* to DARROUGH
HOT SPRINGS (*accommodations*), another camping and picnicking spot. Corn
and potatoes can be boiled in the bubbling waters. Across the range to the east
is another of these hot springs, in a large natural cauldron known as the Devil's
Punchbowl. It is told that an Indian couple decided they wanted some eagles'
eggs laid in a niche on the inner side of the bowl and the man told his wife
to hold tightly to his feet while he descended head first for them. But his wife,
when she saw two small eagles fly near while he was in this precarious position, dropped his heels to catch the birds. The legend is that her husband's
scalp and leggings eventually came through underground channels and up
with the waters at this place.

On Nev. 8A is the junction with an improved road at 55 *m.; L.* here 3 *m.*
to ROUND MOUNTAIN (6,313 alt.), a small lode and placer camp where
ore was discovered in 1906. There is some dispute about the discoverer. Though
Lincoln credits Louis D. Gordon with it, old timers of the neighborhood say
the find was made by Slim Morgan. Placer gravel located in 1907 was worked
by dry washing. A mill was erected in 1907 and later water was brought in
for hydraulic mining. A second mill began operation in 1912. Up to 1922 the
district had produced nearly $5,000,000 worth of ore.

On Nev. 8A at 68 *m.* is the junction with another improved road; L. here
7 *m.* to MANHATTAN (6,905 alt.), near Bald Mountain (9,275 alt.). The
town is in an attractive canyon with wooded slopes nearby. Manhattan was
discovered in 1906 by John Humphrey when all of central and southern Nevada
was being chipped and hammered by prospectors stirred to excitement by the
phenomenal values at Goldfield. Placering began the following year and continued to 1915; then rich ore was found in the lower levels of the White Caps
Mine and there was another boom. A mill erected in 1912 had to be reconstructed and enlarged. Now a huge gold dredge is at work, methodically
swallowing everything in its path and tossing it back to the sides after the
precious metals have been recovered.

The history of no old Nevada mining town is complete without an account
of a badger game. This was the standard method of hazing the tenderfoot
and is still occasionally practiced. In the presence of the newcomer two men
would argue as to whether so-and-so's badger could lick such-and-such a dog.
The argument would wax hot and stop just short of blows, but end in a
respectable bet on the outcome. Posters would then be placed notifying the
town of the coming event and the boys would continue loud arguments over
every detail. On the appointed day a large box containing the "Badger" would
be hauled to the scene, chained and roped. One man would be selected to hold
the dog and another to pull the badger from the box by a chain. Just before
the fight was to begin someone would point out that the man who was to
handle the badger had money on the fight and was disqualified. Arguments
would start again and at last someone would suggest that the newcomer was
the only person present without a stake on the fight. Pieces of stove pipe or

tin would be wrapped around his legs, several pairs of gloves would be put on his hands, and he would be told to grab the chain, pull hard, and run. At the signal the "badger" box would be opened and the newcomer would rush off as fast as he could go in his armor—dragging a "badger" down the street.

The Manhattan road continues to a junction with an unimproved road at 17 m.; L. here 4 m. through sage to the OLD NYE COUNTY COURTHOUSE, a square gaunt structure among the remnants of other buildings—all that remains of the town of BELMONT, a camp that developed with a rush in 1865, two years after discoveries had been made in the district, and immediately became the seat of Nye County. The district had produced about $15,000,000 worth of ore —chiefly lead-silver—by 1885, when large operations ceased. The district gradually declined, having so little activity that Jim Butler, a barely literate rancher of the neighborhood, served as prosecuting attorney for about $50 a year in script. It was Jim who made the Mizpah discovery that was to lift Nevada out of long doldrums and build up Tonopah. He had started for the South Klondyke field and was so casual about his find that it was months before the rush began (see Tour 5b). In Jim's absence Tasker L. Oddie, a young lawyer from the east, had been given Jim's abandoned job. It was through his initiative that the Mizpah was rescued from obscurity. The only inhabitants of the old county seat are occasional prospectors and Indians who camp in the gaunt square building. The town was still active at times long after the court had been moved to booming Tonopah; discovery of turquoise in 1909 attracted some interest and enough ore was still found in 1914 to bring construction of a ten-stamp 100-ton flotation mill—which operated for only two years—and another stamp mill in 1921, but it also closed within a year.

Nev. 8A continues southward to a junction, 103 m., with US 6 (see Tour 6b) at a point 6 miles east of Tonopah.

West of the junction the highway crosses the northernmost rectangle of another division of the Nevada National Forest, and goes over AUSTIN SUMMIT (7,554 alt.), 139 m.

These long stretches of alternate mountain and valley fill those who delight in outdoor life with endless pleasure. No signboards cut off views, and dawn, noon, sunset, and night provide endless changes of color. Fast driving travelers miss the many varieties of flora hidden among the sagebrush, pinenut, greasewood, mountain mahogany, and other conspicuous plants, but botanists still turn up new species in many places along the way. Spring and summer are particularly rewarding with their swaying fields of brilliant flowers but autumn and winter also have their charms.

The white prickly poppy lines the roadside as the route moves westward.

AUSTIN, 148 m. (6,147 alt., 580 pop.), is in the hollow of a steep Toiyabe Canyon, whose high walls are pockmarked with abandoned prospect holes. Austin was the mother town of central and eastern Nevada mining. From this base, Tuscarora, Eureka, Hamilton, and several other camps of more transitory fame were discovered.

With the first rush after William Talcott made his discovery along Reese River in May, 1862, Lander County was formed out of roughly a third of the State and a temporary seat was established at Jacobsville —Jacobs' Well—eight miles southwest of what was to become Austin. This tiny settlement had been a Pony Express station, then a maintenance point on the transcontinental telegraph line. It was named for

General Frederick Jacobs of Indian war fame, who at the time was in charge of construction of a stage road across the State. With men coming in from the east and west to prospect, by 1863 it had two hotels, three stores, and a post office. But the rapidly increasing population decided it preferred Austin to Jacobsville as a center, and Austin formally became the county seat on September 2, 1863; and such it has remained in spite of the whittling away of county lands to form other units.

For a time the discovery here did not attract hordes, for Virginia City was booming and the phenomenal character of the Comstock distracted attention from less startling discoveries. Austin itself began as Clifton, a camp at the foot of the canyon around the cabin and mine of two men named Marshall and Cole. As the camp grew, a townsite farther up the canyon was selected; however, the cost of constructing a road to the more dignified site hindered development until someone put forward the idea of trading town lots for road work. With this incentive the present town was born and the Cliftonites moved up in a body.

Late in 1863 the International Hotel, still in use, was completed and the *Reese River Reveille* was recording fact and rumor for the incoming crowds. Places on the stages of two lines were being booked days ahead and some city lots were bringing $8,000 in gold. By the end of summer 366 houses had been built—far too few to house the 10,000 then on hand. Money was abundant with $20 gold pieces in many pockets—and no change available—but food and shelter were so high that they did not last long. In spite of a duel and several killings, six mills were erected, a Y.M.C.A. was formed, and Reese River stocks were being sold in huge quantities on every street corner in San Francisco. A school was opened in a brush tent in October and a volunteer fire company was organized. In 1864 the upper and lower camps were incorporated as the City of Austin. The following year a lumber mill was at work, 5 clergymen, 12 physicians of one kind or another, and 33 lawyers were at hand—their numbers indicative of the relative importance of the callings in early camps. And Wells Fargo was carrying out millions.

In 1867 the number of mills had increased to 11, their were 6,000 claims, and, in addition to a public school, there were private schools, teaching French, vocal and instrumental music, dancing, and "calisthenics." Three churches—one Roman Catholic, one Protestant Episcopal, and one Methodist—had been erected.

One of the exciting events of Austin's early years was the advent of nine camels, including one that had been presented by the Sultan of Turkey to the United States government. In the pre-war years Jefferson Davis as Secretary of War had been much interested in trying out camels as beasts of burden on the deserts of the Southwest. The experiment was successful but after its sponsor left office and became President of the Confederacy the project lost support, and in 1864 the remaining camels in southern California were sold at auction. The nine were bought up by one of their former keepers, who saw use for them in the booming Austin district. A mining company here took them over to bring salt for the quartz mill from marshes 100 miles to the south. For some years they were seen plodding patiently along the roads.

Probably the best-remembered event of the early years was Reuel Colt Gridley's payment of an election bet. Gridley, a Missouri Democrat, had bet with Dr. H. S. Herrick, Republican, on the outcome of the local election. If the Republicans won Herrick was to carry a sack of flour up from Clifton and if the Democrats won Gridley would have to carry it down the canyon. Later they agreed that the flour should go to the Sanitary Fund for war relief. Gridley lost and on April 20 the town, which was a center of recession sentiment, gathered to watch the fun. Herrick decorated the sack with Union flags and a band headed the procession, followed by the newly-elected officials on horseback and Herrick, carrying Gridley's coat and cane. Behind came the "Reb" with the sack of flour. With mill whistles blowing the flour was ceremoniously delivered in front of the Bank Exchange Saloon. Gridley then proposed that it be auctioned off to swell its value for the fund. The town made this a gala event. Bids began at $200; the successful buyer turned it over for further auctioning, and the process was repeated several times. Before the day was over more than $10,000 in gold and currency had been taken in, and the town had adopted the sack of flour as the city's official seal. Gridley, by this time a convert to the Union cause, decided to take the flour around the State for further sale and made his first offer to Virginia City. Success followed success and eventually the flour went on to California (*see Wilderness to Modern State*) for sale. The sack is now in the Nevada State Historical Society Museum.

Austin, like Eureka, suffered much from the floods of 1868 and 1874. In 1880 a railroad was completed to connect the city with the main line to the north, though when it reached the town Austin had begun to decline and a good part of the $50,000,000 in ore credited to the early years had already gone out. The Manhattan Silver Mining Company, which acquired most of the properties on Lander hill in the early 1870's, continued to operate until 1887. Sporadic operations went on and still do, but in the first 20 years of the 20th century the total output—gold, silver, copper, and lead—was valued at only slightly more than $250,000.

Austin survives today largely as a distributing and educational center of isolated ranching and mining communities, though it now receives supplies by truck, since the railroad was abandoned in 1938.

Austin was the girlhood home of Emma Wixom, who as Emma Nevada was to become one of the great sopranos of her day.

Many of the early public buildings remain, including the three churches, the old county courthouse—which was brought in from Jacobsville and enlarged—and the first hotel. The second LANDER COUNTY COURTHOUSE has numerous pictures of the early days, as well as newspapers that recreate the life of a city that rivaled the queen of the Comstock. Large cemeteries with old-fashioned epitaphs are also reminders of the many who once made this city their home. Former inhabitants who have wandered far like to be assured that they will lie here in the end—a form of devotion that Virginia City also attracts, sure proof that the old camp had more than transient glory.

Austin is at a junction with the northern section of Nev. 8A (*see* *Tour* 1*b*).

1. Left from Austin 1 *m.* on a dirt road to STOKES CASTLE, a tall three-story stone building, 50 feet square, with parapet around its flat roof. It was erected in 1879 by Anson Phelps Stokes and J. G. Stokes of Philadelphia, who had heavy interests in the silver mines and other properties of the area. Used briefly as a residence owing to the decline in production, the strange structure is now the prey of wanton visitors. The first floor held a kitchen and dining room, the second, a living room and bath, the third, bedrooms and a bath, and the roof could be used as a porch. Windows are deep and narrow and there were formerly balconies on each of the upper floors.

There are many local legends of the reason for its construction, one favorite being that the Stokes brothers believed one of their mine foremen was high-grading a great deal of rich ore, and they built this residence on the crown of the hill in order to watch shipping operations. This like the other tales, had no basis in fact.

2. Left at the western end of Austin on Nev. 21, which goes up fertile REESE RIVER VALLEY, 12 miles wide and more than 100 miles long. Reese River, flowing north, has sources in the Toiyabe and Shoshone mountains, and disappears in the sandy wastes south of Battle Mountain, though it was formerly a tributary of the Humboldt. Diminished rainfall, increased use of its water for irrigation, and the early destruction of trees on the watersheds have diminished its flow. Its old, dry channel is still visible northward.

It was from this valley that the notorious L. B. Vail, horse-trader, horse-thief, cattle rustler, and murderer, went to the southward regions in the spring of 1867. Vail was addicted to the playful pastime of killing his associates, sometimes as many as three at once, and of sleeping on their graves for several weeks. He had long been suspected of the murder of Robert Knox, his partner in stock trading, who accompanied him to the Pahranagat Valley (*see Tour* 2*b*). Indians passing one of Vail's camping spots in the valley at a later date discovered a saddle that had been buried, but dug up by coyotes; they took it to Hiko residents who identified it as Knox's, and returned with the Indians to the spot and exhumed the body of the missing trader. Vail was pursued and captured.

Annoyed at delay in bringing him to trial, citizens of Hiko and Pahranagat Valley stormed the jail, took the prisoner, and organized a court of their own. The judge assured Vail that he would have a fair trial. But the proceedings of the self-appointed court were interrupted by sounds of a gallows being erected outside, as well as construction of a coffin within the courtroom itself. The prisoner, nevertheless, was deliberately and gravely tried, found guilty, and hanged an hour later.

Bordering Reese River Valley on the east is the Toiyabe Range, whose wooded slopes comprise the Lander and Reese River Game Refuges. One of the most beautiful ranges in the State, the Toiyabe abounds with deer, quail, grouse, and sage hens. Even an occasional cougar is seen. Dirt roads lead into the higher recesses and camp sites are numerous.

Nev. 21 continues southward, crossing bottoms filled with wild hay. Prospect holes and some old workings can be seen on the hillsides. The mining men have contempt for the cattlemen, whom they call "those river people"; but the prosperous cattle growers have only amusement for this attitude—many of them share the feelings of the prospectors on the excitement of pay-ore.

The road passes two small schools, so remote from any other buildings that the reason for their existence is not immediately clear; the pupils come from the ranchhouses among the cottonwoods by the river, which is some miles from the road at many places, and also from small ranches up the draws. These little school-houses are social centers for the valley and the dances held in them are of the family kind common every where in an earlier day. Music is made by local people—perhaps on jews-harps as well as fiddles. Refreshments are coffee, so strong it curls the hair of those unaccustomed to it, thick ham and deviled egg sandwiches, and huge slices of delicious home-made cake. Chocolate cake is always a favorite but the wonderful creamcakes are almost as popular. Many of the dances are preceded by an afternoon program, worked up by the schoolteacher. After recitations and songs by the pupils, there are games, in which everyone takes part. Then comes a dinner to which every housewife contributes, sometimes large quantities of some special food assigned to her and sometimes a complete meal for as many as are in her family, which is placed on the common table. During the dance the babies sleep on bundles of coats or wherever a place can be found for them, but the older children frolic on the floor between dances until their eyes will no longer stay open. The dance goes on long after midnight.

Some of the ranches up the draws have their own schools, because the State must set one up wherever there are five children of school age. Classes are held in a room of the ranchhouse or in a small separate building. When the teacher has a beau, his visits are not frequent but protracted, as he may have to ride 10 or 15 miles on horseback to see her and must ride that distance back before work begins on the ranch where he lives.

Nev. 21 turns away from Reese River to IONE, 48 *m.*, which is in the shadow of Mount Berlin (9,081 alt.). Berlin and Grantsville, near by, are camps in the Union Mining District, which was discovered in 1863. Enough people were here by 1864 to warrant the establishment of a new county and Ione became the Nye County seat. Ione had only a brief period of prosperity and the court and records were moved to Belmont in 1867. Nonetheless, the district produced about $1,000,000 worth of gold and silver before 1880, and 11,000 flasks of mercury. There have been revivals down to 1940.

US 50 crosses the northern end of the Shoshone Range near EMIGRANT PEAK (8,059 alt.) through a pass, locally called Railroad, that was the scene of many Indian attacks. A three-mile descent leads to a broad valley that was once a lake bed, as terraces (L) of the higher water levels show. The dried-up sedimentary bed (R) is now used as an emergency landing field on the route between Ely and Reno. For miles the highway skirts its edge before turning due west to the base of the Desatoya Mountains, 186 *m.* (*water available*). US 50 now gradually ascends to CARROLL SUMMIT, 195 *m.* (7,452 alt.), in a range heavily wooded and inhabited by deer, coyotes, and wild horses—remnants of former large bands.

At 202 *m.*, near the western base of the Desatoya Mountains, is the junction with a dirt road.

Right on this road to the BIG DEN and LITTLE DEN country, 8 *m.*, and JOHNSON CREEK, 10 *m.*, where deer abound (*camp sites*). The Den area is very beautiful in the fall when the yellow and orange of aspens and brush stand out against evergreens. Great spires of rimrock with jagged points border the deep canyon. Briars and wild berries form thickets along the streams.

EASTGATE, 204 *m.* (5,200 alt., 7 pop.), was for years a stage station. At the mouth of a narrow canyon, it served as a crude stopping place for travelers until 1876, when it was taken over by George B. Williams.

A little tufa-block house was erected by Williams in 1879 with the aid of a Basque mason who had come from Spain to raise sheep. The tufa, lighter than sandstone and ideal for building construction, was obtained from one of the few deposits of commercial value in the state, a small hill four miles west of Eastgate. In 1908 a second tufa structure, of 12 rooms, was erected nearby.

In both buildings hundreds of names and dates have been carved on the soft stone walls—some as early as 1879. The roof of the little old building, composed of a six-inch layer of clay and mud resting on a thatch of willow branches, has never been known to leak.

Eastgate was for years the most-talked-of stopping-place for tenderfoot travelers, for here the buckaroos (*vaqueros*) put on Wild West exhibitions that visitors believed genuine. One of the favorite stunts was a fictitious shooting. After the victim was "murdered" and carried out of sight, presumably for burial, the "killer" was seized, not for murder but for cattle rustling—for it was intended to impress on greenhorns that the slaying of a man was a trifling offense compared with cattle-stealing. While the visitors gazed in horror, the killer-rustler would be strung up by a rope that seemed to be around his neck but was actually around his body under his arms. As the man dangled, the avengers pretended to riddle the body with bullets. Many a traveler left Eastgate, yarn-spinners gleefully relate, convinced that he had seen an actual murder and lynching. A favorite story here is of an eastern woman who arrived to teach in the neighborhood. Enchanted by the soft woolly coats of the lambs she was seen to rush out with a bath towel after the first heavy rain. As she gently rubbed the fleece someone ventured to ask why she was doing it. She explained that she was trying to help the rancher by saving the wool from shrinkage.

For years after the Williams Ranch was established, Indians gathered at the canyon's mouth before a rock in the corral to hold their conferences. These always ended with a huge barbecue and celebration, including dances. Because he had usurped their favorite camping ground for his home, Williams was glad to supply the Indians with beef to keep them in good temper.

US 50 crosses the rolling hills and the flat floor of a narrow valley below the Clan Alpine Range (R).

MIDDLEGATE, an eroded narrow pass through low hills, though barren of any habitation now, once held a station of the Pony Express and later of stage routes. The highway continues through a broad valley to WESTGATE, 214 m. (4,600 alt.), now a C.C.C. camp, whose members preserve water holes and do other range conservation work. On both sides of Westgate are mountains covered with sagebrush.

US 50 crosses a low ridge, 219.5 m., overlooking Fairview and Dixie Valleys. Three miles away (R) is Chalk Mountain, a solitary peak long known for its silver and lead deposits and facing Fairview Peak (8,250 alt.), a noted producer (L), of silver and gold. At the eastern base of this mountain is Gold Basin, where mines are now being worked.

A huge concrete vault (L), all that is left of a former bank, is by the highway toward Fairview Peak. At the Nevada Hills property (L), 6 miles from the highway, is one of the largest glory holes in the State—an immense chasm connecting with tunnels undernearth. The road leading to this mine is very poor.

At 220 m. is the junction with a dirt road.

Right on this road to WONDER, 12 m., discovered in 1906, a year after Fairview and for a few years the most important producer of gold and silver in the area. Nearly $6,000,000 worth had come out by 1921. The remnants of a large mill overlook what is left of the town. At one time single lots in the business section here sold for as much as $8,000, but today they can be had for the asking.

FRENCHMAN'S STATION (*supplies, meals*), 225 m., is in the center of Dixie Valley, on the edge of a dry lake bed. It was a relay and stopping place for teams freighting to the camps of Wonder, Fairview, and points east. On display are mineral specimens from the surrounding area. In the desert to the south mirages are frequent and at sunset the entire valley, as well as the region to the north, swims in purple haze below reddened peaks.

Crossing the Silver Range of the Stillwater Mountains, US 50 dips to Twelve Mile Flat, a vast salt deposit. At the point where the highway first touches the flat is SAND SPRINGS, 233 m., an early stopping-place with only a single shed now standing. Sand Springs was the scene of the old-timer's tall tale about the Chicken Craw gold-rush of 1907. The story is that Larry Hunt, a desert dweller, was operating a wayside inn at the time. Dressing some chickens for a Sunday dinner, Larry discovered fair-sized gold nuggets in the craws of two, and thereupon slew his entire flock. He found more nuggets. Convinced that chickens were not eating gold in the neighborhood, he set out with two companions to learn where the chickens had come from, and discovered they had been purchased from a farmer near Wadsworth, 70 miles away. Confusion was added to distance when he learned that the chickens had been owned by no fewer than four farmers before they were sold to him. The area in which the chickens ate the gold nuggets for gravel remains undiscovered.

Here, too, is the legendary death place of a Shoshone who sprinted into Sand Springs clutching a piece of extremely rich quartz. He collapsed and died, according to the story, but not before he had described the position of his strike. For many years prospectors have tried to find the ledge, but it remains as lost as the fabulous Chicken Craw.

Right from Sand Springs on a dirt road to SINGING MOUNTAIN, 1 m., a high peak of sand deposited by winds blowing down from the north over an abrupt ridge. Singing Mountain is continuously changing its shape. It takes its name from the humming sound caused by the tiny pellets of sand constantly shifting and rubbing one against the other.

SALT WELLS, 245 m., on the western edge of an extensive salt flat, was the base of a salt-refinery. Although the salt is more than 98 per cent pure, and is found to a depth of 80 feet, the plant, built at a cost of $175,000, was abandoned when its operators learned that transportation rates would not allow them to compete with other producers. It was recently dismantled, though a few of the buildings remain standing.

On both sides of the highway across the salt flat are long drainage ditches filled with brackish water that in late spring turns to a deep red, and later, when drying up, to a soda white. Above the flat, on the slopes of hills, are the terraces of ancient Lake Lahontan, one of the outstanding geological features of the Great Basin (*see Natural Setting*). That Indians once lived along the shoreline of the lake is demonstrated by burial grounds, petroglyphs, and an abundance of arrowheads and other primitive weapons. It is believed that the aborigines inhabited this region from 600 to 2,000 years ago.

West of the salt flat is one of the fertile areas of the State. Green fields of alfalfa and corn are in vivid contrast with the salt flats around them.

FALLON, 261 m. (3,749 alt., 1,905 pop.), seat of Churchill County, lies in this large fertile valley, and is the center of the Newlands Irrigation Project. Long a stock-raising center, Fallon did not really come into its own until 1908, with completion of what was begun by the Federal government in 1903 as the Truckee-Carson Project. It was the first undertaking by the Government in accordance with the Reclamation Act of 1902. The total cost to June, 1930, was nearly $8,000,000 financed by the Government and underwritten by water users, the cost to be repaid over a long period; but a considerable number of ranches are now carrying on with Farm Security aid and three-quarters of the cost has been written off by the Government. The project can serve 87,000 acres with all-year irrigation. The products include Hearts of Gold cantaloupe, but alfalfa is the principal crop. High-grade honey comes from the many apiaries in the region, and Fallon turkeys are marketed through the East.

In 1896 a post office was established on Mike Fallon's ranch in a tiny shack but the town did not begin to grow until 1902, when the county seat was moved here after the reclamation project had been approved. With the rush to Fairview and Wonder in 1905, Fallon became a supply base and temporarily a city of tents.

Fallon early set out to make itself a livable town. Sensibly taking into account the large number of people who would come on Saturdays from the widely scattered ranches, it laid out a main street wide enough to afford parking places for all. Cars and trucks can be parked not only in front of the stores on both sides of the streets but also in a double line down the center—with plenty of room left for two-way traffic. The stores lining this street are notably trim and modern in appearance and goods are displayed in broad windows. At the lower end of the street is a handsome school with recessed portico, typical of the educational plants of the State. Another Fallon innovation was establishment of municipal water and power plants; water is stored in a reservoir one mile to the east on Rattlesnake Hill and the power plant is by Lahontan Dam, part of the Newlands project.

With construction of the reservoir and dams it was hoped to make this a beet-sugar district and a $500,000 mill was constructed in 1911 on the northeastern outskirts by the Nevada Sugar Company; this district, however, has been found more suitable for other products.

Though the population of Fallon itself is small, its social life embraces a large number of people. Bridge parties and dances bring people from as far as Reno. The many lodges and societies prominent in the State, including even the Business and Professional Women, have large memberships here.

The oustanding event of the year is the state agricultural fair held in the STATE FAIR GROUNDS at the western end of town; the tract is surrounded by a stockade of upright logs, pioneer fashion. Every district in Nevada is represented in the events. This fair is of the old-fashioned kind, with competing exhibits of various agricultural products, of cattle, and of jellies, cakes, quilts, and other creations of the Nevada farm women. A rodeo is held with prize riders from far and near. Many people from the cities come to the fair to meet old friends—indeed this is really an annual family reunion. Even prospectors are seen comparing bits of ore and telling their tales of the discovery that got away.

The city of Fallon has a New England canniness in its budget planning. Having accepted the problem of relief for the unemployed as a long-time problem, it laid out a program of public improvement to be carried out with W.P.A. labor, and made ample provision in its tentative future budgets for liberal sponsor contributions to carry it out. By this means it has already provided itself with an unusually good athletic field, baseball field, flood-lighted softball field, flood-lighted tennis courts, swimming pool, and a beautiful park; in addition the fair grounds have been extensively improved.

Right from Fallon over an oiled road to STILLWATER, 12 *m.*, on the southern edge of the Carson Sink. This was formerly the county seat. Several years ago it was the scene of oil drilling operations.

Fallon history really begins in Stillwater. In immigrant days a toll bridge was built across an arm of the Carson Sink at this point by Ellen Redman. In 1868 Stillwater, though a small community, became the seat of Churchill County. The first school in the county was started near here in December, 1871, and taught by Lem Allen; the school district was called the Big Adobe. In 1880 an unchartered temperance organization appeared in the town, which then had only 44 residents; three different pledges were offered to the erring —a tobacco abstinence, a whiskey abstinence, or a total abstinence pledge. First religious services were held by the Methodist but did not last long. Then the Seventh Day Adventists organized a congregation. Irrigation was tried, and some farming and stock raising was carried on. When Fallon usurped the position of county seat in 1902, Stillwater became chiefly a village of modern Indians.

Many duck hunters and anglers for catfish come here. To the north is a wintering place of the whistling swan.

Fallon is at a junction with US 95 (*see Tour 5b*).

Section c. FALLON to CALIFORNIA LINE, 88 m.

US 50 goes west from FALLON, 0 m., first through ranches and then rugged country. Before long the Sierra Nevada is seen ahead. The climb to Tahoe begins just west of Carson City.

At 8 m. is the junction with a dirt road.

Right here is the depressions of two old craters, 8 m., whose rims rise about 90 feet above the surrounding desert, and 150 feet above the lakes they hold. These lakes are BIG SODA, without surface inlet or outlet, which covers about 400 acres and has a depth of 150 feet, and LITTLE SODA, covering 16 acres; the latter is nearly dry. The thick deposits of impure sodium carbonates have been intermittently worked, and at one time a two-fifths interest in the property sold for $35,000, and the product for $60 a ton.

These lakes were mined in the early days. Near by are 1,600 acres of borax lands, but only about 400 acres contain salts of borax that were at one time of commercial value.

LEETEVILLE, 11 m., now deserted, began as Ragtown in the days of early overland travel. The first inhabitants lived a few miles south near the Carson River. Ragtown became a station on the early Overland Road and remained a stopping place after the Simpson Road came into general use. Asa L. Kenyon was the only resident in 1854, although a great many other traders camped near by in the summer. There are various stories about the origin of the old town's name, one being that it was given because the cloth shelters had fluttering ends, another because of the ragged clothing travellers washed in the river and spread on the sagebrush to dry. But early diaries indicate that the spot was so named because the area roundabout was covered with rags of mattresses and other household goods discarded as travelers lightened their loads before the long pull over the Sierras. The place might as well have been called Irontown for the hundreds of wagons and farming implements abandoned. Feathertown is supposed to have been a suburb of Ragtown; someone had there thrown away a goose-feather mattress that was later ripped open.

At Leeteville is a burying ground containing about 200 graves of early travelers who died of famine and exhaustion.

Regardless of why or by whom the place was named, Ragtown was a welcome oasis on the overland journey down the Humboldt River and across the Sink (see Tour 1b). With the sheer walls of the Sierra Nevada ahead and pure water at hand after the dreadful barrenness of the Carson Sink, no one wanted to leave. Sometimes as many as five or six trains camped on the bank at one time, trying to recover strength for the last great effort. After a time Indians came here to sell their service as guides in exchange for commodities. Here, too, for many years an enterprising blacksmith had a shop to repair the wagons shrunken and broken by the trip down the Humboldt and across the desert.

Leeteville is at a junction with US 95 (see Tour 5b).

LAHONTAN, 16 m., is the operating headquarters of the Lahontan Dam Reservoir, completed in 1915 and impounding the flood waters of the Carson and Truckee Rivers. The dam creates a lake 23 miles long and at some points 5 miles wide. This lake, whose western shore is followed by US 50, is annually stocked with trout, bass, and catfish; and marshes and sloughs formed by backwaters afford excellent duck and goose hunting. The lake is also used as a motorboat racing course in summer. At the dam is a power plant supplying electricity to the surrounding area.

At 25 *m.* is the junction with Nev. 1B, in a broad valley. Here for many years was an important decision point of early travelers. Those bent on reaching California or the ore deposits of the Comstock Lode continued west up the valley toward Sun Mountain (later renamed Mount Davidson) and the higher Sierra Nevada; those planning to settle on lands along the East and West Walker River turned southward.

Left on Nev. 1B to FORT CHURCHILL, 8 *m.*, garrisoned from 1860 to 1871. Skeleton walls of the former adobe barracks still stand. The post was established just after the rush to the Comstock began and was abandoned soon after completion of the first transcontinental railroad, which greatly lessened the need for military protection on traveled routes. Establishment of the fort by Special Order Number 67 from the Headquarters of the Department of California in July, 1860, was the direct result of the killing of seven men at Williams Station on the Overland Trail. The natives had been attempting to avenge themselves for brutalities by the whites but Comstock and Carson volunteers followed the Paiutes to a point near Pyramid Lake with heavy losses. Following the defeat the Washoe Regiment of Volunteers, under command of Colonel Jack Hays, had been organized for a further expedition against the Indians. The volunteers totalled 544, recruited in California and Nevada. Captains Joseph Stewart and F. F. Flint of the regular army, with 207 men, had been ordered to proceed to Nevada and aid the volunteers. The Indians were completely routed by the combined forces.

After the battle construction of the fort was started; later an officer sent to replace the first commander reported that plans for the fort were much too elaborate; but as long as construction was under way he ordered that a few of the buildings be completed as rapidly as possible.

The reservation was a rhomboid containing about 1,400 acres. Within this was the smaller parade ground, a quadrangle. On its north side were six officers' buildings, on the west stretched the barracks and the mess hall, on the south stood the guardhouse, storeroom, corrals, bakery and blacksmith shop, and on the east were the commandant's office, telegraph office, stores, quartermaster's depot, hospital, and laundry. On a hill near the fort was a post cemetery; the bodies of men buried there were later removed to Carson City or the Presidio in San Francisco.

The military force was detailed here not only to give protection to travelers but also to the rapidly developing mining camps. During Civil War days the post was a recruiting station. From the beginning it was also the eastern terminus of a telegraph line crossing the Sierras from San Francisco, and during the brief Pony Express period it was a station for the mail service.

After the post's abandonment the Government sold the buildings at auction and all of value was removed. Much of the timber is in the large white Towle house at the Carson River crossing on the Fernley-Yerington highway.

In 1935, C.C.C. workers began to clear the old reservation under sponsorship of the State Park Service for the Sagebrush Chapter of the Daughters of the American Revolution. One of the old buildings has been reconstructed for future use as a museum.

US 50 now crosses a valley to DAYTON, 49 *m.* (4,400 alt., 306 pop.), an attractive trade town that grew up in early Comstock days.

The first quartz mill in Nevada was built on the banks of Carson River in Dayton to treat ore from the Comstock Lode (*see Tour 8*). In trail days this place was called Ponderers' Rest, because California bound trains sometimes halted here while they decided whether to continue westward or turn south and settle along the rivers.

1. Right from Dayton on a graveled road to SUTRO TUNNEL (*visitors welcome*), 7 *m.*, constructed to drain the hot waters from lower levels of Comstock mines, to reduce fire hazards, and to enable easier removal of ores. This great project—few have demanded more tact and patience—was planned and consummated by Adolph Sutro, who came to the Comstock with imagination and an unusual knowledge of civil engineering. The manner in which the project was carried out revealed Sutro as a master in dealing with bankers, legislators, and his enemies on the Lode, who did everything they could to thwart him That his plan was fundamentally sound has been proved by time. The project drew the attention of other civil engineers because of problems its builder met and overcame; and modern textbooks acknowledge its importance to the designers and builders of later and greater drainage works.

Sutro was operating a cigar store in Virginia City when he conceived the tunnel idea. The legislature of the new State passed a bill incorporating the tunnel company on February 4, 1865, and the following year an act of Congress chartered the corporation. To guarantee costs of construction Sutro contracted with 19 mining companies for the payment of a royalty of $2 a ton on all ore that should be removed through the tunnel and promised to drain the water free, thereby saving them enormous pumping costs. Before long, however, most of the companies, urged by Sharon and other manipulators on the Lode, repudiated their contracts, and Sutro was forced to sue or raise capital by some other means. It was characteristic of the man that he did not sue.

He had agreed to start work by August 1, 1867, and to spend not less than $400,000 annually driving the tunnel. Unable to raise enough money in the West, he went East, petitioned Congress vainly for a subsidy, tried to interest such men as Commodore Vanderbilt and William B. Astor, and at last turned again to the Nevada Legislature, but without success. After failing everywhere in America he went abroad and obtained promise of aid in France, but it was suddenly nullified by the impending war. William Sharon and the Bank of California were bitterly opposing him, and the Big Four bonanza kings (Mackey, Fair, Flood, and O'Brien) were coming to power on the Comstock. Meanwhile, Sutro had one break; on April 6, 1869, a bad fire in the Yellow Jacket mine cost so many lives and aroused so much anger among the miners that the tunnel-builder, a master showman, saw his chance. With posters and in speeches he called on the miners to support him in building his tunnel, which would lessen the danger of such disasters. He aroused the miners to frenzy, and on October 19, 1869, Sutro himself broke ground on the slope above Carson River where the tunnel was to start.

But he needed more than the support of laborers. He needed millions. Soon after the fire, the influence of Sharon and the Bank of California began to wane; but replacing them were the Big Four. Sharon and the bank had opposed Sutro because the tunnel would have terminated certain profitable Bank of California holdings, but why the four Irishmen opposed him seems largely a mystery. They apparently lacked the vision to understand that the tunnel would be a godsend to them. With four powerful opponents on his hands instead of two, Sutro went again to Congress and persuaded it to send Government experts to investigate the advantage of a tunnel. Then McClamonts' Bank of London, which Sutro had applied to earlier, suddenly pledged $2,500,000.

But his difficulties continued, and it was not until July 8, 1878 that, stripped to the waist, he fired the blast breaking the tunnel through into the first mining shaft. It had taken 13 years for his triumph, and the great Comstock had passed its peak.

Later engineering feats have dwarfed the Sutro Tunnel, but what Sharon had contemptuously dismissed as "Sutro's coyote hole" is still in use. The main tunnel is 20,489 feet long from its mouth to the main shaft of the Savage Mine, and its laterals and side drains aggregate half as much again. The cost was more than $5,000,000, more than repaid in later royalties. In one year, 1880, the tunnel drained more than two billion gallons of water from the Lode.

2. Left from Dayton over a poor road to COMO, 12 m., a mining camp that reached its peak of prosperity in 1864, at a time when it was the seat of Lyon County. In this period Paiute Chief Numaga asked the miner owners to stop the cutting of the pinon trees from which Indians obtained the nuts that were essential foodstuffs to them. The companies, of course, ignored his plea. Late in the dusk of the same day, Indians appeared and wood-choppers, perhaps partly frightened by guilty consciences, fled to the camp from which an alarm was sent to Fort Churchill. After the camp had been placed under military command, a password was devised for the whites, but two late arrivals approached in the darkness without giving the password and were fired on. Hearing the shots, a miner left his cabin in such haste that he accidentally discharged his gun. Immediately the entire male population of the camp sent barrage after barrage down the canyon, where the two cowering whites were hiding. By dawn, soldiers and miners had fired nearly all their ammunition, and, seeing no movement, sailed out to count dead Indians. Their astonishment and chagrin were hardly allayed by Chief Numaga who sauntered into the camp to learn what all the shooting had been for; he said it had disturbed his village and caused his warriors a lot of unnecessary worry.

At 53 m. is the junction (R) with Nev. 17 (see Tour 8). The Virginia Range, which once held the fabulous Comstock Lode, is to the north (R).

CARSON CITY, 61 m. (4,600 alt., 2,474 pop.), (see Tour 4), is at a junction with US 395 (see Tour 4), with which US 50 unites southward.

Through Eagle Valley at the eastern base of the Sierra Nevada, the darker hue of the sagebrush and its unusual height and density indicate that this is a fertile valley. At 64 m. US 395 continues south (see Tour 4) and US 50 turns (R) to ascend beautiful Clear Creek Grade to the summit of the eastern Sierra. Flanking the road are canyon walls and slopes heavily wooded with pine, fir, cedar, aspen, mountain sage, and manzanita. From time to time the valley below is visible, as well as mountain ranges far to the east. There are numerous springs along the highway and deer are occasionally visible in the meadows near the summit.

SPOONER'S STATION, 74 m., a former stagecoach stop, is at the junction with Nev. 28 (see Tour 4). US 50 now makes a rapid descent to the shore of blue Lake Tahoe (see Tour 4) and turns south along the lake, passing fine summer homes.

At 76 m. is the junction with an oiled road.

Right on this road to GLENBROOK (hotel, golf, riding horses), 1 m. (6,225 alt.), one of the resorts on the lake. The inn is on a ranch of 1,100 acres timbered with pine. In 1861 a sawmill was erected here, and for a while Glenbrook was a lumber town. This was the first mill erected on the Nevada side of Lake Tahoe. Many trails lead into the mountains around the inn, and the Tahoe steamer calls here daily in summer with mail and passengers. The steamer circles the blue lake and provides a delightful outing.

US 50 passes south through CAVE ROCK, where a parking spot affords a view of the whole lake. A pointer indicates the places of interest. Cave Rock, when seen in silhouette, has the roughly sculptured likeness of several great stone faces with gazes fixed on the glistening snow-capped high Sierras.

ZEPHYR COVE (*hotels, horses*), 81.8 *m.* (6,280 alt.), is a popular resort surrounded by many summer homes as well as camps. Just above the road at ZEPHYR POINT, 82.3 *m.* (6,380 alt.), are the lodge, dormitory, and dining hall used by the Y.W.C.A. and Y.M.C.A., church groups, Girl Reserves, and others for summer conferences. The Presbyterian Synod also meets here.

EDGEWOOD, 86 *m.*, has several places to offer, dancing and entertainment, in addition to the usual outdoor sports. The STATE LINE COUNTRY CLUB is here.

At 88 *m.* US 50 crosses the CALIFORNIA LINE at a point 112 miles east of Sacramento, California.

Tour 8

Steamboat Springs—Virginia City—Gold Hill—Silver City—Junction US 50; 20.8 *m.*, Nev. 17.

Paved throughout, easy grades; restaurants and one small hotel in Virginia City.

This route, which climbs the new Geiger Grade on the northwestern side of the Virginia Range, crosses to the high eastern flank of Mount Davidson, and descends along Gold Canyon to the bank of the Carson River, runs through country that populated Nevada and made it a State. Slanting along the mountain was the Comstock Lode, the deposit of silver ore that built up enormous fortunes, helped turn San Francisco from a collection of frame cottages into a fashionable city, helped pay the Civil War debt, and financed the laying of telegraph cables under the Atlantic Ocean.

The history of Virginia mining starts at the southern end of the range. In 1848, 1849, and again in 1850, Mormon travelers panned gold at the bottom of what came to be known as Gold Canyon, but the values were so small that they did not greatly impress the hordes rushing westward in search of fortunes. The canyon was named when a strike of some richness was made May 15, 1850, and a year later about 100 men who had returned from Placerville, California, were prospecting and mining at the foot of the canyon. The number doubled during the next year and the camp gradually moved up the canyon. In this period a Brazilian recognized the silver ore but could not make anyone understand what his discovery meant. By 1855 Chinamen who had come over the mountains to dig a canal by the Carson were turning to placer mining and their camp, called Johntown, followed the white camp up the canyon; in time the name of the Chinese camp was applied to both. Arrivals of 1856 were Allen and Hosea Grosch, sons of an eastern clergyman. The Brazilian told them of his discovery and they started prospecting and establishing their own private assay office. While the young men were still patiently making their studies, which had gone on for a year, James Fennimore, called Old Virginny, climbed up through the canyon, crossed Sun Mountain—later called Mount Davidson—and started work in Six Mile Canyon. Immediately a few other Johntowners followed him to discover what he thought was worth the climb. They located various placer claims but soon abandoned them. The Grosch brothers never completed their work for one died of an infected foot in Gold Canyon and the other died on his way over the mountains. Their secret work had attracted the suspicion of Henry Comstock, a lazy fellow who liked to have others do all the arduous prospecting but hoped to stake a rich claim some day, and after their deaths he vainly tried to discover their secret.

The first excitement of 1859 came early in the year when prospectors found a place in Gold Canyon where they got 15 cents worth of gold in each pan. This resulted in a minor building and locating boom and the camp named the site Gold Hill. Johntowners who arrived too late to find any unclaimed spots there decided to try Six Mile Canyon again. Among the latest comers in the second canyon were Peter O'Riley and Patrick McLaughlin, who had to mark off their claims 500 yards above the choice Six Mile Canyon claims. With all this activity the miners decided on June 11 to organize a mining district, which they named Gold Hill; they set its north-south limits at Johntown and Steamboat Springs. In the next day or two O'Riley and McLaughlin discovered the Comstock Lode on their high claims, though they neither understood what they had, nor the richness of the find; to them the "black stuff" with their gold was discouraging. Old Comstock, prowling around as usual, discovered them with the apron of their rocker covered with gold and immediately laid claim to the spot for himself, insisting that he had already taken up claims there. When the Irishmen were unimpressed he went away to find help and the next day came back with Manny Penrod, who cheerfully backed up Comstock's story and said he shared the claim. The discoverers knew they were liars but the site was lonely and they did not like to court attack by the rogues; so they agreed to give them equal shares in the discovery.

Soon all the Gold Canyon men as well as the ranchers of the valleys were rushing over Sun Mountain to locate claims. Comstock left his partners doing the development work while he busily set up location mounuments for himself all over the mountain and canyon, and then, with a supreme burst of imagination, announced claim to a ranch three-quarters of a mile long on high barren rocky Sun Mountain. One of the men attracted by the rush to Washoe was a trader named Stone, who had been operating along the Truckee. He found the Six Mile Canyon men taking out $500 to $1,000 worth of gold a day—but damning the "black-stuff." Stone was curious and carried some discarded ore away with him; a few days later he sent it over the mountains to a friend whom he asked to give it to a reliable assayer. The friend took it to Judge James Walsh, a mining expert, who turned it over to Mel Atwood, best assayer in Grass Valley. That night Atwood did the assay and could not believe his eyes; but test after test showed him ore running $4,791 a ton in silver and $3,196 in gold. When the judge heard the news he swore Atwood to secrecy until he and Stone's friend could cross the Sierras; in return he promised to take up a claim for Atwood. He and two companions started off that night on mules.

Though Atwood had promised to keep the secret, he could not resist writing a letter to Donald Davidson, the Rothschild representative in San Francisco. Davidson also had a few friends to whom he told the news. Overnight all California knew about it and the diggings on the west side of the Sierras were almost deserted as men rode, walked, and staggered up the slopes on the trek eastward to the range they had scorned in passing. Among arrivals on Sun Mountain in 1859 and 1860 were three men who were to play leading roles in its development— William Stewart, who in time came to represent law and order, and Adolph Sutro and John Mackay, who made great contributions in the technical field. George Hearst was also an early arrival and managed to stake the claims that were to be the foundation of a vast fortune.

The rush had an unnerving effect on the early claimants; for all Comstock's boasts on the richness of the claims he held, an offer of a little more than $11,000 in cash was sufficient to buy out all his claims, including the "ranch." He had already sold a quarter interest in one mine; the claims he had sold, later had a total stock-market quotation of $80,000,000. McLaughlin sold out his original interest for $3,500, and Penrod sold his for $8,500.

Before long, the whole range was covered with new camps going under the names of Winnemuc, Ophir Diggins, and Mount Pleasant Point. The story is that it was Old Virginny who in a bibulous moment christened the new community Virginia in order to get some use out of liquor he had managed to spill on the ground. This was in November of 1859; Wells Fargo and the post office between them later added the word "city" as fitting for the new metropolis. That first winter was very severe; winds tore over the breast of the mountain and carried away all tents and similarly flimsy structures. No wagon road yet existed for the transportation of lumber and Sun Mountain itself was treeless, so the men who did not die or leave for warmer spots dug holes in the hills for shelter. Food and water were at such a premium that everyone lived on whiskey, the one staple that seemed to come through even better than the mail. Brush was the only fuel and a ton hardly gave a respectable fire.

The new Virginians were a sorry lot when spring arrived, what with filth, scurvy, and lack of food. But they were cheered when snow left the Sierra passes and a new horde swept over and up the long slopes to join them. By mid-summer of 1860 the community was taking on some of the aspects of civilization; real estate speculation was reaching its stride, a road was being constructed through Gold Canyon, and ore was going down on muleback to quartz mills at Gold Hill and in Washoe Valley. The whole valley westward (*see Tour 4*) was covered with tents and shacks as the quartz mills grew in number and the wooded slopes of the Sierras were being denuded to provide lumber, mine timbers, and firewood for Virginia City and its satellite camps. The Gould and Curry claims acquired by Hearst and Henry Meredith revealed a bonanza in July.

In 1861 construction on the Geiger Grade was begun to provide a better approach; this was the predecessor of the modern road that approaches Virginia from the north. In this year also Joseph T. Goodman became editor and part owner of the *Daily Territorial Enterprise.* Another important event of the year was the beginning of construction on the 3,200-foot Latrobe Tunnel, to be pushed back into the hill 400 feet below Virginia City; and Washoe was providing enough traffic to cause construction of a toll road over the mountains from California.

Three years after the first discovery of silver the mountain was feeding ore to 80 mills and speculation was so active that Washoe had its own stock exchange. The San Francisco Exchange was organized a year later. Washoe also had five newspapers and gas lights in its streets by 1862. In the same year Gould and Curry stock reached $6,300 a foot on the exchange (Comstock shares were first sold in units of feet).

Though the range produced $15,600,000 worth of ore in 1864 and even more in the following year, the years between 1864 and 1868 were counted slack times on the Comstock. But the State government was bringing order out of chaos; the rowdies and gunmen who had hindered production were being run out of the State, and a good part of the surplus Virginia population had suddenly run off to new discoveries in the central part of the State, hoping to make the strikes that would put them into the millionaire class.

The Sutro Tunnel Company (*see Tour 7c*) was incorporated in 1865 to reach the lode at a low level. In the next year the owners of the Belcher met unusual heat at the 900-foot level. In 1868, 1869, and 1870 production averaged only about half that of the earlier peak years. But construction of the Virginia and Truckee went on and reached the high silver city in 1869. Then the output again began to climb, with more than $12,000,000 worth in 1872 and nearly double that in the next year; the Belcher and Crown Point stocks made the market highs. The new peak year saw the first water siphoned down and then up from the Sierra to Virginia City, and it also saw low pay development reached in the Gould and Curry mine. Virginia's population was 35,000, in another 12 months, after a bonanza in the Ophir had been discovered at the 1,300-foot level. That fall William Sharon began to manipulate Comstock shares, sending them up and down, and in the following spring financial panic hit the Pacific Coast, with a big break in the price of Comstock stock; in August the Bank of California closed its doors. Production reached a new high in spite of the juggling with silver prices in Washington. Late in the year Virginia City had one of its worst fires with losses reaching $10,000,000. This fire, and others in mines, did not hinder production of $36,500,000 worth of ore in 1876, and nearly the same amount in the succeeding 12 months, with discovery of another bonanza in the Ophir. Then the returns dropped nearly in half, though the Sutro Tunnel had at last reached the Savage Mine. The next year saw a drop of more than half from the 1878 production and within two years only a little more than $1,000,000 worth of ore was being removed annually. That was the low of the period; a very slow rise began but with the devaluation of silver there was no hope for a return of the high profits of the past. The population of the whole range began to leave. The last year of the century did not see $200,000 worth of bullion go out. At intervals there were slight rises and declines in output, which did not again reach a value of $2,000,000 until 1923, when the cyanide process of recovery was in use. The all-time low was reached in 1932 with only about $32,000 worth of bullion recovered; but four years later the output again passed $1,000,000 in value, entirely from low-grade ore of the kind that Virginia had used in 1876 to pave C Street.

The Virginia that was a great industrial center is usually ignored in popular accounts of the Comstock; rather, the chaotic camp of the first five years, with its gunfights and over-night millionaires, is stressed. But even Mark Twain had to do considerable fine-combing to find enough gaudy stories to make up his book about his two years on the range during the most turbulent period. Actually, the towns on Sun Mountain early reached social stability, and life there was no more wild and woolly by 1870 than it was in New York. Fluctuating production caused hard times and good in rapid succession and the population rose and fell at about the same rate as the profits. The towns are not ghosts; in 1934 Silver City saw more activity than it had in 40 years. And there is not a Comstocker alive who would be surprised if new bonanzas were discovered, even though experts are pessimistic.

Nev. 17 branches southwest from US 395 (*see Tour 4*) at STEAMBOAT SPRINGS, 0 *m.,* and the ascent of one of the most beautiful routes in the State soon begins. Nothing hides the views as the road winds back and forward around the slopes and gullies.

Whereas the old Geiger Grade road had steep stretches that taxed the ability of even the best motor cars, the new Geiger Grade can be driven to the top in high gear. The foothills are dotted with second-growth juniper. Mile after mile the road climbs, offering many broad views of the valley with the magnificent Sierras beyond in the west.

The broad expanse of mountains, forests, and valleys is best viewed from the GEIGER LOOKOUT, 4.8 *m.,* an area of about two acres at a strategic point nearly 1,000 feet above the Truckee Meadows and below the road level. Fireplaces, lookouts, and picnicking facilities have been constructed of vividly colored local rock, and rock-lined paths lead to Geiger, Tilton, and Thorp points, whose names honor the partners who constructed the original road. Groups gather here for supper, particularly during the waning hours of the day and on evenings when the moon is bright. Star study groups sometimes set up their telescopes here.

The view from the lookout is not more impressive than that at many other points; it merely offers a convenient parking spot. Far down near the valley floor feathers of trailing smoke are seen, marking Steamboat Springs; far across the valley is the white ribbon of the road that zigzags up the hazy blue side of towering Mount Rose. In near by and distant hills every color of the spectrum is seen, with the soft blues, violets, and gray-greens accented by vivid red spots of highly mineralized earth. In spring the meadows are bright green with new crops. The dull green of the forests on the high flanks of the Sierras, mauve shadows on far-away hills, white roads lacing the foreground and background, the deep rich black of freshly turned fields, the brown of drying weeds—all run together to provide a magnificent spectacle.

Directly below the lookout the original Geiger Grade, built in 1861-62, sweeps up a steep canyon, ascending some 2,000 feet in five miles. Over it on October 16, 1869, 14 yoke of oxen hauled the first locomotive of the V. & T. During the 1860's both the Wells Fargo and Pioneer Stage companies kept a continuous procession of swift carts shuttling over the route and there were several hotels and stores along the way; not a trace of these remains. When the Central Pacific Railroad reached Reno in 1868, the Geiger became a veritable race-track. Virginia City turned out en masse, and thousands of dollars changed hands as the stages of the two companies wheeled into town. The best time from Reno to Virginia was an hour and 32 minutes, but a horse once made the trip in two minutes less than an hour.

At the GEIGER SUMMIT, 9.1 *m.,* the old Geiger Grade rejoins the modern highway from the west, and between this point and Virginia City the routes of the old and new roads are nearly the same. During the wild 1860's stagecoach holdups were such ordinary occurrences on roads entering Virginia City that they received little mention in the newspapers. One that took place on the Geiger Summit in October, 1866, received more than usual mention, however, probably because other news was momentarily scarce. Stages of the Pioneer Company arriving at the summit in the early morning hours, were stopped by seven masked men with levelled shotguns and the warning "You'll find us the damndest, roughest set of citizens you ever fell in with." This was quite sufficient to unload the coaches and stand 38 men, one woman, and a Chinaman in line with hands reaching for the sky. The horses were led away and the strongbox on one of the coaches was blown open with gunpowder. All it contained was $6,000 in gold coin, so the passengers were next considered. The leader of the band courteously waved the lady aside and remarked to the stage drivers, "You men earn whatever you get hard enough and you have damned little anyhow," and then turned to the remaining passengers. "Gentlemen, we don't like to do this. It's not in our line, but the fact is that we haven't made so good a haul as we expected, and since we've made a night of it, we may as well play our hand out." Each man was relieved of his valuables, the robbers helped the drivers hitch up the horses, and bade the passengers a pleasant journey.

At the Geiger Summit (6,799 alt.), the road crosses to the eastern side of the range but descends very little as it winds past old workings.

VIRGINIA CITY, 13.6 m. (6,500 alt., 948 pop.), once the center of the greatest mining activity in North America, sits high on the eastern slope of Sun Mountain—now named Mount Davidson for the Rothschild representative who vainly tried to interest his firm in the early Comstock. Friends among the Virginians renamed the mountain in his honor during a convivial trip to the summit.

The view from Virginia City is both sublime and picturesque. Rocky and barren mountains form an amphitheater in air so clear that the snow-capped Humboldt Range, more than 150 miles away to the northeast, is a distinct blue-purple mass, far beyond the green fields and cottonwoods along the Carson River and the white sands of the Forty Mile Desert, 2,000 feet below. To the south is Dayton by the Carson River, which winds around the towering pink-tinged Como Range from the yet higher Sierra Nevada. The scene when the sun is low has few rivals in America.

The highway follows C Street, the core of the town; both high above it and far below are parallel streets—though not nearly as many as in the days when many thousands of people lived here. Cross streets climb steeply and motor cars of Virginia learn to do acrobatics without a groan. Below C Street the remaining buildings are largely industrial, above it are the old, fine residential sections—and others not so fine. Only a few houses are left from the bonanza days; some were torn down for firewood or to build other structures in the valleys below, or even in distant camps, and some were taken apart and re-erected in Reno, Carson, and other towns. Yet enough still cling to B and A streets to vivify the days when Virginia ladies delicately shook their hands above their heads to render them properly white and bloodless before receiving guests and called for their carriages to make calls on next door neighbors. Most of the houses have long been unpainted and the elaborately turned wooden balustrades along the high retaining walls are beginning to sag. The few that still have most of their decorative urns and finials are marked exceptions. Here and there is an old house in good condition and showing continuous habitation; yet even the freshest show beyond question that they belong to the days when the jigsaw was creating domestic Gothic Revival decorations.

C Street is lined with old places making a mild bid to attract attention from curious visitors; the Only and Original This-and-That offers its faded charms and many windows display huddles of photographs, chunks of Comstock ores, and similar curios. Wooden awnings are still supported by spindling cast-iron columns and cast-iron pilasters still frame the show windows. Here and there are iron shutters, reminders of the day when many of the offices and stores handled daily receipts that would have tempted some fairly honest men. Each year there are a few less buildings, for annually in the spring the undermined earth sags a little more at one spot or the other. Though sidewalks tilt and walls crack no one is seriously concerned about a collapse of any large section of town.

Many of the saloons that so readily catch the eye of the tourist are in reality museums of relics. The fixtures in some are as suggestive of the past as are their formal displays. One in particular has awe-inspiring early lighting fixtures, lamps of red and green dripping with pendant prisms in tiers. The chief relic of an earlier magnificence in one is an old piano, now fixed to play electrically the hit tunes of its youth.

Visitors lingering in Virginia City are sure to find someone sooner or later who will tell them of the days when affluent Comstockers hired gunmen at $20 a day to protect their claims, of "601" vigilante episodes, of this gunman and that who daily ticked off his man before breakfast. Some of the tales are true, some have a grain of truth, but piled together they represent the violence of a few short years kept alive for outsiders who would be much disappointed if they did not hear of them. Old Comstockers rarely refer to any of these hoary tales among themselves. Instead they love to remember when an agile youngster could pick up $20 in the course of a day running errands for liberal-handed men; when no saloonkeeper was expected to give change for a $5 gold piece, and change of any kind was so scarce that it could be exchanged at a premium.

Old timers are also particularly fond of remembering the formal parties that were the delight of the day and how the $5 dances of the Ivy Social Club could always be depended on for some daring novelty, as on the occasion when the committee collected all the canaries in town—every Virginia household had at least one—kept them with an attendant for a few days in a darkened cellar, and then hung the cages in rows from the ceiling of the armory. "We didn't much need the orchestra that night," they tell triumphantly. More elaborate and formal were the dances of the exclusive *Entre Nous* Club, with its quadrilles, schottisches, mazurkas, and waltzes. Oysters from the Coast, strawberries from Lamoille Valley, squab from heaven knows where, were regular fare at public dinners and even the miners could not indulge in a dinner or celebration without a few dozen cases of champagne. It wasn't that they really liked the drink; it was merely a symbol of wealth and the Comstock had it.

In 1878 Virginia had 20 laundries, 8 dairies, 4 hay-yards, 4 banks, 50 drygoods merchants, 2 pawnbrokers, 20 insurance agents, 18 barbers, 1 josshouse, 6 churches, 30 lodging and boarding houses, 150 places where liquor was sold, 11 faro games, 1 keno and 2 pan games, 2 homeopathic doctors and 35 physician-surgeons—a list that provides a fair index to the demands of the population. The list does not tell whether the insurance men wrote fire or life policies but both were sorely needed because the fire loss here was as high as was usual in mining camps, and loss of life and serious injury were almost daily events. An average month—August, 1877—saw 15 killed by cave-ins, falls in shafts, blasts, and other mine accidents, and several others seriously injured.

A favorite diversion was climbing Mount Davidson, and from 1863 on there was a pole on the summit from which to unfurl a huge flag on special occasions. One of Mark Twain's most vivid memories was of the tense period during the battle of Gettysburg, when the fate of the Nation was in the balance, and of how the black clouds mantling the Davidson summit suddenly parted to reveal the Stars and Stripes lit by the rays of the sun.

During the Civil War, sentiment in Virginia City favored the Union and two regiments were raised and sent to Fort Churchill. Southern sympathizers caused some trouble and the proprietress of the Tahoe House shot a man in the act of raising the Stars and Stripes over her hotel. No people contributed more liberally to the soldiers engaged in the Civil War than the people of Virginia City and when news came that Lee had surrendered to Grant and the war was terminated, the Lode went frantic with excitement and the air was filled with the sound of bells, whistles, exploding anvils, music, and cheers. All the saloons were crowded, and men drinking over the bars and in the streets pledged one hero and then another, saluting "The Old Flag," "Old Everybody," and "Old Everything," until they lost all power of recollection.

In April, 1869, occurred the worst fire in any American metal mine up to that time. At seven o'clock in the morning several hundred men of the day-shift were standing about the shaft mouths of the Yellow Jacket, Crown Point, and Kentuck mines, waiting their turn to go underground. More than 100 had already gone underground when smoke was seen coming out of the shafts of all three mines. Station tenders heroically boarded the cages and rescued all but 49 of the men who were underground. Rescue work continued all day and far into the night, even though they knew no man could live in the burning mines.

On May 31, 1882, at 8:30 a. m., the pump column broke in the Alta shaft and seven men working 2,150 feet below the surface in a drift 1,400 feet from the shaft were imprisoned by the rising hot water. The water rose 18 feet over the drift in which the miners were imprisoned before the pumps were repaired. There did not seem to be one chance in a million to rescue the men, but the policy of mine owners on the Comstock was to recover bodies regardless of expense. On the third day after the accident, the water in the shaft had been lowered sufficiently to allow a boat to be navigated in the drift, and two miners volunteered to go down. When they did not return a middle aged Civil War veteran, Yank Van Dusen, volunteered to don an ice mask invented by a local man, Fred Ritter, and enter the drift. On his way in, with his helmet and boots filled with ice, Van Dusen saw the dead bodies of the two men who had gone to the rescue in the boat, and several hundred feet farther in, within 100 feet of the face of the drift, he found the seven imprisoned miners alive, but nearly dead from heat and exhaustion. It required more than 100 men, inured to working in the hot mines to rescue the seven. Sixty-two hours after the pump broke the last of the victims landed on the surface at midnight, and the steam whistle of every mine and mill on the Comstock was tied down for 15 minutes as the Lode celebrated.

Practically all men and women living in Virginia City during its prosperous years speculated in mining shares. Female domestic servants, earning from $50 to $75 a month were particularly incorrigible stock gamblers and had opportunities, time and time again, to sell their shares to advantage; but they held onto their stock, waiting for better offers, and all died poor. Many among the working class had opportunities to sell their shares for more than $100,000, and all who speculated persistently over a period of years had at least one opportunity to sell for at least $25,000. Few did, however, and eventually those who held on had only bundles of green certificates to show for their investments.

Speculation in Comstock shares was usually on a 20 per cent margin. Market prices depended on many factors, of which production was not always the most important. Manipulation by powerful speculators caused frantic fluctuations that at times endangered even the soundest West Coast banking houses. Even more important was public sentiment; tips and rumors, panic on the part of one man, sensational success on a wild gamble by another—alone or together these would send shares from quotations of a few cents up to thousands, and down again to the gutter.

Even when the Crown Point and Belcher mines were extracting their bonanzas and the companies were paying millions in dividends, shares in all Comstock mines decreased steadily in value under prophecies of doom from those who had lost faith. Then came the Big Bonanza of 1873—probably the richest body of gold and silver ore ever found on earth. Within a little more than a year the stock of the Consolidated Virginia and the Consolidated California, which together owned the bonanza, had a total stock exchange value of $159,000,000. Mackay, Fair, Flood, and O'Brien—who became known as the Bonanza Kings—had been able to buy control of the two mines for about $100,000 only two years before the discovery was made. In 1870, before the Crown Point bonanza had appeared to rouse new hopes, the Consolidated Virginia, with 1,010 feet on the Lode, had 11,000 shares of stock listed at $1 a share, and two small claims adjoining it, with 300 feet on the Lode that were later part of the reorganized Consolidated Virginia and Consolidated California, were considered too worthless for regular listing.

Another factor causing confusion in Lode market values was the lack of accurate surveys. Claims conflicted and overlapped and litigation often swallowed all profits. Mackay worked endlessly to clarify the holdings of Consolidated Virginia and Consolidated California; and at the time when their stock prices were at their peak, with monthly dividends of $1,080,000, the reorganized Consolidated Virginia had only 710 feet on the Lode.

Of the thousands of young men who came to the Comstock to make their fortunes, comparatively few succeeded. The great majority had great wealth within their grasp a hundred times, but guessed wrong on their gambles over discoveries, feet, and shares. Some lacked faith in the magnitude of what they owned and sold out for pittances; others lacked the vision to go on with patient grubbing on the claims they had located when richer surface deposits showed in some other area. It is true that many of the successful men got quick riches with little work, but many others worked long and hard for their returns; this was notably the case with Sutro and Mackay. Sutro went through endless difficulties and heartbreaks in digging his great tunnel and received far less from it than he had hoped; he did, however, lay the foundation for a very solid estate and later, as mayor of San Francisco, was notable for his civic contributions.

John W. Mackay was a poor miner who went to work in the Kentuck for feet, not shares; while others, including his comrade, Jack O'Brien, roistered and drank, he worked and horded to enable him to continue with small returns. When Mackay's patience was rewarded he became one of the few Comstockers who, with his family, never forgot to contribute to the State that had given him his start; his early gifts were to churches but the Mackay School of Mines is his real monument.

William Stewart was a lawyer with a keen analytical mind and his monument is found in the basic mining laws of the United States; he was a rough and tumble fighter, suited to the lawless period in which he entered Washoe, and the stories of how he forged ahead in politics make lusty reading. He was one of the first pair of Senators sent to Washington by Nevada and served in the Senate for 28 years.

James G. Fair was another Comstock millionaire who went to the Senate, but from California, not Nevada. He was the principal stockholder of the Nevada Bank in San Francisco, whose history belongs to the days of uncontrolled banking. James L. Flood was a saloonkeeper whose name is associated with the Comstock but he made his money by lucky speculation in shares. His home down the Peninsula below San Francisco became a symbol of new-rich pretentiousness. John P. Jones, who was United States Senator from Nevada for 30 years, was an ardent promoter who could not resist the call of any prospect, from mines to real estate. William Sharon was another Comstocker whose millions took him to the United States Senate, in his case for one term. It was Sharon's manipulations of Comstock shares

POINTS OF INTEREST IN VIRGINIA CITY

1. Sierra Nevada Glory Hole
2. Union Shaft
3. Site of International Hotel
4. Piper's Opera House
5. Storey County Courthouse
6. Crystal Bar
7. Episcopal Church
8. St. Mary's In the Mountains
9. Odd Fellow's Hall
10. Gould and Curry Office
11. Savage Office
12. Fourth Ward School
13. Chollar Cut

that created such havoc in the 1870's and resulted in at least one notable suicide.

Lucky Baldwin, one of the first men to come to Washoe mines, was a spectacular gambler in stocks, losing and winning millions in Nevada, and later in California. George Hearst was an earnest young miner who joined the first rush and made a lucky choice; he later showed dogged perseverance in developing the holdings that were eventually to finance the great publishing interests expanded by his son.

Sam Clemens (Mark Twain) was the outstanding literary product of Nevada; Virginia stimulated his imagination and taught him his pace. His *Roughing It* is the most read book on the State.

Though much of old above-ground Virginia City has disappeared, it still rewards visitors who have imagination to fill in the gaps; the most important part of the city is still there—the vast workings underground. The great surface workings have appeared only since about 1920. These glory holes are made by operators working the low-grade surface ores, which give good returns under modern processes of recovery.

POINTS OF INTEREST

1. High on the slope of Cedar Hill at the northern end of town is (R) the SIERRA NEVADA GLORY HOLE. Steam shovels can be seen on the upper terraces chewing away at the hill. The Sierra Nevada mine marks the northern end of the Comstock Lode.

2. Down the hill (L), not far south of the Sierra Nevada, are the galvanized iron buildings and tall tumbling gallows of the UNION SHAFT, which goes down 3,000 feet and meets the north lateral of the Sutro Tunnel at a point 1,650 feet below the surface. The side road leading to the Union also goes to the cemetery spread far over hillocks; legends on tombstones and markers here provoke speculation, amusement, and pity.

3. On the west side of C Street, at the corner of Union—opposite the post office—is an empty lot, the SITE OF THE INTERNATIONAL HOTEL, which was the boast and glory of the Comstock. The tall, elaborately appointed brick building was destroyed by the inevitable fire in the 1920's.

4. Up Union Street one block, at the corner of B Street, is PIPER'S OPERA HOUSE, whose long one-story recessed porch received the beauty and wealth of the Virginia Range when such stars as Edwin Booth came to town. The stage boxes are now tarnished and most of the old interior fittings are gone.

5. On B Street, half a block south of Union, is the STOREY COUNTY COURTHOUSE, whose records reveal the source of many American fortunes.

6. On the northwestern corner of C Street and Taylor, the first cross street south of Union, is the CRYSTAL BAR, of the astonishing chandeliers. The Crystal was formerly in another building but the fittings were moved complete to this place. Among the many

photographs and relics on display is the register of the International Hotel, an autograph book of the mighty dead. One of the most prominently displayed photographs shows U. S. Grant at the mouth of the Sutro Tunnel. Even Grant had thoughts of recouping his badly managed finances by investing in Comstock.

7. Down the hill, Taylor Street leads (L) to the deserted EPISCOPAL CHURCH and its rectory; gaunt, with peeling paint, on the edge of a high jumping-off place with 100 miles of magnificent, brilliantly colored scenery as a back-drop, this old structure is a symbol of dead hope.

8. Southwest of the Episcopal Church, with a side paralleling Taylor St., is ST. MARY'S IN THE MOUNTAINS, most beautiful church in the State and in some ways one of the loveliest of its period in America. The large red brick building accented with white limestone and entered through three pointed-arch vestibules, has two pinnacles on its facade and a rose window high in the gabled center front; above rises a white, turreted bell-tower supporting a steeple. The cross on the steeple has one curious adjunct, a water pipe installed to place the church under a powerful fountain—with the aid of the high pressure engendered during the water's course from the high Sierras—in case one of the perennial fires should endanger it. The pews and appurtenances of the auditorium are pleasing but not notable; the real glory of St. Mary's is in its tall, slender, clustered redwood columns and in the delicately carved redwood trusses and arches supporting the ceiling. The capitals of the columns are also finely carved. The redwood has never been marred by shellac or varnish and its color has been enhanced by oil alone. The high ceiling is painted a delicate powdery blue of the kind seen in the Sistine Chapel at Rome; the effect of the traceried redwood against this color is breath-taking.

In the rear of the church are many fine vestments, some of them 200 years old. Virginia's first Roman Catholic church, built in 1860, was blown down by a Washoe "zephyr"; the second, a frame structure, was soon replaced by one of brick, costing $65,000. This was destroyed in the great fire of 1875; the present church was completed two years later—its bell was made of Comstock silver. All but the first little chapel were the result of efforts by the Reverend Patrick Manogue, an Irishman who was as devout as he was energetic. It is told that on one occasion at least he knocked down a bully who was trying to keep him from visiting a dying woman.

9. On the east side of C Street, south of Taylor, is the ODD FELLOWS HALL, which was the National Theater of Bonanza days. Modjeska appeared there when the early opera house burned shortly before her arrival. The rear of the building suddenly dropped away in the night, early in 1940, as the undermined earth settled slightly after winter rains.

10. Close to the road, about 100 yards farther south on the west side of C Street, is seen the roof of a large square brick building, the

GOULD AND CURRY OFFICE, where John Mackay once lived for a short time. The large solid structure, which is entered from the street below, looks more like a mansion than an office; its Victorian trim is among the most delightful in town.

11. A short distance south of the Gould and Curry office is the large frame SAVAGE OFFICE, entered from D Street. Grant lived here during most of his stay in the city. Not far from the office is a heap of rubble, head of the Savage shaft, which was reached by the main Sutro Tunnel in 1876.

12. As C Street begins to rise toward the southern end of town the large square deserted FOURTH WARD SCHOOL, built in 1876, is seen at a point where the eastern side of C Street does not slope quickly downward. It is no longer used.

13. Not far south of the school, on the opposite side of the road, is the CHOLLAR CUT, a large glory hole made by the Arizona Comstock Mining Company to extract low-grade ore. This place used to be covered with houses and streets; old-time workings came within 100 feet of them but never caused trouble.

At the southern end of town is the low DIVIDE. Slightly north of the Divide the modern highway turns L.

Left here 9 *m.* on the modern highway, which is a better paved alternate to the old road and unites with it near the southern end of the range.

The old Gold Canyon Road, which at this point becomes an alternate route to the modern route, is much used by visitors; it turns R. from the modern highway, soon meeting the old Ophir Grade, a little used road that climbs over the range and descends to the Washoe Lake area (*see Tour* 4). It was constructed in 1860.

The Gold Canyon Road winds down steeply, passing the BULLION MINE, an unfortunate venture that absorbed much money before it was discovered to be at a point where the Comstock Lode was broken. Some old houses dripping jigsaw work still stand in the canyon. Wild roses are particularly abundant here in the spring.

GOLD HILL, 15.3 *m.,* is the remnant of the first highly prosperous camp on the range (*see before*). At its upper end is an old firehouse, typical of these built in early camps. After Virginia City reached the stage of expansive civic development the people of Gold Hill objected to the levies made on them and broke away to form their independent town. Then, the Gold Hillers, feeling that Virginia was stealing too much glory, tried to form a new county for which their town would be the seat. The attempt failed.

The first building in the Gold Hill camp was the small frame shack of Nicholas Ambrosia, "Dutch Nick," the next was a small boarding house and restaurant, run by Mrs. Alexander Cowan, later Mrs. Sandy Bowers (*see Tour* 4). Soon a town hall was erected, then an Odd Fellow's Building, and elegant residences, churches, schools, and other lodge halls appeared.

Opposite the firehouse is the BOWERS MINE, one of the first fortune makers on the mountain. It paid for the Bowers Mansion. Near it is a recent glory hole.

Gold Canyon Road descends through DEVIL'S GATE, which was guarded by a cannon during the Indian scare of 1860. But the cannon was more dangerous to those who fired it than to possible victims. Around the gate was a rebel stronghold during the days when Secessionists were rampant in the camps.

SILVER CITY, 17.5 *m.*, third in importance among the old camps on the range, shows some vigor after long inactivity. At the northern end is the Crown Point Ravine, which was once spanned by a high frame railroad trestle. Not far from it is the ALTA SHAFT, end of the southern lateral of the Sutro Tunnel.

Up and down this canyon the first prospectors did desultory panning for gold for 10 years before the Lode was discovered to bring hordes to build a city on the side of Sun Mountain.

In the canyon the first marriage and divorce of Western Utah took place. An emigrant, Powell by name, came to Gold Canyon in the summer of 1853, and left his motherless family there while he went on to seek a home for them in California. A young man, Benjamin Cole, persuaded the 15-year-old daughter Mary to marry him. The ceremony was performed by civil law, and the young man took his bride of half an hour to Mother Cosser, one of the few women in the country, while he sought a cabin in which to set up housekeeping. Interested in the child-bride, Mother Cosser advised her to await her father's return before going with her husband. The whole camp took sides, some for the husband, some against. When the father returned he was grateful to Mrs. Cosser for her care and started hastily with his brood for California. The young husband, however, immediately followed with the avowed intention of abducting his bride, and the rest of the camp trailed along to prevent trouble. The decision was finally left to the girl, and she elected to stay with her father.

The next attempt at marriage in the territory was made July 1, 1854, when an immigrant and his sister camped at the mouth of Gold Canyon. One of the miners proposed marriage with the girl and she was willing, but they could find neither magistrate nor minister. A woman in the camp solved the dilemma by drawing up a triplicate contract of marriage on July 4, which each signed. The document read:

> By these presents we hereby certify, in the presence of witnesses, that we will from this time henceforth to the end of our lives, live together as man and wife, obeying all the laws of the United States as married persons. In witness we set our hands and seals, this fourth day of July, in the year of our Lord, one thousand eight hundred and fifty-four.

But the lady tired of her husband after living with him for eight years and left to join her brother in California.

Silver City is the southern junction with the modern highway, which here becomes the tour route again.

At 20.8 *m.* on Nev. 17, is the junction with US 50 (*see Tour 7c*), at a point 8 miles west of Carson City.

Part III

Appendices

Chronology

1775   First attempt was made to find a route north of Colorado River between Santa Fe and California missions.

1826   Jedediah Strong Smith with a party of fifteen men crossed Nevada near Las Vegas from the Great Salt Lake.

1827   Jedediah Smith and his party returned from California, crossing the center of what became Nevada.

1828   Peter Skene Ogden, heading party of Hudson's Bay trappers, trapped on Mary River, later Ogden, now Humboldt.

1833-   Joseph Walker led a group from Captain Bonneville's party
'34   along the Humboldt on a secret reconnaissance of California.

1841   The Bartelson-Bidwell party, including one woman and a child, crossed Nevada by the way of the Humboldt, Carson Sink, and Walker River.

1843   Immigrant party led by Joseph Walker through Walker Pass took first wagons across the Sierra.
        In December Lieutenant John C. Fremont entered Nevada from Oregon with Kit Carson as guide; he discovered and named Pyramid Lake and Carson River before crossing into California.

1844   In April and May Fremont party returned across southern Nevada through what is now Clark County.
        The Stevens-Townsend party led by Old Greenwood, went down Humboldt with wagons, the first taken across what became Donner Pass.

1845   Captain John C. Fremont crossed Nevada again, this time from east to west in a general line running from Flowery Lake to Walker Lake.

1846   The Donner Party, traveling along the Humboldt and Truckee Rivers, made its ill-fated trip, following on the heels of Lansford W. Hastings and party. The Hastings party left the Humboldt somewhere near Wells.

1847   Mormon immigrants reached Salt Lake Valley in July and sent two parties to California, one under Jefferson Hunt, the other under Porter Rockwell, to buy seed grain and cattle. They went south through Utah and then followed the Old Spanish Trail. House possibly erected at Kane Springs, Wahmonie, near Salt Lake-Los Angeles Trail.

1848   On February 2, by Treaty of Guadalupe-Hidalgo, Mexico ceded to the United States a great region in which was the present Nevada.

1849 Mormons organized the State of Deseret, which included Nevada. The gold rush across Nevada began; possibly 25,000 came through the area.

The Jayhawkers and others left a party guided on Mormon Trail by Hunt, cut westward across Nevada and then through Death Valley.

H. S. Beatie, a Mormon, opened a summer trading station on the overland trail at Carson Valley.

Allen Hardin while crossing the Black Rock Desert found a piece of hornsilver that weighed about 25 pounds.

1850 On September 9 Territory of Utah including most of Nevada was created; also Territory of New Mexico, which included southern Nevada.

Brigham Young was appointed governor of Utah Territory.

1851 John Reese and other Mormons arrived in Carson Valley with thirteen wagons loaded with supplies for a trading post, which became Mormon Station.

United States mail was carried for the first time across Nevada between Carson Valley and Salt Lake City. The "jackass" mail began trips across Nevada, between Sacramento and Salt Lake City under contract with Absalom Woodward and George Chorpenning. On November 12 settlers in Carson and near-by valleys set up a squatters' government.

1852 Gold coin began to circulate in Carson Valley. This money was made by the Mormons at Salt Lake City in the Church Mint.

The first toll bridge in Nevada was built by John Reese, over the Carson River not far from Mormon Station.

The first crop of turnips, fruit, and watermelons was harvested at Mormon Station.

C. D. Jones brought about 30 milk cows and a few hogs into Carson Valley.

The first land claim was granted by the Mormon Station squatters' government, to John Reese.

1853 Gentiles of Carson and near-by valleys petitioned California to take jurisdiction over their lands. Petition was refused.

1853 Near Mormon Station the first Nevada marriage, the first divorce, and the first dance took place.

1854 Carson County was created by the Utah government.

George Chorpenning again obtained a contract to carry the mail and changed the route to pass through southern Nevada from Salt Lake City to Los Angeles.

1855 Mormons established a stockaded trading post at Las Vegas and soon opened a lead mine near by.

Judge Orson Hyde, who was appointed probate judge over Carson County by Brigham Young, organized county government September 20.

A meeting house was built by the Mormons at Mormon Station, which became Genoa.

1856   During the early spring between 60 and 70 Mormon families from Salt Lake City arrived in Carson Valley.

Many Gentiles moved into Carson Valley from California.

The Grosh Brothers discovered and recognized silver ore in Gold Canyon.

1857   Brigham Young ordered all Latter-Day Saints to return to Utah because of approach of government forces sent out to subdue the resistance to federal rule.

1858   The newspaper, *Territorial Enterprise,* was established at Genoa.

Mormons were settling Pahranagat Valley in eastern Nevada.

The name Nevada was first used for Western Utah by Delegate Crane when petitioning for territorial government for it.

1858   The Comstock Lode was discovered in the spring when the Ophir and Little Gold Hill ore bodies were found by placer miners from Gold Canyon.

For a third time George Chorpenning received the contract to carry the mail between Salt Lake City and California. He used the shorter northern route called the Egan Trail; also improved the road and rolling stock.

1859   On July 18 a constitution was drawn up by settlers at Genoa, and under it on September 7, the voters of Carson County elected Isaac Roop governor of this unofficial government.

The silver rush from California and the east began.

A trail that became the Simpson Route across central Nevada was explored by Captain J. H. Simpson under orders of General A. S. Johnson.

1860   Population of Nevada, 6,857.

On April 3 Pony Express began service between the Missouri River and Placerville, California, by way of Salt Lake City.

A battle between Indians and whites near Pyramid Lake cost the lives of 46 Indians and 66 white men, including Major William M. Ormsby.

On July 20 Fort Churchill was established.

1861   On March 2 the bill creating the Territory of Nevada was signed by President Buchanan.

On July 11 Governor James W. Nye proclaimed establishment of the Territorial government.

The Diedesheimer square sets of timber were being put into the mines of the Comstock.

In September the transcontinental telegraph line was completed and in October the Pony Express came to an end.

Mail for California was ordered carried over the central route.

1862   Camp Ruby was established by Colonel P. E. Connor and the Territory of Nevada recruited 1,100 men for Civil War service.

Gold and silver ore was discovered near Austin and the Reese River Mining District was organized.

1863   The Plumas-Roop County quarrel between Nevada and California was settled, with California gaining land east of the summit of the Sierra.

A ferry boat was operated on Walker Lake by J. H. Rose.

On November 2 a state constitutional convention was held at Carson City.

1864   Camels were used to carry salt from the salt marshes near Walker Lake to Austin for milling purposes.

On July 4 a second state constitutional convention was held at Carson City.

On October 18 construction of Sutro Tunnel was started.

On October 31 Nevada was admitted as a State by presidential proclamation.

H. G. Blasdel was elected first State governor.

Silver-lead ore was discovered at Eureka.

1865   During February Captain T. E. Trueworthy took a boat-load of lumber up the Colorado River to Black Canyon.

Colonel Charles McDermit was killed near Quinn River Station, with the result that a fort was established at that place.

1866   In May by act of Congress the eastern boundary of the State of Nevada was set at the 114th degree of west longitude.

On February 24 the seal of state for Nevada was provided for by the legislature.

The southern boundary line of the State of Nevada between the 35th and 39th parallels was surveyed and accepted by Nevada and California.

1867   In order to cross at the Donner Pass toward Nevada the Central Pacific Railroad was forced to dig eighteen tunnels, most of them between 1,000 and 1,400 feet long.

The Carson Mint was built.

The first V-flume in Nevada was built near Carson City.

1868   On May 4, the Central Pacific reached the site of Reno and established a camp.

Two thousand head of cattle were driven into White Pine County.

The town of Hamilton in White Pine County was laid out.

1869   On May 10 the formal completion of the transcontinental railroad took place at Promontory, Utah.

A mining boom began at Mountain City in Elko County.

The first big bonanza at Virginia City became exhausted.

The boundary between Arizona Territory and Nevada was determined.

Elko County was created.

William Sharon's milling company was operating seventeen mills along the Carson River.

The V. & T. R. R. between Carson City and Virginia City was completed.

In the latter part of December a heavy earthquake shook Reno.

1870 Population of Nevada 42,491.

State capitol was being erected in Carson City.

1871 In August the state capitol was occupied.

1873 Eureka County was created from part of Lander County.

In March the Big Bonanza at Virginia City was discovered.

The great siphon to conduct water from the Sierra Nevada to Virginia City was laid across Washoe Valley.

1874 Walker River and Pyramid Lake Indian reservations were established.

The State University was opened at Elko.

1875 Virginia City was destroyed by fire.

A fire laid waste to Eureka.

Part of Elko County, the Mineral Hill Strip, was annexed to Eureka County.

1877 The state legislature enacted a law against dueling.

1878 John H. Kinkead was elected governor of Nevada. He became an outstanding supporter of law enforcement.

On July 8 the Sutro Tunnel reached the Comstock mines.

1879 The Fish Creek War between charcoal burners and officers of the law occurred at Eureka. Five coal burners were killed.

An ostrich farm was started by Theodore Glancy near Carson City.

1880 Population of Nevada was 62,266.

The U. S. Census found 700 work-oxen and 31,550 work-horses in Nevada.

In October old Chief Winnemucca died.

The rainfall for the year at Carson City was thirteen and one-tenth inches.

1881 Fifty silver-lead mines were producing in the Eureka District.

The Mormons were re-settling the Muddy Valley in southern Nevada.

The Big Bonanza at Virginia City became exhausted and the mines began to close.

1882 In February Sutro Tunnel was completed.

1883 The Eureka mines were producing enough lead to effect all markets of the world.

Jewett Adams, a farmer and stock raiser, was elected Governor of Nevada. "Free silver" was the main issue of his administration.

1884 The Mexican-Ophir winze reached a depth of 3,300 feet—deepest working on the Comstock.

1885 The Carson Mint ceased operation.

In July 275 tons of Nevada hay were shipped to New York; the hay delivered in New York cost $200 a ton.

The legislature provided for removal of the state university from Elko to Reno.

1886 Christopher C. Stevenson was elected Governor of Nevada.

Fort Halleck in Elko County was abandoned and the troops were moved to Fort Douglas in Utah.

1887 An effort was made to add southern Idaho to Nevada.

On March 3 the governor of Nevada approved an "anti-Mormon" bill, taking the right of franchise from all members of that church.

1889 Fort McDermitt Indian Reservation was established.

In April the Carson Mint was re-opened with $1,600,000 in gold bars on hand.

1890 The population of Nevada was 47,355.

1891 Roswell K. Colcord, an engineer and contractor, became governor of the State.

Nevada received first prize for wheat at the New Orleans Exposition.

1892 In January the Ghost Dance led by an Indian, Jack Wilson, on the Walker Reservation caused great excitement; Wilson said he was the Indian Messiah.

1895 John E. Jones was elected governor.

The Elko County board of education organized the first county high school.

1898 Reinhold Sadler became governor, elected by a majority of only 25 votes.

The mint at Carson City was dismantled and re-equipped for assaying.

1900 Population of Nevada was 42,335.

There were nearly 6,000 Indians in Nevada distributed among the Paiute, Western Shoshoni, and Washoe.

The Washoe Indians were given 160 acres of land apiece in the Pine Nut Mountains.

Tonopah was discovered.

Development of the copper zone in the Ely Mining District was begun.

1901 A law was passed making it unlawful to sell horse-meat without informing the purchaser of its nature.

It became unlawful to have in operation any form of nickel-in-the-slot machine.

Dan Stewart led a losing fight to have lotteries legalized.

1902 John W. Mackay, most famous of all the Comstockers, died in London, England, at the age of 72.

Goldfield was discovered.

1903 Francis G. Newlands became United States Senator, succeeding John P. Jones.

John Sparks became governor on the Silver-Democratic ticket.

Construction of a railroad through southern Nevada was begun to connect Salt Lake City and Los Angeles.

1904 Rhyolite was enjoying a "boom."

1905 The first Nevada State Flag was adopted.

Construction on a copper mill at McGill was begun.

William M. Stewart retired from the United States Senate after 29 years of service; he was succeeded by George S. Nixon. The Truckee-Carson Irrigation project was under way.

1907   The state was divided into five school districts.

Federal Troops were called to Goldfield in a labor strike. There were no fatalities.

1908   Denver S. Dickerson became governor upon the death of Governor John Sparks.

1909   Clark County was formed out of a part of Lincoln County and Las Vegas made county seat.

In December a snow storm at Las Vegas left twelve inches of snow in the city.

1910   Population of Nevada was 81,875 with 220 men to every 100 women; school children numbered only two-fifths of the average in other states.

Tasker L. Oddie became governor.

1911   Nevada mines were producing about $35,000,000 annually.

1912   Key Pittman became United States Senator, succeeding W. A. Massey.

1913   The first state motor vehicle law passed, the license fee to be 12.5 cents per horsepower of the motor. Minimum horsepower rating to be 20.

The per capita cost of state government was $10.45 and of county government $17.18.

The six-months divorce law was repealed by the legislature.

1915   Emmet D. Boyle became governor on the Democratic ticket.

The second state flag was adopted.

The legislature restored the six-months divorce law.

1917   The state legislature adopted the sagebrush as the state emblem. Nevada was the first State in the Union to subscribe her quota to the first Liberty Loan and over-subscribed 92 per cent.

1918   Nevada adopted by initiative a stringent prohibition law.

1919   Pershing County was created from part of Humboldt County. Extensive irrigation canals were dug in Mason and Smith valleys.

In November S. Frank Hunt discovered Rio Tinto Mine.

1920   Population of Nevada 77,407.

1921   The mines of Osceola were still producing much gold, with some silver.

The Coppermines Company at Ruth, and the Nevada Consolidated Copper Company of Ely closed down because of the low price of copper.

1922   Lehman Cave was set aside as a National Monument.

Just a little more than three per cent of Nevada's land was privately owned and less than one per cent of it was under irrigation.

1923   James G. Scrugham elected governor on the Democratic ticket.

The first State recreation grounds were set aside.

1924   A Chinaman was executed at the state prison by means of lethal gas, the first execution by this means.

Lost City in Clark Coupnty was explored, revealing Nevada habitation 8,000 to 10,000 years ago.

1925   The State inheritance tax was repealed.

A law was passed making the use of a common towel unlawful in public places.

1926   A fire in the mountains west of Carson City destroyed much timber and burned five men to death.

1927   A three-month divorce law was adopted.

Fred B. Balzar was elected governor on the Republican ticket.

A federal ammunition depot was established at Hawthorne.

1928   On December 21 President Coolidge signed the Swing-Johnson Bill authorizing the construction of Boulder Dam.

1929   The third State flag was adopted.

The federal government paid the State of Nevada $595,076.53 as a "full and final settlement for claims against the federal government . . . for money advanced during the Civil War."

1930   Population of Nevada was 91,058, includinug 4,871 Indians.

Work on Boulder Dam begun.

Stockraising and allied agricultural activities were employing more people than any other industry.

1931   More money was in circulation in Nevada than in any year since the Comstock days.

On March 22 a six-weeks divorce law was passed.

A wide open gambling law was passed.

1933   Patrick A. McCarran was elected United States senator, replacing Tasker L. Oddie.

A State song, "Home Means Nevada," was adopted.

1934   Nevada became eligible to receive 18 per cent of the power generated at Boulder Dam.

1935   Richard Kirman was elected governor on the Democratic ticket.

1936   An artesian well at Winnemucca was driven to a depth of 525 feet and gave a flow of 550 gallons a minute.

The value of cattle grazing on the Nevada ranges was estimated at $11,000,000.

1937   A flowing well at Las Vegas, drilled by Union Pacific to 650 feet, flowed three and a half million gallons a day.

The Taylor-Grazing Act was put into effect.

1938   A full-blood Paiute, Dewey Sampson, was elected state assemblyman from Washoe County.

A mammoth gold-dredging machine was placed in operation at Manhattan.

E. P. Carville became governor after election on the Democratic ticket.

Supplementary Reading List of Nevada Books

Adams, Romanzo. *Taxation in Nevada.* Published at Reno, Nevada, by Nevada State Historical Society, Inc., Carson City, Nevada, State Printing Office, 1918. 199 p.

Adams, George I. *The Rabbit Hole Sulphur Mines near Humboldt House.* Washington, Government Printing Office, 1916. 361 p. illus., maps. (U. S. Geological Survey, Bulletin 620).

Angel, Myron, ed. *History of Nevada.* Oakland, California, Thompson and West, 1881. 680 p. illus. Valuable for pages copied from Book of Records, Carson Valley.

Armstrong, Margaret and J. J. Thornber. *Field Book of Western Wild Flowers.* New York, G. P. Putnam's Sons, 1915. 596 p. illus., col. plates.

Bancroft, Hubert Howe. *Nevada, Colorado and Wyoming.* San Francisco, History Company, 1889. 827 p. (Vol. XXV of *History of Pacific States of North America.* 34 v.)

Banning, Capt. William and George H. *Six Horses.* New York, Century Company, 1930. 410 p.

Book of Nevada Poems. Selected and arranged by Nevada Federation of Women's Clubs. Reno, Nevada, Reno Printing Company, 1927. 214 p.

Bradley, Glen D. *The Story of the Pony Express:* An account of the Most Remarkable Mail Service ever in Existence, and Its Place in History. 4th edition. Chicago, A. C. McClurg and Company, 1920. 175 p. illus. Route and riders.

Brennen, C. A. *The Main Reason Why Range Cattle Ranches Succeed or Fail.* Carson City, Nevada, State Printing Office, 1933. 22 p. illus. (Agricultural Experiment Station, University of Nevada, Bulletin 133).

Brown, George R. ed. *Reminiscences of Senator William M. Stewart of Nevada.* New York, Neale Publishing Company, 1908. 308 p.

Burton, Richard F. *City of the Saints: And Across the Rocky Mountains to California.* New York, Harper and Brothers, Publishers, 1862. 574 p. illus. Only a small section deals with Nevada.

Carr, Harry. *The West Is Still Wild:* Romance of the Past and Present. Boston, Houghton Mifflin, 1932. 275 p. illus. Anecdotes and short stories.

Carson, Kit. *Kit Carson's Life and Adventures from Facts Narrated by Himself.* Embracing events in the life-time of America's great-

est trapper, scout and guide, including vivid accounts of the every
day life, inner character, and peculiar customs of all Indian Tribes
of the far west. Edited by Dewitt C. Peters. Hartford, Connecticut, Dustin, Gilman and Company, 1873. 604 p. illus.
Little on Nevada.

Chandlers, William. *Visit to Salt Lake*: Being a journey across the
plains and a residence in the Mormon Settlements at Utah. London, Smith, Elder and Company, 1857. 346 p. fold map.

Chapman, H. R. *Deserts of Nevada and Death Valley*. Scientific
American Supplement 63: 26125-9. April 6, 1907, illus., map.
An address before the National Geographic Society.

Chittenden, Hiram Martin. *The American Fur Trade of the Far
West*. Corrected edition. New York, Pilgrim Press, 1938. 2 v.

Clemens, Samuel L. *Roughing It*. Hartford, American Publishing
Company, 1871. 419 p.

Clements, Edith S. *Flowers of Coast and Sierra*. New York. H.
W. Wilson Company, 1928. 226 p. col. front., col. illus.

Coy, Owen C. *The Great Trek*. Los Angeles, San Francisco, Powell
Publishing Company, 1931. 349 p. illus., plates, maps. Overland Journeys to the Pacific Coast.

Dale, Harrison Clifford, ed. *The Ashley-Smith Explorations and the
Discovery of a Central Route to the Pacific, 1822-1829, with the
Original Journals*. Cleveland, Arthur H. Clark Company, 1918.
352 p., plates, maps.

Davis, Sam P. ed. *History of Nevada*. Los Angeles, Elms Publishing Company, 1913. 2 v. 1279 p. Compilation of articles written by pioneers and contemporaries, some of much value.

Dellenbaugh, Frederick S. *Fremont and '49*: The story of a remarkable career and its relation to the exploration and development
of our western territory, especially California. New York, G. P.
Putnam's Sons, 1914. 547 p. illus., maps.

——. *Breaking the Wilderness*. New York, G. P. Putnam's Sons,
1905. 360 p. illus.

De Voto, Bernard Augustine. *Mark Twain's America*. Boston,
Little, Brown and Company, 1932. 353 p. illus.

Drago, Henry Sinclair. *Following the Grass*. New York, Macauley
Company, 1924. 320 p. Story.

Drury, Wells. *An editor on the Comstock Lode*. New York, Farrar
and Rinehart, 1936. 343 p. illus.

Eckel, Edwin C. *Portland Cement Materials and Industries in the
United States*. Washington, Government Printing office, 1913.
401 p. maps. (U. S. Geological Survey, Bulletin 522). Contributions by E. F. Burch, A. F. Crider, G. B. Richardson, E. A.
Smith, J. A. Taff, E. O. Ulrich and W. H. Weed.

Emmons, William Harvey. *A Reconnaissence of Some Mining Camps
in Elko, Lander and Eureka Counties, Nevada*. Washington,
Government Printing Office, 1910. 130 p. map. (U. S. Geological Survey, Bulletin 408).

Everett, Willis E. *Genesis of the Formation and Deposition of the Nevada Desert Gold, Silver and Copper Mines.* Scientific American Supplement, 65: 61. Jan. 25, 1908.

Fletcher, Fred Nathaniel. *Early Nevada*: The Period of Exploration, 1776-1848. Reno, Carlisle and Company, 1929. 183 p. mounted fold. map.

Fremont, Brevet Col. J. C. *The Exploring Expedition to the Rocky Mountains, Oregon and California.* Buffalo, George H. Derby and Company, 1851. 456 p. Fremont was in Nevada, January 1844.

Fulton, Robert Lardin. *Epic of the Overland.* San Francisco, A. M. Robertson, 1924. 109 p. front plates, ports, fold. map.

Glasscock, Carl Burgess. *The Big Bonanza: The Story of the Comstock Lode.* Indianapolis, Bobbs-Merrill Company, 1931. 368 p. illus. Historical recital of the flourishing days of Virginia City. Somewhat melodramatic.

——. *A Golden Highway*: Scenes of History's greatest gold rush yesterday and today. Indianapolis, Bobbs-Merril Company, 1934. 333 p. front plate.

——. *Gold in Them Hills*: The story of the West's last wild mining days. Indianapolis, Bobbs-Merrill Company, 1932. 330 p. illus.

Goodwin, Charles C. *As I Remember Them.* Salt Lake City, Published by special committee of Salt Lake Commercial Club, 1913. 360 p.

Hafen, Leroy R. *The Overland Mail, 1849-1869*: Promoter of Settlement, Procursor of Railroads. Cleveland, Arthur H. Clark Company, 1926. 361 p. plates, map.

Hardman, George and M. R. Miller. *The Quality of the Water of Southern Nevada*: Drainage Basins and Water Resources. Carson City, Nevada, State Printing Office, 1934. 62 p. (Agricultural Experiment Station, University of Nevada, Bulletin 136).

Harrington, Mark R. *Archeological Explorations in Southern Nevada.* Los Angeles, Southwest Museum, 1930. 126 p. illus., map. (Southwest Museum Papers No. 4).

——. *Gypsum Cave.* Los Angeles, Southwest Museum, 1933. 197 p. illus., plates, maps. (Southwest Museum Papers No. 8). Nevada prehistoric man.

Harvey, Charles M. *Trail of the Argonauts.* Atlantic Monthly, 106; 115-125. July, 1911.

Hayden, Irwin. *Last Stand of the Nevada Pueblos.* Scientific American, 142; 132-134. Feb. 1930.

Higginbotham, A. L. *A Mountain University.* Overland, 82; 387-90. Sept. 1924.

Hill, J. M. *Notes on the Economic Geology of the Ramsey, Tallapoose and White Horse Mining Districts in Washoe and Lyon counties, Nevada.* Washington, Government Printing Office, 1911. p. 99-108. (U. S. Geological Survey, Bulletin 470).

Hodge, Frederick Webb. *Handbook of American Indians.* Washington, Government Printing Office, 1912. 2 v. (Smithsonian Institution, Bureau of American Ethnology, Bulletin 30).

Hopkins, Sarah Winnemucca. *Life Among the Piutes*: Their Wrongs and Claims. Edited by Mrs. Horace Mann. New York, G. P. Putnam's Sons, 1883. 268 p. Mrs. Hopkins was an educated Piute.

Hutchins, Wells A. *Summary of Irrigation District Statutes of Western States.* Washington, Government Printing Office, 1931. 127 p. (U. S. Department of Agriculture, Miscellaneous Publications 103).

Johnson, Clifton. *Highways and Byways of the Pacific Coast.* New York, Macmillan, 1908. 323 p. illus.

Kelly, Charles. *Salt Desert Trails;* A History of the Hastings' Cut-off and other early Trails which Crossed the Great Salt Lake Desert seeking a Shorter Road to California. Salt Lake City, Western Printing Company, 1930. 178 p. illus., maps.

Kelly, J. Wells. *First Directory of Nevada Territory.* San Francisco, Valentine and Company, 1862. 266 p. Contains historical sketch, lists of residents in the principal towns and descriptions of quartz mills.

Kniess, Gilbert H. *The Virginia and Truckee Railroad.* Boston, the Railway and Locomotive Historical Society, Inc., 1938. 32 p. illus., map. (Railway and Locomotive Historical Society, Inc., Bulletin 45).

Knopf, Adolph. *Some Cinnabar Deposits in Western Nevada.* Washington, Government Printing Office, 1916. 361 p. illus., maps. (U. S. Geological Survey, Bulletin 620).

———. *A gold-platinum-palladium lode in southern Nevada.* Washington, Government Printing Office, 1916. 361 p. illus., maps. (U. S. Geological Survey, Bulletin 620).

Kroeber, Alfred L. *American Archeology and Ethnology.* Berkeley, University of California Press, 1903-1923. 20 v. *Includes Language of the Washoes.*

Leonard, Zenas. *Fur Trader and Trapper, 1831-1836, Adventures of.* Reprinted from the rare original of 1839. Edited by W. F. Wagner. Cleveland, Burrows Brothers Company, 1904. 317 p. illus., maps.

Lewis, Oscar. *The Big Four*: The Story of Huntington, Stanford, Hopkins and Crocker, and the building of the Central Pacific. New York, and London, Alfred A. Knopf, 1938. 418 p.

Lincoln, Francis Church. *Mining Districts and Mineral Resources of Nevada.* Reno, Nevada, Newsletter Publishing Company, 1923. 295 p. tables. Extended bibliographies. (Paper cover). Invaluable statistics and condensed technical material.

Linsdale, Jean M. *The Birds of Nevada.* Berkeley, California,

Cooper Ornithological Club, 1936. 145 p. (Pacific Coast Avifauna 23). (Paper cover).

Loomis, Leander Vaness. *A Journal of the Birmingham Emigrating Company*: The Record of a Trip from Birmingham, Iowa, to Sacramento, California, in 1850. Edited by Edgar M. Ledyard. Salt Lake City, Legal Printing Company, 1928. 198 p. plates, ports., fold. maps. (From Randolph B. Marcy's *The Prairie Traveler,* London, 1863).

Lord, Eliot. *Comstock Mining and Miners.* Washington, Government Printing Office, 1883. 451 p. maps. (U. S. Geological Survey, Monographs V., 4).

Loud, Llewellyn L. and Mark R. Harrington. *Lovelock Cave.* Berkeley, University of California Press, 1929. 183 p. illus., plates, tables, diagrs., maps. (University of California publications in *American Archeology and Ethnology* V. 25 No. 1). Piute Indians.

Luke, Mrs. C. H. *The Geography of Nevada.* Chicago, Rand McNally, 1932. 20 p. illus., maps. (Paper cover).

Lyman, George D. *Saga of the Comstock Lode.* New York, Charles Scribner's Sons, 1934. 407 p. illus. Melodramatic.

——. *Ralston's Ring.* California Plunders the Comstock Lode. New York, Charles Scribner's Sons, 1937. 368 p. plates, ports.

Mack, Effie Mona. *Nevada*: A History of the State from the Earliest Times through the Civil War. Glendale, California, Arthur H. Clark Company, 1936. 495 p. illus., maps.

McGlashan, C. F. *History of the Donner Party*: A Tragedy of the Sierra. Sacramento, H. S. Crocker Company, 1890. 125 p. illus.

McNaughton, Clara. *Native Indian Basketry.* New West, I: 17-20. Reno, New West Publishing Company, Oct. 1912.

Manly, William Lewis. *Death Valley in '49*: The Autobiography of a Pioneer, detailing his life from a humble home in the Green Mountains to the gold mines of California; and particularly reciting the sufferings of the band of men, women and children who gave "Death Valley" its name. San Jose, California, The Pacific Tree and Vine Company, 1894. 498 p.

Marsh, Andrew J., official reporter. *Constitutional Convention,* 1864. Official report of the debates and proceedings—at Carson City, July 4, 1864. San Francisco, F. Eastman, printer, 1866. 943 p.

Martin, Anne. *Nevada, Beautiful Desert of Buried Hopes.* Nation, 115: 88-92. July 26, 1922.

Marye, George T., Jr. *From '49 to '83 in California and Nevada*: Chapters from the Life of George Thomas Marye, a Pioneer of '49 (by his son). San Francisco, A. M. Robertson Company, 1923. 212 p. plates, ports.

Meinzer, O. E. *Geology and Resources of Big Smoky, Clayton and Alkali Springs valleys, Nevada.* Washington, Government Printing Office, 1917. 167 p. maps. (U. S. Geological Survey, Water supply paper 423).

Muir, John. *Steep Trails*. Edited by William Frederic Bade. Boston and New York, Houghton Mifflin Company, 1918. 382 p. illus. Chapter XVI "Nevada's Dead Towns."

Myers, Harriet Williams. *Western Birds*. New York, Macmillan Company, 1923. 391 p. front., plates.

Nevada. *Constitution of State of Nevada*: Its Formation and Interpretation by A. J. Maestretti and Charles Roger Hicks. Reno, University of Nevada, 1933. 120 p. (University of Nevada, Bulletin 27: 4. Sept. 1933).

——. Department of Highways: *Nevada's Parks*. Carson City, Nevada, State Printing Office, 1938. 80 p. illus., maps, tables, diagrs.

——. *Nevada's Golden Stars*. Prepared under the direction of Maurice J. Sullivan, the adjutant general of Nevada. Reno, A. Carlisle and Company of Nevada, 1924. 303 p. illus., ports.

Nevada. State Board of Stock Commissioners. *Nevada Brand Book and a Compilation of Laws Affecting Live Stock*. Reno, Nevada Brand Book Company, 1924. 292 p.

——. State Engineer. *Biennial Reports, 1930-1938*. Carson City, Nevada, State Printing Office, 1931-39. 4 v.

Nevada State Historical Society, Inc. *Reports*. Published biennially 1907-1918. Edited by Jeanne Elizabeth Wier, Secretary of Nevada State Historical Society, Inc. Carson City, Nevada, State Printing Office, 1909-19. 3 v. plates, ports., maps. Reminiscences of pioneers, theses, and memorial sketches of members.

——. *Papers*. 1913-1926. Edited by Jeanne Elizabeth Wier, Secretary of Nevada State Historical Society, Inc. Carson City, Nevada, State Printing Office, 1913-1927. 5 v. illus., ports., maps. Published periodically by the Society, Reno, Nevada. Carfeully selected materials for history, theses and reprints.

Nevada. State Mineralogist. *Biennial Reports, 1866-1877 and 1878*. Carson City, Nevada, State Printing Office, 1867-1879. 7 v. fold. tables.

——. Surveyor General. *Biennial Reports, 1915-16, 1917-18, 1931-32, 1933-34*. Carson City, Nevada, State Printing Office, 1915-1934. 4 v. tables.

Nevada State University. *Tri-decennial Celebration*: May 28 to June 2, 1904. Edited by J. E. Church, Jr. Reno, Press of Barndollar and Durley, 1904. 204 p. front. plate, ports.

Nevins, Allen. *Fremont, Pathmarker of the West*. New York, D. Appleton-Century Company, Inc., 1939. 649 p. front. (port.), illus., maps.

Oetteking, Bruno. *The Skeleton from Mesa House*: A Physical Investigation. Los Angeles, Southwest Museum, 1930. 48 p. illus. (Southwest Museum Papers No. 5).

Ogden, Peter Skene. *Report of Peter Skene Ogden to the Hudson's Bay Company*. Copied in London, copy in possession of Robert A. Allen, Nevada State Engineer.

Pelzer, Louis. *The Cattlemen's Frontier*: A Record of the trans-Mississippi Cattle Industry from Oxen Trains to Pooling Companies, 1850-1890. Glendale, California, Arthur H. Clark Company, 1936. 351 p. front. illus., plates.

Powell, John J. *Nevada: the Land of Silver*. San Francisco, Bacon and Company, 1876. 305 p. plates.

Rand-McNally. *Commercial Atlas and Marketing Guide*. Chicago, Rand-McNally, 1936-1939. 4 v. maps, tables.

Requa, Mark L. *Grubstake*: A Story of Early Mining days in Nevada, time 1874. New York, C. Scribner's Sons, 1933. 360 p.

Ridgway, Robert. *Ornithology*. (In IV, Part III, of U. S. Geological Survey *Exploration of the Fortieth Parallel*). Washington, Government Printing Office, 1877. p. 305-643.

Rollins, Phillip A. *The Cowboy*: His Characteristics, his Equipment and his Part in the Development of the West. New York, Charles Scribner's Sons, 1922. 353 p.

Royce, Sarah. *Frontier Lady*: Recollections of the Gold Rush and Early California; with a foreword by Katherine Royce. Edited by Ralph Henry Gabriel. Yale University Press, 1932. 144 p.

Sabin, Edwin L. *Building the Pacific Railway*. Philadelphia and London, J. B. Lippincott Company, 1919, 308 p. illus., map. Ulysses S. Grant's visit to Nevada.

Saunders, Charles Francis. *Western Wild Flowers and Their Stories*. Garden City, New York, Doubleday, Doran and Company, Inc., 1933. 320 p.

Scrugham, James G. ed. *Nevada*: A Narrative of the Conquest of a Frontier Land. Chicago, American Historical Society, Inc., 1935. 3 v. illus., ports.

Shearer, Frederick E. ed. *William's Pacific Tourist and Guide Across the Continent*. New York, Adams and Bishop, 1881. 352 p. illus. Union and Central Pacific Railroads.

Shinn, Charles Howard. *The Story of the Mine, as Illustrated by the Great Comstock Lode of Nevada*. New York, D. Appleton and Company, 1908. 272 p. illus.

Schrader, Frank Charles. *Reconnaisance of the Jarbidge, Contact and Elk Mountain Districts, Elko County, Nevada*. Washington, Government Printing Office, 1912. 162 p. map. (U. S. Geological Survey, Bulletin 497).

Smythe, William E. *The Conquest of Arid America*. New York, Macmillan Company, 1905. 360 p. illus.

Spurr, J. E. *Alum Deposit near Silver Peak, Esmeralda County, Nevada*. pp. 501-502. Washington, Government Printing Office, 1904. 527 p. illus., maps. (U. S. Geological Survey, Bulletin 225).

——. *Coal Deposits between Silver Peak and Candelaria, Esmeralda County*. pp. 289-292.

——. *Notes on the Geology of the Goldfields District*. pp. 118-119.

——. *Ore Deposits of the Silver Peak quadrangle.* pp. 111-117.

——. Preliminary Report on the Ore Deposits of Tonopah. pp. 89-110.

Stacey, May Humphreys. *Uncle Sam's Camels.* Edited by Lewis Burt Lesley. Cambridge, Harvard University Press, 1929. 298 p. plates, ports., fold. map. The journal of May H. Stacey. Southwestern U. S.

Strobridge, Idah Meacham. *In Miners' Mirage-Land.* Los Angeles, Baumgardt Publishing Company, 1904. 129 p.

Sullivan, Maurice S. *Jedediah Smith, Trader and Trail-breaker.* New York, Press of the Pioneers, Inc., 1936. 233 p. front. illus., plates, ports.

Taylor, L. H. *Water Storage in the Truckee Basin, California-Nevada.* Washington, Government Printing Office, 1902. 90 p. (U. S. Geological Survey, Water Supply 68).

Traner, F. W. *Nevada Supplement.* New York, Macmillan Company, 1923. 16 p. illus., tables. Nevada geography.

United States. Geological Survey. *Geographical Surveys West of the 100th Meridian.* Capt. George M. Wheeler, Corps of Engineers U. S. Army in charge. Washington, Government Printing Office, 1875-1889. 7 v., Supplement and 2 Atlases. V. 1. *Geographical Report,* 1889. 780 p. plates, maps. v. 6. *Botany,* 1878.

——. *Geological Exploration of the Fortieth Parallel.* Clarence King, Geologist-in-charge. Washington, Government Printing Office, 1870-1880. 7 v. and Atlas. V. 3. *Mining Industry,* 1870. 647 p. plates, maps. V. 4. *Zoology and Paleontology,* 1877.

Wier, Jeanne Elizabeth. *Nevada Politics. In Intermountain Politics.* Edited by T. C. Donnelly, 1940.

Wright, William (Dan De Quille, pseud.) *History of the Big Bonanza.* Hartford, Connecticut, American Publishing Company; San Francisco, A. L. Bancroft and Company, 1877. 569 p. illus., plates, ports. One of the most accurate accounts.

——. *A History of the Comstock Lode Mines, Nevada* and the Great Basin Regions, Lake Tahoe and the High Sierras. Virginia City, Nevada, F. Boegle, 1889, 158 p.

Most of the foregoing items are found in the library of the Nevada State Historical Society, Inc., in Reno, or in the libraries at the University of Nevada.

INDEX

PRINCIPAL REFERENCE FIRST